ISBN 0-312-28935-9

First published in Great Britain by Virgin Books.

First U.S. Edition

10 9 8 7 6 5 4 3 2 1

ACKNOWLEDGEMENTS

Thanks to the following production companies, distributors, publications, PR firms and film archives for their continued co-operation and assistance:

Alpha, Anglo American, Artificial Eye, Blue Dolphin, Brent Walker, BFI Productions, The British Film Institute, Bordeaux, Cannon, Cinegate, Columbia, Connoisseur, Contemporary, Dennis Davidson Associates, Embasssy, Enterprise, Entertainment, Flashbacks, Gala, Golden Era GTO, Hemdale, ICA Projects, ITC, MGM-UA, The National Film Archive, PIC Publicity, PSA, Palace, Paramount, Poseidon Productions, Premier Releasing, Rank, Richard Laver, Screen International, Society of Film Distributors, Thorn EMI, Tigon, Time Out, Topham Picture Library, Tri-Star, 20th Century-Fox, UIP, Universal, Variety, Video Form, Virgin Films, Walt Disney, Warner Bros, Zakiya and Associates.

To all the contributors in general; and to Myron Meisel, Tim Pulleine, Paul Taylor and Geoff Andrew in particular.
To Rachel Marks who typed up the credits, and Linda Wood who assembled the reference section and answered our many questions.

To
Jane Charteris – cheerful, unremitting perseverance.
Sue Walliker – improvisation in the face of uncertainty.
Ursula Shaw – certainty in the face of improvisation.
Mary Volk – soundness and support.
Ginny Turnbull – (very) long distance telephone.

Just for a change: no resignation.
A.C.

For Clare

THE FILM YEARBOOK 1986

EDITED BY AL CLARK

St. Martin's Press
New York

EDITOR

AL CLARK is the author of *Raymond Chandler in Hollywood*, the editor of three volumes of the *The Rock Yearbook*, and the editor of the *The Film Yearbook* since its inception in 1982. He is Head of Production at Virgin Films, executive producer of *Secret Places*, *Absolute Beginners* and *Heroine*, and co-producer of *Nineteen Eighty-Four* and *Castaway*.

CONTRIBUTORS

GEOFF ANDREW is a film critic for *Time Out*. He has also contributed to the *Radio Times*, and has written a book on *Hollywood Gangster Movies*. Before becoming a journalist he was manager and co-programmer of London's Electric Cinema.

TONY CRAWLEY is the author of *The Films of Sophia Loren*, *Bébé: The Films of Brigitte Bardot*, *Screen Dreams: The Hollywood Pin-Up* and *The Steven Spielberg Story*. He has written on films for publications throughout the world and now lives in France. He is foreign editor of *Starburst*.

DAVID EHRENSTEIN is a freelance writer, contributing to the *Los Angeles Herald Examiner*, *Village Voice*, *Rolling Stone*, *Cahiers du Cinema*, *Film Culture*, *Film Comment*, *Film Quarterly* and the anthologies *Jean-Luc Godard* and *The New American Cinema*. He is also the co-author, with Bill Reed, of *Rock on Film* and is currently editor of *Laserworks* magazine and *On Film*. His book *Film: The Front Line – 1984* was published in December 1984.

QUENTIN FALK is a contributor to *Anatomy of the Movies* and the author of *Travels in Greeneland: The Cinema of Graham Greene*. He is a past editor of *Screen International* and now writes for *Punch*, the *Guardian* and the *Sunday Times*.

HARLAN KENNEDY is the European correspondent for *Film Comment* and a member of the Critics' Circle. For four years he was the London contributing editor of *American Film*, and now writes regularly for *Film Review*, *The Face* and *Emmy* magazine.

TODD McCARTHY was co-editor of *Kings of the Bs*. He has contributed to many film publications including *Film Comment*, *American Film* and *Cahiers du Cinema*. He is also a critic and reporter on *Variety*.

DAVID McGILLIVRAY has, since 1970, written and appeared in sixteen films, the best-known of which are *House of Whipcord* and *Frightmare*. He also dabbles in other branches of the media, notably radio and theatre (he runs the touring company, *Entertainment Machine*). He is the author of *The History of British Sex Movies 1957-1981*.

MYRON MEISEL is a writer-producer based in Los Angeles. His credits include *Final Exam*, *A Savage Hunger*, *I'm a Stranger Here Myself: A Portrait of Nicholas Ray* and the forthcoming French production, *Machete!* A member of the National Society of Film Critics, his reviews appear in *Movies on TV*. He also works as a lawyer and marketing consultant.

BART MILLS writes about films and television from Hollywood for such publications as the *Guardian*, the *Los Angeles Times* and *American Film*.

JAMES PARK has covered the film beat for *Variety* for the past three years. The author of *Learning to Dream: The New British Cinema*, he is currently preparing a more substantial tome recounting the joys and nightmares of producing six recent British features. It will be published in late 1986.

CHRIS PEACHMENT is the film editor of *Time Out* and also writes for *The Times*. He was once a pilot.

DILYS POWELL was the film critic of the *Sunday Times* from 1939 to 1976, and has since written for the same newspaper about films on television. She is also the film critic of *Punch*, a frequent broadcaster and the author of several books about Greece.

TIM PULLEINE is deputy film critic of the *Guardian* and also contributes reviews and articles to various publications, including *Films and Filming*, *Radio Times* and *Monthly Film Bulletin*.

PAUL TAYLOR currently works for the British Film Institute as a programme advisor to regional cinemas. While continuing to write on movies and television for various publications, he is also chairman of the Leicester City Supporters Club, London Branch.

JOHN WALKER is the author of *The Once and Future Film* and the *Which? Software Guide*. He writes on the arts for many of the world's leading newspapers and magazines and on microcomputing for most of Britian's biggest-circulation regional newspapers.

CONTENTS

THE FILMS   7

THE FILMS RELEASED ONLY IN THE US   74

THE US YEAR   82

THE UK YEAR   84

FILMS OF THE YEAR   86

TURKEYS OF THE YEAR   108

FACES OF THE YEAR   118

QUOTES OF THE YEAR   129

FEATURES   140

THE AWARDS   152

BOOKS   155

OBITUARIES   170

REFERENCE   179

THE FILMS

Reviews by *Al Clark, Tim Pulleine, Paul Taylor, Myron Meisel, David Ehrenstein, Geoff Andrew, Anne Billson, John Walker* and *David Thompson*

1 JULY 1984 – 30 JUNE 1985

Like the book in general, this covers the year as indicated above. The first section includes all the feature films – excluding documentaries, reissues and 16mm movies – released in both the US and the UK during this time, plus those which opened only in the UK. Note is made if a film has appeared in the US prior to the book's coverage period. A second section lists in further detail those films (this year including a selection of noteworthy documentaries as an addendum) released only in the US between the dates in question. Wherever there is a descrepancy between British and American titles, the original is used, with the appropriate cross-reference. Foreign language films are listed under the title by which they are best known.

Abbreviations are as follows: *dir* director *pro* producer *exec pro* executive producer *scr* screenplay *ph* director of photography *ed* editor *pro des* production designer *art dir* art director *mus* music.

A*a*

THE ADVENTURES OF BUCKAROO BANZAI: ACROSS THE 8TH DIMENSION: See US section

ALAMO BAY: See US section

ALL OF ME
(Kings Road/Universal/Thorn EMI)
dir Carl Reiner *pro* Stephen Friedman *scr* Phil Alden Robinson, based on the novel 'Me Two' by Ed Davis *ph* Richard H Kline, in Technicolor *ed* Bud Molin *pro des* Edward Carfagno *mus* Patrick Williams *r time* 91 mins *US opening* Sep 21 *UK opening* Jan 18.
cast Steve Martin, Lily Tomlin, Victoria Tennant, Madolyn Smith, Richard Libertini, Dana Elcar, Jason Bernard, Selma Diamond, Eric Christmas, Gailard Sartain, Neva Patterson, Michael Ensign, Peggy Feury, Nan Martin, Basil Hoffman, Hedley Mattingly, Harvey Vernon, Stu Black.

Sooner or later, the Reiner/Martin partnership will be inspired to turn out something like 'The Plaid-Suited Jerk With Half A Brain' – and it'll work. This comes close, being the regular amalgam of cherishable craziness, comedic cannibalism and more-hit-than-miss hilarity, as Martin finds his body occupied to overcrowding with the mislaid soul and psyche of Lily Tomlin. Semi-predictable embarrassments in bathrooms, bedrooms and boardrooms ensue, but even the glorious slapstick gags are strung along a line on sexual identity that makes the supposed 'audacity' of a 'Tootsie' look decidedly tame.

Left: All of Me. Above: Amadeus

ALMOST YOU: See US section

AMADEUS
(Orion/Thorn EMI)
dir Milos Forman *pro* Saul Zaentz *exec pro* Michael Hausman, Bertil Ohlsson *scr* Peter Schaffer, based on his own play *ph* Miroslav Ondricek, in Technicolor *ed* Nena Danevic, Michael Chandler *pro des* Patrizia Van Brandenstein *art dir* Karel Cerny, Francesco Chianese *mus* Mozart, Salieri, Pergolesi and others *r time* 160 mins *US opening* Sep 19 *UK opening* Jan 18.
cast F Murray Abraham, Tom Hulce, Elizabeth Berridge, Simon Callow, Roy Dotrice, Christine Ebersole, Jeffrey Jones, Charles Kay, Kenny Baker, Lisabeth Bartlett, Barbara Bryne, Martin Cavani, Roderick Cook, Milan Demjanenko, Peter DiGesu, Richard Frank, Patrick Hines, Nicholas Kepros, Philip Lenkowsky.

Shaffer's award-winning play was a successful entertainment that promised to turn into an inferior movie, one of those overstuffed, costumed composer biopics. Forman's film instead converts Shaffer's clever conceit into a profoundly moving and scintillating work of art that vastly overshadows its antecedent. (See Films of the Year.)

THE AMBASSADOR
(Cannon)
dir J Lee Thompson *pro* Menahem Golan, Yoram Globus *scr* Max Jack, suggested by the novel '52 Pick-Up' by Elmore Leonard *ph* Adam Greenberg, in colour *ed* Mark Goldblatt *art dir* Yoram Barzilai *mus* Dov Seltzer *r time* 95 mins *US opening* Jan 11 *UK opening* Apr 26.
cast Robert Mitchum, Ellen Burstyn, Rock Hudson, Fabio Testi, Donald Pleasance, Heli Goldenberg, Michal Bat-Adam, Ori Levy, Uri Gavriel, Zachi Noy, Joseph Shiloah, Shmulik Kraus, Yossi Virginsky, Iftah Katzur, Shai Scwartz, Ran Vered, Assi Abaiov.

Somewhere in the labyrinth of plots and sub-plots which criss-cross this tepid, torpid, would-be topical farrago is a routine liberal message about how Arabs and Israelis should live in peace, spelt out in neon at the film's climax. An interesting cast is largely wasted.

7

AMERICAN DREAMER
(CBS Theatrical/Warner/Rank)
dir Rick Rosenthal *pro* Doug Chapin *exec pro* Barry Krost *scr* Jim Kouf, David Greenwalt, based on a story by Ann Biderman *ph* Giuseppe Rotunno, Jan De Bont, in Technicolor *ed* Anne Goursaud *pro des* Brian Eatwell *mus* Lewis Furey and others *r time* 105 mins *US opening* Oct 26 *UK opening* May 17.
cast JoBeth Williams, Tom Conti, Giancarlo Giannini, Coral Browne, James Staley, C B Barnes, Huckleberry Fox, Pierre Santini, Pierre Olaf, Jean Rougerie, Brian Eatwell, Guy Montagni, Fernand Guiot, Yanou Collart, Michael Bardinet, Leon Zitrone, André Valardy, Nancy Stephens, Rick Rosenthal.

Lame-brained comedy-thriller involving JoBeth Williams (stridently trying) and Tom Conti (wearisomely laid-back in frightfully British fashion) with arch-villain Giancarlo Giannini (apparently seeking to emulate Inspector Clouseau in the matter of tortured vowels). Some sort of comic pastiche of pulp fiction protocols seems to be intended; only slow-motion inanity transpires.

L'AMOUR À MORT
(Ariane-A2-Acteurs Auteurs Associés/Cannon-Gala)
dir Alain Resnais *pro* Philippe Dussart *scr* Jean Gruault *ph* Sacha Vierny, in Eastman Colour *ed* Albert Jurgenson, Jean-Pierre Besnard *mus* Hans-Werner Henze, Jeffery Cotton *r time* 93 mins *UK opening* Feb 22.
cast Sabine Azéma, Fanny Ardant, Pierre Arditi, André Dussollier, Jean Dasté, Geneviève Mnich, Jean-Claude Weibel, Françoise Rigal, Louis Castel, Françoise Morhange.

Resnais' leading character is killed off in the first minute, but brought back to life shortly afterwards – only to hanker after a return to the country of the dead. Unsettling in its combination of romanticism and (anti?) religious seriousness, this is a work of genuine originality, yet one which fails to mitigate an impression that its maker has somehow become divorced from his audience.

L'AMOUR PAR TERRE
(Cannon-Gala)
dir Jacques Rivette *pro* Martine Marignac *scr* Pascal Bonitzer, Marilu Parolini, Jacques Rivette, Suzanne Schiffman *ph* William Lubtchansky, in colour *ed* Nicole Lubtchansky, Louise de Champfleury *art dir* Roberto Plate *r time* 127 mins *UK opening* Nov 16.

cast Geraldine Chaplin, Jane Birkin, André Dussollier, Jean-Pierre Kalfon, Facundo Bo, Laszlo Szabo, Sandra Montaigu, Isabelle Linnartz, Eva Roelens.

Inevitably, if slightly uncharitably, re-dubbed 'Celine and Julie Spring a Leak', this particular import from Rivette offers poor encouragement to those mantaining that too few of his idiosyncratically playful entertainments cross the Channel these days. As usual, 'the play's the thing...', but even with Birkin and Chaplin involved in the whimsically puppeteered charades around an eccentric dramatist's chateau, the shifting relations between artistes, authors and audiences this time seem almost academic, and the fantasy dimension fails to take flight.

ANNIE'S COMING OUT [US Title: A TEST OF LOVE]
(Film Australia/Enterprise/Universal)
dir Gil Brearly *pro* Don Murray *exec pro* Don Harley *scr* John

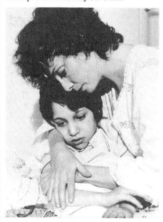

Patterson, Chris Borthwick, based on the book by Rosemary Crossley, Anne McDonald *ph* Mick Van Borneman, in Eastman Colour *ed* Lindsay Frazer *art dir* Mike Hudson *mus* Simon Walker *r time* 93 mins *UK opening* Nov 23 *US opening* Apr 12.
cast Angela Punch-McGregor, Drew Forsythe, Liddy Clark, Monica Maughan, Philippa Baker, Tina Arhondis, Mark Butler, John Frawley, Wallas Eaton, Lyn Collingwood, Laurie Dobson, Carl Bleazby, Esme Melville, Judith Graham, Alistair Duncan, Simon Chilvers, James Wright.

Above: Baby – Secret of the Lost Legend. Right: Bachelor Party

The fact that this Australian drama-doc, about a supposedly 'hopeless case' teenage girl rescued by a devoted teacher from incarceration in a mental hospital, is based on actual events makes one approach it with respect. But admiration for the real participants does not override a feeling that the film's method is heavily reliant on blandness and sentimental short cuts. In documentary terms, we do not discover enough of the hard facts of the matter; on the other hand, the gestures toward dramatization, including a semi-humorous love interest for the teacher, tend to be forced and somewhat irrelevant.

THE AVIATOR: See US section

BABY, IT'S YOU
(Double Play/Paramount/Mainline)
dir-scr John Sayles, based on a story by Amy Robinson *pro* Griffin Dunne, Amy Robinson *ph* Michael Ballhaus, in colour *ed* Sonya Polonsky *pro des* Jeffrey Townsend *r time* 105 mins *US opening* prior to Jul 1984 *UK opening* Oct 26.
cast Rosanna Arquette, Vincent Spano, Joanna Merlin, Jack Davidson, Nick Ferrari, Dolores Messina, Leora Dana, William Joseph Raymond, Sam McMurray, Liane Curtis, Claudia Sherman, Marta Kober, Tracy Pollan, Rachel Dretzin, Susan Derendorf.

John Sayles gets back on the right track (after nearly derailing himself with 'Lianna') in this sweet, thoughtful, boy-meets-girl romance set in the early

sixties. Not all the socio-economic points Sayles wishes to make about this Jewish Princess heroine and Italian lumpenprole hero come across, but the behavioral details of male/female emotional interplay are well observed. Best of all is the film's finale in which the possibility of friendship between a man and a woman is posited with insightful aplomb. Photographed by Michael Ballhaus (of Fassbinder fame), this is the first Sayles film to actually look like something.

BABY – SECRET OF THE LOST LEGEND
(Touchstone)
dir B W L Norton *pro* Jonathan T Taplin *exec pro* Roger Spottiswoode *scr* Clifford Green, Ellen Green *ph* John Alcott, in Technicolor *ed* Howard Smith, David Bretherton *pro des* Raymond G Storey *mus* Jerry Goldsmith *r time* 93 mins *US opening* Mar 22 *UK opening* Mar 29.
cast William Katt, Sean Young, Patrick McGoohan, Julian Fellowes, Kyalo Mativo, Hugh Quarshie, Olu Jacobs, Eddie Tagoe, Edward Hardwicke, Julian Curry, Alexis Meless, Susie Nottingham, Stephane Krora, Anthony Sarfoh, Jeannot Banny, Roger Carlton, Thérèse Taba.

'Darkest Africa' hokum of an old-fashioned, not to say pretty silly sort, with conservation-minded American interlopers coming to the rescue of dinosaurs (which, according to the climax, are capable of outrunning a speeding vehicle). Put together, nonetheless, with an unassuming narrative skill which perhaps renders it closer to bygone genre movie-making than some more ostentatious efforts to revive the form.

BACHELOR PARTY
(Fox)
dir Neal Israel *pro* Ron Moler, Bob Israel *exec pro* Joe Rorth *scr* Neal Israel, Pat Proft, based on a story by Bob Israel *ph* Hal Trussell, in DeLuxe colour *ed* Tom Walls *art dir* Kevin Conlin, Martin Price *mus* Robert Folk *r time* 105 mins *US opening* prior to Jul 1984 *UK opening* Sep 14.
cast Tom Hanks, Tawny Kitaen, Adrian Zmed, George Grizzard, Barbara Stuart, Robert Prescott, William Tepper, Wendie Joe Sperber, Barry Diamond, Gary Grossman, Michael Dudikoff, Bradford Bancroft, Martina Finch, Deborah Harmon, Tracy Smith, Florence Schauffler, Sumant, John Bloom, Kenneth Kimmins.

One of the more detestable examples of a scurrilous genre, this vulgar comedy propagates the ugliest aspects of the

values and attitudes of contemporary American youth. Naturally, they loved it and made it a major hit. Tom Hanks maintains some semblance of dignity as a wisecracking school bus driver about to marry a wealthy but down-to-earth girl. His buddies are determined to throw him a raunchy send-off with hookers despite his protestations. Meanwhile, the girls crash the party dressed as prostitutes to set the debased farce in motion. Director/co-writer Neal Israel showed some promise with 'Americathon' but this witless exercise dashes any reasonable future expectations.

LE BAL
(Cineproductions SA-Film A2-Massfilm Oncic/Almi/Warner)
dir Ettore Scola *pro* Giorgio Silvagni *scr* Jean-Claude Penchenat, Ruggero Maccari, Furio Scarpelli, Ettore Scola, based on the stage production by the Théâtre du Campagnol *ph* Ricardo Aranovich, in Fujicolor *ed* Raimondo Crociani, Pina Triumveri, Elvira Zincone *mus* various, arranged by Vladimir Cosma *r time* 112 mins *US opening* prior to Jul 1984 *UK opening* Nov 29.
cast Etienne Guichard, Régis Bouquet, Francesco de Rosa, Arnault

Lecarpentier, Lilian Delval, Martine Chauvin, Danielle Rochard, Nani Noël, Aziz Arbia, Marc Berman, Geneviève Rey-Penchenat, Michel Van Speybroeck, Rossana di Lorenzo, Michel Toty, Raymonde Heudeline, Anita Picchiarini, Olivier Loiseau, Monica Scattini, Christophe Allwright, François Pick, Chantal Capron, Jean-François Perrier, Jean-Claude Penchenat.

French history over the past fifty years summoned up – not a word of dialogue is spoken – in a series of tableaux

vivants (or dansants) in a huge dance hall. With its origins in a stage production, Ettore Scola's film remains theatrically stylized, yet in its deployment of framing and movement it could hardly be more cinematic in effect. The transitions from one setpiece to the next are often brilliantly managed, and while the view of events might by any realistic yardstick be considered sentimental (did German officers really have much difficulty in finding dancing partners during the Occupation?), as a fantasia on popular memory, the movie is both ingenious and highly appealing.

THE BAY BOY
(Hachette Fox Prods–Antenne 2-Films A2-CTV-Telefilm Canada-HBO/Orion/Rank)
dir-scr Daniel Petrie *pro* John Kemeny, Denis Héroux *exec pro* Susan Cavan, Frank Jacobs *ph* Claude Agostini, in colour *ed* Susan Shanks *pro des* Wolf Kroeger *mus* Claude Bolling and others *r time* 101 mins *US opening* Sep 19 *UK opening* May 3.
cast Liv Ullmann, Kiefer Sutherland, Peter Donat, Allan Scarfe, Mathieu Carrière, Chris Wiggins, Thomas Peacocke, Isabelle Mejias, Jane McKinnon, Leah Pinsent, Peter

Spence, Joséphine Chaplin, Pauline Laffont, Roy McMullin, Kathy McGuire, Robbie Gallivan, Robert Rose.

Daniel Petrie's memoir of his Catholic boyhood in Depression Canada treads familiar coming-of-age terrain without any new perspectives. Kiefer Sutherland makes a congenial impression in the lead rôle, but Liv Ullmann is again embarrassingly ill-cast. Winner of the several Genie awards, it is the conventional cinema that national institutions love to recognize as official art. Not bad, but hardly of any real merit, either.

BEAT STREET
(Orion/Rank)
dir Stan Lathan *pro* David V Picker, Harry Belafonte *scr* Andy Davis, David Gilbert, Paul Golding *ph* Tom Priestly, in DeLuxe colour *ed* Dov Hoenig *pro des* Patrizia Von Brandenstein *mus* Harry Belafonte, Arthur Baker *r time* 105 mins *US opening* prior to Jul 1984 *UK opening* Jul 6.
cast Rae Dawn Chong, Guy Davis, John Chardiet, Leon Grant, Robert Taylor, Dean Elliott, Franc Reyes.

Le Bal

The plot is little more than a patchwork of elements from 'Fame' 'Footloose', 'Breaking' 'Wild Style'; and the rather anodyne view of life in the Bronx (populated largely by aspiring graffiti artists, breakdancers and deejays) wears thin very quickly. But the vitality of the dancing, an energetic score and an engaging quartet of central characters make it a cheerful and professional entertainment.

THE BEAR: See US section

BENVENUTA

(La Nouvelle Imagerie-UGC-Europe 1-FR3-Opera Film/Artificial Eye) *dir-scr* André Delvaux, based on the novel 'La Confession Anonyme' by Suzanne Lilar *pro* Jean-Claude Batz *ph* Charlie Van Damme in Eastman Colour *ed* Jean Goudier *art dir* Claude Pignot *mus* Frédéric Devreese *r time* 106 mins *UK opening* Jul 19.
cast Fanny Ardant, Vittorio Gassman, Françoise Fabian, Mathieu Carrière, Claire Wauthion, Philippe Geluck, Anne Chappuis, Armando Marra, Rénato Scarpa, Franco Trevisi, Giufrida, Goddart, Franco Angrisano, Tamara Trifez, Béatrice Palme, Franz Joubert, Franco Bruno, Bert André.

Memories, fantasies, parallel fictions... Delvaux has nimbly trodden the tricky obstacle courses of surreal ambiguity in the past, but this time only manages an elegantly glacial plod. Would-be screenwriter Carrière elicits from ageing authoress Fabian a shadow version of her once-scandalous romantic novel, his ears cocked for any plaintive echoes of autobiography in the tragic love affair acted out by Ardant and Gassman, and finds himself seductively haunted by both tale and teller. Labyrinthine stuff, but oppressively laboured.

BEST DEFENSE: See US section

BEVERLY HILLS COP

(Paramount) *dir* Martin Brest *pro* Don Simpson, Jerry Bruckheimer *exec pro* Mike Moder *scr* Daniel Petrie Jr *ph* Bruce Surtees, in Technicolor *ed* Billy Weber, Arthur Coburn *pro des* Angelo Graham *mus* Harold Faltermeyer *r time* 105 mins *US opening* Dec 5 *UK opening* Jan 25.

cast Eddie Murphy, Judge Reinhold, John Ashton, Lisa Eilbacher, Ronny Cox, Steven Berkoff, James Russo, Jonathan Banks, Stephen Elliott, Gilbert R Hill, Art Kimbro, Joel Bailey, Bronson Pinchot, Paul Reiser, Michael Champion, Frank Pesce, Gene Borkan, Michael Gregory, Alice Cadogan, Philip Levien, Karen Mayo-Chandler, Gerlad Berns, William Wallace, Israel Juarbe.

Setting up a neat comic variation on the old Siegel/Eastwood 'Coogan's Bluff' formula, the latest customised star vehicle for Murphy does little more than coast on its premise of a street-smart, no-shit, out-of-Motown 'tec shaking up the by-the-book computer-complacency of the bureaucratic Beverly Hills police force. But at least Murphy's patent jive-patter is in overdrive, fostering the amiable (and profitable) illusion that the whole movie's in fast-forward. (See Films of the Year.)

Benvenuta

Left: Birdy. Above: Blame It on Rio

BIRDY
(A & M/Tri-Star-Delphi III/Columbia)
dir Alan Parker *pro* Alan Marshall *exec pro* David Manson *scr* Sandy Kroopf, Jack Behr, based on the novel by William Wharton *ph* Michael Seresin, in Metrocolor *ed* Gerry Hambling *pro des* Geoffrey Kirkland *art dir* Armin Ganz, Stu Campbell *mus* Peter Gabriel *r time* 120 mins *US opening* Dec 21 *UK opening* Jun 14.
cast Matthew Modine, Nicolas Cage, John Harkins, Sandy Baron, Karen Young, Bruno Kirby, Nancy Fish, George Buck, Dolores Sage, Robert L Ryan, James Santini, Maude Winchester, Marshall Bell, Elizabeth Whitcraft, Sandra Beall, Victoria Nekko, Crystal Field, John Brumfield, Joe Lerer.

Alan Parker flies high in a post-Vietnam movie whose oblique approach, through two damaged survivors, is more telling than a direct confrontation. The camera circles the two protagonists obsessively, working in close-up to maintain a tension that is released by the final funny dénouement.

BIZET'S CARMEN: See CARMEN

BLAME IT ON RIO
(Fox)
dir-pro Stanley Donen *exec pro* Larry Gelbart *scr* Charlie Peters, Larry Gelbart *ph* Reynaldo Villalobos, in Metrocolor *ed* George Hively *art dir* Marcos Flaksman *mus* Ken Wannberg, Oscar Castro Neves *r time* 110 mins *US opening* prior to Jul 1984 *UK opening* Aug 17.
cast Michael Caine, Joseph Bologna, Valerie Harper, Michelle Johnson, Jose Lewgoy, Lupe Gigliotti.

Someone should be blamed for this strained farce (based on an inconsequential Claude Berri film of several years ago, 'One Wild Moment') but it shouldn't be Rio – or star Michael Caine. As a businessman on vacation who finds himself sexually entangled with his daughter's best friend – who also happens to be the daughter of his best friend – Caine manages to

maintain his dignity against nearly insurmountable odds. Larry Gelbart's script leaves no innuendo unturned. Stanley Donen's direction is professional but hardly inspired – which, considering what he was working with, is quite understandable.

BLAME IT ON THE NIGHT: See US section

BLESS THEIR LITTLE HEARTS: See US section

BLOOD SIMPLE
(River Road Prods/Circle Releasing/Palace)
dir Joel Coen *pro* Ethan Coen *exec pro* Daniel F Bacaner *scr* Joel Coen, Ethan Coen *ph* Barry Sonenfeld in DuArt colour *ed* Roderick Jaynes, Don Wiegmann, Peggy Connolly *pro des* Jane Musky *mus* Carter Burwell *r time* 99 mins *US opening* Jan 18 *UK opening* Feb 1.
cast John Getz, Frances McDormand, Dan Hedaya, Samm-Art Williams, M Emmet Walsh, Deborah Neumann, Raquel Gavia, Van Brooks, Señor Marco, William Creamer, Loren Bivens, Bob McAdams, Shannon Sedwick, Nancy Ginger, Reverend William Preston Robertson.

A truly stylish thriller in the modern noir mould, this inventive debut from the Coen brothers features a plot so serpentine as to defy synopsis. Barman hires private eye to kill faithless wife and lover: eye fakes killing, decides to kill employer. Fails, and everyone else starts believing everyone else has committed the crime. It's not merely the sheer joy to be taken in following the taut threads interwoven throughout the plot that makes this such a stunner; it is also the acutely ironic depiction of human motivation, with characters killing or being killed simply because someone, somewhere, doesn't understand what's going on. This sense of universal misapprehension and corruptability, coupled with the determinedly sordid Texas setting, evokes nothing less than the guiding spirit of James M Cain. But unlike, say, 'Body Heat', the film is a true original rather than pastiche, and – with its heady brew of adultery, murder, blackmail, and greed – never loosens its gruesome, greasy grip from start to finish.

BMX BANDITS
(Rank)
dir Brian Trenchard-Smith *pro* Tom Broadbridge, Paul F Davies *scr* Patrick Edgeworth, based on a screenplay by Russell Hagg *ph* John Seale in Panavision, colour *ed* Alan Lake *pro des* Ross Major *mus* Colin Stead, Frank Strangio *r time* 90 mins *UK opening* Jul 20.
cast David Argue, John Ley, Nicole Kidman, Angelo D'Angelo, James Lugton, Bryan Marshall, Brian Sloman, Peter Browne, Bill Brady, Linda Newton, Bob Hicks, Guy Norris, Chris Hession, Norman Hodges, Tracey Wallace, Michael Gillette, Brian Best, Jerry D'Angelo, Malcom Day, Ray Marshall.

The danger with trend-related movies, inevitably, is that the trend is usually on its way out by the time the film appears, leaving as the potential audience only the committed die-hards who haven't found something new to

satisfy their curiosity. People still ride BMX bicycles, of course, but they clearly didn't ride them to cinemas playing this cheerful, fluffy anachronism.

BODY DOUBLE: See US section

BODY ROCK
(New World/Thorn EMI)
dir Marcelo Epstein *pro* Jeffrey Schechtman *exec pro* Phil Ramone, Charles J Weber, Jon Feltheimer *scr* Desmond Nakano, based on a story by Desmond Nakano, Kimberly Lynn White *ph* Robby Müller, in CFI colour

Body Rock

ed Richard Halsey, Lorenzo DeStephano *pro des* Guy Comtois *mus* Sylvester Levay *r time* 94 mins *US opening* Sep 28 *UK opening* Feb 8.
cast Lorenzo Lamas, Vicki Frederick, Cameron Dye, Michelle Nicastro, Ray Sharkey, Seth Kaufman, La Ron A Smith, Rene Elizondo, Oz Rock, Joseph Whipp, Grace Zabriskie, Tony Ganios, Shashawnee Hall, Carola Ita White, Ellen Gerstein, Russell Clark, Robin Menken, Mimi Kinkade, Shawn Patrick Whittington.

Cinematography by Robby Müller gives this breakdance opus an unexpected edge of visual distinction. But in other respects this is very much par for a pretty ropy course, with a clapped-out scenario about local boy who makes good in showbiz, gets swollen head, but ends up by doing right by his erstwhile chums. Even the dancing, though shot from a multiplicity of bizarre angles, comes out looking on the tame side.

Bolero

BOLERO

(Cannon)

dir-scr-ph John Derek, in colour *pro* Bo Derek *exec pro* Menahem Golan, Yoram Globus *pro des* Alan Roderick-Jones *mus* Peter Bernstein, Elmer Bernstein *r time* 104 mins *US opening* Aug 31 *UK opening* Oct 26.

cast Bo Derek, George Kennedy, Andrea Occhipinti, Ana Obregon, Greg Bensen, Olivia D'Abo, Ian Cochrane, Mirta Miller, Mickey Knox, Paul Stacey, James Stacey.

Exhibiting every sign of their consistent confusion between the lubricious and the ludicrous, the latest fleshy farce from the deadly Derek duo is a thoroughly un-Ravelled affair about reluctant virgin Bo offering herself in turn to a sleepy sheik and an unfortunately groin-gored bullfighter. The focus is soft, the action coreless, and the final simulated stimulation takes place amid a dry-ice-and-neon setting in which the word 'ecstasy' is doubly abused by misspelling and abject misapplication. (See Turkeys of the Year.)

THE BOSTONIANS

(Rediffusion/Almi/Curzon)

dir James Ivory *pro* Ismail Merchant *exec pro* Al Schwarz, Michael Landes *scr* Ruth Prawer Jhabvala, based on the novel by Henry James *ph* Walter Lassally, in colour *ed* Katherine Wenning, Mark Potter *pro des* Leo Austin *mus* Richard Robbins *r time* 122 mins *US opening* Aug 2 *UK opening* Sep 28.

cast Christopher Reeve, Vanessa Redgrave, Madeleine Potter, Jessica Tandy, Nancy Marchand, Wesley Addy, Barbara Bryne, Linda Hunt, Nancy New, Charles McCaughan, John Van Ness Philip, Wallace Shawn, Maura Moynihan, Martha Farrar, Peter Bogyo, Dusty Maxwell, Lee Doyle, J Lee Morgan.

James Ivory invariably works with fascinating projects that he generally butchers, but once in a while he makes a good film ('Shakespeare Wallah', 'Heat and Dust'), so he compels attention despite a history of bad experiences. The adaptation blunts the impact of the great Henry James novel, and Ivory as usual can get no handle on the material. Nevertheless, the magnetism of James remains palpable, and the acting by a superb cast is uniformly excellent. Maybe Ivory ought to be an executive producer, or some such.

THE BOUNTY

(Orion/Thorn EMI)

dir Roger Donaldson *pro* Bernard Williams *scr* Robert Bolt, based on the book 'Captain Bligh and Mr Christian' by Richard Hough *ph* Arthur Ibbetson, in Technicolor *ed* Tony Lawson *art dir* Tony Reading *mus* Vangelis *r time* 130 mins *US opening* prior to Jul 1984 *UK opening* Sep 24.

cast Mel Gibson, Anthony Hopkins, Laurence Olivier, Edward Fox, Daniel Day-Lewis, Bernard Hill, Philip Davis, Liam Neeson, Wi Kuki Kaa, Tevaite Vernette, Philip Martin Brown.

Robert Bolt's two-part epic (based more on history than on Nordhoff-Hall) had been a dream project for a decade for David Lean, but this condensed single

feature version disappointingly lacks sweep and credible conflict. Anthony Hopkins' neurotic but heroic conception of Bligh sustains interest, but Mel Gibson makes a weak Christian, undermining the whole dramatic structure. Gibson isn't helped by surprisingly impersonal direction from Roger Donaldson (of the inspired 'Smash Palace'), which garbles the action in key passages.

BRAZIL

(Fox/Universal)

dir Terry Gilliam *pro* Arnon Milchan *scr* Terry Gilliam, Tom Stoppard, Charles McKeown *ph* Roger Pratt, in colour *ed* Julian Doyle *pro des* Norman Garwood *mus* Michael Kamen *r time* 142 mins *UK opening* Feb 22.

cast Jonathan Pryce, Robert De Niro, Katherine Helmond, Ian Holm, Bob Hoskins, Michael Palin, Ian Richardson, Peter Vaughan, Kim

Greist, Jim Broadbent, Barbara
Hicks, Charles McKeown, Derrick
O'Connor, Kathryn Pogson, Bryan
Pringle, Sheila Reid, John Flanagan,
Ray Cooper, Brian Miller, Simon
Nash.

*Gilliam's tragicomic improvisation on
themes familiar from Orwell's
'Nineteen Eighty-Four' is one of the
most genuinely bizarre movies to
emerge in recent years. Pryce is the
Ministry of Information clerical worker
who dreams endlessly of gaining both
the power of flight and the love of a
mysterious revolutionary girl, and
despairs of ever getting his central
heating system fixed. But try as he
might to sort out his various problems,
he is thwarted by the intricacies and
absurdities of bureaucracy at every
turn. With a story that is often
wayward – hardly surprising given the
outrageous fertility of Gilliam's manic
imagination – and a climactic ending
that goes on rather too long, the film
nevertheless succeeds through its blend
of black humour and horrific brutality,
its hyperbolic satire, and its stunning
sets which combine grimy forties'
metallurgy, futuristic fantasy and
Pythonesque surrealism with
remarkable coherence. As original,
invigorating comedy with a serious
point to make, it stands alone, while the
hesitant renditions of the song 'Brazil'
that echo throughout provide an
appropriately wistful backdrop for a
film that cherishes and mourns love
and freedom.*

THE BREAKFAST CLUB
(A&M/Universal)
dir-scr John Hughes *pro* Ned Tanen,
John Hughes *exec pro* Gil Friesen,
Andrew Meyer *ph* Thomas Del Ruth,
George Bouillet, in Technicolor *ed*
Dede Allen *mus* Keith Forsey and
others *r time* 97 mins *US opening*
Feb 15 *UK opening* Jun 7.
cast Emilio Estevez, Paul Gleason,
Anthony Michael Hall, John Kapelos,
Judd Nelson, Molly Ringwald, Ally
Sheedy, Perry Crawford, Mary
Christian, Ron Dean, Tim Gamble,
Fran Gargano, Mercedes Hall.

The Breakfast Club

*Clichéd recipe – take half a dozen
assorted strangers, isolate them and
watch what happens – given an
adolescent twist as a group of students
serve a day's school detentions. Filmed
in the style of a rock video, the movie's
message beneath its surface rebellion is
depressingly conformist: suppress your
individuality and you, too, can become
sexually attractive.*

BREWSTER'S MILLION: See US
section

BROADWAY DANNY ROSE
(Orion/Rank)
dir-scr Woody Allen *pro* Robert
Greenhut *exec pro* Charles H Joffé *ph*
Gordon Willis, in monochrome *ed*
Susan E Morse *pro des* Mel Bourne
mus Dick Hyman *r time* 86 mins
US opening prior to Jul 1984
UK opening Aug 17.
cast Woody Allen, Mia Farrow, Nick
Apollo Forte, Milton Berle, Sandy
Baron, Corbett Monica, Jackie Gayle,
Morty Gunty, Will Jordan, Howard
Storm, Jack Rollins, Craig
Vandenburgh, Herb Reynolds.

Broken Mirrors

Broadway Danny Rose

*Woody Allen's most straightforwardly
enjoyable film since 'Annie Hall'. This
story of a small-time agent falling in
love with the abrasive girlfriend of his
one halfway successful client may
produce more in the way of gentle
smiles than raucous belly laughs, but
they're nonetheless welcome. For once
not wearing his intellectual martyr
outfit, Allen sports the appeal that
made him a star in the first place. As
the lounge singer he manages, Nick
Apollo Forte (a singer in real life) is
delightful. Mia Farrow is equally
charming as his – and Allen's – girl,*

*though the conception of her character
(and to some extent her performance)
owes a shade too much to Cathy
Moriarty in 'Raging Bull'.*

BROKEN MIRRORS
(Sigma Films/Thorn EMI Classics)
dir-scr Marleen Gorris *pro* Matthijs
van Heijningen *ph* Frans Bromet, in
Eastman Colour *ed* Hans van Dongen
art dir Harry Ammerlaan *mus*
Lodewijk De Boer, Haydn *r time* 112
mins *UK opening* Apr 5.
cast Lineke Rijxman, Henriette Tol,
Edda Barends, Coby Stunnenberg,
Carla Hardy, Marijke Veugelers,
Arline Renfurm, Anke Van't Hoff,
Hedda Tabet, Elja Pelgrom, Johan
Leyssen, Rolf Leendeerts, Eddy
Brugman, Beppie Melissen, Wim
Wama, Truus Dekker, Elsje De Wijn,
Matthias Maat, Mara Peelen.

*A reductive feminist/separatist polemic
cast in the inappropriately comforting
form of an art movie, Marleen Gorris's
disappointing follow-up to 'A Question
of Silence' interweaves two story-lines –
about everyday brothel life and about
the victim of a sadistic kidnapper/killer
– while settling for a single, absolutist
vision of gender-determined rôles and
functions based exclusively on sexual
hatred and fear. There's clearly much
off-screen space for argument over
what's omitted from this narrow
schema, but also room enough to query*

*why such an innately voyeuristic
approach to the material should have
been adopted in the first place.*

THE BROTHER FROM
ANOTHER PLANET
(A-Train Films/Cinecom/Virgin)
dir-scr-ed John Sayles *pro* Peggy
Rajski, Maggie Renzi *ph* Ernest R
Dickerson, in colour *pro des* Nora
Chavooshian *mus* Mason Daring
r time 108 mins *US opening* Sep 14
UK opening Nov 30.
cast Joe Morton, Tom Wright,
Caroline Aaron, Herbert Newsome,
Dee Dee Bridgewater, Darryl
Edwards, Leonard Jackson, Bill
Cobbs, Steve James, Edward Baran,
John Sayles, David Strathairn,
Maggie Renzi, Olga Merediz, Minnie
Gentry, Ren Woods, Reggie Rock
Bythewood, Alvin Alexis.

*Born of both the imagination that
unleashed 'Alligator' and his
'Secaucus Seven' sensibility, John
Sayles' wry and funky variant on 'ET'
has the wonderful premise of a black
alien crash-landing in Harlem, and no
one noticing. Mutely observing the sub-
cultural niceties (and nastinesses) as
an impressionably innocent
immigrant, Joe Morton is helped in
sidestepping the pitfalls of
sentimentality by Sayles' wackier
interventions – especially those made
in his acting guise as one of a pair of
incompetent inter-planetary bounty
hunters. The colourful character
gallery around him is suitably
accommodated in an endlessly
digressive ramble that jars only when it
ODs on a story strand about drug-
dealing.*

Cc

CAL
(Enigma-Goldcrest/Warner)
dir Pat O'Connor *pro* Stuart Craig,
David Puttnam *exec pro* Terence A
Clegg *scr* Bernard MacLaverty, based
on his own novel *ph* Jerzy Zielinski, in
colour *ed* Michael Bradsell *pro des*
Stuart Craig *mus* Mark Knopfler
r time 102 mins *US opening* Aug 24
UK opening Sep 14.
cast Helen Mirren, John Lynch, Donal
McCann, John Kavanagh, Ray
McAnally, Stevan Rimkus, Catherine
Gibson, Louis Rolston, Tom Hickey,
Gerard Mannix Flynn, Edward Byrne,
J J Murphy, Audrey Johnston, Brian
Munn, Daragh O'Malley, George
Shane, Julia Dearden, Yvonne
Adams, Laurence Foster, Scott
Frederick, Gerard O'Hagan.

*Lugubrious treatment of a potentially
compelling subject, as a Catholic youth
in Northern Ireland is drawn against
his inclination into terrorist activity
and then begins to grow emotionally
through a love affair with the widow of
the Protestant policeman he helped to
murder. Though honest in its
portrayals and faultless in its integrity,
the movie fails to discover any artistic
insight beyond accurately sketching its
situations and characters. Helen
Mirren won the Best Actress award at
Cannes, but the keenest work comes
from Donal McCann as Cal's ill-fated
father.*

CANNONBALL RUN II
(Golden Harvest/Warner/Miracle/
Videoform)
dir Hal Needham *pro* Albert S Ruddy
exec pro Raymond Chow, Andre
Morgan *scr* Hal Needham, Albert S
Ruddy, Harvey Miller *ph* Nick
McLean in Technicolor *ed* William
Gordean, Carl Kress *art dir* Tho E
Azzari *mus* Al Capps *r time* 108 mins
US opening prior to Jul 1984
UK opening Jul 27.
cast Burt Reynolds, Dom DeLuise,
Jack Elam, Mel Tillis, Charles Nelson
Reilly, Doug McClure, Henry Silva,
Sammy Davis Jr, Molly Picon, Jamie
Farr, Michael Gazzo, Marilu Henner,
Alex Rocco, Abe Vigoda, Joe
Theismann, Shirley MacLaine, Dean

Caravan of Courage

Carmen

Martin, Tony Danza, Richard Kiel,
Susan Anton, Telly Savalas,
Catherine Bach, Arte Johnson, Jilly
Rizzo, Lee Kolima, Shawn Wetherly,
Jack Smith, Tim Conway, Don Knotts,
Marty Allen, Avery Schreiber, Dub
Taylor, Ricardo Montalban, John See,
George Lindsey, Frank Sinatra, Fred
Dryer, John Worthington Stuart, Debi
Greco, C James Lewis, Harry Gant,
Hal Needham, Robert B Chandler,
Frank O Hill.

*To all intents and purposes, a remake
of the unappealing 'Cannonball Run',
with Burt Reynolds tirelessly flashing
his teeth as the Juanesque master of the
revels while Dean Martin and Sammy*

*Davis lurk about on the sidelines like
pale shadows of their former Rat Pack
selves. A sub-plot about an inept Mafia
family, the Cannelonis, raises a few
lugubrious laughs; the rest of the
picture expires in a welter of mugging
and mistiming.*

CARAVAN OF COURAGE
(Lucasfilm/Korty Films/Fox)
dir John Korty *pro* Thomas G Smith
exec pro George Lucas *scr* Bob Carrau,
from a story by George Lucas *ph* John
Korty, in DeLuxe colour *ed* John Nutt,
Howard Stein *pro des* Joe Johnston
r time 120 mins *US opening* on
television *UK opening* Dec 14.
cast Eric Walker, Warwick Davis,
Fionnula Flanagan, Guy Boyd,
Aubree Miller, Dan Frishman, Debbie
Carrington, Tony Cox, Kevin
Thompson, Margarita Fernandez,
Pam Grizz, Bobby Bell.

*A pre-Christmas kiddie-special on
American TV, this mop-up release for
very undemanding British moppets
must have looked tacky even there. An
extended ad for Ewok cuddlies left
unsold after 'Return of the Jedi', it
features the cutesy critters in a wan
adventure to reunite crash-landed
space-kids (nauseous) with their
imperilled parents (ditto), and
attempts to flavour the ladled-on
sentiment with some of the most
poverty-stricken special effects the
Lucasfilm cynics could contrive.*

THE CARE BEARS MOVIE: See
US section

**CAREFUL, HE MIGHT HEAR
YOU:** See US section

CARMEN [US Title: Bizet's
Carmen]
(Gaumont-Opera/Columbia-Triumph/
Virgin)
dir Francesco Rosi *pro* Patrice Ledoux
exec pro Alessandro Von Normann *scr*

THE FILMS

Francesco Rosi, Tonino Guerra, based on the opera by Georges Bizet, Meilhac, Halévy, from the novel by Prosper Mérimée *ph* Pasqualino De Santis, in Eastman Colour *ed* Ruggero Mastroianni, Collete Semprun *pro des* Enrico Job *mus* Georges Bizet *r time* 152 mins *US opening* Sep 20 *UK opening* Mar 14.
cast Julia Migenes-Johnson, Plácido Domingo, Ruggero Raimondi, Faith Esham, François Le Roux, Jean-Paul Bogart, Susan Daniel, Lilian Watson, Jean-Philippe Lafont, Gérard Garino, Julien Guiomar, Accursio Di Leo, Maria Campano.

After the glut of recent Carmens, it comes as something as a relief to get back to basic Bizet. Rosi's treatment, filmed in sun-bleached Spanish locations, could almost be described as naturalistic were it not for the orchestral score and singing. This is the poppiest of popular operas and the principals play it to the hilt amidst the heat and dust of the barracks and corridas. Domingo's Don José is slightly wooden, but Raimondi's toreador is the epitome of banderilla-slinging elegance, and Julia Migenes-Johnson's Carmen smoulders in time-honoured sex-bomb fashion, flashing her dusky thighs left, right and centre. (See Films of the Year.)

CAT'S EYE: See US section.

THE CHAIN
(Quintet-County Bank-Film 4 International/Rank)
dir Jack Gold *pro* Victor Glynn *exec pro* David Deutsch *scr* Jack

Rosenthal *ph* Wolfgang Suschitzky, in Eastman Colour *ed* Bill Blunden *pro des* Peter Murton *mus* Stanley Myers and others *r time* 100 mins *UK opening* May 24.
cast Herbert Norville, Denis Lawson, Rita Wolf, Maurice Denham, Nigel Hawthorne, Billie Whitelaw, Judy Parfitt, Leo McKern, Tony Westrope, Bernard Hill, Warren Mitchell, Gary Waldhorn, Ron Pember, Carmen Munroe, David Troughton, Phyllis Logan, Anna Massey, Ann Tirard.

Portmanteau (or pantechnicon) British comedy which engagingly exploits the trauma of moving house. Evocatively shot London settings – the action moves in an upwardly mobile arc from Hackney to Holland Park – and a gamut of staunch performances from both familiar faces and newcomers happily overcome a periodic over-calculation at script level.

CHEECH AND CHONG'S THE CORSICAN BROTHERS: See US section

CHILDREN OF THE CORN
(New World-Cinema Group Venture/Thorn EMI)
dir Fritz Kiersch *pro* Donald P Porchers, Terrence Kirby *exec pro* Earl Glick, Charles J Weber *scr* George Goldsmith, based on a story by Stephen King *ph* Raoul Lomas, in colour *ed* Harry Keramidas *art dir* Craig Stearns *mus* Jonathan Elias *r time* 93 mins *US opening* prior to Jul 84 *UK opening* Jul 27.
cast Peter Horton, Linda Hamilton, R G Armstrong, John Franklin, Courtney Gains, Robby Kiger, Anne Marie McEvoy, Julie Maddalena, Jonas Marlowe, John Philbin.

The Stephen King movie adaptation machine blows a fuse with this version of one of the pulpmeister's shorter works – a rip-off of Shirley Jackson's 'The Lottery'. Some of the worst performances given by children in recent memory are the featured attraction of this limp melodrama about a coven of murderous moppets under the spell of Old Nick who sacrifice their elders to the 'Corn God'.

A Christmas Carol

CHINESE BOXES
(Road Movies/Palace)
dir Christopher Petit *pro* Chris Sievernich *exec pro* Stephen Woolley, Nik Powell *scr* L M Kit Carson, Christopher Petit *ph* Peter Harvey, in colour *ed* Fred Srp *art dir* Edgar Hinz,

Klaus Beiser *mus* Günther Fischer and others *r time* 87 mins *UK opening* Jun 21.
cast Will Patton, Gottfried John, Adelheid Arndt, Robbie Coltrane, Beate Jensen, Susanne Meierhofer, Jonathan Kinsler, L M Kit Carson, Chris Sievernich, Martin Müller, Jochen von Vietinghoff, Ben De Jong, Michael Büttner, Michael Maichle, Edgar Hinz, Christopher Petit.

Petit may be one of Britain's most cine-literate and idiosyncratic film-makers, but it still seems that he would benefit from adhering a little more closely to the disciplines of genre. On a simplistic level, this could be described as a thriller, although far from conventional, despite its evocative use of sordid, colourful locations and its sporadic bursts of efficiently handled action. Fragmented and elliptical, so that the already difficult plot becomes

virtually incomprehensible in places, it works less like a straightforward thriller than as an experiment with the narrative conventions of B-movie mysteries and as an investigation of various forms of entrapment. These art-movie concerns coexist rather awkwardly with the crime format, while some scenes jar with unspeakably solemn dialogue. However, there are enough moments of purely cinematic inspiration – Petit deploys his camera with intelligence and style – to confirm his status as an ambitious director to watch.

CHOOSE ME
(Island Alive/Tartan)
dir-scr Alan Rudolph *pro* Carolyn Pfeiffer, David Blocker *exec pro* Shep Gordon, Chris Blackwell *ph* Jan Kiesser, in Movielab colour *ed* Mia Goldman *pro des* Steven Legler *mus* Luther Vandross and others *r time* 106 mins *US opening* Aug 24 *UK opening* Apr 19.
cast Geneviève Bujold, Keith Carradine, Lesley Ann Warren,

Patrick Bauchau, Rae Dawn, John Larroquette, Edward Ruscha, Gailard Sartain, Robert Gould, John Considine, Jodi Buss, Sandra Will, Mike E Kaplan, Russell Parr, Teresa Velarde, Henry G Sanders, Margery Bond, Debra Dusay, Minnie Lindsay.

Alan Rudolph finally walks through Orpheus' mirror with a smashingly original romantic farce that conveys the spirit of the eighties. With deliciously witty and passionate performances by all concerned, this low budget independent work provides a model for film-making in an era of specialized markets.

A CHRISTMAS CAROL
(Entertainment Partners/Enterprise)
dir Clive Donner *pro* William F Storke, Alfred R Kelman *exec pro* Robert E Fuisz *scr* Roger O Hirson, based on the novel by Charles Dickens *ph* Tony Imi, in colour *ed* Peter Tanner *pro des* Roger Murray-Leach *mus* Nick Bicát *r time* 101 mins *US opening* on television *UK opening* Dec 6.
cast George C Scott, Frank Finlay, Angela Pleasence, Edward Woodward, David Warner, Susannah York, Roger Rees, Nigel Davenport, Timothy Bateson, Michael Gough, Liz Smith, John Sharp, Anthony Walters, Caroline Langrishe, Lucy Gutteridge, Mark Strickson, Joanne Whalley.

Made for American television and it shows. Nothing particularly wrong with it – certainly not in the performances which are uniformly excellent – but suffused with an air of blandness which makes it seem lost on a cinema screen.

A CHRISTMAS STORY
(MGM-UA)
dir Bob Clark *pro* Bob Clark, Rene Dupont *scr* Jean Shepherd, Leigh Brown, Bob Clark, based on the novel 'In God We Trust, All Others Pay Cash' by Jean Shepherd *ph* Reginald H Morris, in colour *ed* Stan Cole *pro des* Gavin Mitchell *mus* Carl Zittrer, Paul Zaza *r time* 94 mins *US opening* prior to Jul 1984 *UK opening* Nov 23.
cast Melinda Dillon, Darren McGavin, Peter Billingsley, Ian Petrella, Scott Schwartz, R D Robb, Tedde Moore, Zack Ward.

Radio humourist Jean Shepherd's folksy anecdotes about growing up in the Midwest in the forties transfer to the big screen better than might be expected – especially considering the director is Bob 'Porky's' Clark. But with "Ol' Shep" doing the narration, this tale of a small boy's desire for a quasi-lethal pop gun is moderately pleasant.

C.H.U.D.
(Bonime Assocs/New World/Premier Releasing)
dir Douglas Cheek *pro* Andrew Bonime *exec pro* Larry Abrams *scr* Parnell Hall *ph* Peter Stein, in TVC colour *ed* Claire Simpson *art dir* Jorge Luis Toro *mus* Cooper Hughes *r time* 110 mins *US opening* Aug 31 *UK opening* Jan 10.
cast John Heard, Kim Greist, Daniel Stern, Christopher Curry, George Martin, John Ramsey, Eddie Jones.

Enjoyable, low-budget piece of eco-horror, based on the premise that if you dump hazardous radioactive waste in a city's sewers, don't be surprised if the tramps who live there evolve into flesh-eating monsters.

CITY HEAT
(Malpaso-Deliverance/Warner)
dir Richard Benjamin *scr* Sam O Brown (Blake Edwards), Joseph C Stinson, based on a story by Sam O Brown (Blake Edwards) *ph* Nick McLean, in Technicolor *ed* Jacqueline Cambas *pro des* Edward Carfagno *mus* Lennie Niehaus and others *r time* 97 mins *US opening* Dec 7 *UK opening* Mar 1.
cast Clint Eastwood, Burt Reynolds, Jane Alexander, Madeline Kahn, Rip Torn, Irene Cara, Richard Roundtree, Tony Lo Bianco, William Sanderson, Nicholas Worth, Robert Davi, Jude Farese, John Hancock, Tab Thacker, Gerald S O'Loughlin, Jack Nance, Dallas Cole, Lou Filippo, Michael Maurer.

City Heat

Kansas City, 1933, is the backdrop for the starring and sparring partnership of Reynolds and Eastwood, in what amounts to a superannuated variation on the 'buddy' movies prevalent a few years back. Graphic mayhem, running to defenestration and burning alive, sorts uneasily, not to say tastelessly, with intimations of farcical comedy. Fringe benefits: some effective camerawork and an enjoyably over-the-top cameo by Rip Torn.

CITY OF PIRATES
(Les Films du Passage-Metro Films/The Other Cinema)
dir-scr Râúl Ruiz *pro* Anne-Marie La Joisin *exec pro* Paulo Branco *ph* Acacio De Almeida, in colour *ed* Valeria Sarmiento, Rodolfo Wedeles, Monique Soussan, Claudio Martinez *mus* Jorge Arriagada *r time* 121 mins *UK opening* Apr 19.
cast Hugues Quester, Anne Alvaro, Melvil Fouquad, André Engel, Duarte De Almeida, Clarisse Dole, André Gomes.

Ruiz has a vocal clique of admirers; to those outside it, however, this movie will seem extraordinary in quite the wrong way. An interminable shaggy dog story set on a remote island, it brandishes a genre of experimentalism which seems a good half-century out of date, resembling nothing so much as an update of something like 'The Seashell and the Clergyman', only at double the length and to not even half the putative point.

CLOAK AND DAGGER: See US section

COCOON: See US section

CODENAME WILDGEESE
(Ascot-Gico Cinematografica/Entertainment)
dir Anthony M Dawson (Antonio Margheriti) *pro* Erwin C Dietrich *scr* Michael Lester *ph* Peter Baumgartner, in colour *mus* Jan

Nemec *r time* 101 mins *UK opening* Mar 1.
cast Lewis Collins, Lee Van Cleef, Ernest Borgnine, Klaus Kinski, Manfred Lehmann, Mimsy Farmer, Thomas Danneberg, Frank Glaubrecht, Wolfgang Pampel, Hartmut Neugebauer.

As crude, gloating and excessive as this director's previous exercises in jungle madness, this has nothing to do with the other Wild Geese despite the subject overlap and the appropriation of the name. Destined for a short, sharp life on video.

CODE OF SILENCE: See US section

CONSTANCE
(Mirage-New Zealand Film Commission/Miramax/Enterprise)
dir Bruce Morrison *pro* Larry Parr *scr* Jonathan Hardy, Bruce Morrison *ph* Kevin Hayward, in colour *ed* Phillip Howe *pro des* Richard Jeziorny *mus* Dave Fraser *r time* 103 mins *US opening* prior to Jul 1984 *UK opening* Jan 18.
cast Donogh Rees, Shane Bryant, Judie Douglass, Martin Vaughan, Donald McDonald, Mark Wignall, Graham Harvey, Hester Joyce, Dana Purkis, Lee Grant, Don Kjestrup, Susan Trainer, Jules Regal, Miranda Pritchard, Roman Watkins, Beryl Te Wiata, Elric Hooper, Lenore Truscott, Stephen Taylor.

Handsomely mounted and full of judicious period reconstruction, Bruce Morrison's movie proceeds from the initially intriguing notion of a Kiwi Mademoiselle Bovary pining for a life of elevating style and elevated passion amid the unpropitious surroundings of post-war Auckland. As the film goes

on, however, the tone seems to falter, first into exaggerated satire, then into contrived melodrama, culminating in a last sequence which unwisely appears to have been lifted from 'Sunset Boulevard'. As a whole, the film confirms a belief that the New Zealand cinema, adventurous though it may be, has yet to acquire the fluency of the best 'new' Australian movies.

COMFORT AND JOY
(Thorn EMI/Universal)
dir-scr Bill Forsyth *pro* Davina Belling, Clive Parsons *ph* Chris Menges, in colour *ed* Michael Ellis *pro des* Adrienne Atkinson *mus* Mark Knopfler *r time* 106 mins *UK opening* Aug 31 *US opening* Oct 10.
cast Bill Paterson, Eleanor David, C P Crogan, Alex Norton, Patrick Malahide, Rikki Fulton, Roberto Bernardi, George Rossi, Peter Rossi, Billy McElhaney, Gilly Gilchrist, Caroline Guthrie, Ona McCraken, Elizabeth Sinclair, Katie Black, Robin Black, Ron Donachie, Arnold Brown, Iain McColl, Billy Johnstone.

Taking for its story content a gang war between rival Glaswegian ice-cream manufacturers, Bill Forsyth's latest film might sound like something rather forced in the way of neo-Ealing whimsicality. But in the upshot Forsyth has created something beguilingly original, a kind of fairy-tale which manages to dissolve the line between fantasy and reality. A disc jockey (endearingly played by Bill Paterson) has his complacency shattered when his girlfriend walks out on him; he begins to see himself as a character in search of maturity, and in a way he finds it as arbitrator in the ridiculous, yet sinister, ice-cream war. More distinctively (at least to some) than in 'Local Hero', Forsyth here finds the extraordinary in the everyday, to achieve in his audience a willing suspension of disbelief, summed up in the way that Chris Menges' camerawork makes the murk of Glasgow on a wintry afternoon affectingly real, yet at the same time contrives through its gliding motion to create an enveloping atmosphere of dream.

Above: Codename Wildgeese. Right: Comfort and Joy

THE COMPANY OF WOLVES
(Palace/ITC/Cannon)
dir Neil Jordan *pro* Chris Brown, Stephen Woolley *exec pro* Stephen Woolley, Nik Powell *scr* Angela Carter, Neil Jordan, based on the stories 'The Company of Wolves' and 'Wolf Alice' by Angela Carter *ph* Bryan Loftus, in colour *ed* Rodney Holland *pro des* Anton Furst *mus* George Fenton *r time* 95 mins
UK opening Sept 21 *US opening* Apr 19.
cast Angela Lansbury, David Warner, Graham Crowden, Brian Glover, Kathryn Pogson, Stephen Rea, Tusse Silberg, Micha Bergese, Sarah Patterson, Georgia Slowe, Susan Porrett, Shane Johnstone, Dawn Archiblad, Richard Morant, Danielle Dax, Vincent McClaren, Ruby Buchanan.

For all that 'The Company of Wolves' is markedly different in both style and content from Neil Jordan's earlier 'Angel', it shares with its predecessor a turning away from an ostensibly realistic premise into a heightened world of its own. And the world that 'Wolves' turns to is, it might be claimed, that of the 'alternative' history of British cinema: the Hammer horror movies and the romantic fantasies of Powell and Pressburger, sharing with the former a concern with the gruesome and supernatural, with the latter an ambience of stylized studio settings,

and with both a readiness to delve into the realm of the suppressed. The movie is also, of course, highly literary, a good joke at the expense of those pundits who would seek to use the term pejoratively, but a bit of a stumbling-block nonetheless: the faux-naif balance is not always maintained and we do not consistently feel that the assorted anecdotes function as projections of the pubescent heroine's sensibility. Even if it does not quite come off, however, this is an achievement of real note, with sumptuous visuals, terrific effects, and – most important of all – a capacity to strike a provocative balance between 'highbrow' and 'popular'. (See Films of the Year.)

CONAN THE DESTROYER
(Universal)
dir Richard Fleischer *pro* Raffaella De Laurentiis *exec pro* Stephen F Kesten *scr* Stanley Mann, based on a story by Roy Thomas, Gerry Conway *ph* Jack Cardiff, in Technicolor *ed* Frank J Urioste *pro des* Pier Luigi Basile *mus* Basil Poledouris *r time* 103 mins
US opening prior to Jul 1984
UK opening Oct 19.
cast Arnold Schwarzenegger, Grace Jones, Wilt Chamberlain, Mako, Tracey Walter, Sarah Douglass, Olivia D'Abo, Pat Roach, Jeff Corey, Sven Ole Thorsen, Bruce Fleischer, Ferdinand Mayne.

Country

Perhaps it's the presence of veteran director Richard Fleischer, perhaps it's the fact that star Arnold Schwarzenegger has grown into his rôle (a rather frightening idea if you think about it) but the plain fact of the matter is this sequel to 'Conan the Barbarian' has it all over the original. Good, dirty, brawny fun, with Arnold squaring off against all comers – mortal or supernatural – helped immeasurably by the presence of disco diva Grace Jones as a warrior woman ally.

THE COTTON CLUB
(Zoetrope/Orion/Rank)
dir Francis Coppola *pro* Robert Evans *exec pro* Dyson Lovell *scr* William Kennedy, Francis Coppola, from a story by William Kennedy, Francis Coppola, Mario Puzo *ph* Stephen Goldblatt, in Technicolor *ed* Barry Malkin, Robert Q Lovett *pro des* Richard Sylbert *mus* John Barry *r time* 128 mins *US opening* Dec 14 *UK opening* May 3.
cast Richard Gere, Gregory Hines, Diane Lane, Lonette McKee, Bob Hoskins, James Remar, Nicolas Cage, Allen Garfield, Fred Gwynne, Gwen Verdon, Lisa Jane, Maurice Hines, Julian Beck, Novella Nelson, Larry Fishburne, John Ryan, Tom Waits, Ron Karabatsos, Glenn Withrow, Jennifer Grey, Wynonna Smith.

No one figured out what this film was about while it was shooting and it wasn't discovered in the editing either. Brilliantly directed scenes are stranded without any meaningful context, as ideas are used and discarded like tissue paper. On lower budgets, such risks can be salutary; at this level of production, it is merely arrogant.

COUNTRY
(Far West Prod/Pangaea Corporation/Touchstone)
dir Richard Pearce *pro* William D Wittliff, Jessica Lange *scr* William D

Wittliff *ph* David M Walsh, in Technicolor *ed* Bill Yahraus *pro des* Ron Hobbs *mus* Charles Gross *r time* 109 mins *US opening* Sep 29 *UK opening* Mar 1.
cast Jessica Lange, Sam Shepard, Wilford Brimley, Matt Clark, Therese Graham, Levi L Knebel, Jim Haynie, Sandra Seacat, Alex Harvey, Stephanie-Stacie Poyner, Jim Ostercamp, Robert Somers, Frank Noel Jr, Reverend Warren Duit, Conrad Doan, James Harrell, Dean French, Betty Smith.

Elements of sentimentality and melodrama obtrude into this account of the hardships of life among a Midwest farming community, but they are assimilated into the movie's understated naturalism and the manner in which the narrative is anchored in semi-documentary observation. Strong playing by Shepard and Lange assists the sincerity of a modest, likeable movie.

CRACKERS
(Universal/Enterprise)
dir Louis Malle *pro* Edward Lewis, Robert Cortes *scr* Jeffrey Fiskin *ph* Laszlo Kovacs, in Technicolor *ed* Susanne Barron *pro des* John J Lloyd *mus* Paul Chihara *r time* 92 mins
US opening prior to Jul 1984
UK opening Jan 25.
cast Donald Sutherland, Jack Warden, Sean Penn, Wallace Shawn, Larry Riley, Trinidad Silva, Christine Baranski, Charlaine Woodard, Tania Valenza, Irwin Corey, Edouard

Crackers

DeSoto, Anna Maria Horsford, Mitchell Lichtenstein, Marjorie Eaton.

Stepping only slightly aside from Hollywood's recent fad for rehashing French comedies, Louis Malle here wastes a fair few dollars of time and talent on an unimaginatively slavish crib of Mario Monicelli's Italian hit of 1958, 'I Soliti Ignoti'/'Persons Unknown', wringing out a disappointingly facile multi-ethnic morality tale with a fatally low laugh-count. Security guard Sutherland leads a cross-section of the dispossessed in an incompetent heist attempt on skinflint Warden's empty pawnshop safe, but Malle never gets beyond this outline irony in doodling a riposte to prevalent Reaganomic wisdoms.

CRIMES OF PASSION:
See US section

Left: Conan the Destroyer. Above: The Cotton Club

D d

DANCE WITH A STRANGER
(First Film Co-Goldcrest-NFFC-Film 4 International/Fox)
dir Mike Newell *pro* Roger Randall-Cutler *scr* Shelagh Delaney *ph* Peter Hannan, in colour *ed* Mick Audsley *pro des* Andrew Mollo *mus* Richard Hartley *r time* 102 mins *UK opening* Mar 1.

cast Miranda Richardson, Rupert Everett, Ian Holm, Matthew Carroll, Tom Chadbon, Jane Bertish, David Troughton, Paul Mooney, Stratford Johns, Joanne Whalley, Susan Kyd, Lesley Manville, Sallie-Anne Field, David Beale, Martin Murphy, Tracy-Louise Ward, Michael Jenn, Alan Thompson, Nicholas McArdle.

Marvellously meticulous recreation of fifties' urban sleaze and its tawdry passions. Miranda Richardson, as Ruth Ellis, the last woman to be hanged in Britain, gives a brilliant, nervy performance. But the reticence of Shelagh Delaney's script, concentrating on display rather than explanation, robs the movie of lasting resonance.

D.A.R.Y.L: See US section

LE DERNIER COMBAT: See THE LAST BATTLE

DESPERATELY SEEKING SUSAN: See US section

DIARY FOR MY CHILDREN: See US section

THE DOGS (LES CHIENS)
(A J Films-AMS Prods-Les Films de la Drouette-Pacific Films/Connoisseur) *dir* Alain Jessua *pro* Laurent Meyniel *exec pro* Daniel Deschamps *scr* André Ruellan, Alain Jessua, based on an idea by Alain Jessua *ph* Etienne Becker, in Eastman Colour *ed* Hélène Plemiannikov *art dir* Jean-Louis Poveda *mus* René Koering, Michel Portal, Djiby *r time* 99 mins *UK opening* Jan 8.

cast Gérard Depardieu, Victor Lanoux, Nicole Calfan, Pierre Vernier, Gérard Séty, Pierre Londiche, Stéphane Bouy, Henri Labussière, Gérard Caillaud, Philippe Mareuil, Anna Gaylor, Guy Saint-Jean, Denyse Roland, Fanny Ardant, Marc Chpill, Philippe Klébert, Régis Porte.

Given the commercial fates of such disparate canine parables as 'Cujo' and 'White Dog', it's less surprising that few decided to engage with Jessua's biting observation on the rise of the New Right than that its long (post-1978) shelf-life was interrupted at all. Lanoux is the appalled liberal discovering a New Town ruled by fear, and roamed unhealthily by both numerous guard-dogs and their rabidly racist owners; Depardieu the fascistic philosopher who trains them to kill in the name of law-and-order. For all its continuing timeliness, though, an overly-dogged dossier rather than a pedigree thriller.

DREAMSCAPE
(Zuplein-Curtis/Fox/Thorn EMI) *dir* Joseph Ruben *pro* Bruce Cohn Curtis *exec pro* Stnaley R Zupnik, Tom Curtis *scr* David Loughery, Chuck Russell, Joseph Ruben, based on a story by David Loughery *ph* Brian Tufano, Kevin Kutchaver, in CFI colour *ed* Richard Halsey *art dir* Jeff Staggs *mus* Maurice Jarre *r time* 99 mins *US opening* Aug 15 *UK opening* Oct 26.
cast Dennis Quaid, Max Von Sydow, Christopher Plummer, Eddie Albert, Kate Capshaw, David Patrick Kelly, George Wendt, Larry Gelman, Cory 'Bumper' Yothers, Redmond Gleeson, Peter Jason, Chris Mulkey, Jana Taylor, Madison Mason, Kendall Carly Browne, Kate Charleson, Eric Gold, Virginia Kiser.

A tacky but enjoyable sci-fi thriller that presaged 'A Nightmare on Elm Street' in its device of having much of the action take place within a number of disturbed human psyches. With the central scenes thrown up by various characters' nightmares, the story is inevitably episodic and variable, veering queasily between lame comedy (a middle-aged man's ludicrous fears about his wife's infidelity) and all-out horror (an eight-year-old's monstrous bogeyman fantasies). But the basic idea and the effects are strong enough to carry the film, and a talented cast manages to deflate the rather overblown and muddled political ideas introduced, almost like an afterthought, towards the end.

DUNE
(Dino De Laurentiis/Universal) *dir-scr* David Lynch, based on the novel by Frank Herbert *pro* Raffaella De Laurentiis *ph* Freddie Francis, in Technicolor *ed* Antony Gibbs *pro des* Anthony Masters *art dir* Pierluigi Basile, Benjamin Fernandez *mus* Toto, Brian Eno, Daniel Lanois, Roger Eno, Marty Paich *r time* 137 mins *US opening* Dec 14 *UK opening* Dec 14.
cast Francesca Annis, Leonardo Cimino, Brad Dourif, José Ferrer, Linda Hunt, Freddie Jones, Richard Jordan, Kyle MacLachlan, Virginia Madsen, Silvana Mangano, Everett McGill, Kenneth McMillan, Jack Nance, Sian Phillips, Jurgen Prochnow, Paul Smith, Patrick Stewart, Sting, Dean Stockwell, Max Von Sydow, Alicia Roanne Witt, Sean Young.

Hamstrung by the apparently imposed need to pictorialize (or wordily synopsize) every single page of Frank Herbert's weighty and highly-resistant sci-fi 'classic', David Lynch just about maintains his own reputation as a master of visual imagination ('Eraserhead', 'Elephant Man') while haplessly demonstrating the inevitable misguidedness of notions of film-of-the-book fidelity. More, in this case, is less; with the skeletal politics of the novel sticking out like a sore thumb from the narrative overload and the numbing morass of characters, causes, creeds and alliances inhabiting Herbert's parallel universe. (See Turkeys of the Year.)

Dune

E*e*

EDDIE AND THE CRUISERS

(Embassy/Media Releasing)
dir Martin Davidson *pro* Joseph
Brooks, Robert K Lifton *exec pro* Rich
Irvine, James L Stewart *scr* Martin
Davidson, Arlene Davidson, based on
the novel by P F Kluge *ph* Fred
Murphy, in Technicolor *ed* Priscilla
Nedd *art dir* Gary Weist *mus* John
Cafferty *r time* 95 mins *US opening*
prior to Jul 1984 *UK opening* Apr 26.
cast Tom Berenger, Michael Paré, Joe
Pantoliano, Matthew Laurance, Helen
Schneider, David Wilson, Michael
'Tunes' Antunes, Ellen Barkin, Kenny
Vance, Joan Stockwell, Joe Cates,
Barry Sand, Vebe Borge, Howard
Johnson, Joey Balin, Bruce Brown,
Robin Karfo, Rufus Harley.

*A sort of where-are-they-now exposé,
with a pushy reporter sniffing out the
remnants of a sixties rock band twenty
years after their lead singer did a
high-drive off a pier in his Chevy. Or
did he. . .? It should have been great,
but the narrative gets bogged down in
red herrings (has Eddie's ghost come
back to haunt his old girlfriend?), the
film totally flunks its flashbacks, and
the music sounds more like watered-
down Springsteen than raunchy period
rock'n'roll.*

EDITH AND MARCEL

(Film 13-Parafrance Film/Miramax/
Cannon-Gala)
dir-scr Claude Lelouch *pro* Tania
Zazulinsky *ph* Jean Bofféty, in
Eastman Colour *ed* Hugues Darmois,
Sandrine Péry *art dir* Jacques Bufnoir
mus Francis Lai and others *r time* 140
mins *US opening* prior to Jul 1984
UK opening Jan 18.

Edith and Marcel

cast Evelyne Bouix, Jacques Villeret,
Francis Hustler, Jean-Claude Brialy,
Jean Bouise, Charles Gérard, Marcel
Cerdan Jr, Charlotte de Turckheim,
Micky Sebastian, Maurice Garrel,
Ginette Garcin, Charles Aznavour,
Philippe Khorsand, Jany Gastaldi,
Candice Patou, Tanya Lopert, Jean
Rougerie.

*Lelouch is hardly a fashionable name
in critical circles but his movies are
consistently popular at the French box
office, and with 'Edith and Marcel' it is
easy to see why. Concerning itself with
Edith Piaf's love affair with the boxer
Marcel Cerdan, ended tragically by the*
*latter's death in a 1949 air crash, this is
not so much a dramatization as an
evocation of the relationship. Quite
daringly, a substantial part of the
running-time is given over to a fictional
sub-plot about a wartime romance and
its sequel – a device which serves to
bring out both the tenor of the times and
the flavour of Piaf's songs. The film is
certainly grandiose in style, full of
elaborate, sometimes almost dizzying,
camera movements; yet somehow the
grandiosity, together with the
formidable production values, elevates
the novelettish elements of the material.
Kitsch it may be, but undeniably kitsch
de-luxe.*

ELECTRIC DREAMS

(Virgin Pictures/MGM-UA/Virgin-
Fox)
dir Steve Barron *pro* Rusty
Lemorande, Larry De Waay *exec pro*
Richard Branson *scr* Rusty
Lemorande *ph* Alex Thomson, in
Metrocolor *ed* Peter Honess *pro des*
Richard MacDonald *mus* Giorgio
Moroder and various *r time* 112 mins
US opening Jul 20 *UK opening* Oct 5.
cast Lenny Von Dohlen, Virginia
Madsen, Maxwell Caulfield, Bud Cort,
Don Fellows, Alan Polonsky, Wendy
Miller, Harry Rabinowitz, Miriam
Margolyes, Holly De Jong, Stella
Maris, Mary Doran, Diana Choy, Jim
Steck, Gary Pettinger, Bob Coffey,
Mac McDonald, Regina Walden,
Howland Chamberlin, Patsy Smart.

*When a young West Coast architect
falls for the concert cellist who lives
upstairs, he finds himself competing
for her affections with his own
computer which he has programmed to
compose tunes for her delectation. This
is the first full-length feature from
pop-promo director Steve Barron, and
in some respects it shows: the bare
bones of a soppy romance have been
dressed up in all manner of video-
assisted gimmickry and high-tech
graphics and doused with a saleable
synthesized soundtrack.*

THE ELEMENT OF CRIME

(Per Holst Filmproduktion-Danish
Film Institute/Palace)
dir Lars von Trier *exec pro* Per Holst
scr Lars von Trier, Niels Vørsel *ph*
Tom Elling, in colour *ed* Tómas
Gislason *pro des* Peter Høimark *mus*
Bo Holton *r time* 104 mins *UK opening*
Jun 7.
cast Michael Elphick, Esmond
Knight, Me Me Lai, Jerold Wells,
Ahmed El Shenawi, Astrid Henning-
Jensen, Janos Hersko, Stig Larsson,
Harry Harper, Roman Moszkowicz,
Lars von Trier, Frederik Casby, Duke
Addabayo, Jon Bang-Carlsen, Leif
Magnusson, Preben Leerdorff-Rye,
Camilla Overbye.

*Trailered by the most ludicrously
pretentious statement about
'heterosexual films' from its young
director, bearing no apparent relation
to his over-allusive, semi-surreal mish-
mash of second-hand movie references,
this slice of Danish dementia subsumes
both a convoluted psychodrama plot
about sex-crime detection and a
hapless multi-national cast to a
succession of drippingly arty
compositions in the mode of jaundiced
neo-noir. Some sort of nadir in
desolation chic.*

The Element of Crime

Falling in Love

THE FALCON AND THE SNOWMAN

(Hemdale/Orion/Rank)
dir John Schlesinger *pro* Gabriel Katzka, John Schlesinger *exec pro* John Daly *scr* Steven Zaillian, based on the book by Robert Lindsey *ph* Allen Daviau, in DeLuxe colour *ed* Richard Marden *pro des* James D Bissell *mus* Pat Metheny, Lyle Mays and others *r time* 131 mins *US opening* Jan 25 *UK opening* Apr 19.
cast Timothy Hutton, Sean Penn, Pat Hingle, Joyce Van Patten, Richard Dysart, Dorian Harewood, Mady Kaplan, Kavid Suchet, Boris Leskin, Lori Singer, Jennifer Runyon, Dan McDonald, Carlos Romano, Valerie Wildman, George Belanger, Nicholas Pryor, Betty Lou Henson, Macon McCalman.

Schlesinger seizes the bull by the horns to turn this factually based account of two unlikely and inept spies into a thuddingly emphatic, elaborately edited mosaic. But not for the first time, truth proves to be duller than fiction, or at least less amenable to dramatization. The bizarre facts cannot be left to speak for themselves, and in the latter half even the facts of the matter cease to be altogether clear. The director has retained his skill with actors, but the performances begin to look like exercises in making bricks without much straw. One is finally left wondering not why these ingenuous young men acted as they did, but rather why on earth anyone felt it worthwhile to make an expensive film about them.

The Falcon and the Snowman

FALLING IN LOVE

(Paramount)
dir Ulu Grosbard *pro* Marvin Worth *scr* Michael Cristofer *ph* Peter Suschitzky, in Technicolor *ed* Michael Kahn *pro des* Santo Loquasto *mus* Dave Grusin *r time* 106 mins *US opening* Nov 21 *UK opening* May 3.
cast Robert De Niro, Meryl Streep, Harvey Keitel, Jane Kaczmarek, George Martin, David Glennon, Dianne Wiest, Victor Argo, Wiley Earl, Jesse Bradford, Chevi Colton, Richard Giza, Frances Conroy, James E Ryan, Sonny Abagnale, George Barry, L P McGlynn, J S Klinetob.

The most brazen of recent attempts to sell on star-power alone, this epic of mock-romantic, 'women's picture' twaddle was surely over-dignified by reviewers repeatedly comparing it with 'Brief Encounter' – although emotional reticence and railways are indeed much to the fore as New York commuters De Niro and Streep fret guiltily over whether they should capitalise on the coincidences of meeting cute at every trip and turn.

THE FAMILY GAME: See US section

FANDANGO: See US section

FAST FORWARD

(Delphi III/Columbia)
dir Sidney Poitier *pro* John Patrick Veitch *exec pro* Melville Tucker *scr* Richard Wesley, from a story by Timothy March *ph* Matthew F Leonetti, in Metrocolor *ed* Harry Keller *mus* Tom Scott, Jack Hayes and others *r time* 109 mins *US opening* Feb 15 *UK opening* May 10.
cast John Scott Clough, Don Franklin, Tamara Mark, Tracy Silver, Cindy McGee, Gretchen F Palmer, Monique Cintron, Debra Varnado, Noel Conlon, Karen Kopins, Irene Worth, Sam McMurray, Michael DeLorenzo, Doris Belack, David White, Robin Bach, Constance Towers, Phyllis Ehrlich.

Formula bopsical which follows the fortunes of eight peachy-clean, all-singing, all-dancing teens who arrive in New York fresh from Ohio, and have to battle against various forms of moneyed corruption and antagonistic streetlife before they can triumph in the requisite big dance contest. Despite having Sidney Poitier at the helm, the film's spotlight shines steadfastly on the three white members of the octet, while the blacks fade anonymously into the background.

FAST TALKING

(Oldata-Australian Film Commission-Merchant Ivory/Filmtrex)
dir-scr Ken Cameron *pro* Ross Matthews *ph* David Gribble, in Eastman Colour *ed* David Huggett *des* Neil Angwin *mus* Sharon Calcraft *r time* 95 mins *UK opening* Mar 29.
cast Rod Zuanic, Toni Allaylis, Chris Truswell, Gail Sweeny, Steve Bisley, Peter Hehir, Tracy Mann, Dennis Moore, Julie McGregor, Garry Cook, Peter Collingwood, Ric Carter, Frank Lloyd, Ron Hackett, John Cobley, Bill McCluskey, Alistair Duncan, Genevieve Moy, Mariette Rups-Donnelly.

Underprivileged Aussie teenagers up against the uncomprehending adult world in a movie whose occasional flashes of spontaneity lose out against the-kids-are-alright sentiment of the most banal and loaded kind. A dispiriting follow-up by Ken Cameron to the interesting 'Monkey Grip'.

FAVOURITES OF THE MOON

(FR3-RAI/Artificial Eye)
dir Otar Iosseliani *pro* Philippe Dussart *exec pro* Michel Choquet *scr* Otar Iosseliani, Gérard Brach *ph* Philippe Theaudière, in Eastman Colour *ed* Dominique Bellfort *pro des* Claude Sune *mus* Nicolas Zourabichvili *r time* 102 mins *UK opening* Mar 28.
cast Katia Rupe, Hans Peter Cloos, Alix De Montaigu, Maïté Nahyr, François Michel, Mathieu Amalric, Jean-Pierre Beauviala, Pascal Aubier, Christiane Bailly, Vincent Blanchet, Bernard Eisenschitz, Marie-Claude

Pouvesle, Fanny Dupin, Marie Parra Aledo, Gabriella Scheer, René Vo Van Minh.

An overly-cultured attempt at kaleidoscopic comedy, busy yet banal in its complex criss-crossing of the paths of such characters as arms dealers, anarchists and art thieves, this first French feature from the transplanted Georgian director Iosseliani toys rather pedantically with variations on a theme of property as/ and theft. A Parisian circus of conspiracy and confusion, it looks all too much like an academic try at hybridizing the eccentric spirits of Vigo and Rivette; while symptomatic of its failure is that amid all the freneticism, only a couple of very slow-burn sight gags raise more than a knowing smile.

FINDERS KEEPERS

(CBS/Warner/Rank)
dir-exec pro Richard Lester *pro* Sandra Marsh, Terence Marsh *scr* Charles Dennis, based on the novel 'The Next-to-Last Train Ride' by Charles Dennis *ph* Brian West, in Technicolor *ed* John Victor Smith *art dir* J Dennis Washington *mus* Ken Thorne *r time* 96 mins *US opening* prior to Jul 1984 *UK opening* Jan 11.
cast Michael O'Keefe, Beverly D'Angelo, Louis Gossett Jr, Pamela Stephenson, Ed Lauter, David Wayne, Brian Dennehy, Jack Riley, John Schuck, Timothy Blake, Jim Carrey, Robert Clothier, Jayne Eastwood, Alf

Humphreys, Barbara Kermode, Paul Jolicoeur, Blu Mankuma, Richard Newman, Frances Flanagan, Campbell Lane, Wayne Robson, Margaret Martin, Judy Leigh-Johnson, Kevin Cork, John Stocker, Harvey Atkin, J C Roberts, Peter Haworth, Kymm Dungy, Margaret Hertlein.

A rather conventional, and rather hit-and-miss, caper from Lester. It gets off to a lively start, compressing exposition into a series of gags, and culminates in a well managed farcical imbroglio involving an ultra-mobile home. But between times there is some forced and mismanaged business aboard a train (a setting which somewhat suffocatingly invokes an earlier tradition of comedy-thrillers), and some uneasy gestures toward calculated bad taste concerning the supposed coffin of a Vietnam war victim. Full marks, though, to Ed Lauter, granted more of an opportunity than usual as the mock-villain of the piece, and playing up to the hilt beneath an alarming black wig.

FIRE AND ICE
(PSO/Fox/Thorn EMI Classics)
dir Ralph Bakshi *pro* Ralph Bakshi, Frank Frazetta *exec pro* John W Hyde, Richard R St Thomas *scr* Roy Thomas, Gerry Conway *ed* A Davis Marshall *mus* William Kraft *r time* 81 mins *US opening* prior to Jul 1984 *UK opening* July 27.
cast Susan Tyrrell, Maggie Rosewell, William Ostrander, Stephen Mendel, Clare Nono, Alan Koss, Hans L Howes, Ray Oliver, Nathan Purdee, Le Tari.

No, not the Revlon story, just another noxious bit of Ralph Bakshi rotoscoping. This time out, fantasy illustrator Frank Frazetta is added to the usual stew of sex and violence in a cartoon tale out of prehistoric times when men were blond surfer ubermensch, women pouting Playboy bunnies, and the forces of evil drooling non-whites referred to as "sub-humans". It is a small miracle that theatres that played this repulsive trash remained standing.

FIRESTARTER
(Dino De Laurentiis/Universal)
dir Mark L Lester *pro* Frank Capra Jr *scr* Stanley Mann, based on the novel by Stephen King *ph* Guiseppe Ruzzolini, in Technicolor *ed* David Rawlins *art dir* Giorgio Postiglione *mus* Tangerine Dream *r time* 115 mins *US opening* prior to Jul 1984 *UK opening* Jul 6.
cast David Keith, Drew Barrymore, Freddie Jones, Martin Sheen, George C Scott, Art Carney, Heather Locklear, Louise Fletcher, Moses Gunn, Antonio Fargas, Drew Synder, Curtis Credel, Keith Colbert, Richard Warlock, Jeff Ramsey, Jack Magner,

Lisa Anne Barnes, Larry Sprinkle, Cassandra Ward-Freeman, Scot R Davis, Nina Jones, William Alspaugh.

Yet another Stephen King adaptation. Ripping himself off this time, the story centres on a young miss with telekinetic powers capable of provoking blazes at will. Drew Barrymore isn't as winsome as she was in 'ET' largely because of the script and direction. George C Scott, however, hams it up to the great effect as the chief villain.

FIRSTBORN: See US section

THE FLAMINGO KID: See US section

A FLASH OF GREEN: See US section

FLASHPOINT: See US section

FLETCH: See US section

LES FLEURS SAUVAGES
(Cinak/Cinegate)
dir-scr Jean Pierre Lefebvre *pro-ed* Marguerite Duparc *ph* Guy Dufaux, in colour *mus* Raoul Duguay, Jean Corriveau *r time* 153 mins *UK opening* Jan 10.
cast Marthe Nadeau, Michele Magny, Pierre Curzi, Claudia Aubin, Eric Beausejour, Georges Belisle, Sarah Mills, Michel Viala, Edoin Family, Thibert Family, Monique Thouin, Raoul Duguay, Marie Esterez, Philippe Esterez, Esterez Children, Rosie Godbout, Claudie Haustrate, Brigitte Lecours, Christian Marcotte, Anna Girouard, Vincent Graton.

This long and slow-moving French-Canadian film makes an initially sympathetic impression with its look at a three-generational family group (elderly widow visiting married daughter and offspring), but sympathy

Fire and Ice

and interest drain away in the face of a non-narrative and some tiresome stylistic mannerisms. Well before the end, the viewer has been overcome by a sense of pointlessness, not to mention a strong dose of ennui.

FOREVER YOUNG
(Enigma-Goldcrest-Channel 4/Fox)
dir David Drury *pro* Chris Griffin *exec pro* David Puttnam *scr* Ray Connolly *ph* Norman Langley, in colour *ed* Max Lemon *art dir* Jeffrey Woodbridge *mus* Peter Maxwell-Davies *r time* 84 mins *UK opening* Sep 28.
cast James Aubrey, Nicholas Gecks, Karen Archer, Alex McCowen, Liam Holt, Jane Forster, Ruth Davies, Joseph Wright, Jason Carter, Julian Firth, Oona Kirsch, Eileen Fletcher,

Carol MacReady, Philip McGough, Pamela Miles, Martin Duncan, Robin Wentworth, Shelley Borkum, Kate Percival, James Wynn.

Preciously written, stolidly performed television drama which looked lost on the few cinema screens it briefly played.

Les Fleurs Sauvages

A Funny Dirty Little War

THE FOURTH MAN

(De Verenigde Nederlandsche Filmcompagnie/Spectrafilm/Mainline)
dir Paul Verhoeven *pro* Rob Houwer *scr* Gerard Soeteman, based on the novel by Gerard Reve *ph* Jan De Bont, in colour *ed* Ine Schenkkan *art dir* Roland De Groot *mus* Loek Dikker *r time* 102 mins *US opening* prior to Jul 1984 *UK opening* Jul 13.
cast Jeroen Krabbé, Renée Soutendijk, Thom Hoffman, Dolf De Vries, Geert De Jong, Hans Veerman, Hero Muller, Caroline De Beus, Reinout Bussemaker, Erik J Meijer, Ursul De Geer, Filip Bolluyt, Hedda Lornie, Paul Nygaard, Guus van der Made, Pamela Teves, Hella Faassen, Helen Hedy.

Scabrous murder comedy from Dutch director Paul Verhoeven buoyed by a

demonically inventive portrayal by Jeroen Krabbé as a homosexual Catholic writer who seduces a literary club hostess out of an obsession with her boyfriend. Teeming with fruity Freudian symbols pouring out of the author's feverish imagination, the film sports a flamboyant cleverness that only wanes with an unsatisfying dénouement.

Full Moon in Paris

FRIDAY THE 13TH – A NEW BEGINNING: See US section

FULL MOON IN PARIS

(Les Films du Losange-Les Films Ariane/Orion Classics/Artificial Eye)
dir-scr Eric Rohmer *pro* Margaret Ménégoz *ph* Renato Berta, in colour *ed* Cécile Decugis *art dir* Pascale Ogier *mus* Elli, Jacno *r time* 101 mins *US opening* Sep 7 *UK opening* Nov 8.
cast Pascale Ogier, Tchéky Karyo, Fabrice Luchini, Virginie Thévenet, Christian Vadim, Laszlo Szabo, Lisa Garneri, Mathieu Schiffman, Anne Séverine Liotard, Hervé Grandsart, Noël Coffman.

The fourth entry in Eric Rohmer's series of 'Fables and Proverbs' presents yet another obtuse heroine setting up her own romantic misfortunes out of a confusion of values and attitudes. The late Pascale Ogier won the Best Actress award at Venice for her superb incarnation of the Rohmer woman. Rohmer's formal command of his solemn farces remains peerless, as he penetrates the rather superficial plotting of his scenario to elicit the philosophical and tragic implications of contemporary living.

A FUNNY DIRTY LITTLE WAR

(Aries Cinematográfica Argentina/ICA Projects)
dir Héctor Olivera *pro* Fernando Ayala, Luis Osvaldo Repetto *scr* Roberto Cossa, Héctor Olivera, based on the novel by Osvaldo Soriano *ph* Leonardo Rodriguez Solis, in Eastman Colour *ed* Eduardo López *art dir* Emilio Basaldúa, Mariá Julia Bertotto *mus* Oscar Cardoza Ocampo and others *r time* 79 mins *UK opening* May 10.
cast Federico Luppi, Hector Bidonde, Victor Laplace, Rodolfo Ranni, Miquel Angel Sola, Julio De Grazia, Lautaro Murua, Graciela Dufau, Ulises Dumont, Raul Rizzo, Arturo Maly, José Maria Lopez.

Provocatively wrought in kinetic comic-book style as a joltingly jaunty black farce, Olivera's scrutiny of the civil strife that attended the last encore of Peronism in Argentina in the seventies is a distinctly troubling exercise in sinister political slapstick. A small-town siege acts as microcosmic harbinger of the militarist terror to come, with a ragtag collection of harmless eccentrics the first in the firing line, doomed to torture, death or disappearance despite their winningly absurd antics in defence of political sanity. Some of the satirical specifics remain obscure, but not a chortle remains unchoked.

THE FUTURE OF EMILY

(Les Films du Losange-Helma Sanders Filmproduktion-Literarisches Colloquium-ZDF-BMI-FFA-Berliner Film-förderung/Mainline)
dir Helma Sanders-Brahms *pro* Nicole Flipo, Ursula Ludwig *ph* Sacha Vierney, in colour *ed* Ursula West *art dir* Jean-Michel Hugon, Rainer Schaper *mus* Jürgen Knieper *r time* 107 mins *UK opening* Apr 26.
cast Brigitte Fossey, Hildegarde Knef, Ivan Desny, Herman Treusch, Camille Raymond, Mathieu Carrière.

After 'Germany Pale Mother' and 'No

Mercy, No Future', this represents a move by its director towards a kind of chamber movie, in which a successful actress returns to the home of her upper-crust parents on the Normandy coast. On the whole, though, the effect is more like an echo chamber. Intriguing correspondences are evoked between the personal histories of Fossey (the actress) and Knef (the mother), but the mixture of elements is not synthesized in such a way as to make the film grip as either drama or dialectic.

GABRIELA

(The Sultana Corporation/UIP)
dir Bruno Barreto *pro* Harold Nebenzal, Ibrahim Moussa *scr* Leopoldo Serran, Bruno Barreto, based on the novel 'Gabriela, Cravo e Canela' by Jorge Amado *ph* Carlo Di Palma, in Technicolor *ed* Emmanuelle Castro *art dir* Hélio Eichbauer *mus* Antônio Carlos Jobim *r time* 99 mins *US opening* prior to Jul 1984 *UK opening* Oct 26.
cast Sonia Braga, Marcello Mastroianni, Antonio Cantáfora, Paulo Goulart, Nelson Xavier, Nuno Leal Maia, Fernando Ramos, Nicole Puzzi, Tânia Boscoli, Joffre Soares, Paulo Pilla, Claudia Gimenez, Ricardo Petraglia, Antônio Pedro, Yvan Mesquita, Zeni Pereira, Flávio Glavão.

A solid citizen of a small village takes a sultry wench under his protective wing. So far so good, especially as he is Marcello Mastroianni and she is Sonia Braga. The only problem is that director Bruno Baretto ('Dona Flor and Her Two Husbands') hasn't given his leads enough to do.

GARBO TALKS: See US section

GHOSTBUSTERS
(Columbia)
dir-pro Ivan Reitman *exec pro* Bernie
Brillstein *scr* Dan Aykroyd, Harold
Ramis *ph* Laszlo Kovacs, Herb
Wagreitch, in Panavision, Metrocolor
ed Sheldon Kahn, David Blewitt
pro des John de Cuir *mus* Elmer
Bernstein *r time* 107 mins *US opening*
prior to Jul 1984 *UK opening* Dec 7.
cast Bill Murray, Dan Aykroyd,
Sigourney Weaver, Harold Ramis,
Rick Moranis, Annie Potts, William
Atherton, Ernie Hudson, David
Margulies, Steven Tash, Jennifer
Runyon, Slavitza Jovan, Michael
Ensign, Alice Drummond.

*Not by any stretch of the imagination a
great movie – which isn't to say it
doesn't provide a good time. Bill
Murray's special brand of 'laid back'
wise-guyism has never been more
irresistible than in this souped-up
Abbott-and-Costello vehicle about a
trio of paranormal investigators who
are out to rid Manhattan of things that
go bump in the night. Sigourney
Weaver is quite fetching as a lady in
distress. Rick Moranis is hilarious as
her nerd of a neighbour. In a season
chocked full of films aimed at kids, this
is one of the few you could actually take
one to see. (See Films of the Year.)*

GIVE MY REGARDS TO BROAD STREET
(MPL Communications/Fox)
dir Peter Webb *pro* Andros
Epaminondas *scr* Paul McCartney *ph*
Ian McMillan, in colour *ed* Peter
Beston *pro des* Anthony Pratt *mus*
various, arranged by George Martin
r time 108 mins *US opening* Oct 26
UK opening Nov 30.
cast Paul McCartney, Bryan Brown,
Ringo Starr, Barbara Bach, Linda
McCartney, Tracey Ullman, Ralph
Richardson, George Martin, Ian
Hastings, John Bennett, Luke
McMasters, Philip Jackson, Marie
Collett, John Harding, Mark
Kingston, Frank Duncan, John
Salthouse, Christopher Ellison, John
Burgess.

*Popular audiences seem to have found
something in Paul McCartney's
expensive piece of indulgence, but it's
mighty difficult to see what it might be.
For one thing, the whole film seems so
middle-aged – hardly anyone on the
screen looks to be under forty – and the
plot, though it looms large in the
scheme of things, is painfully inept. A
couple of the musical numbers are quite
inventively produced – but even on the
strictly musical front, the inclusion of
'Eleanor Rigby' and 'Yesterday' all too
clearly show up the thinness of
McCartney's more recent compositions.
(See Turkeys of the Year.)*

Grace Quigly

THE GLITTER DOME
(Tele-pictures-Trincomali-HBO/
Thorn EMI Classics)
dir Stuart Margolin *pro* Stuart
Margolin, Justis Greene *scr* Stanley
Kallis, based on the novel by Joseph
Wambaugh *ph* Michael Watkins, Fred
Murphy, in colour *ed* M S Martin
pro des Douglas Higgins *mus* Stuart
Margolin *r time* 94 mins *US opening*
on television *UK opening* Nov 23.
cast James Garner, Margot Kidder,
John Lithgow, John Marley, Stuart
Margolin, Paul Koslo, Colleen
Dewhurst, Alex Diakun, Billy Kerr,
William Taylor, Dusty Morean,
Christianne Hirt, Tom McBeath,
Dixie Seatle, Dale Wilson, Julian
Muñoz, Sal Lopez, Real Andrews,
Stephen Chang.

*A curiously erratic made-for-cable
crossover, unexpectedly spicing
Wambaugh's 'Police Story' grittiness
with Garner and Margolin's 'Rockford
Files' grins. The Hollywood-set saga of
murder among the kiddie-porn movie
colony mixes its media metaphors quite
engagingly at times, aiming at a sort of
'TV noir', but cameo-rôle clichés and
between-commercials construction
almost scupper it. A solid lower-case
programmer, nonetheless.*

THE GOODBYE PEOPLE: See US
section

THE GOONIES: See US section

GOTCHA: See US section

GRACE QUIGLEY
(Cannon)
dir Anthony Harvey *pro* Menaham
Golan, Yoram Globus *exec pro* A
Martin Zweiback, Adrienne Zweiback
scr A Martin Zweiback *ph* Larry Pizer,
in colour *ed* Robert Reitano *pro des*
Gary Weist *art dir* Jack Blackman
mus John Addison *r time* 87 mins *US
opening* May 17 *UK opening* Jun 21.
cast Katharine Hepburn, Nick Nolte,
Kit Le Fever, Chip Zien, William
Duell, Elizabeth Wilson, Walter Abel,
Frances Pole, Truman Gaige, Paula
Trueman, Christopher Murney,
Nicholas Kepros, William Cain,
Howard Sherman, Jill Eikenberry,
Michael Charters, Christopher
Charters.

*Finally surfacing in re-edited form
with an abbreviated title a year after its
screening at Cannes, this could well be
the most twee, condescending view of
old age in recent cinema, with Hepburn
and Nolte struggling to impart some
charm to proceedings which
continually defy it.*

GRANDVIEW, USA: See US section

The Glitter Dome

Give My Regards to Broad Street

GREMLINS
(Warner)
dir Joe Dante *pro* Michael Finnell
exec pro Steven Spielberg, Frank
Marshall, Kathleen Kennedy *scr*
Chris Columbus *ph* John Hora, in
Technicolor *ed* Tina Hirsch *pro des*
James A Spencer *mus* Jerry
Goldsmith *r time* 111 mins
US opening prior to Jul 1984
UK opening Dec 7.
cast Zach Galligan, Hoyt Axton,
Frances Lee McCain, Phoebe Cates,
Polly Holliday, Scott Brady, Glynn
Turman, Corey Feldman, Dick Miller,
Keye Luke, Judge Reinbold, Jonathan
Banks, Edward Andrews.

*Expanding on the vein of cartoon
'black' humour he mined in his episode
of 'Twilight Zone – The Movie', Joe
Dante offers a film overflowing with
movie in-jokes and nasty fun. It wears a
bit thin after a while, but there's no
denying Dante's skill in keeping afloat
this minimal tale-cum-toy-store-sales-
pitch about a youth whose unusual pet
spawns an army of less friendly
critters.*

Gremlins

THE GREY FOX
(Mercury Pictures/UA Classics/
Palace)
dir Phillip Borsos *pro* Peter O'Brian
exec pro David H Brady *scr* John
Hunter *ph* Frank Tidy, in Eastman
Colour *ed* Frank Irvine *pro des* Bill
Brodie *art dir* Ian Thomas *mus*
Michael Conway, the Chieftans *r time*
91 mins *US opening* prior to Jul 1984
UK opening May 17.
cast Richard Farnsworth, Jackie
Burroughs, Ken Pogue, Wayne
Robson, Timothy Webber, Gary
Reineke, David Petersen, Don
Mackay, Samantha Langevin, Tom
Heaton, Ray Michael, Stephen E
Miller, Gary Chalk, Jack Leaf, Isaac
Hislop, Sean Sullivan, Peter Jobin,
Anthony Holland, Jon York.

*Attractive and distinctive Canadian
western, wherein a veteran stage robber
embarks on a new career of holding up
trains, then has to take refuge north of
the border. The raw little British
Columbia town where much of the
action is set is sketched in with a
freshness and edge which offsets the
occasionally studied visual style; and
veteran stuntman turned character*

The Grey Fox

*actor Richard Farnsworth brings to the
leading rôle not just a leathery
conviction and fine economy of gesture
but a legacy of faithful service in the
movie west.*

GUNEY'S THE WALL
(MK 2-TFI/Contemporary)
dir Yilmaz Güney *pro* Marin Karmitz
ph Izzet Akay, in Fujicolor *ed* Sabine
Mamou *mus* Ozan Garip Sahin, Setrak
Bakirel, Ali Dede Altuntas, Robert
Kempler *r time* 116 mins *UK opening*
Sep 7.
cast Tuncel Kurtiz, Ayse Emel Mesci,
Saban, Sisko, Ziya, Garip, Zapata,
Mankafa, Malik Berrichi, Nicolas
Hossein, Habes Bounabi, Isabelle
Tissandier, Ali Berktay, Sema Kuray,
Ahmet Ziyrek, Selahattin Kuzuoglu,
Jean-Pierre Colin, Jacques Dimanche,
Ali Dede Altuntas, Necdet Nakiboglu

*The sad fact of Yilmaz Güney's death
only a few days after the UK opening of
'The Wall' makes one all the more
regretful at failing to respond more
deeply to this unmistakably personal
and committed film. An episodic*

*an increasingly self-defeating one.
Intended as a celebration of its
victimised protagonists, it ends up
uneasily like an exploitation of their
suffering. Because the repressive
system concerned is not analysed, the
effect becomes gratuitous.*

GYMKATA: See US section

H h

HAMSIN
(Nachsom Films/Contemporary)
dir Daniel Wachsman *pro* Jacob
Lifshin *scr* Daniel Wachsman, Danny
Verete, Jacob Lifshin *ph* David
Gurfinkel, in colour *ed* Levi Zinni
art dir Frank Gempel, Bashire Abu-
Rabia *mus* Raviv Gazit *r time* 88 mins
UK opening Nov 9.
cast Schlomo Tarshish, Hemda Levy,
Ruth Geler, Shawaf Yassin, Daou
Selim, Zvika Cornfield, Shmuel Shilo,
Yussuf Halil Nassrat, Ilam Toren,
Tarak Copti, Yossi Kenan, Yossi
Savoya, Alon Paz.

*Nominated for an Oscar as best foreign
film, and partially funded by the
Israeli Film Board, 'Hamsin' is a
complex, politically incisive study of
racial conflict, social distinction and
sexual unrest; impressively played,
articulately expressed.*

HEART OF THE STAG: See US
section

HEARTBREAKERS: See US section

HEAVEN HELP US: See US section

HEAVENLY BODIES: See US
section

HEIMAT
(Edgar Reitz-WDR-SFB/Artificial
Eye)
dir-pro Edgar Reitz *scr* Edgar Reitz,
Peter Steinbach *ph* Gernot Roll, part
in colour *ed* Heidi Handorf *art dir*
Franz Bauer *mus* Nikos Mamangakis
r time 924 mins *UK opening* Feb 16
US opening Mar 15.
cast Marita Breuer, Michael Lesch,
Dieter Schaad, Karin Kienzler, Eva
Maria Bayerswaltes, Rüdiger
Weigang, Getrud Bredel, Willi Berger,
Johannes Lobewein, Kurt Wagner,
Marliese Assmann, Eva Maria
Schneider, Wolfram Wagner,
Alexander Scholz, Arno Lang, Otto
Henn, Manfred Kuhn, Karin
Rasenack, Helga Bender.

*Partly conceived in reaction to the soap
operatics of 'Holocaust', Reitz's 16-
hour marathon of twentieth-century
German life is a magnificent
achievement. Focusing on one fictional
village – Schabbach, in the South West
– Reitz describes the changes, political
and personal, that successive
generations underwent from World
War I to the present day. His actors are
wholly convincing (especially Marita
Breuer as Maria, the pivot of all these
lives), the emotions and situations
universal. And for once the appeal of
Nazism to the petit-bourgeoisie is
precisely shown, with none of the comic
strip fascism of Bertolucci's '1900'. A
film 'event' that began life as a
television series but transcends any
categorization.*

**THE HIGHEST HONOUR – A
TRUE STORY**
(Southern International Films/
Enterprise)
dir Peter Maxwell *pro* Lee Robinson
exec pro John McCallum *scr* Lee
Robinson, in association with Katsuya
Suzaki, Takeo Ito *ph* John McLean, in
colour *ed* David Stiven *pro des*
Bernard Hides *art dir* Virginia
Bieneman *mus* Eric Jupp *r time* 108
mins *UK opening* Oct 12.
cast John Howard, Atsuo Nakamura,
Stuart Wilson, Steve Bisley, Michael
Aikens, George Mallaby, Tony
Bonner, John Ley, Harold Hopkins,
Garry Waddell, Tim Elston, Neil
Redfern, Michael Harris, Hu Inn
Mong, Ken Goodlet, Hohsei Komatsu,
Mizuho Suzuki, Allan Cassell.

*A curiously old-fashioned Australian-
Japanese co-production, made in 1982
and cut by thirty-five minutes from its
original running time. Difficult to see
the point of releasing it now.*

The Highest Honour – A True Story

HIGHWAY TO HELL
(Lucky 13/Highbroad Prods/Anglo-American)
dir-scr Mark Griffiths *pro* David Calloway *exec pro* Dimitri T Skouras *ph* Tom Richmond, in colour *ed* Andy Blumenthal *pro des* Katherine Vallin *art dir* Anthony Cowley *mus* Al Capps *r time* 95 mins *US opening* prior to Jul 1984 *UK opening* Jul 27.
cast Monica Carrico, Eric Stoltz, Stuart Margolin, Richard Bradford, Joe George, Virgil Frye, Louise Baker, Laurel Patrick, Sorrells Pickard, Ben Hammer, Juliette Cummins, Bob Carroll, Lesley Woods, Clark Howat, Geno Havens, Seth Kaufman, Richard Walsh, Matt Boston.

The couple-on-the-run theme, which once fuelled movies like 'They Live By Night' and 'Gun Crazy', here dwindles away into the prop for sleazy exploitation. Hooker and escaped teenage killer (transparently innocent, of course) take it on the lam in a corpse-strewn, and visibly cut-price, odyssey in which occasional details (electrical equipment causes one character's shocking demise when it rips into his water bed) suggest that Mark Griffiths might be worthy of better things.

THE HIT
(Zenith/Recorded Picture Co/Palace/Island Alive)
dir Stephen Frears *pro* Jeremy Thomas *scr* Peter Prince *ph* Mike Molloy, in Technicolor *ed* Mick Audsley *pro des* Andrew Sanders *mus* Paco De Lucia *r time* 98 mins *UK opening* Sep 7 *US opening* Mar 8.
cast John Hurt, Tim Roth, Laura Del Sol, Terence Stamp, Bill Hunter, Fernando Rey, Lennie Peters, Bernie Searl, Brian Royal, Albie Woodington, Willoughby Gray, Jim Broadbent, Manuel De Benito, Juan Calot, Freddie Stuart, Ralph Brown, A J Clarke.

A London bank robber gives evidence against his associate, whereupon the scene shifts to southern Spain ten years later and the snatching of the grass from his rural retreat by a couple of hard men detailed to transport him to Paris for summary justice at the hands of his erstwhile employer. Striking performances – Terence Stamp as the

laconic victim, Tim Roth as the cocksure tyro gunman, John Hurt as the hooded-eyed, chain-smoking first murderer – and at least one excitingly managed passage of action in a lethal contretemps at a filling station. On the other hand, the tone of the script is sometimes uncertain, with the ambience wavering between hard-boiled realism and a vein of Pinter-like black comedy.

THE HOLY INNOCENTS: See US section

THE HOME AND THE WORLD
(National Film Development Corporation of India/Artificial Eye/European Classics)
dir-scr-mus Satyajit Ray, based on the novel by Rabindranath Tagore *ph* Soumendu Roy, in Eastman Colour *ed* Dulal Dutt *art dir* Ashoke Bose *r time*

140 mins *UK opening* Sep 13 *US opening* Jun 21.
cast Soumitra Chatterjee, Victor Banerjee, Swatilekha Chatterjee, Gopa Aich, Jennifer Kapoor, Manoj Mitra, Indrapramit Roy, Bimal Chatterjee.

The Hit

Satyajit Ray's valedictory work summarizes the themes of his career with precise power. Liberal landowner Victor Banerjee pushes his wife from the purdah into the turmoil of turn-of-the-century Raj politics, watching as she becomes enthralled by his charismatic friend (Soumitra Chatterjee), a radical opportunist, and his own wealth and values are fatally undermined. Ray's film is suffused with passion and intellect in every frame. Shot in a richly-hued, flat visual style, its measured impact recalls masterpieces like Carl Dreyer's 'Gertrud'.

HOT MOVES: See US section

THE HOTEL NEW HAMPSHIRE
(Woodfall/Orion/Rank)
dir-scr Tony Richardson, based on the novel by John Irving *pro* Neil Hartley *exec pro* George Yaneff, Kent Walwin, Grahame Jennings *ph* David Watkin,

in DeLuxe colour *ed* Robert K Lambert *art dir* John Meighen *mus* Jacques Offenbach *r time* 110 mins *US opening* prior to Jul 1984 *UK opening* Nov 16.
cast Jodie Foster, Beau Bridges, Rob Lowe, Nastassja Kinski, Wilford Brimley, Dorsey Wright, Jennie Dundas, Matthew Modine, Paul McCrane, Anita Morris, Amanda Plummer, Lisa Banes, Seth Green, Wallace Shawn, Gayle Garfinkle, Jonelle Allen.

This is about as good a film as can be made from John Irving's grotesquely whimsical tome – which is not to say it is per se a good movie. Director Tony Richardson and a fine cast give it all they've got, but it's not enough to convert this leaden conceit about a hotel-owner, his family and friends, and the horrors and indignities they stolidly suffer at the hands of various parties.

The Hotel New Hampshire

I i

The Ice Pirates

THE ICE PIRATES
(MGM-UA)
dir Stewart Raffill *pro* John Foreman *scr* Stewart Raffill, Standford Sherman *ph* Matthew F Leonetti, in Metrocolor *ed* Tom Walls *art dir* David M Haber, Ronald Kent Foreman *mus.* Bruce Broughton *r time* 96 mins *US opening* prior to Jul 1984 *UK opening* Nov 23.
cast Robert Urich, Mary Crosby, Michael D Roberts, Anjelica Huston, John Matuszak, Ron Perlman, John Carradine.

A rousing, deliberately mindless sci-fi swashbuckler that strikes a deft balance between intentional camp and earnest derring-do. The requisite hardware and special effects are skilfully deployed for maximum amusement, and the sound in particular is strikingly well done. Best encountered as a surprise lark, it will have to do as the contemporary version of a Louis Hayward vehicle.

IMPULSE: See US section

THE INNOCENT
(Tempest-TVS/Curzon)
dir John MacKenzie *pro* Jackie Stoller *exec pro* Dickie Bamber *scr* Ray Jenkins, based on the novel 'The Aura and the Kingfisher' by Tom Hart *ph* Roger Deakins, in colour *ed* Tony Woollard *pro des* Andrew Mollo *art dir* Philip Elton *mus* Francis Monkman *r time* 96 mins *UK opening* May 31.

cast Andrew Hawley, Kika Markham, Kate Foster, Liam Neeson, Patrick Daley, Paul Askew, Lorraine Peters, Tom Bell, Richard Hope, Jack Carr, Clive Wood, Miranda Richardson, Richard Laxton, Alison Lloyd, Denis Lill, Bill Rodgers.

Into the Night

A nother one of those tastefully photographed coming-of-age-in-Yorkshire-in-the-thirties films. The innocent of the title is a young epileptic who wanders over the Dales when he's not acting as wide-eyed witness to the traumatic affairs of the grown-ups, most of whom are on the dole. Performances – particularly those of Neeson, Bell and Richardson – are excellent, but the central concept is thin and one wonders why it was made at all.

INTO THE NIGHT
(Universal)
dir John Landis *pro* George Folsey Jr, Ron Koslow *exec pro* Dan Allingham *scr* Ron Koslow *ph* Robert Paynter, in Technicolor *ed* Malcolm Campbell *pro des* John Lloyd *mus* Ira Newborn and others *r time* 115 mins *US opening* Feb 22 *UK opening* Apr 19.
cast Jeff Goldblum, Michelle Pfeiffer, Dan Aykroyd, David Cronenberg, John Landis, Waldo Salt, Daniel Petrie, Jack Arnold, Paul Mazursky, Jonathan Lynn, Paul Bartel, Carl Perkins, Don Siegel, Jim Henson, David Bowie, Amy Heckerling, Roger Vadim, Lawrence Kasdan, Richard Farnsworth, Vera Miles, Irene Papas.

John Landis' contemporary version of the comedy-thriller – evoking memories not only of Hitchcock but of lowlier Bob Hope vehicles like 'They Got Me Covered' – is somewhat more mechanical in tone than was his 'Trading Places' as an update of thirties' populist comedy. But as a well-upholstered entertainment it has a good deal going for it – a likeably uncharismatic leading man (Jeff Goldblum) and a strikingly charismatic leading lady (Michelle Pfeiffer); a gallery of bizarre subsidiary characters (several played by movie directors, but it doesn't spoil the fun if you don't recognize them); above all, an unshowy narrative command, supported rather than slowed down by the impressive production values, which for the two hours it is on the screen converts the casually far-fetched plot into something genuinely diverting.

IRRECONCILABLE DIFFERENCES
(Lantana/Warner/Guild International)
dir Charles Shyer *pro* Arlene Sellers, Alex Winitsky *exec pro* Nancy Meyers *scr* Nancy Meyers, Charles Shyer *ph* William A Fraker, in Technicolor *ed* John F Burnett *pro des* Ida Random *art dir* Jane Bogart *mus* Paul De Senneville, Olivier Toussaint *r time* 113 mins *US opening* Sept 28 *UK opening* Feb 15.
cast Ryan O'Neal, Shelley Long, Drew Barrymore, Sam Wanamaker, Allen Garfield, Sharon Stone, Hortensia Colorado, Richard Michenberg, Lorinne Vozoff, Stuart Pankin, David Graf, Jenny Gago, David Paymer, Beverlee Reed, Charlotte Stewart, Rex Reed, Kelly Lange, Steffen Zacharias, Ken Lerner.

O'Neal and Long's marriage gets wrecked on the swings and roundabouts of transient fame, while their chubby-cheeked offspring whinges words of precocious wisdom in the middle. What could have been another tedious tug-of-love saga is jiffed up by a witty script and amiable performances into a wry look at Hollywood lifestyles and the excesses of fame, complete with film industry in-jokes and intriguing peeks at the screenwriting process.

J j

JOHNNY DANGEROUSLY
(Fox)
dir Amy Heckerling *pro* Michael Hertzberg *exec pro* Bud Austin, Harry Colomby *scr* Norman Steinberg, Bernie Kukoff, Harry Colomby, Jeff Harris *ph* David M Walsh, in DeLuxe colour *ed* Pem Herring *pro des* Joseph R Jennings *mus* John Morris *r time* 90 mins *US opening* Dec 21 *UK opening* May 17.
cast Michael Keaton, Jo Piscopo, Marilu Henner, Maureen Stapleton, Peter Boyle, Griffin Dunne, Glynnis

The Innocent

Johnny Dangerously

Kaos

Colour *ed* Roberto Perpignani *art dir* Francesco Bronzi *mus* Nicola Piovani *r time* 187 mins *UK opening* Oct 4. *cast* Margarita Lozano, Claudio Bigagli, Enrica Maria Modugno Massimo Bonetti, Anna Malvica, Ciccio Ingrassia, Franco Franchi, Biagio Barone, Salvatore Rossi, Franco Scaldati, Pasquale Spadola, Laura Mollica, Omero Antonutti, Regina Bianchi.

Comprising dramatizations of four stories by Pirandello set in his native Sicily, plus an epilogue in which the writer is seen returning to the scene of his youth, the Tavianis' film is a work of real scale, resonantly folkloric in its imagery, and especially in its response to harsh, wild landscape. But it remains somewhat diffuse, and it is perhaps unfortunate that the two most effective stories, both in the melodramatic register, come at the beginning; the third episode, the comic 'The Jar', tends to outstay its welcome, and the fourth, elegiac story is rather muddled. With due qualification entered, though, this is among the most personal movies to emerge from Italy, or anywhere else, during the year – and among other things, intimates that its directors are Pasolini's natural heirs.

THE KARATE KID
(Columbia)
dir John G Avildsen *pro* Jerry Weintraub *exec pro* R J Lewis *ph* James Crabe, in Metrocolor *ed* Bud Smith, Walt Mulconery, John G Avildsen *pro des* William J Cassidy *mus* Bill Conti *r time* 126 mins *US opening* prior to Jul 1984 *UK opening* Aug 31.
cast Ralph Macchio, Noriyuki (Pat) Morita, Elisabeth Shue, Martin Kove, Randee Heller, William Zabka, Ron Thomas, Rob Garrison.

Taking two hours to retail an anecdote that might merit three or four pages of the 'Readers Digest', this is a slumbrous and cumbrous affair. Some sentimental truth attaches to the central relationship between adolescent hero and the elderly Japanese gardener who becomes his mentor at karate and helps him to best a band of bullies. But precious little sense of reality obtrudes into the attempted social observations that surround it.

O'Connor, Dom DeLuise, Richard Dimitri, Danny DeVito, Ron Carey, Ray Walston, Dick Butkus, Byron Thames, Alan Hale, Scott Thomson, Sudie Bond, Mark Jantzen, Gary Watkins.

Misfired parody-burlesque of Warner Brothers gangster films, teeming with talented comic actors, all of whom are wasted on stodgy, uninventive bits. The model was 'Airplane!' but this lacks both the requisite tomfoolery and the underlying conviction of that inspired piece. Instead, it is simply dumb.

A JOKE OF DESTINY: See US section

JOY OF SEX: See US section

JUST ONE OF THE GUYS: See US section

JUST THE WAY YOU ARE: See US section

KAOS
(Filmtre-RAI Channel 1/Cannon-Gala)
dir-scr Paolo Taviani, Vittorio Taviani, based on short stories from the collection 'Novelle per un anno' by Luigi Pirandello *pro* Giuliani G De Negri *ph* Guiseppe Lanci, in Eastman

The Karate Kid

THE KEY

(San Francisco Film/Enterprise)
dir-scr-ed Tinto Brass, based on the
novel 'Kagi' by Junichiro Tanizaki *pro*
Giovanni Bertolucci *ph* Silvano
Ippoliti, in Technicolor *art dir* Paolo
Biagetti *mus* Ennio Morricone *r time*
116 mins *UK opening* Jan 25.
cast Frank Finlay, Stefania Sandrelli,
Franco Branciaroli, Barbara Cupisti,
Armando Marra, Maria Grazia Bon,
Gino Cavalieri, Piero Bortoluzzi, Irma
Veithen, Milly Codinaldi, Giovanni
Michelagnoli, Elo Capritti, Maria Pia
Colonnello, Edgardo Fugagnoli,
Luciano Gasper, Osiride Pevarello,
Sara Tagliapietra, Mirella Zardo,
Arnaldo Momo.

*Transposing a Japanese novel
(previously filmed by Ichikawa), about
an ageing man whose flesh is weaker
than his spirit is willing, to the setting
of Venice in 1940, Brass plays down the
'decadent' atmosphere and the
historical context and plays up the
scratchy humour. And he achieves not
just a quality of the bizarre (though
there is no shortage of that, including
Frank Finlay besporting himself in
ladies' lingerie) but also a real feeling
of pathos. Moreover, the film is realized
with considerable dash and
momentum. Surely it might be time to
forget about 'Caligula'? (For a different
view, see Turkeys of the Year.)*

THE KILLING FIELDS

(Enigma-Goldcrest/Warner)
dir Roland Joffé *pro* David Puttnam
scr Bruce Robinson *ph* Chris Menges,
in Eastman Colour *ed* Jim Clark
pro des Roy Walker *r time* 142 mins
US opening Nov 2 *UK opening* Nov 24.
cast Sam Waterston, Doctor Haing S
Ngor, John Malkovich, Julian Sands,
Craig T Nelson, Spalding Gray, Bill
Paterson, Athol Fugard, Graham
Kennedy, Katherine Kragum Chey,
Oliver Pierpaoli, Edward Entero
Chey, Tom Bird, Monirak Sisowath,
Lambool Dtangpaibool, Ira Wheeler.

*Cambodia revisited by British movie-
makers, who, from their post-
imperialist position, can more easily
come to terms with an all-American
catastrophe. Roland Joffé's first film is
an impressive debut: well-made,
intelligent, gripping. Yet, for all its
skill, it is soft-centred – willing to
wound, but afraid to strike and
settling, in the final analysis, for being
a variation on the buddy-buddy movie.
Huckleberry Finn and Jim ride again.
(See Films of the Year.)*

THE KING AND MISTER BIRD

(Les Films Paul Grimault-Les Films
Corona-Les Films Gibé-Antenne 2/
ICA Projects)
dir-pro Paul Grimault *scr* Jaeques
Prévert, Paul Grimault, based on 'The
Shepherdess and the Chimney Sweep'
by Hans Christian Andersen *ph*
Gérard Soirant, in Eastman Colour
mus Wojciech Kilar, songs by Joseph
Kosma, Jacques Prévert *r time* 82
mins *UK opening* Jul 20.

*Emerging in this form after a
chequered production history lasting
over thirty years 'The King and Mr
Bird' is an animated feature of
considerable wit and ingenuity. Some
of the spirit of its fairy-tale fantasy
seems to hark back not so much to 1947,
when the project was conceived, as to*

The Killing Fields

the thirties, with jokes about mass
production and a somewhat simple-
minded view of the power of the people.
But simply because it enshrines a
certain vanished brand of Gallic
populist whimsy, the film is intriguing;
and many of the visual conceits – the
action is set in a crenellated castle
replete with high-tech mod cons – are
engaging in their own right. The
strident American voices of this
English-language version, however,
prove something of a hindrance.

KINGS AND DESPERATE MEN

(Kineversal/Blue Dolphin)
dir-pro Alexis Kanner *scr* Edmund
Ward, Alexis Kanner *ph* Henry Lucas
(Alexis Kanner), Paul van der Linden,
in colour *ed* Henry Lucas (Alexis
Kanner) *art dir* Will McGow *mus*
Michel Robidoux, Pierre F Brault
r time 118 mins *UK opening* Dec 28.
cast Patrick McGoohan, Alexis
Kanner, Andrea Marcovicci, Margaret
Trudeau, Jean-Pierre Brown, Robin
Spry, Frank Moore, Budd Knapp,
Kevin Fenlon, Peter McNeil, David
Patrick, August Schellenberg, Neil
Vipond, Kate Nash, Frederic Smith-
Bolton, Jane Hooper.

*Long-gestating, long-shelved and
terminally long-winded, Kanner's
initial shot at all-round auteurism
reunites him with old 'Prisoner' cohort*

The King and Mister Bird

The Key

McGoohan in a tricksily dramatized ding-dong of hammy egos, that may well have worked better as a product of the Canadian radio station in which its central hostage-siege confrontation is set. The obscure political motivations for Kanner's gang seizing the airwaves are soon forgotten in the by-play paraphernalia of a phone-in trial and battling broadcast oratory between the man with a gun and a grievance and his media-literate control-freak 'host'. The developing question of whose 'show' this is marks the movie as little more than an inflated private joke.

KING DAVID: See US section

KIPPERBANG: See P'TANG, YANG, KIPPERBANG

LADIES ON THE ROCKS
(Komme Films-Danish Film Institute/ Artificial Eye)
dir Christian Braad Thomsen *scr* Christian Braad Thomsen, Helle Rysling, Annemarie Helger *ph* Dirk Brüel, in colour *ed* Grete Møldrup *mus* Helle Ryslinge, Pernille Grumme, Annemarie Helger *r time* 100 mins *UK opening* Mar 8.
cast Helle Ryslinge, Annemarie Helger, Flemming Quist Møller, Hans Henrick Clemmensen, Gyda Hansen, Aksel Erhardsen, Gotha Andersen, Bent Conradi, Peter Ronild, Lotte Olsen, Lene Vasgaard, Lis Frederiksen, Knud Ditmar, Asta Esper Andersen, Arne Simsen, Kim Weisgaard, Anne Grethe Finnerup.

A feminist road movie, in which two cabaret artists travel through Denmark with their comedy show, making a living out of their problems, as they put it. Charmingly played, sharply observed, deftly directed.

LADYHAWKE: See US section

LASSITER
(Pan Pacific/Golden Harvest/Warner/ Rank)
dir Roger Young *pro* Albert S Ruddy *exec pro* Raymond Chow, André Morgan *scr* David Taylor *ph* Gil Taylor, in Technicolor *ed* Benjamin A Weissman, Richard Hiscott *pro des* Peter Mullins *mus* Ken Thorne *r time* 100 mins *US opening prior to Jul 1984*

Lassiter

UK opening Sep 21.
cast Tom Selleck, Jane Seymour, Lauren Hutton, Bob Hoskins, Joe Regalbuto, Ed Lauter, Warren Clarke, Edward Peel, Paul Antrim, Christopher Malcolm, Barrie Houghton, Peter Skellern, Harry Towb, Belinda Mayne, Morgan Sheppard, Brian Coburn, Jane Wood, Tristram Jellinek, David Warbeck.

Tom Selleck shrewdly maintains his low-key likeability from his television series in this attempted throwback to the days of elegant spy thrillers. As an American jewel thief blackmailed into a dangerous mission by British intelligence, Selleck effortlessly carries the production without recourse to tempting Cary Grant or David Niven flourishes. Lauren Hutton makes a

kinky impression as a formidable Nazi agent, and there are some mildly surprising twists, but generally the formula is both too familiar and too dated to register any more than very mild entertainment. (See Turkeys of the Year.)

THE LAST BATTLE
[US Title: Le Dernier Combat]
(Les Films du Loup/Columbia-Triumph/ICA Projects)
dir-pro-scr Luc Besson *ph* Carlo Varini, in Scope *ed* Sophie Schmit *mus* Eric Serra *r time* 92 mins *US opening* prior to Jul 1984 *UK opening* Aug 10.
cast Pierre Jolivet, Jean Bouise, Fritz Wepper, Jean Reno, Maurice Lamy, Pierre Carrive, Jean-Michel Castanié, Michel Doset, Bernard Have, Petra Müller, Christiane Krüger, Marcel Berthomier, Garry Jode.

Revelling in the monochrome stylishness and silent samurai posings of post-Holocaust chic, Besson constructs a cheap (and occasionally even cheerful) slice of slowed-down Gallic Mad-Maxery, with both obligatory sci-fi nods to the likes of Ballard and Bradbury and a few more unexpected tips of the imagination to screen surrealists like Buñuel and Borowczyk. Touted for a cultdom it never actually achieved here, this knowing film may well have been the first victim of audience apathy brought on by rock-video overkill in the futuristic face-off stakes.

THE LAST DRAGON: See US section

LAST NIGHT AT THE ALAMO: See US section

The Last Battle

THE LAST STARFIGHTER
(Lorimar/Universal/Miracle/
Videoform)
dir Nick Castle *pro* Gary Adelson,
Edward O Denault *scr* Jonathan
Betuel *ph* King Baggot, in Technicolor
ed C Timothy O'Meara *pro des* Ron
Cobb *mus* Craig Safan *r time* 101 mins
US opening Jul 13 *UK opening* Dec 12.
cast Lance Guest, Dan O'Herlihy,
Catherine Mary Stewart, Barbara
Bosson, Norman Snow, Robert
Preston, Kay E Kuter, Dan Mason,
Chris Herbert, John O'Leary, George
McDaniel, Charlene Nelson, John
Maio, Robert Starr, Al Berry, Scott
Dunlop, Vernon Washington.

*Marred only by its unwise investment
in computer-generated space battles, a
genuinely witty kid-flick on the theme
of upward mobility. A trailer-park
gofer who can't wait to get out and get
on has his dreams fulfilled in aces
courtesy of his video-game wizardry
and the good offices of inter-stellar
con-man Robert Preston, who recruits
him for a real battle beyond the stars.
Leaving, to complicate things
amusingly, a replicant on earth to cover
the kid's absence. Deft and daft by
turns, making a neat follow-up to Nick
Castle's little-seen low-budgeter, the
equally playful 'Tag'.*

The Last Starfighter

LAUGHTERHOUSE
(Greenpoint/Palace)
dir Richard Eyre *pro* Ann Scott
exec pro Simon Relph *scr* Brian Glover
ph Clive Tickner, in colour *ed* David
Martin *art dir* Jamie Leonard *mus*
Dominic Muldowney *r time* 93 mins
UK opening Jul 20.
cast Ian Holm, Penelope Wilton, Bill
Owen, Richard Hope, Stephen Moore,
Rosemary Martin, Patrick Drury,
Aran Bell, Stephanie Tague, C J
Allen, Norman Fisher, Clare Laine,
Denise Summers, Kenneth
MacDonald, Barbara Burgess, Ben
Wright, Tim Seely, Johnny Golde,
Stephen Phillips, Gillian Barge.

*Set mainly in rural East Anglia, this
'miniaturised western' (writer Brian
Glover's description) about a 'goose
drive' from Norfolk to Smithfield could
at one level hardly be further removed
from the media smart set of the same
director's 'The Ploughman's Lunch'.
Yet it has an equal particularity in
observing aspects of how we live now,
and the growing purposiveness of its
participants might be seen as a positive
obverse of the cynical opportunism of
the earlier film's protagonist. In its
modest, low-key fashion
uncomplacently reminiscent of the
Ealing tradition, the film even
manages to evoke something of a
different kind of England, one less in
the grasp of admass and a quick
turnover. A generally underrated
achievement – though the punning title
is perhaps a liability.*

LIES
(New Empire Films-Westcom Prods/
Alpha)
dir-scr Ken Wheat, Jim Wheat *pro*
Ken Wheat, Jim Wheat, Shelley
Hermann *exec pro* James Hart,
Lawrence Taylor-Mortoff *ph* Robert
Ebinger in DeLuxe colour *ed* Michael
Ornstein, Dennis Hill *pro des*
Christopher Henry *mus* Marc
Donahue *r time* 102 mins *UK opening*
Sep 14.
cast Ann Dusenberry, Gail Strickland,
Bruce Davison, Clu Gulager, Terence
Knox, Bert Remsen, Stacy Keach Sr,
Douglas Leonard, Patience Cleveland,
Julie Philips, Ann Gibbs, Dick Miller,
Walter Wood, Jerry Vaughn, Guy
Remsen, Tony Miller, Jean Howell, B
J Davis, Eddie Braun, Jane Lillig.

*An out-of-work actress, initially hired
to impersonate a mad heiress, finds
herself incarcerated in an asylum and
unable to convince anyone (except the
bad guys who put her there) of her
sanity. The first half of this cheapo
psycho-thriller is a promising farrago
of imposture and plot twists, but the
action degenerates into routine
woman-in-peril, with the heroine
stranded helpless in her straitjacket as
she awaits rescue by her boyfriend.*

Laughterhouse

Lonely Hearts

LIFEFORCE: See US section

THE LITTLE DRUMMER GIRL: See US section

LITTLE TREASURE: See US section

LONELY HEARTS
(Adams Packer Film Productions/
Gala)
dir Paul Cox *pro* John B Murray
exec pro Phillip Adams *scr* Paul Cox,
John Clarke *ph* Yuri Sokol, in
Eastman Colour *ed* Tim Lewis *art dir*
Neil Angwin *mus*Norman Kaye *r time*
95 mins *UK opening* Aug 2.
cast Norman Kaye, Wendy Hughes,
John Finlayson, Julia Blake,
Jonathan Hardy, Irene Inescort, Vic
Gordon, Ted Grove-Rogers, Ronald
Falk, Chris Haywood, Diana
Greentree, Margaret Steven, Kris
McQuade, Maurie Fields.

*Made before (though released in
Britain after) the same director's 'Man
of Flowers', this is both a more
conventional film and a more
completely achieved one. In outline it is
a Melbourne 'Marty', charting the
awkward progress of a middle-aged
romance with wry humour that never
lapses into condescension. The playing
of Wendy Hughes and Norman Kaye is
faultless, and there is a sharply etched
cameo from a sardonic policeman from the
ever-reliable Chris Haywood. With
intimations of mortality to keep the
sentiment in proportion, and a
judicious control of background
observation, the film is both highly
pleasurable and a thoroughgoing
vindication of cinematic naturalism.*

LOST IN AMERICA: See US section

A LOVE IN GERMANY
(CCC Filmkunst-Gaumont-TFL-
Stand'Art/Artificial Eye)
dir Andrzej Wajda *pro* Arthur Brauner
exec pro Peter Hahne *scr* Boleslaw
Michalek, Agnieszka Holland,
Andrzej Wajda, based on the novel by
Rolf Hochhuth *ph* Igor Luther, in
colour *ed* Halina Prugar-Ketling
art dir Allan Starski, Gotz Heymann,
Jürgen Henze *mus* Michel Legrand
r time 107 mins *UK opening* May 9.
cast Hanna Schygulla, Marie-
Christine Barrault, Armin Mueller-
Stahl, Elisabeth Trissenaar, Daniel
Olbrychski, Piotr Lysak, Gérard
Desarthe, Bernhard Wicki, Ralf
Wolter, Otto Sander, Ben Becker,
Thomas Ringelmann, Friedrich G
Beckhaus, Gernot Duda, Sigfrit
Steiner, Erika Wackernagel.

*Andrzej Wajda's story of impossible
romance between a German woman
and a Jewish prisoner during World
War II suffers from his usual*

*didacticism and structural
deficiencies, but before the message
engulfs the drama, the dynamics of the
affair and the social context of the small
town are realized with compelling
detail. Hanna Schygulla, though good,
doesn't reach the required mythic
dimensions of her rôle, while Marie-
Christine Barrault reveals herself a
character actress of striking affect.*

LOVELINES: See US section

LUST IN THE DUST: See US section

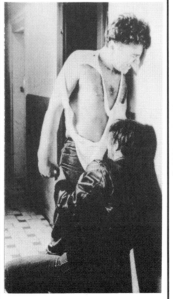

A Man Like Eva

MACARTHER'S CHILDREN: See
US section

MAKING THE GRADE [US TITLE:
PREPPIES]
dir Dorian Walker *pro-scr* Gene
Quintano *exec pro* Menahem Golan,
Yoram Globus *ph* Jacques Haitkin, in
colour *ed* Daniel Wetherbee, Roy
Watts *art dir* Joseph T Garrity *mus*
Basil Poledouris *r time* 104 mins *US
opening* prior to Jul 1984 *UK opening*
Sep 28.
cast Judd Nelson, Jonna Lee, Gordon
Jump, Walter Olkewicz, Ronald
Lacey, Dana Olsen, Carey Scott, Scott
McGinnis, Andrew Clay, John Dye,
Daniel Schneider, John Stevens,
Waldo Zimmerman.

*One of those disposable, pandering
youth comedies centred around the
fraternal antics of schoolboys in which
even a glimmer of care and quality is
noteworthy, if not remotely enough to
make it worthwhile. Though much of
the humour is coarse and imitative,
there are at least intermittent attempts
at class satire (mostly in a stylish
performance by Dana Olsen as a
sybaritic scion) and a certain
awareness of classic comedy narrative
structure in both writing and directing.*

A MAN LIKE EVA
(Schier-Straub-Trio Film-Impuls
Film-Maran Film/Cinevista/Blue
Dolphin)
dir Radu Gabrea *pro* Horst Schier,
Laurens Straub *scr* Radu Gabrea,
Laurens Straub, based on an idea by
Horst Schier, Laurens Straub *ph* Horst
Schier, in colour *ed* Dragos-Emmanuel
Witkowski *art dir* Herbert
Buchenberger *mus*Verdi *r time* 89
mins *US opening* prior to Jul 1984
UK opening Jan 3.
cast Eva Mattes, Lisa Kreuzer,
Werner Stocker, Charles Regnier,
Carola Regnier, Charly Muhamed
Huber, Albert Kitzl, Towje Kleiner,
Lothar Borowsky, Maria Mettke, Loek
Dikker, Frank Büssing, Heinz
Kowalczyk, Sybelle Rauch, Frederike
Wilde.

*Slightly scabrous film á clef based on
Rainer Werner Fassbinder, redeemed
by the tour de force casting of Eva
Mattes as the self-destructive creative
genius. Mattes illuminates the
character in ceaselessly fascinating
ways, even as the parodistic and
exploitative elements of the scenario get
out of hand. Charles Regnier achieves
a legitimate pathos in a supporting rôle
as a loyal crew member.*

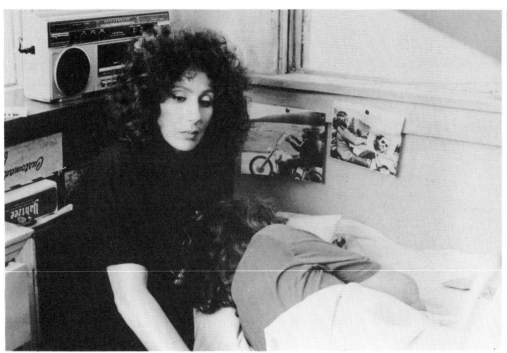

Above: Mask. Right: Mata Hari

MARIA'S LOVERS
(Cannon)
dir Andrei Konchalovsky *pro* Bosko Djordjevic, Lawrence Taylor-Mortoff *exec pro* Menahem Golan, Yoram Globus *scr* Gérard Brach, Andrei Konchalovsky, Paul Zindel, Marjorie David *ph* Juan Ruiz-Anchia, in colour *ed* Humphrey Dixon *pro des* Jeannine Oppewall *mus* Gary S Remal *r time* 109 mins *UK opening* Nov 23 *US opening* Jan 18.
cast Nastassja Kinski, John Savage, Robert Mitchum, Keith Carradine, Anita Morris, Bud Cort, Karen Young, Tracy Nelson, John Goodman, Danton Stone, Vincent Spano, Lela Ivey, Elena Koreneva, Anton Sipos, Larry John Meyers, Anna Levine, Tania Harley, Bill Smitrovich.

Remaining aloof from the usual Cannon-fodder approach to erotica, Soviet director Konchalovsky transplants to the American melting-pot a simple folk-tale of impotence and experience, but shows himself only slightly better assimilated than his hero, a returning POW who can't quite cope with the reality of a virginal Kinski after having lived for so long with a fantasy of her. The downbeat melodrama of lusts and losses is rather embalmed in images, and the tone wavers alarmingly between the tremulously moving and the risible. But if some of the symbols grate, at least the icons (Kinski, Mitchum, post-war Pennsylvania) shine.

MARTIN'S DAY: See US section

MASK
(Universal)
dir Peter Bogdanovich *pro* Martin Starger *scr* Anna Hamilton Phelan *ph* Laszlo Kovacs, in Technicolor *ed* Barbara Ford *art dir* Norman Newberry *mus* various *r time* 120 mins *US opening* Mar 8 *UK opening* Jun 28.
cast Cher, Sam Elliott, Eric Stoltz, Estelle Getty, Richard Dysart, Laura Dern, Micole Mercurio, Harry Carey

Jr, Dennis Burkley, Lawrence Monoson, Ben Piazza, Craig King, Alexandra Powers, Kelly Minter, Todd Allen, Howard Hirdler, Jeannie Dimter Barton, Steven James.

Peter Bogdanovich's compassionate study of a deformed, doomed teenager avoids all the sentimental and didactic pitfalls of its genre by exploring the complex emotions involved honestly

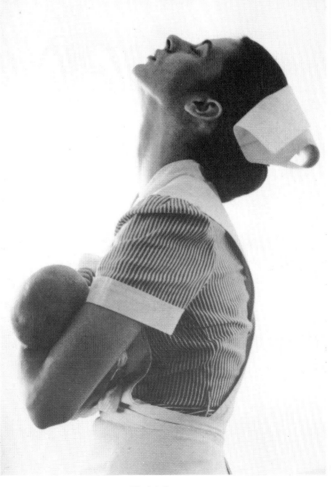

Maria's Lovers

and with respect for the human frailty that inevitably accompanies courage and triumph. Though missing two scenes and the Springsteen songs the director wanted, the release version still displays the most acute visual narrative sense in American film today. Cher manages to create a multifaceted character despite the preponderance of madonna-nimbus close-ups, and Eric Stoltz is perfect as the resilient true-life Rocky.

MASS APPEAL: See US section

MATA HARI
(Cannon)
dir Curtis Harrington *pro* Rony Yacov *exec pro* Menaheim Golan, Yoram Globus *scr* Joel Ziskin *ph* David Gurfinkel, in Eastman Colour *ed* Henry Richardson *art dir* Tivadar Bertalan *mus* Wilfred Josephs, Sri Hastanto *r time* 108 mins *UK opening* May 10.
cast Sylvia Kristel, Christopher Cazenove, Oliver Tobias, Gaye Brown, Gottfried John, William Fox, Michael Anthony, Vernon Dobtcheff, Anthony Newlands, Brian Badcoe, Tutte Lemkow, Taylor Ryan, Tobias Rolt, Victor Langley, Nicholas Selby, Malcolm Terris, Carlos Sutton.

Or 'Emmanuelle Goes to War', both as a spy in World War II and as a pawn in the personal sub-war between old pals Christopher Cazenove (German) and Oliver Tobias (French). Quite risible in its po-faced banality, the only mystery is how a director like Curtis Harrington came to be involved.

THE MEAN SEASON
(Turman-Foster Company/Orion/Rank)
dir Phillip Borsos *pro* David Foster, Lawrence Turman *scr* Leon Piedmont, based on the novel 'In the Heat of the Summer' by John Katzenbach *ph* Frank Tidy, in DeLuxe colour *ed* Duwayne Dunham *pro des* Philip Jefferies *mus* Lalo Schifrin *r time* 104 mins *US opening* Feb 15 *UK opening* May 31.
cast Kurt Russell, Mariel Hemingway, Richard Jordan, Richard Masur, Joe Pantoliano, Richard Bradford, Andy Garcia, Rose Portillo, William Smith, John Palmer, Lee Sandman, Dan Fitzgerald, Fred Buch, Bruce McLaughlin, Jill Beach, Peter Lundquist, Tamara Jones, Joan Murphy, Lillian Zuckerman.

A crime reporter finds himself singled out as a murderer's confidant – a promising idea which manages to ignore intriguing questions of journalistic involvement and responsibiity in favour of straight TV-movie-style action heroics. The torrid Florida locations and threatening skies are presumably intended in some way to be analogous to the plot.

Micki and Maude

MEATBALLS PART II: See US section

METROPOLIS
(UFA-Giorgio Moroder/Cinecom/
Virgin)
dir Fritz Lang *pro* Erich Pommer
exec pro Michele Cohen, Keith Forsey,
Laurie Howard, George Naschke *scr*
Thea von Harbou, Fritz Lang *ph* Karl
Freund, Günther Rittau *art dir* Otto
Hunte, Erich Kettelhut, Karl
Vollbrecht *mus* Giorgio Moroder
r time 83 mins *US opening* Aug 3
UK opening Nov 30.
cast Brigitte Helm, Gustav Frölich,
Alfred Abel, Rudolph Klein-Rogge,
Theodor Loos, Fritz Rasp, Erwin
Biswanger, Heinrich George, Olaf
Strom, Hans Leo Reich, Heinrich
Gotho, Margarete Lanner, Max
Dietze, Georg John, Walter Kühle,
Arthur Reinhard, Erwin Vater.

*Sniffed at by some critics as the
ultimate rock video, there's no question
Moroder has given Lang's classic
renewed life. The worker-ruler/strife-
reconciliation theme is as dubious as
ever, but the visual brilliance has been
heightened by imaginative tinting.
Tightened by a quarter of its original
length, there's not a great setpiece
missing and the pacing is breathless.
The drawback is the awful songs, but*

*these are easily ignored while
Moroder's synthetic motor rhythms are
seductively apt.*

MICKI AND MAUDE
(Delphi III/Columbia)
dir Blake Edwards *pro* Tony Adams
exec pro Jonathan D Krane, Lou
Antonio *scr* Jonathan Reynolds *ph*
Henry Stradling, in Metrocolor *ed*
Ralph E Winters *pro des* Rodger Maus
mus Lee Holdridge *r time* 117 mins
US opening Dec 21 *UK opening* Apr 5.
cast Dudley Moore, Amy Irving, Ann

Mikey and Nicky

Reinking, Richard Mulligan, George
Gaynes, Wallace Shawn, John
Pleshette, H B Haggerty, Lu Leonard,
Priscilla Pointer, Robert Symonds,
George Coe, Gustav Vintas, Ken
Olfson, Philippe Denham, Emma
Walton, Ruth Silveira, Wiley Harker.

*A rare instance of Blake Edwards
directing another's screenplay, this
farce about a bigamist whose wives are
both expecting babies at the same time
has a certain manufactured quality to
it, but the farce mechanics are deftly*

*oiled, and the relationships, notably
between Dudley Moore and his boss-
mentor, Richard Mulligan, have
authentic Edwards flavour.*

MIKEY AND NICKY
(Paramount/Enterprise)
dir-scr Elaine May *pro* Michael
Hausman *exec pro* Bud Austin *ph*
Victor J Kemper, in colour *ed* John
Carter, Sheldon Kahn *pro des* Paul
Sylbert *mus* John Strauss *r time* 106
mins *UK opening* Oct 25.
cast Peter Falk, John Cassavetes, Ned
Beatty, Rose Arrick, Carol Grace,
William Hickey, Sanford Meisner,
Joyce Van Patten, M Emmet Walsh,
Sy Travers, Peter Scoppa, Virginia
Smith, Jean Shevlin, Danny Klein,
Martin Wolfson, Eugene Hobgood,
David Pendleton, William Gill,
Marilyn Randall, Reuben Greene.

*Elaine May, whose script contributions
to numerous major movies have often
remained uncredited, here takes self-
effacement a stage further. This is an
edgily indulgent, noir-ish
psychodrama straight out of the
Cassavetes catalogue, directed as if by
conspiratorial proxy. 'The Killing of a
Chinese Bookie' writ even more
claustrophobically, in fact, with small-
time scufflers Falk and Cassavetes
upping the improvisatory hysteria
quotient as one-time best-buddies now
haplessly sparring as hit-man and
mark, adrift in the darker reaches.
Startlingly uncomfortable stuff.*

MISCHIEF: See US section

MISSING IN ACTION
(Cannon)
dir Joseph Zito *pro* Menahem Golan,
Yoram Globus *exec pro* Lance Hool *scr*
James Bruner, based on characters
created by Arthur Silver, Larry
Levinson, Steve Bing *ph* Joao
Fernandes, in Metrocolor *ed* Joel
Goodman *art dir* Ladi Wilheim, Toto
Castillo *mus* Jay Chattaway *r time*
101 mins *US opening* Nov 21
UK opening Feb 22.
cast Chuck Norris, M Emmet Walsh,
David Tress, Leonore Kasdorf, James
Hong, Ernie Ortega, Pierrino
Mascarino, E Erich Anderson, Joseph
Carberry, Avi Kleinberger, Willy
Williams, Ric Segreto, Bella Flores,
Gil Arceo, Roger Dantes, Sabatini
Fernandez, Renato Morado, Jim
Crumrine, Jeff Mason, Stephen
Barbers, Nam Moore.

*Preparing the world for 'Rambo – First
Blood 2', Chuck Norris gives the
Vietnamese plenty of chop-socky in his
crusade to prove that there are still
American servicemen held captive after
the war.*

**MISSING IN ACTION 2 – THE
BEGINNING:** See US section

MORONS FROM OUTER SPACE
(Thorn EMI)
dir Mike Hodges *pro* Barry Hanson *exec pro* Verity Lambert *scr* Griff Rhys Jones, Mel Smith *ph* Phil Meheux, in colour *ed* Peter Boyle *pro des* Brian Eatwell *mus* Peter Brewis and others *r time* 91 mins *UK opening* Mar 22.
cast Mel Smith, Griff Rhys Jones, Joanne Pearce, Jimmy Nail, Paul Brown, James B Sikking, Dinsdale Landen, Jimmy Mulville, Miriam Margolyes, Tristram Jellinek, George Innes, John Joyce, Mark Jones, Leonard Fenton, André Maranne Joanna Dickens, R J Bell, Peter Whitman, Olivier Pierre, Edward Wiley.

An unmitigated disaster from start to finish. Three "interplanetary pillocks" crashland their hired mobile space home on the M1 and are pushed by newsboy-turned-entrepreneur Rhys-Jones into becoming international celebrities and rock stars. There is also what looks like a misguided attempt to pull in an American audience with a barely relevant subplot about a fourth alien wandering alone and unacknowledged through the Midwest. The parodies of films like 'Close Encounters' and 'One Flew Over the

Moscow on the Hudson

Cuckoo's Nest' are crass, the jokes are unfunny, the performers lack charm and the whole enterprise smacks of desperation.

MOSCOW ON THE HUDSON
(Columbia)
dir-pro Paul Mazursky *scr* Paul Mazursky, Leon Capetanos *ph* Donald McAlpine, in Metrocolor *ph* Richard Halsy *pro des* Pato Guzman *mus* David McHugh *r time* 115 mins *US opening* prior to Jul 1984 *UK opening* Oct 5.
cast Robin Williams, Maria Conchita Alonso, Cleavant Derricks, Alejandro Rey, Savely Kramarov, Elya Baskin, Oleg Rudnik, Alexander Beniaminov, Ludmila Kramerevski, Ivo Vrzal, Natlie Iwanow, Tiger Haynes, Edye Byrde, Robert MacBeth.

Paul Mazursky's contribution to Reagan's resumption of the Cold War/ Curdled Capra centres on a Russian who defects via Bloomingdales (New York's choicest department store) – thus providing a hook for upwardly mobile ex-liberals wishing to defect to recession-era Republicanism. Robin Williams' allegedly 'inventive' frenetic comedy style is beginning to wear very thin.

Morons from Outer Space

MOVERS & SHAKERS: See US section

MOVING VIOLATIONS: See US section

MRS SOFFEL
(MGM-UA)
dir Gillian Armstrong *pro* Edgar J Scherick, Scott Rudin, David A Nicksay *scr* Ron Nyswaner *ph* Russell Boyd, Peter Norman, Darwin Dean, in Metrocolor *ed* Nicholas Beauman *pro des* Luciana Arrighi *art dir* Roy Forge Smith, Ed Pisoni *mus* Mark Isham *r time* 111 mins *US opening* Dec 26 *UK opening* Jun 27.
cast Diane Keaton, Mel Gibson, Matthew Modine, Edward Herrmann, Trini Alvarado, Jennie Dundas, Danny Corkill, Harley Cross, Terry O'Quinn, Pippa Pearthree, William Youmans, Maury Chaykin, Joyce Ebert, John W Carroll, Dana Wheeler-Nicholson, Wayne Robson, Les Rubie, Paula Trueman.

Utterly unoriginal and passionless period piece, based on true story of warden's wife who escaped with two condemned prisoners, which for some reason attracted critical nods. Artsy and superficial, the style and content are rigorously 'correct' and pompously uninspired.

MS 45 – ANGEL OF VENGEANCE
(Navaron Films/Warner Home Video)
dir Abel Ferrara *exec pro* Rochelle Weisberg *scr* N G St John *ph* James Momèl, in colour *ed* Christopher Andrews *art dir* Ruben Masters *mus* Joe Delia *r time* 76 mins *US opening* prior to Jul 1984 *UK opening* Jan 18.
cast Zoë Tamerlis, Bogey, Albert Sinkys, Darlene Stuto, Helen McGara, Nike Zachmanoglou, Jimmy Laine (Abel Ferrara), Peter Yellen, Editta Sherman, Vincent Gruppi, S Edward Singer, Stanley Timms, Faith Peters, Lawrence Zavaglia, Alex Jachino, Jack Thibeau, Jane Kennedy.

Mrs Soffel

Tight and taut, raw yet infinitely reverberating, Abel 'Driller Killer' Ferrara's feminist vigilante movie restores faith in the radical potential of the B-pic. Appearing here late (but with the bonus of following and seeming to answer such interim obscenities as 'Sudden Impact'), it plays provocative havoc with the rape-revenge format as silently-screaming victim Zoë Tamerlis turns the street-level iconographies and ideologies of sex and violence back in on themselves, intensifying the troubling echoes from each gunshot ricochet.

THE MUPPETS TAKE MANHATTAN: See US section

MY BEST FRIEND'S GIRL
(Renn Prods/Sara Films/Cannon-Gala)
dir Bertrand Blier *pro* Alain Sarde *exec pro* Pierre Grunstein *scr* Bertrand Blier, Gérard Brach *ph* Jean Penzer,

Yves Agostini, Michel Coteret, Eric Vallée, in Eastman Colour *ed* Claudine Merline, Sylvie Quester, Annick Ménier, Jeanne Kef *mus* J J Cale and others *r time* 100 mins *UK opening* Jun 7.
cast Coluche, Isabelle Huppert, Thierry Lhermitte, Farid Chopel, François Perrot, Daniel Colas, Frédérique Michot.

Virtually a three-hander, this latter-day approximation to boulevard cinema tends to fall between the stools of artificial comedy (not fast enough) and genuine feeling (too glib and superficial). Despite some attractive performances, an air of pointlessness prevails.

MY BROTHER'S WEDDING
(Charles Burnett Prods-Zweites Deutsches Fernsehen/Blue Dolphin)
dir-scr-ph Charles Burnett *pro* Charles Burnett, Gaye Shannon-Burnett *exec pro* Gaye Shannon-Burnett, in colour *ed* Thomas M Penick *mus* various *r time* 116 mins *UK opening* Mar 28.
cast Everette Silas, Jessie Holmes, Gaye Shannon-Burnett, Ronald E Bell, Dennis Kemper, Sally Easter, Hobert Durham Jr, Angela Burnett, Tim Wright, Cora Lee Day, Monte Easter, Frances Nealy, Sy Richardson, Garnett Hargrave, Margarita Rodriguez, Jackie Hargrave, Lynda Gypcy Lewis.

A worthwhile example of black independent film-making by Charles Burnett, limited visually by a low budget but an expressive accomplishment withal. A ghetto youth confronts the meaning of family responsibility as he sorts out his social values amidst the pressures of urban life. Burnett's determination to

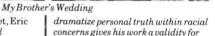
My Brother's Wedding

dramatize personal truth within racial concerns gives his work a validity for any audience.

MY NEW PARTNER: See US section

MY OWN COUNTRY
(Malaya Films-Stephen Films/ICA Projects-BFI)
dir Lino Brocka *pro* Vera Belmont *exec pro* Jeric Soriano *scr* José F Lacaba, based on his articles 'The Strike' and 'The Hostage' *ph* Conrado Baltazar, in colour *ed* George Jarlego, Robert Yucejo, Hero Reyes *art dir* Joey Luna *mus* Jess Santiago *r time* 108 mins *UK opening* Mar 29.
cast Phillip Salvador, Gina Alajar, Claudia Zobel, Carmi Martin, Raoul

MS 45 – Angel of Vengeance

My Best Friend's Girl

Aragonn, Rez Cortez, Venchito Galvez, Aristo Reyes Jr, Lorli Villanueva, Nomer Son, Gloria Guinto 'Mona Lisa', Lucita Soriano, Joe Taruc, Paquito Diaz, Jess De La Paz, Bongchi Miraflor, Tanya Shpilevoy.

A powerfully felt, though in some ways simplified, exercise in fatalistic melodrama, this Filipino film was joint-winner of the 1984 BFI Award. The fact that its director has subsequently suffered imprisonment under the Marcos regime is a grim testament in itself to the nerves this film has touched, though it is perhaps inevitable that some of its network of local allusions and nuances remains inaccessible to a foreign viewer.

The Natural

Nadia

NADIA
(Tribune-Jadran Films/Odyssey)
dir Alan Cooke *pro* James E Thompson *exec pro* Dave Bell *scr* Jim McGinn *ph* Frank Beascoechea, in Foto-Kem colour *ed* Raymond Bridgers *pro des* George Becket *art dir* Zeljko Senecic *mus* Christopher L Stone *r time* 99 mins *UK opening* Oct 26.
cast Talia Balsam, Jonathan Banks, Joe Bennett, Simone Blue, Johann Carlo, Conchata Ferrell, Carrie Snodgress, Carl Strano, Karrie Ullman, Leslie Weiner, Sonja Kereskenji, Pat Starr, Gregory Cooke, Geza Poszar, Vjenceslav Kapural, Tom Vukusic, Bozo Smiljanic, Gheorghe Berechet.

The true story of gymnast Nadia Comaneci, who at the age of fourteen wins three Olympic gold medals at Montreal, becoming in the process the first person ever to score a perfect ten. Despite illustrating the perils of being the Most Famous Person in Rumania (Nadia gets fat and drinks bleach in a fit of friendless pique), this is a weary little biopic which can only be of interest to budding baby gymnasts and paedophiles who like to watch little girls doing handstands

THE NATURAL
(Tri-Star)
dir Barry Levinson *pro* Mark Johnson *exec pro* Roger Towne, Philip M Breen *scr* Roger Towne, Phil Dusenberry, based on the novel by Bernard Malamud *ph* Caleb Deschanel, in Technicolor *ed* Stu Linder *pro des* Angelo Graham, Mel Bourner *art dir* James J Murikami, Speed Hopkins *mus* Randy Newman *r time* 134 mins *US opening* prior to Jul 1984 *UK opening* Oct 19.
cast Robert Redford, Robert Duvall, Glenn Close, Kim Basinger, Wilford Brimley, Barbara Hershey, Robert Prosky, Richard Farnsworth, Darren McGavin, Joe Don Baker, John Finnegan, Alan Fudge, Paul Sullivan Jr, Rachel Hall, Robert Rich III, Michael Madsen.

A monument to Robert Redford's narcissism and the quasi-religious regard for baseball held by upper middle-class American pseudo-intellectuals. The star doesn't so much play a character as mount every frame in which he appears – glowing with a glacéd wholesomeness so aggressively displayed as to make the 'charm' Lucille Ball plastered over 'Mame' seem restrained by comparison. If any actress tried to get away with what Redford brings to this vapid miasma she'd be laughed out of town. Directed by Barry Levinson in a style that might be likened to late period George Stevens on valium, and lit by Caleb Deschanel in a manner that suggests that Harrison Ford and the gang from 'Blade Runner' are about to trundle in at any moment, this tale of a do-no-wrong ball player who saves a down-and-out team in some deco-bedecked past of an over-ambitious art director's imagination is enough to make any intelligent American want to go out and register as a Communist agent. (See Turkeys of the Year.)

The Neverending Story

THE NEVERENDING STORY
(Neue Constantin Filmproduktion-
Bavaria Studios-WDR/Warner)
dir Wolfgang Petersen *pro* Bernd
Eichinger, Dieter Geissler *exec pro*
Mark Damon, John Hyde *scr*
Wolfgang Petersen, Herman Weigel
ph Jost Vacano, in Technicolor *ed* Jane
Seitz *pro des* Rolf Zehetbauer *mus*
Klaus Doldinger, Giorgio Moroder
r time 94 mins *US opening* Jul 20
UK opening Apr 5.
cast Barret Oliver, Gerald McRaney,
Drum Garrett, Darryl Cooksey,
Nicholas Gilbert, Thomas Hill, Deep
Roy, Tilo Prückner, Moses Gunn,
Noah Hathaway, Alan Oppenheimer,
Sydney Bromley, Patricia Hayes,
Tami Stronach.

*Expensive venture into juvenile fantasy
which occasionally delivers the goods*

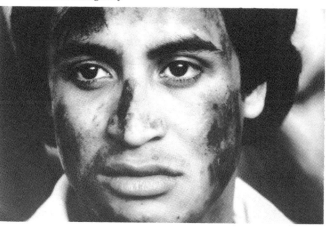

El Norte

in terms of surreal conceits (what
seems to be a small mountain turns out
to be a large and mournful talking
snail) but fails to achieve the
allegorical dimension that might have
made it more than an inconsequential
comic strip. Even on this level, it leaves
something to be desired, with the
ferocious beast that pursues our hero
turning out to look like nothing so
much as a domestic dog with a funny
set of false teeth.

THE NEW KIDS: See US section

NIGHT OF THE COMET
(Atlantic Releasing/Entertainment)
dir-scr Thom Eberhardt *pro* Andrew
Lane, Wayne Crawford *exec pro*
Thomas Coleman, Michael Rosenblatt
ph Arthur Albert, in colour *ed* Fred
Stafford *pro des* John Muto *mus* David
Richard Campbell *r time* 95 mins *US
opening* Nov 16 *UK opening* Jun 21.
cast Robert Beltran, Catherine Mary
Stewart, Kelli Maroney, Sharon
Farrell, Mary Woronov, Geoffrey
Lewis, Peter Fox, John Achorn,
Michael Bowen, Devon Ericson, Lissa
Layng, Ivan E Roth, Janice Kawaye,
Chance Boyer, Andrew Boyer, Stanley
Brock, Mark Poppel, Raymond Lynch,
Bob Perlow.

*Terrific low-budget sci-fi/horror about
two spunky teenage sisters who suppose
themselves to be the only survivors after
a passing comet has turned the rest of
the populace into little piles of fine red
dust. Luckily, the girls are not your
average screeching heroines and know
how to wield a submachine gun, so they
acquit themselves admirably when
threatened by flesh-eating zombies and
mad scientists. There are thrills and
chills, but the accent is on humour
rather than gore – the girls discover the
joys of unfettered consumerism in a
deserted apartment store and bicker in
sisterly fashion over the last boy in the
world, when they find him.*

NIGHT PATROL: See US section

**A NIGHTMARE ON ELM
STREET:** See US section

1918: See US section

NINETEEN EIGHTY-FOUR
(Virgin/Umbrella-Rosenblum/Fox/
Atlantic)
dir-scr Michael Radford, based on the
novel by George Orwell *pro* Simon
Perry *co pro* Al Clark, Robert
Devereux *exec pro* Marvin J
Rosenblum *ph* Roger Deakins, in
Eastman Colour *ed* Tom Priestley
pro des Allan Cameron *mus* Dominic
Muldowney, Eurythmics *r time* 110
mins *UK opening* Oct 12 *US opening*
Dec 14.
cast John Hurt, Richard Burton,
Suzanna Hamilton, Cyril Cusack,
Gregor Fisher, James Walker,
Andrew Wilde, David Trevena, David
Cann, Anthony Benson, Peter Frye,
Pam Gems, Joscik Barbarossa, John
Boswall, Bob Flag, Roger Lloyd Pack,
Rupert Baderman, Corinna Seddon.

*As 1984 dawned, it was inevitable, as
well as appropriate, that we should be
hearing a good deal in reappraisal of
Orwell's novel and its continuing
influence in imaginatively penetrating
the protocols of totalitarianism. To*

release a film of the book in the year of its projected setting was thus altogether worthwhile, and – quite apart from the ingenuity involved in getting the finished product on to the screen only a year after its inception – the picture Michael Radford has written and directed bears every sign of being a labour of love. It is true that in a sense the original is a work of impassioned journalism, deploying narrative as a pretext, which occasions some lack of dramatic momentum in the adaptation. But atmosphere and performances are what count most here. A variety of claustrophobically decrepit surroundings are fastidiously lit in penumbral colours. John Hurt as a haggard Winston Smith and Suzanna Hamilton as his partner in a gruesomely foreshortened brief encounter are admirable, but the strongest impression of all is left by Richard Burton, who in his final appearance makes of the interrogator a truly chilling embodiment of perverted ideological mania. (See Films of the Year.)

NINJA III – THE DOMINATION:
See US section

NO SMALL AFFAIR: See US section

EL NORTE
(Independent Productions/Cinecom International-Island Alive/Mainline) *dir* Gregory Nava *pro* Anna Thomas *scr* Gregory Nava, Anna Thomas *ph* James Glennon, in colour *ed* Betsy Blankett *mus* various *r time* 140 mins *US opening* prior to Jul 1984 *UK opening* Jul 20.
cast Zaide Silvia Gutierrez, David Villalpando, Ernesto Gomez Cruz, Alicia del Lago, Eraclio Zepeda, Stella Quan, Rodolfo Alejandre, Emilio del Haro, Rodrigo Puebla, Trinidad Silva, Abel Franco, Mike Gomez, Lupe Ontiveros, John Martin, Ron Joseph, Larry Cedar, Sheryl Bernstein, Gregory Enton, Tony Plana, Diana Civita, Jorge Moreno.

With an expansiveness that belies its modest budget, Gregory Nava's film paints a vivid portait, at once direct and stylized, of the attempts by a victimised Guatemalan brother and sister to escape to the US and then to adapt to a precarious new life there. Sentimental, certainly, but in the most affirmative sense of the term, this is popular movie-making at its sympathetic and worthwhile best.

NOT FOR PUBLICATION
(Northstreet/Samuel Goldwyn/Thorn EMI Classics)
dir Paul Bartel *pro* Anne Kimmel *exec pro* Mark Forstater *scr* John Meyer, Paul Bartel *ph* George Tirl, in colour *ed* Alan Toomayan *pro des* Robert Schulenberg *mus* John Meyer *r time* 87 mins *US opening* Nov 1 *UK opening* Nov 23.

cast Nancy Allen, Don Peoples, Katherine Schultz, Richard Blackburn, Sonia Petrovna, Cork Hubbert, Richard Paul, Warrington Winters, Jeanne Evans, J David Moeller, Desmond Dhooge, Alan Rosenberg, Leslie Lyon, Laurence Luckinbill, Randy Moore, Frances Galvan, Christopher Wycliff, Bill Engvall.

An amiable, doomed conceit: the promise of delirious bad-taste schlock, actually delivered in the innocuously twee tones of lightweight thirties' screen farce and featherbrained fifties' sitcom TV. Buffeting sleaze and sweetness even more audaciously than in 'Eating Raoul', Bartel reorientates Allen's scandal-sheet hackette rôle from 'Strange Invaders' and sets her on a crusade against both gutter politics and the gutter press itself, with fancy-dress song 'n' dance acts along the way. Commercially speaking, this was always beyond subbing, and should have been spiked. To at least this critic, though, it was good news.

NOT QUITE JERUSALEM
(Acorn/Rank)
dir-pro Lewis Gilbert *exec pro* Herbert Oakes *scr* Paul Kember, based on his own play *ph* Tony Imi, in colour *ed* Alan Strachan *pro des* John Stoll *mus* Rondo Veneziano, Gian Reverberi *r time* 114 mins *UK opening* Mar 29.
cast Sam Robards, Todd Graff, Kevin McNally, Bernard Strother, Selina Cadell, Ewan Stewart, Joanna Pacula, Zafrir Kochanovsky, Libby Morris, Bernard Spear, Juliano Mer, David Menachem, Sawally Srinonton, Kate Ingram, Gary Cady, Poli Reshef, Yaacov Ben Sira, Shlomo Tarshish.

The questionable joys of living and working on a kibbutz, as seen through the stereotyped eyes of a group of young English and American volunteers who don't seem to mind having to muck out the chickens, feed the cows and do the washing up. Personalities clash, characters are formed, but it's all little more than an excuse for an Israeli

travelogue, climaxing in a totally misjudged finale in which the kubbutzniks are held hostage by Arab terrorists and rescued by the super-efficient Israeli military. The very beautiful Joanna Pacula manages to ooze charisma in the thankless rôle of stroppy kibbutz crossed with romantic interest. She deserves better.

Not Quite Jerusalem

Nineteen Eighty-Four

Number One

NOTHING LASTS FOREVER: See US section

NOTRE HISTOIRE: See Our Story

NUMBER ONE
(Stageform/Videoform)
dir Les Blair *pro* Mark Forstater, Raymond Day *exec pro* Warren Goldberg *scr* G F Newman *ph* Bahram Manocheri, in Technicolor *ed* Jon Gregory *pro des* Martin Johnson *mus* David Mackay *r time* 106 mins *UK opening* Apr 19.
cast Bob Geldof, Mel Smith, Alison Steadman, P H Moriarty, Phil Daniels, Alfred Molina, James Marcus, David Howey, Ian Dury, David Squire, Ron Cook, Alun Armstrong, Tony Scott, Kate Hardie, Ray Winstone, Albie Woodington, Jack Eden, A J Clark, Harry Scott, Eric Richard, Jimmy Tippett.

Despite a script by G F Newman ('Law and Order') and a supporting cast packed with sterling British television actors, this is a disappointment. What could have been a zesty slice of low-life (much of it filmed in seedily picturesque South London) degenerates into implausible lowbrow farce as Geldof's cheeky but charming snooker ace refuses to bow to his bent manager's demands that he throw the world championship.

Once Upon a Time in America

OH, GOD! YOU DEVIL: See US section

OLD ENOUGH
(Silverfilm Prods/Orion Classics/Connoisseur)
dir-scr Marisa Silver *pro* Dina Silver *ph* Michael Ballhaus, in colour *ed* Mark Burns *pro des* Jeffrey Townsend *art dir* Leslie Hope *mus* Julian Marshall *r time* 92 mins *US opening* Aug 24 *UK opening* May 23.
cast Sarah Boyd, Rainbow Harvest, Neill Barry, Alyssa Milano, Danny Aiello, Susan Kingsley, Roxanne Hart, Fran Brill, Gerry Bamman, Anne Pitonlak, Charlie Willinger, Michael Monetti, Manny Jacobs, Gina Batiste, Paul Butler, Judith Drake, Primy Rivera, Nance Kass.

The kind of intimate, genuinely felt movie for which charming is an inevitable but inadequate description. There is no shortage of charm, or humour, in this look at a summer friendship between two thirteen-year-old New York girls from different sides of the tracks, but above all there is a sense of truth, of everyday experience made universal by an art that conceals art. Occasional touches of contrivance in the scripting and of academicism in the visual treatment do little to diminish that sense, all too rare in today's cinema, of not a camera and actors but a privileged window on a private world.

ONCE UPON A TIME IN AMERICA
(Ladd Company/Warner)
dir Sergio Leone *pro* Arnon Milchan *exec pro* Claudio Mancini *scr* Leonardo Benvenuti, Piero De Bernardi, Enrico Medioli, Franco Arcalli, Franco Ferrini, Sergio Leone, based on the novel 'The Hoods' by Harry Grey *ph* Tonino Delli, in Technicolor *ed* Nino Baragli *pro des* Carlo Simi, James Singelis *mus* Ennio Morricone *r time* 227 mins *US opening* prior to Jul 1984 *UK opening* Oct 5.
cast Robert De Niro, James Woods, Elizabeth McGovern, Treat Williams, Tuesday Weld, Burt Young, Joe Pesci, Danny Aiello, William Forsythe, James Hayden, Darlanne Fleugel, Larry Rapp, Amy Ryder, Scott Tiler, Rusty Jacobs, Jennifer Connelly, Mike

Monetti, Adrian Curran, Brian Bloom, Julie Cohen, Noah Moazezi, James Russo, Karen Shallo.

Even though it seems to have alienated some audiences through its excessive violence, length and lack of sympathetic characters (in this last respect the film is far more honest than 'The Godfather'), Leone's Kosher Nostra epic is simply a masterpiece of modern cinema. Spanning over forty years, it recounts the story of Noodles (De Niro in yet another immaculate performance), from his street-urchin boyhood on the Lower East Side in 1922, through fully-blown gangsterdom during the Prohibition years, to 1968 when he returns from self-imposed exile to New York to discover the truth about his criminal colleagues and confront the nightmare of his past. Performance, recreation of place and period, and camerawork are all of the highest order, lent a tone of ironic nostalgia by Ennio Morricone's haunting score. But what makes the film so remarkable, as Leone cross-cuts from era to era with the logic of a dream, is the way the film works on so many levels: as a portrait of a critical period in American history, as an account of one man's coming to terms with his own overwhelming guilt, as a critique of a whole history of gangster-movie mythology, and as a meditation on the effects of time. Strangely, the bloodbaths and gunfights of the film's first half subside into a sad, sombre and incredibly moving elegy for wasted lives and lost love. (See Films of the Year.)

ORDEAL BY INNOCENCE

(Cannon)
dir Desmond Davis *pro* Jenny Craven *exec pro* Menahem Golan, Yoram Globus *scr* Alexander Stuart, based on the novel by Agatha Christie *ph* Billy Williams, in Eastman Colour *ed* Timothy Gee *pro des* Ken Bridgeman *mus* Dave Brubeck *r time* 88 mins *UK opening* Feb 15 *US opening* May 17.
cast Donald Sutherland, Faye Dunaway, Christopher Plummer, Sarah Miles, Ian McShane, Diana Quick, Annette Crosbie, Michael Elphick, George Innes, Valerie Whittington, Phoebe Nichols, Michael Maloney, Cassie Stuart, Anita Carey, Ron Pember, Kevin Stoney, John Bardon, Brian Glover, Billy McColl.

Set, rather shakily, in the fifties and featuring an assortment of revenants of the sixties (Sutherland, Miles, Dunaway – though the last, playing the guest victim, only gets to be glimpsed in flashback), this distinctly plodding Agatha Christie adaptation doesn't really seem to have much to do with filmgoing in the eighties. Dave Brubeck's non-stop Muzak score is a particular liability.

OUR STORY (NOTRE HISTOIRE)

(Adel Productions-Sara Films-A2/Artificial Eye)
dir-scr Bertrand Blier *pro* Alain Sarde *exec pro* Alain Delon *ph* Jean Penzer, in Eastman Colour *ed* Claudine Merlin *art dir* Bernard Evien *mus* Bohuslav Martinu, Ludwig van Beethoven, Franz Schubert, and others *r time* 111 mins *UK opening* Jun 20.

Ordeal by Innocence

Our Story

cast Alain Delon, Nathalie Baye, Michel Galabru, Geneviève Fontanel, Jean-Pierre Darroussin, Gérard Darmon, Sabine Haudepin, Norbert Letheule, Vincent Lindon, Bernard Farcy, Jean-Louis Foulquier, Philippe Laudenbach, Paul Guers, Frimin, Jean-François Stevenin, Nathalie Nell.

Providing downcast train-traveller Delon with two far-from-obscure objects of desire – indiscreet charmer Baye and an endless supply of beer – Blier nonetheless overreaches into Buñuel territory with a succession of stop-start narratives of frustrated wish-fulfilment, and loses the sure black-comedy footing he's previously demonstrated in the likes of 'Buffet Froid' or 'Les Valseuses'. Even the outrageously inconsequential excesses of Delon's participant fantasies – a whole Swiss village in self-destructive thrall to Baye's bedroom manner, for

instance – are eventually grounded in pat psychologising, prompting little stronger reaction than a Gallic shrug.

OUT

(Eli Hollander/Cinegate)
dir-pro-ed Eli Hollander *scr* Eli Hollander, Ronald Sukenick, based on the novel by Ronald Sukenick *ph* Robert Ball, in colour *pro des* Antony Chapman *mus* David Cope *r time* 85 mins *US opening* prior to Jul 84 *UK opening* Oct 4.
cast Peter Coyote, O-Lan Shepard, Jim Haynie, Grandfather Semu Haute, Scott Beach, Danny Glover, Michael Grodenchik, Gail Dartez.

Looking more as if it were made in 1968 than in 1982, this bizarre, low-budget independent road-movie would be extremely irritating if one were forced to take the pretensions of its plot and symbolism seriously. Coyote wants out – from what is never made clear – and

starts off on a geographical and spiritual odyssey that sees him meeting various Protean weirdos, experimenting with his own wavering identity, and experiencing explosively paranoid situations. Standard pseudo-significant stuff – except that it's all realized with tongue apparently firmly in cheek: anarchists devise their subversive plots by fishing letters out of alphabet soup; an aged Indian sage witters profoundly about Life and his New Pair of Boots; intensely meaningful dialogue degenerates into absurdly banal banter. Quite what, exactly, the film is all about remains a mystery.

OVER THE EDGE

(Orion/Mainline)
dir Jonathan Kaplan *pro* George Litto *scr* Charlie Haas, Tim Hunter *ph* Andrew Davis, in Technicolor *ed* Robert Barrère *pro des* Jim Newport *mus* Sol Kaplan *r time* 94 mins *US opening* prior to Jul 1984 *UK opening* Jul 6.
cast Harry Northup, Andy Romano, Ellen Geer, Julia Pomeroy, Michael Kramer, Matt Dillon, Pamela Ludwig,

Vincent Spano, Tom Fergus, Kim Kliner, Tiger Thompson, Richard Jamison, Lane Smith, Eric Lalich, Frank Mugavero, Kristina Hanson, Diane Reilly, Jeff Fleury, Bill Whedbee.

A wholly welcome, long-overdue dusting-down for the panic-shelved late-seventies classic of early-teen revolt. Yuppie-spawned kids discover they're the only unplanned-for element of a new suburban sleepytown development and, multiple provocations later, shuck their ennui with a suitably inflammatory rampage. Kaplan's B-pic punch, the intelligent detailing of the exploitation outline by Haas and Hunter, and the convincing teenage cast combine to make this the perfect riposte to the burgeoning ranks of Reaganite kid-pix. Pre-punk in styling, but the ultimate portrait of the No Wave ethos.

OXFORD BLUES: See US section

P p

narrative. For all the quality of Harry Dean Stanton's performance as the quintessential Wenders wanderer, some may find the film's middle passages over-extended. But the concluding sequence in the encounter booth, daring in its metaphoric theatricality, of Stanton's reunion with his wife, Nastassja Kinski, triumphantly pulls the existential loose ends into a gripping dramatic fabric. (See Films of the Year.)

PALE RIDER: See US section

PARIS, TEXAS
(Road Movies/Palace/TLC)
dir Wim Wenders *pro* Don Guest, Anatole Dauman *exec pro* Chris Sievernich *scr* Sam Shepard, from a story adapted by L M Kit Carson *ph* Robby Müller, in colour *ed* Peter Przygodda *art dir* Kate Altman *mus* Ry Cooder *r time* 148 mins
UK opening Aug 23 *US opening* Nov 9.
cast Harry Dean Stanton, Dean Stockwell, Aurore Clement, Hunter Carson, Nastassja Kinski, Bernhard Wicki, Sam Berry, Claresie Mobley, Viva Auder, Socorro Valdez, Edward Fayton, Justin Hogg, Tom Farrell, John Lurie, Jeni Vici, Sally Norwell, Sharon Menzel, The Mydolls.

Wim Wenders' odyssey movie displays an intense response to the nuances of American lifestyle and topography, yet its sensibility remains darkly European. There are echoes of Ford (the opening and closing shots directly evoke their counterparts in 'The Searchers') but also of Lang in the fatalistic symbolism (freight trains, railroad tracks) that is woven into the

PARKER
(Moving Picture Company/Virgin)
dir Jim Goddard *pro* Nigel Stafford-Clark *scr* Trevor Preston *ph* Peter Jessop, in colour *ed* Ralph Sheldon *art dir* Andrew McAlpine *mus* Richard Hartley, Hector Berlioz *r time* 97 mins
UK opening May 3.
cast Bryan Brown, Cherie Lunghi, Kurt Raab, Bob Peck, Beate Finkh, Gwyneth Strong, Simon Rouse, Uwe Ochsenknecht, Micha Lampert, Dana Gillespie, Ingrid Pitt, Phil Smeeton, Tom Wilkinson, Hennlore Elsner, Klaus Fuchs, Colin Gilder, Marie-Charlott Schüler, Alexander Duda, Klaus Menzel, Jane Bertish.

An intriguingly labyrinthine thriller with, at times, a genuinely hallucinatory quality, this never really delivers as much as it promises in its

first few reels, ultimately remaining stranded in some ill-defined limbo between mainstream television and art-house cinema.

THE PARTY ANIMAL: See US section

A PASSAGE TO INDIA
(GW Films-HBO/Columbia/Thorn EMI)
dir-scr-ed David Lean, based on the novel by E M Forster and the play by Santha Rami Rau *pro* John Brabourne, Richard Goodwin *ph* Ernest Day, in Technicolor *pro des* John Box *mus* Maurice Jarre *r time* 163 mins *US opening* Dec 14
UK opening Mar 19.
cast Judy Davis, Victor Banerjee, Peggy Ashcroft, James Fox, Alec Guinness, Nigel Havers, Richard

Wilson, Antonia Pemberton, Michael Culver, Art Malik, Saeed Jaffrey, Clive Swift, Ann Firbank, Roshan Seth, Sandra Hotz, Rashid Karapiet, H S Krishnamurthy, Ishaq Bux, Moti Makan, Mohammed Ashiq, Phyllis Bose.

David Lean's triumphant return to film-making after a long absence confounded epic expectations by reverting to his earlier Dickensian manner. It might not have been Forster, though it was true to the novel's theme of mutual incomprehensibility between English and Indian. But it was popular cinema at its well-crafted best. (See Films of the Year.)

PAVLOVA – A WOMAN FOR ALL TIME
(Mosfilm-Sovinfilm/Poseidon)
dir-scr Emil Lotianou *pro* Eric Weissberg, Serafim Karalexis *exec pro* Frixos Constantine *ph* Evgeni Guslinsky, Vladimir Nakhabtsev, in colour *ed* I Kalatikova, E Galkina, J Connock, *Western version sup* Michael Powell *art dir* Boris Blank *mus* Evgeny Dogas *r time* 133 mins
UK opening Mar 11.
cast Galina Beliaeva, James Fox, Sergei Shakourov, Vsevolod Larionov, Lina Boultakova, Georgio Dimitriou, Ivan Shkyra, P Gusev, Martin Scorsese, Bruce Forsyth, Roy Kinnear, Jacques Debari, Michael Kradunin, Alkis Kritikos, Anastasia Stakis.

A British-Russian co-production, the involvement of Michael Powell brought hopes of the delirious glories of 'The Red Shoes'. But the celebrated octogenarian simply edited a sprawling, anonymous biopic down to an indigestible two hours plus. Pavlova's life is reduced to noisy highlights, with brief encounters with the greats and some bizarrely unconnected globe-leaping. Atrocious dubbing adds to the dislocation, alongside temperamental Sovcolor and bloated re-orchestration of Tchaikovsky's greatest hits. Few pleasures here for aspiring swans, and only the bizarre cameos of Kinnear, Forsyth and Scorsese provide a few seconds of relief.

Above: Parker. Right: A Passage to India

Pavlova – A Woman for All Time

PERFECT: See US section

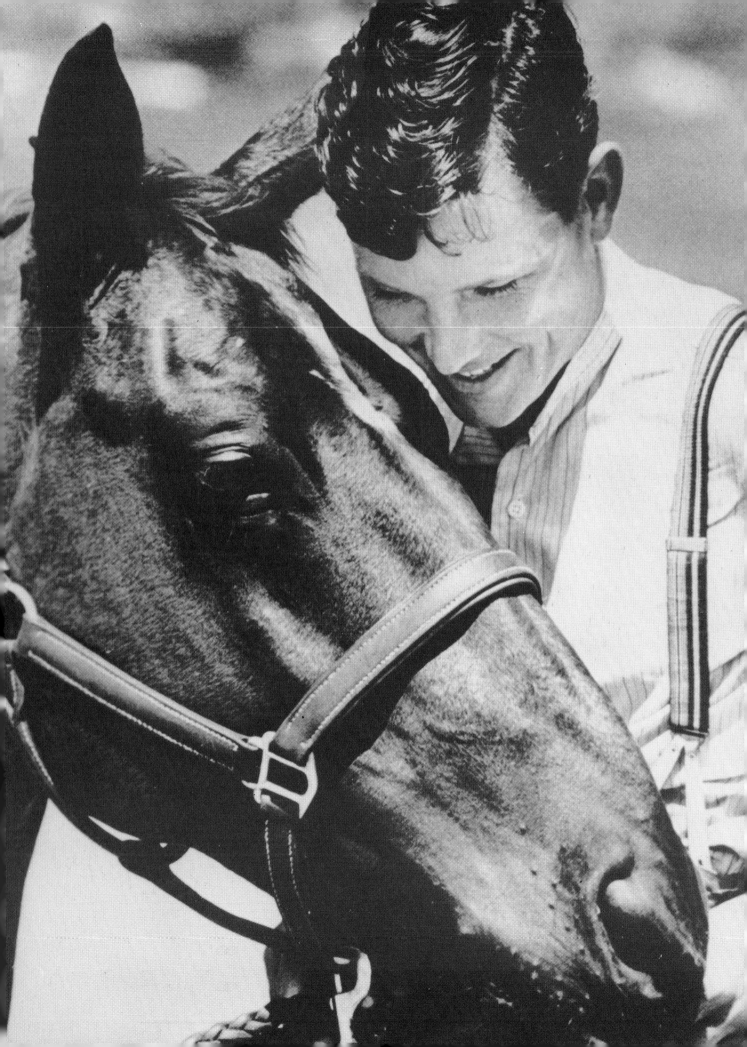

LA PETITE SIRENE: See US section

PHAR LAP
(John Sexton Prods-Michael Edgley International/Fox/Touchstone) *dir* Simon Wincer *pro* John Sexton *exec pro* Richard Davis *scr* David Williamson *ph* Russell Boyd, in colour *ed* Tony Paterson *pro des* Laurence Eastwood *mus* Bruce Rowland and others *r time* 118 mins *US opening* Aug 10 *UK opening* Mar 15.
cast Tom Burlinson, Martin Vaughan, Judy Morris, Celia de Burgh, Ron Liebman, Vincent Ball, John Stanton, Peter Whitford, Robert Grubb, Richard Morgan, Georgia Carr, James Steele, Steven Bannister Richard Terrill, Warwick Moss, Henry Duvall, Pat Thompson, Redmond Phillips, Maggie Miller.

Folkloric, cliché-ridden celebration of the brief career of a popular Australian race horse in the early thirties, with side-swipes at the snobbery and anti-semitism of the racing world. With its 'stirring' music and slow-motion photography, it often resembles an equine would-be 'Chariots of Fire'.

THE PHILADELPHIA EXPERIMENT
(New World-Cinema Group Venture/ Thorn EMI)
dir Stewart Raffill *pro* Joel B Michaels, Douglas Curtis *exec pro* John Carpenter *scr* William Gray, Michael Janover, from a story by Wallace Bennett, Don Jakoby, based on the book by William I Moore, Charles Berlitz *ph* Dick Bush, in CFI/ Eastman Colour *ed* Neil Travis, William Hoy *art dir* Chris Campbell *mus* Ken Wannberg *r time* 101 mins *US opening* Aug 3 *UK opening* Oct 12.
cast Michael Paré, Nancy Allen, Eric Christmas, Bobby Di Cicco, Louise Latham, Kene Holliday, Joe Dorsey, Michael Currie, Stephen Tobolowsky, Garry Brockette, Debra Troyer, Miles McNamara, Ralph Manza, James Edgcomb, Glenn Morshower, Rodney Saulsberry, Vivian Brown, Stephenie Faulkner.

A vastly entertaining slice of sci-fi hokum in the 'Twilight Zone' vein. In 1943, an experiment in radar evasion goes horribly wrong: a US battleship is sucked into a whirling limbo between time zones and two of its crew members deposited in the Nevada Desert, forty-one years later. While the heroes go on

the run from the understandably inquisitive military and try to stop their molecules from drifting, the whirling limbo gets out of hand: "If we don't stop this thing soon," says a scientist, "the whole damn planet's in trouble."

PLACES IN THE HEART
(Tri-Star-Delphi/Columbia)
pro-scr Robert Benton *pro* Arlene Donovan *exec pro* Michael Hausman *ph* Nestor Almendros, in Technicolor *ed* Carol Littleton *pro des* Gene Callahan *art dir* Sydney Z Litwak *mus* John Kander *r time* 111 mins *US opening* Sep 21 *UK opening* Feb 22.
cast Sally Field, Lindsay Crouse, Ed Harris, Amy Madigan, John Malkovich, Danny Glover, Yankton Hatten, Gennie James, Lane Smith, Terry O'Quinn, Bert Remsen, Ray Baker, Jay Patterson, Toni Hudson, DeVoreaux White, Jerry Haynes, Lou Hancock, Shelby Brammer, Norma Young, Arthur Pugh.

Unlike its rural companion pieces ('Country', 'The River') Robert Benton's scrupulously well-made tale of everyday Texan folk is rooted in the thirties. After the accidental death of her sheriff husband, fiery Edna

The Pope of Greenwich Village

Spaulding decides to farm cotton despite pressure from the bank, and takes in an itinerant negro worker and a blind lodger. Triumph over adversity is coolly yet sympathetically observed, Nestor Almendros's pellucid photography is without fault, and Sally Field is as plucky as ever with the sure hand of Benton forestalling the subsequent gush of her Oscar acceptance speech.

Places in the Heart

POLICE ACADEMY 2: THEIR FIRST ASSIGNMENT: See US section

THE POPE OF GREENWICH VILLAGE
(Koch-Kirkwood Prods/MGM-UA) *dir* Stuart Rosenberg *pro* Gene Kirkwood *scr* Vincent Patrick, based on his novel *ph* John Bailey, in Metrocolor *ed* Robert Brown *pro des* Paul Sylbert *mus* Dave Grusin *r time* 120 mins *US opening* prior to Jul 1984 *UK opening* Nov 30.
cast Eric Roberts, Mickey Rourke, Daryl Hannah, Geraldine Page, Kenneth McMillan, Tony Musante, M Emmet Walsh, Burt Young, Jack Kehoe, Philip Bosco, Val Avery, Joe Grifasi, Tony DiBenedetto, Ronald Maccone, Betty Miller.

Apparently clueless as to how Martin Scorsese made the nervy excess energies of 'Mean Streets' leap from the screen, Stuart Rosenberg maintains a static blank stare throughout this perversely pointless near-remake, and indulges the manically mannered mumblings of hustler-buddies Roberts and Rourke to a point some distance beyond the sublimely silly. Haunted by memories of Keitel and De Niro's similar shuffles between small-time crime and Little Italy loan sharks, the former pair both react with Methodical hysteria, and Roberts somehow manages to go even further OTT than he did as the sleazoid of last year's turkey, 'Star '80'.

PREPPIES: See MAKING THE GRADE

PRIME RISK: See US section

A PRIVATE CONVERSATION
(Mosfilm/Contemporary)
dir Nikita Mikhalkov *exec pro* Villi Geller *scr* Nikita Mikhalkov, Sofia Prokofieva, Ramiz Fataliev, based on the play 'Conversation Without Witnesses' by S Prokofieva *ph* Pavel Lebeshev, in colour *ed* E Praksina *art dir* Aleksandr Adabashyan, Igor Makarov, Aleksandr Samulekin *mus* Eduard Artemyev, C W Gluck *r time* 93 mins *UK opening* May 24.
cast Irina Kupchenko, Mikhail Ulyanov.

A film with only two characters, and those designated merely 'He' and 'She', arouses ample fears of pretension and obscurantism; and unfortunately such fears are only too fully realized in this strident, claustrophobic affair, in which a woman and her ex-husband seem confusingly to relive vicissitudes both marital and otherwise. A degree of technical trickery provides inadequate compensation for the lack of thematic clarity or even basic involvement.

Left: Phar Lap. Above: The Philadelphia Experiment

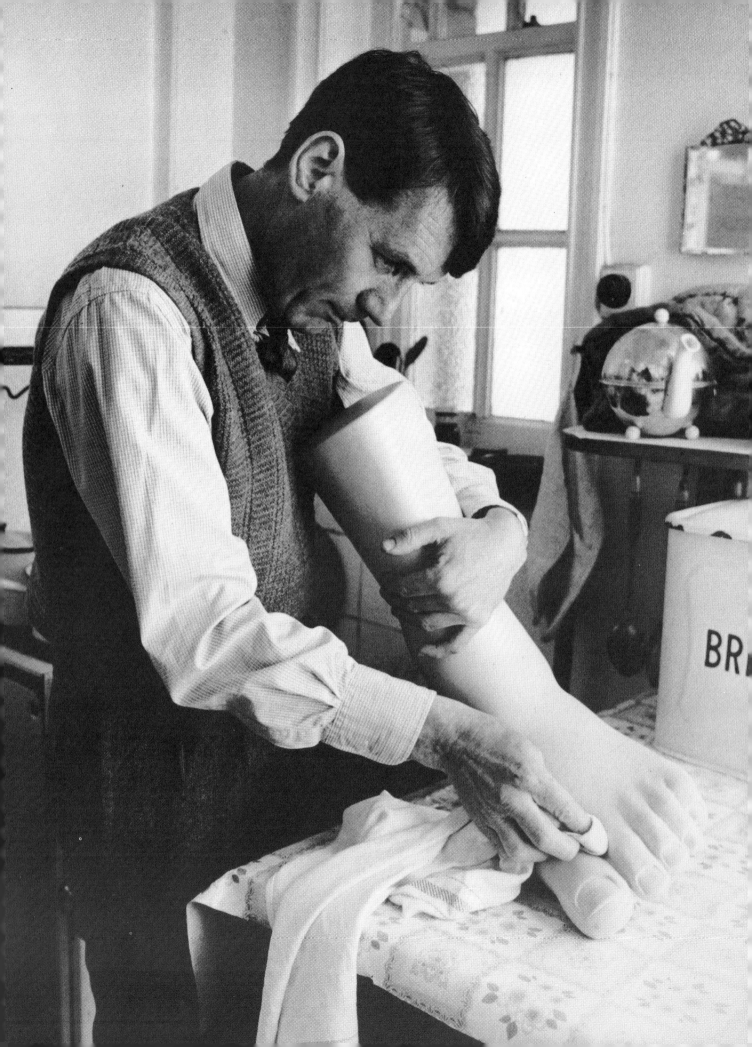

A PRIVATE FUNCTION

(HandMade/Island Alive)
dir Malcolm Mowbray *pro* Mark Shivas *exec pro* George Harrison, Denis O'Brien *scr* Alan Bennett, from a story by Alan Bennett, Malcolm Mowbray *ph* Tony Pierce-Roberts, in colour *ed* Barrie Vince *pro des* Stuart Walker *mus* John du Prez *r time* 94 mins *UK opening* Nov 30 *US opening* Mar 1.
cast Michael Palin, Maggie Smith, Denholm Elliot, Richard Griffiths, Tony Haygarth, John Normington, Bill Paterson, Liz Smith, Alison Steadman, Jim Carter, Pete Postlethwaite, Eileen O'Brien, Rachel Davies, Reece Dinsdale, Philip Wileman, Charles McKeown, Susan Porrett.

Alan Bennett's first script for the big screen is located in the West Riding territory of much of his TV work and takes a farcical-cum-satirical look at post-war attitudes through the microcosm of a stiff-collared clique in a small Yorkshire town making black market preparations to celebrate the wedding of the then Princess Elizabeth. Michael Palin is the mild-mannered chiropodist who finds himself man in the middle, and Maggie Smith his gorgon of a wife, determined at any price to ascend the class ladder from lower-middle to middle. The caricature is often gruesomely persuasive, though an element of parochialism, allied to some lack of cinematic momentum, sometimes tilts the film back toward the telly sphere.

PRIVATE LIFE

(Mosfilm/Contemporary)
dir Yuli Raizman *exec pro* Vladimir Tseitlin *scr* Anatoly Grebnyev, Yuli Raizman *ph* Nikolai Olonovsky, in colour *ed* V Belova *art dir* Tatyana Lapshina *mus* none *r time* 104 mins *UK opening* Nov 2.
cast Mikhail Ulyanov, Iya Savvina, Irina Gubanova, Tatyana Dogileva, Aleksei Blokhin, Elena Sanayeva, Liliya Gritsenko.

Octogenarian Soviet director Yuli Raizman recaptured international attention with this Oscar-nominated character study of a suddenly retired civil servant who is forced to grapple with his failures as a husband and father. Raizman displays wisdom in honestly portraying his protagonist without harshly judging him, and his functional visual style makes its points clearly. Still, by any standard this is a minor work of limited vision and ambition.

PRIZZI'S HONOUR: See US section

P'tang, Yang, Kipperbang

PROTOCOL

(Warner)
dir Herbert Ross *pro* Anthea Sylbert *exec pro* Goldie Hawn *scr* Buck Henry, based on a story by Charles Shyer, Nancy Meyers, Harvey Miller *ph* William A Fraker, in Technicolor *ed* Paul Hirsch *pro des* Bill Malley *art dir* Tracy Bousman, Enrico Fiorentini *mus* Basil Poledouris and others *r time* 95 mins *US opening* Dec 21 *UK opening* May 3.
cast Goldie Hawn, Chris Sarandon, Richard Romanus, André Gregory, Gail Strickland, Cliff De Young, Keith Szarabajka, Ed Begley Jr, James Staley, Kenneth Mars, Jean Smart, Maria O'Brien, Joel Brooks, Grainger Hines, Kenneth McMillan, Richard Hamilton, Mary Carver, Jack Ross Obney, Kathleen York.

Lame sub-Capraesque vehicle for the irksome Goldie Hawn, who seems to think that acting like a dumb blonde precludes any necessity for comedy founded on wit and imagination. Here she plays a peabrained cocktail waitress who stops a bullet bound for a Middle East potentate. She gets caught up in the wheeling and dealing whirl of Washington diplomatic life and ends up, predictably, gushing on about the Declaration of Independence.

Left: A Private Function. Above: Protocol

Basically, it's the old chestnut of naive idealism versus corruption in high places, done badly.

P'TANG, YANG, KIPPERBANG

[US TITLE: KIPPERBANG]
(Enigma-Goldcrest-Channel 4/Fox/MGM-UA Classics)
dir Michael Apted *pro* Chris Griffin *exec pro* David Puttnam *scr* Jack Rosenthal *ph* Tony Pierce-Roberts, in colour *ed* John Shirley *art dir* Jeff Woodbridge *mus* David Earl *r time* 80 mins *US opening* prior to Jul 1984 *UK opening* Aug 3.
cast John Albasiny, Abigail Cruttenden, Maurice Dee, Alison Steadman, Mark Brailsford, Chris Karallis, Frances Ruffelle, Robert Urquhart, Garry Cooper, Maurice O'Connell, Tim Seeley, Richenda Carey, Peter Dean, Dave Atkins, Eric Richard, Arthur Whybrow, John Arlott, Nicola Prince.

Adolescent love and schoolboy passions; well directed, sensitively acted and blessed with Jack Rosenthal's gently witty script.

PUMPING IRON II: THE WOMEN:
See US section

PURPLE RAIN

(Warner)
dir Albert Magnoli *pro* Robert Cavallo, Joseph Ruffalo, Steven Fargnoli *scr* Albert Magnoli, William Blinn *ph* Donald E Thorin, in Technicolor *ed* Albert Magnoli *pro des* Ward Preston *mus* Michel Colombier *r time* 111 mins *US opening* Jul 27 *UK opening* Aug 31.
cast Prince, Apollonia Kotero, Morris Day, Olga Karlatos, Clarence Williams III, Jerome Benton, Billy Sparks, Jill Jones, Charles Huntsberry, Dez Dickerson, Brenda Bennett, Susan, Sandra Claire Gershman, Kim Upsher, Alan Leeds,

Israel Gordon, Gil Jacobson, Joseph F Ferraro.

Showcase for the peculiar talents of Prince, in which His Royal Badness plays a young singer struggling to rise above a fraught family background. It wouldn't be so bad if he were merely preening, narcissistic and effeminate; but the guy has to come on like a macho jerk and slap his girlfriend around as well.

THE PURPLE ROSE OF CAIRO:
See US Section

Racing with the Moon

Rr

RACING WITH THE MOON
(Jaffe-Lansing Prods/Paramount)
dir Richard Benjamin *pro* Alain
Bernheim, John Kohn *scr* Steven
Kloves *ph* John Bailey, in colour *ed*
Jacqueline Cambas *pro des* David L
Snyder *mus* Dave Grusin *r time* 108
mins *US opening* Prior to Jul 1984
UK opening Sep 14.
cast Sean Penn, Elizabeth McGovern,
Nicolas Cage, John Karlen, Rutanya
Alda, Kate Williamson, Suzanne
Adkinson, Shawn Schepps, Julie
Philips, Michael Talbott.

*The only sense of energy to be found in
this film is in its title. A listless tale of
three 'nice' (ie vapid) teenagers in a
small American town at the outset of
World War II. The model is 'Summer of
'42', which was no great shakes as a
movie either, but at least managed to
keep viewers awake. If Penn, McGovern
and Cage are American film acting's
bright young hopes, then we're in
bigger trouble than we thought.*

RAMBO: FIRST BLOOD, PART II:
See US section

THE RAZOR'S EDGE: See US
section

RAZORBACK: See US section

O'Neal, William Smith, Vladek
Sheybal, Powers Boothe, Franke
McRae, Roy Jenson, Pepe Serna, Lane
Smith.

*Paradoxically made with too little care
or conviction to emerge as the
dangerous Reaganite obscenity
anticipated from Hollywood's most
self-consciously provocative rogue
rightist, Milius's sub-comic book vision
of World War Three (Reds vs The Rest)
turns out rather comfortingly to be a
monumentally silly exercise in
survivalist teen-fantasy. Guerrilla
groups in the movies always have all
the romance and all the fun; so
America should have some of its own,
even if it's got to get itself invaded first.
Much farcical macho mysticism, much
transparent Commie/Nazi conflation,
much sound and fury. Defused,
thankfully, by its own dumbness. (See
Turkeys of the Year.)*

RED SONJA: See US section

REPO MAN
(City Prods/Universal/Artificial Eye)
dir-scr Alex Cox *pro* Jonathan Wacks,
Peter McCarthy *exec pro* Michael
Nesmith *ph* Robby Müller, in DeLuxe
colour *ed* Dennis Dolan *art dir* J Rae
Fox, Linda Burbank *mus* Tito Larriva,
Steven Hufsteter *r time* 92 mins
US opening prior to Jul 1984
UK opening Jan 10.
cast Harry Dean Stanton, Emilio
Estevez, Tracey Walter, Olivia
Barash, Sy Richardson, Susan Barnes,
Fox Harris, Tom Finnegan, Del
Zamora, Eddie Velez, Zander Schloss,
Jennifer Balgobin, Dick Rude,

RED DAWN
(MGM-UA)
dir John Milius *pro* Buzz Feitshans,
Barry Beckerman *exec pro* Sidney
Beckerman *scr* Kevin Reynolds, John
Milius, from a story by Kevin
Reynolds *ph* Ric Waite, in Metrocolor
ed Thom Noble *pro des* Jackson De
Govia *mus* Basil Poledouris *r time* 114
mins *US opening* Aug 10 *UK opening*
Nov 9.
cast Patrick Swayze, C Thomas
Howell, Lea Thompson, Charlie
Sheen, Darren Dalton, Jennifer Grey,
Brad Savage, Doug Toby, Ben
Johnson, Harry Dean Stanton, Ron

Michael Sandoval, Vonetta McGee,
Richard Foronjy, Bruce White, Biff
Yeager.

*One of the most original and
invigorating independent movies to
emerge in years: part comedy, part
sci-fi, part thriller and part socio-
political satire, all gathered with
tireless invention into a bizarre but
coherent unity. (See Films of the Year.)*

RESTLESS NATIVES
(Oxford Film Company/Thorn EMI)
dir Michael Hoffman *pro* Rick
Stevenson *exec pro* Mark Bentley *scr*
Ninian Dunnett *ph* Oliver Stapleton,
in Technicolor *ed* Sean Barton
pro des Adrienne Atkinson *mus* Stuart
Adamson *r time* 89 mins *UK opening*
Jun 28.
cast Vincent Friell, Joe Mullaney,
Teri Lally, Bed Beatty, Robert
Urquhart, Bernard Hill, Anne Scott-
Jones, Rachel Boyd, Iain McColl, Mel
Smith, Bryan Forbes, Nanette
Newman, Lawrie McNicol, Neville
Watchurst, Dave Anderson, Eiji
Kusuhara, Sabu Kimura, Michael
Stroud, Ed Bishop.

*Irredeemably awful comedy that
plagiarises the work of Bill Forsyth –
the semi-realist style, the theme of
culture clash between winsome Scots
and invading Americans – to
disastrous effect. Two canny young
lads, bored with their jobs, take to
highway robbery by stealing cash and
jewellery from charmed coachloads of
American tourists, while zooming
around the Edinburgh environs on a
moped wearing jokeshop masks and
toting toy guns. Initial notoriety turns
to legend as the lads become media
heroes, and the entire project spirals off
into a tiresomely cute never-never
world of fairy-tale fantasy full of dire
stereotypes spouting dreadful lilting
dialogue. If this had not been set in
Scotland, one can only imagine that it
would never even have been made.*

RETURN TO OZ: See US section

Repo Man

Revenge of the Nerds

REVENGE OF THE NERDS
(Interscope Communications/Fox)
dir Jeff Kanew *pro* Ted Field, Peter
Samuelson *exec pro* David Obst, Peter
Bart *scr* Steve Zacharias, Jeff Buhai
ph King Baggot, in DeLuxe colour *ed*
Alan Balsam *pro des* James L Schoppe
mus Thomas Newman *r time* 90 mins
US opening Jul 20 *UK opening* Mar 8.
cast Robert Carradine, Anthony
Edwards, Ted McGinley, Bernie
Casey, Julian Montgomery, Tim
Busfield, Andrew Cassese, Curtis
Armstrong, Larry B Scott, Brian
Tochi, Donald Gibb, David Wohl, John
Goodman.

*Predictable addition to the cycle which
began with 'Animal House'. The only
difference here is that the underdogs
who win the day are all either
bespectacled or black or gay or ugly or
Japanese, which must represent some
kind of social breakthrough in
American winner-psychology.*

RHINESTONE
(Fox)
dir Bob Clark *pro* Howard Smith,
Marvin Worth *exec pro* Sandy Gallin,
Ray Katz *scr* Phil Alden Robinson,
Sylvester Stallone *ph* Timothy Galfas,
in Panavision, DeLuxe colour *ed* Stan
Cole, John Wheeler *pro des* Robert
Boyle *mus* Dolly Parton *r time* 111
mins *US opening* prior to Jul 1984
UK opening Nov 16.

cast Sylvester Stallone, Dolly Parton,
Richard Farnsworth, Ron Leibman,
Tim Thomerson, Steven Apostle Pec,
Penny Santon, Russell Buchanan,
Ritch Brinkley, Jerry Potter, Jesse
Welles, Phil Rubenstein.

*The question of whether America
wants to know whose chest expansion is
greater – the only valid reason for a
teaming such as this one – has been
answered. They don't. Taking its cue
from 'My Fair Lady' this unromantic,
unfunny comedy about a country-and-
western singer who, on a bet, teaches a
New York cabbie how to be a Good Ol'
Boy is as grisly a superstar spectacle as
has ever been conceived by a pack of
agents, lawyers, and studio flunkies.*

**RICHARD PRYOR HERE AND
NOW**
(Columbia)
dir-scr Richard Pryor *pro* Bob
Parkinson, Andy Friendly *exec pro*
Jim Brown *ph* Vincent Singletary,

Richard Pryor Here and Now

Kenneth A Patterson, Joe Epperson,
Tom Geren, John Simmons, Dave
Landry, in Metrocolor *ed* Raymond M
Bush *pro des* Anthony Sabatino,
William Harris *r time* 94 mins
US opening prior to Jul 1984
UK opening Aug 3.
cast Richard Pryor.

*Pryor's latest concert film finds him
mellowing to point of near
marshmellow softness. A comic
without edge has no point. Still, it's a
less depressing spectacle than 'The
Toy'.*

LES RIPOUX: See MY NEW PARTNER

THE RIVER

(Universal)
dir Mark Rydell *pro* Edward Lewis,
Robert Coates *scr* Robert Dillon,
Julian Barry, based on a story by
Robert Dillon *ph* Vilmos Zsigmond, in
Technicolor *ed* Sidney Levin *pro des*
Charles Rosen *mus* John Williams
r time 124 mins *US opening* Dec 19
UK opening Mar 22.
cast Mel Gibson, Sissy Spacek, Shane
Bailey, Becky Jo Lynch, Scott Glenn,
Don Hood, Billy Green Bush, James
Tolkan, Bob W Douglas, Andy Stahl,
Lisa Sloan, Larry D Ferrell, Susia
Toomey, Kelly Toomey, Frank Taylor,
Ivan Green, Desmond Couch, Charles
G Riddle, Jim Antonio, Samuel Scott
Osborne.

*Rare among recent populist Americana
in airing its own contradictions quite
so blatantly (albeit on the way to a
predictably rousing conservative
finale), Mark Rydell's contribution to
the year's cycle of rural dramas throws
its emotional weight behind a working-
class hero at the same time as it
demontrates clearly his (literal) stick-
in-the-mud wrong-headedness.
Farmer Gibson tries outfacing both
floods and the financial inducements of
dambuilder Glenn to maintain an
illusion of patriarchal control over
land, fate and family, unshaken even
by an enforced spell of cautionary
moonlighting as an industrial scab.*

THE RIVER RAT: See US section

ROADHOUSE 66: See US Section

ROMANCING THE STONE

(El Corazón/Fox)
dir Robert Zemeckis *pro* Michael
Douglas *scr* Diane Thomas *ph* Dean
Cundey, in Panavision, DeLuxe colour
ed Donn Cambern, Frank Morriss
pro des Lawrence G Paull *art dir*
Augustin Ituarte *mus* Alan Silvestri
r time 105 mins *US opening* prior to
Jul 1984 *UK opening* Aug 17.

The River

cast Michael Douglas, Kathleen
Turner, Danny DeVito, Zack Norman,
Alfonso Arau, Manuel Ojeda, Holland
Taylor, Mary Ellen Trainor.

*A pleasant rip-off-cum-send-up of
'Raiders of the Lost Ark' about a
mousey writer of true romances who
stumbles into an adventure beyond
even her fervid imagination. Kathleen*

*Turner pours on the pizzazz – almost
making up for co-star Michael
Doulgas' lack of same.*

R.S.V.P.

(Playboy Channel-Chuck Vincent
Prods/New Realm)
dir Lem Amero *exec pro* Chuck
Vincent *scr* LaRue Watts, based on a
story by Joel Bender *ph* Larry
Revenue, in colour *ed* Lem Amero
pro des LaRue Watts, Fabian Stuart
mus Ian Shaw *r time* 89 mins
US opening prior to Jul 1984
UK opening Jul 27.
cast Adam Mills, Lynda Wiesmeier,
Veronica Hart, Ray Colbert, Harry
Reems, Katt Shea, Lola Mason, Allene
Simmons, Dustin Stevens, Carey
Hayes, Judith Cassmore, Paul Coufos,
Robert Pinkerton, Steve Nave, Bob
Gorman, Jimmy Jue, Arlene Steger,
Laurie Senit, Tamara Landry, Cindy
Kirby.
Desperately un-funny playboy frolic.

RUNAWAY

(Tri-Star-Delphi III/Columbia)
dir-scr Michael Crichton *pro* Michael
Rachmil *exec pro* Kurt Villadsen *ph*
John A Alonzo, in Panavision,
Metrocolor *ed* Glenn Farr *pro des*
Douglas Higgins *mus* Jerry Goldsmith
r time *US opening* Dec 14 *UK opening*
Jun 21.
cast Tom Selleck, Cynthia Rhodes,
Gene Simmons, Kirstie Alley, Stan
Shaw, Joey Cramer, G W Bailey, Chris
Mulkey, Anne-Marie Martin, Michael
Paul Chan, Elizabeth Norment, Caro,l
Teesdale, Jackson Davies, Paul
Batten, Babs Chulla, Marilyn
Schreffler, Cec Verrell, Natino
Bellentino.

*Lighthearted and lightheaded futurist
thriller from Michael Crichton. A
detective specializing in defusing rogue
robots confronts a mad genius. Tom
Selleck makes a credible hero and Gene
Simmons a memorably hammy villain.
Routine plotting enhanced by some
competently rendered suspense
sequences.*

RUSTLER'S RHAPSODY: See US
section

Left: Romancing the Stone. Above: Runaway

ST ELMO'S FIRE: See US section

SAM'S SON: See US section

SCREAM FOR HELP
(Lorimar/Videoform/Miracle)
dir-pro Michael Winner *exec pro* Irwin
Yablans *scr* Tom Holland *ph* Robert
Paynter, Dick Kratina, in colour
exec ed Christopher Barnes *art dir*
Tony Reading *mus* Howard Blake,
Johnny Pearson *r time* 90 mins
UK opening Mar 15.
cast Rachael Kelly, David Brooks,
Marie Masters, Rocco Sisto, Lolita
Lorre, Corey Parker, Tony Sibbald,
Sandra Clark, Stacey Hughes David
Baxt, Leslie Lowe, Michael Corby,
Morgan Deare, Sarah Brackett, Clare
Burt, Matthew Peters, Marlene
Marcus, Diane Ricardo, Burnell
Tucker.

*A teenager is convinced that her
stepfather is plotting to murder her*

Scream for Help

mom, but no one will believe her.
Michael Winner combines the teen-in-
peril with the coming-of-age and comes
up with a golden turkey. The
screenplay is awe-inspiringly awful,
the soundtrack is screamingly
inappropriate, the acting is out of the
soap-opera school and the direction is
bursting with irrelevant zooms. The
result is hard to resist. (See Turkeys of
the Year.)

SECRET ADMIRER: See US section

SECRET HONOR
(Sandcastle 5/Blue Dolphin)
dir-pro Robert Altman *exec pro* Scott
Bushnell *scr* Donald Freed, Arnold M
Stone, based on their own play *ph*
Pierre Mignot, in Movielab colour *ed*
Juliet Weber *art dir* Stephen Altman
mus George Burt *r time* 90 mins
US opening Jul 20 *UK opening* Feb 8.
cast Philip Baker Hall.

*Provocative fantasia on Nixon's career,
as the man drunkenly dictates tapes
from his den of disgrace, spinning
paranoid alibis of conspiracies behind
Watergate. The figure of Nixon is
daringly used as a Shakespearean
figure of tragedy, and the*

She'll Be Wearing Pink Pyjamas

extraordinary theatricality of Philip
Baker Hall actually achieves unlikely
pathos. Robert Altman mounts the one-
man show with few visual flourishes,
and those at least enhance rather than
distract from the histrionic spectacle.

SHEENA
(Delphi II-Columbus)
dir John Guillermin *pro* Paul Aratow
exec pro Yoram Ben-Ami *scr* David
Newman, Lorenzo Semple Jr, based on
a story by David Newman, Leslie
Stevens *ph* Pasqualino De Santis, in
Metrocolor *ed* Ray Lovejoy *pro des*
Peter Murton *mus* Richard Hartley
r time 115 mins *US opening* Aug 17
UK opening May 10.
cast Tanya Roberts, Ted Wass,
Donovan Scott, Elizabeth of Toro,
France Zobda, Trevor Thomas, Clifton
Jones, John Forgeham, Errol John,
Sylvester Williams, Bob Sherman,
Michael Shannon, Nancy Paul,
Kathryn Grant, Kirsty Lindsay, Nick
Brimble, Paul Gee, Dave Cooper, Tim
Ward-Booth.

*Distaff Tarzan played tongue-in-cheek
but without wit. Delightful animal
stunts don't redeem the failure to
achieve either conviction or camp. John
Guillermin provides amiable direction,
but the screenplay recycles sprightly
stratagems from the 'Superman' films
without delight or new invention.*

SHE'LL BE WEARING PINK PYJAMAS
(Film Four International/Virgin)
dir John Goldschmidt *pro* Tara Prem,
Adrian Hughes *scr* Eva Hardy *ph*
Clive Tickner, in colour *ed* Richard
Key *pro des* Colin Pocock *mus* John Du
Prez *r time* 90 mins *UK opening* Jun
14.
cast Julie Walters, Anthony Higgins,
Jane Evers, Janet Henfrey, Paula
Jacobs, Penelope Nice, Maureen
O'Brien, Alyson Spiro, Jane Wood,
Pauline Yates, Bill Lund, Paul
Butterworth, Nicky Putnam, Paul
Atkinson, Gail Herring.

*A wholly inept and insincerely
'feminist' comedy of strained
sisterhood, this telefilm hybrid about
an assorted octet of women on a Lake
District outward-bound course boils
down to a succession of monologues on
self-defining relationships with or to
men. Julie Walters' familiar comic
voice is naturally the loudest in merely
reversing the old 'can't-live-with-'em,
can't-live-without-'em' clichés.
Retrograde open-air sitcom.*

THE SHOOTING PARTY
(Edenflow-Geoff Reeve Film &
Television/Curzon/European Classics)
dir Alan Bridges *pro* Geoffrey Reeve
exec pro Jeremy Saunders *scr* Julian
Bond, based on the novel by Isabel
Colegate *ph* Fred Tammes, in
Technicolor *ed* Peter Davies *pro des*
Morley Smith *mus* John Scott *r time*
96 mins *UK opening* Feb 1 *US opening*
May 24.
cast James Mason, Edward Fox,
Dorothy Tutin, John Gielgud, Gordon
Jackson, Cheryl Campbell, Robert
Hardy, Aharon Ipalé, Joris Stuyck,
Rebecca Saire, Sarah Badel, Rupert
Frazer, Judi Bowker, John J Carney,
Ann Castle, Daniel Chatto, Mia
Fothergill, Thomas Heathcote, Frank
Windsor.

The Shooting Party

Sheena

Silver City

*Impeccably detailed, perceptively
evoked view of a weekend in the country
that signals the end of an era – in this
case, the unquestioned upper-class rule
which collapsed, for a while at least,
with the beginning of World War I and
under the weight of its own internecine
warfare. The tone is elegiac, the mood a
little ponderous, the speech rather
stagy, but there's a first class
performance from James Mason,
whose last film this was.*

SILENT NIGHT, DEADLY NIGHT:
See US section

SILVER CITY
(Limelight Prods/Artificial Eye)
dir Sophia Turkiewicz *pro* Joan Long
ph John Seale, in Eastman Colour *ed*
Don Saunders *art dir* Igor Nay *mus*
William Motzing and others *r time* 102
mins *UK opening* Jun 13.
cast Gosia Dobrowolska, Ivar Kants,
Anna Jemison, Steve Bisley, Debra
Lawrance, Ewa Brok, Joel Cohen, Tim
McKenzie, Dennis Miller, Annie
Byron, Steve Jacobs, Halina
Abramowicz, Joseph Drewniak, Ron
Blanchard, Kathleen Allen, Robert
Lkenner, Urszula Hooker, Ron
Graham.

*A feature debut, drawing indirectly on
its director's own family background,
'Silver City' annotates the experience of
post-war immigrants to Australia with
a vivid sense of physical detail, though
a shade too much cosmetic top-
dressing, and does not feel altogether
assured in handling a somewhat
novelettish narrative. Touching
though many of the incidental
observations are, the final effect is on
the artificial side.*

SKYLINE: See US section

THE SLUGGER'S WIFE: See US section

SNOWDROP FESTIVAL: See US section

A SOLDIER'S STORY
(Delphi/Columbia)
dir Norman Jewison *pro* Norman
Jewison, Ronald L Schwary, Patrick
Palmer *exec pro* Charles Schultz *scr*
Charles Fuller, based on his play 'A
Soldier's Play' *ph* Russell Boyd, in
Metrocolor *ed* Mark Warner, Caroline
Biggerstaff *pro des* Walter Scott
Hernden *mus* Herbie Hancock *r time*
101 mins *US opening* Sep 14
UK opening Mar 15.
cast Howard E Rollins Jr, Adolph
Caesar, Art Evans, David Alan Grier,
David Harris, Dennis Lipscomb, Larry
Riley, Robert Townsend, Denzel
Washington, William Allen Young,
Patti LaBelle, Wings Hauser, Scott
Paulin, John Hancock, Trey Wilson,
Patricia Brandkamp, Carl Dreher,
Vaughn Reeves.

*Norman Jewison revisits the territory
of 'In the Heat of the Night' in this
detective story set against the
background of a segregated US army
unit in 1944 Louisiana. The well-
crafted result wins respect by
addressing itself in popular terms to a
topic both substantial and
uncomfortable, with the military
context used to throw into relief a
moment of incipient social change.
Moreover, the movie seeks to engage*

A Soldier's Story

*with a black perspective on the toll
taken by segregation, rather than
remain at the level of white liberal
guilt. Finally, though, the mystery plot,
with its artificial construction of
interviews and flashbacks fails to
illuminate the social theme. Writer and
director fall back on overstatement and
rhetoric, and one unfortunate result –
however contrary the intentions – is
that a hint of patronage attaches to the
way the characters are viewed.*

SONGWRITER: See US section

SPRING SYMPHONY
(Allianz Filmproduktion-Peter
Schamoni Filmproduktion/Blue
Dolphin)
dir-pro-scr Peter Schamoni *ph* Gerard
Vandenberg, in colour *ed* Elfi Tillack
pro des Alfred Hirschmeier *mus*
Robert Schumann
r time 103 mins
UK opening Sep 14.
cast Nastassja Kinski, Herbert
Grönemeyer, Rolf Hoppe, André
Heller, Bernhard Wicki, Gidon
Kremer, Edda Seippel, Margit
Geissler, Inge Marschall, Christine
Preussler, Sonja Tuchmann, Wolfgang
Gresse, Günter Krää, Uwe Müller,
Gisela Rimpler, Helmut Oskamp.

Spring Symphony

Biopic about Schumann and Clara Wieck; well acted, handsomely photographed but sketchily drawn, with a rather arbitrary non-ending.

STAR TREK III: THE SEARCH FOR SPOCK
(Paramount)
dir Leonard Nimoy *pro* Harve Bennett *exec pro* Gary Nardino *ph* Charles Correll, in Panavision, Movielab colour *ed* Robert F Shugrue *art dir* John E Chilberg *mus* James Horner, Alexander Courage *r time* 105 mins *US opening* prior to Jul 1984 *UK, opening* Jul 27.
cast William Shatner, Leonard Nimoy, DeForrest Kelley, James Doohan, George Takei, Walter Koenig, Nichelle Nichols, Mark Lenard, Merrit Butrick, Judith Anderson, Robin Curtis, Christopher Lloyd, James B Sikking, Allan Miller, Robert Hooks, Cathie Shiriff, Phil Morris, Scott McGinnis, Philip Richard Allen, Stephen Liska, John Larroquette, Sharon Thomas, Miguel Ferrer.

Not as lively as II, not as deadly as I, this third expedition by the starship Enterprise *appears designed more for Trekkies than the rest of us. Much in the way of moral-uplift mumbling as the gang get together to bring the pointy-eared pal Mr Spock back to their dimension in space and time.*

STARMAN
(Delphi II-Columbia)
dir John Carpenter *pro* Larry J Franco *exec pro* Michael Douglas *scr* Bruce A Evans, Raynold Gideon *ph* Donald M Morgan, in Metrocolor *ed* Marion Rothman *pro des* Daniel Lomino *mus* Jack Nitzsche *r time* 115 mins *US opening* Dec 14 *UK opening* May 10.
cast Jeff Bridges, Karen Allen, Charles Martin Smith, Richard Jaeckel, Robert Phalen, Tony Edwards, John Walter Davis, Ted White, Dirk Blocker, M C Gainey, Sean Faro, Buck Flower, Russ Benning, Ralph Cosham, David Wells, Anthony Grumbach, Jim Deeth, Alex Daniels, Carol Rosenthal.

John Carpenter expands his expressive range with this sweet romantic road-movie, an 'ET' with adult emotions. Jeff Bridges' alien visitor takes endearing cartoonish chances in his movements, while Karen Allen's mature sensuality helps overcome a sticky, silly sentimentality at the film's core. Thematically consistent with the rest of his work, however much a generic departure, 'Starman' is Carpenter's most fully realized work since 'Halloween'. (See Films of the Year.)

Steaming

STEAMING
(World Film Services/Columbia)
dir Joseph Losey *pro* Paul Mills *exec pro* Richard F Dalton *scr* Patricia Losey, based on the play by Nell Dunn *ph* Christopher Challis, in colour *ed* Reginald Beck *pro des* Maurice Fowler *art dir* Michael Pickwoad *mus* Richard Harvey *r time* 95 mins *UK opening* May 31.
cast Vanessa Redgrave, Sarah Miles, Diana Dors, Patti Love, Brenda Bruce, Felicity Dean, Sally Sagoe, Anna Tzelniker.

Joseph Losey's last, posthumously released, film seems a sadly inadequate envoi. An unreconstructed adaptation of the stage success, wholly (and on the screen, improbably) set in a women's municipal bath-house, it addresses topics of class and sexuality with a coarseness astonishing by comparison with the director's earlier Pinter-scripted movies, while even the visual possibilities of the ornate, enclosed setting manage to count for next to nothing.
STICK: See US section

STOP MAKING SENSE
(Cinecom/Island Alive/Palace)
dir Jonathan Demme *pro* Gary Goetzman *exec pro* Gary Kurfirst *scr* conceived for the stage by David Byrne *ph* Jordan Cronenweth, in Technicolor *ed* Lisa Day *mus* Talking Heads *r time* 88 mins *US opening* Oct 19 *UK opening* Nov 26.
cast David Byrne, Chris Frantz, Jerry Harrison, Tina Weymouth, Edna Holt, Lynn Mabry, Steve Scales, Alex Weir, Bernie Worrell.

A note-perfect meltdown of three 1983 Talking Heads concerts, classily choreographed for cinema as a suitably simmering spectacle of art-rock

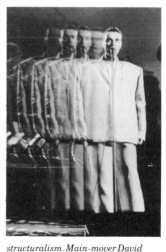

structuralism. Main-mover David Byrne gradually surrounds himself with band and backing to pile on the digitally-recorded polyrhythms, while Jonathan Demme's cameras scrutinize the storyboarded stagecraft with long-take respect.

Star Trek III: The Search for Spock

Stranger Than Paradise

STRAIGHT THROUGH THE HEART: See US section

STRANGER THAN PARADISE
(Cinesthesia-Grokenberger/Samuel Goldwyn/Artificial Eye)
dir-scr Jim Jarmusch *exec pro* Otto Grokenberger *ph* Tom Dicillo *ed* Jim Jarmusch, Melody London *mus* John Lurie, Aaron Picht *r time* 89 mins
US opening Oct 1 *UK opening* Oct 4.
cast John Lurie, Eszter Balint, Richard Edson, Cecilia Stark, Danny Rosen, Rammellzee, Tom Dicillo, Richard Boes, Rockets Redglare, Harvey Perr, Brian J Burchill, Sara Driver, Paul Sloane.

Jim Jarmusch's exercise in single-take hipness not only won the Director's Fortnight at Cannes, it was also the first work of post-Warhol sensibility to achieve broad audience popularity. Two layabouts strike up a comradeship with a young Hungarian emigrée, finding that from a depressed perspective, all America looks alike. Knowing in its deliberate wit and flattened grey images, the film seems daringly original to those unaware of the more resonant work of Edgar G Ulmer.

STREETS OF FIRE
(Hill-Gordon-Silver Prods/Universal-RKO)
dir Walter Hill *pro* Lawrence Gordon, Joel Silver *exec pro* Gene Levy *scr* Walter Hill, Larry Gross *ph* Andrew Laszlo, in Technicolor *ed* Freeman Davies, Michael Ripps *pro des* John Vallone *mus* Ry Cooder *r time* 94 mins

US opening prior to Jul 1984
UK opening Sept 21.
cast Michael Paré, Diane Lane, Rick Moranis, Amy Madigan, Willem Dafoe, Deborah Van Valkenburgh, Richard Lawson, Rick Rossovich, Bill Paxton, Lee Ving, Stoney Jackson, Grand Bush, Robert Townsend, Mykel T Williamson.

Walter Hill's bone-crushing rock fantasy may be irretrievably pretentious, playing ostensibly like an overripe outgrowth of 'The Warriors' but more often like the deader patches of 'The Driver', but it is honestly imagined, elaborately expressive, and stylistically astounding. If Hill were more self-conscious, his more personal projects might be less obtuse about their vulnerability to audience scepticism. As always, the physical production and action sequences are superb in every respect, and if one can indulge the determined avoidance of characterization, the film delivers kinetic cinema with intense integrity.

STRIKEBOUND
(TRM Prods/Mainline)
dir-scr Richard Lowenstein, based on the book 'Dead Men Don't Dig Coal' by Wendy Lowenstein *pro* Miranda Bain, Timothy White *exec pro* Erik Lipins, Miranda Bain *ph* Andrew De Groot, in colour *ed* Jill Bilcock *pro des* Tracy Watt *mus* Declan Affley *r time* 100 mins *UK opening* Nov 2.
cast Chris Haywood, Carol Burns, Hugh Keays-Byrne, Rob Steele, Nik Forster, David Kendall, Anthony Hawkins, Marion Edward, Lazar Rodic, Reg Evans, Rod Williams, Ian Shrives, Tiriel Mora, May Howlett, Declan Affley, Denzil Howson, Charles Gilroy, Ivor Bowyer, Kirsty Grant, Alice Lowenstein, Hardy Stow.

Strikebound

Streets of Fire

A dispiritingly simplistic slab of 'right-onnery' from young Aussie pop-promo wiz Lowenstein, turning conscientiously serious with a docu-drama on a Depression-era pit strike, yet contriving to make socialist struggle look like a saleable commodity. A would-be affective populism suffuses the over-lyrical logging of lock-out, stay-in scabbing and solidarity, with notions of deepening politicisation inadequately indexed in the gradual accommodation of a pit-wife's staunch Salvationism to her organizer-husband's activism.

SUBURBIA

(Suburbia Productions/New World-Vestron Video International)
dir-scr Penelope Spheeris *pro* Bert Dragin *ph* Timothy Suhrstedt, in colour *ed* Ross Albert *art dir* Randy Moore *mus* Alex Gibson *r time* 94 mins *US opening* prior to Jul 1984 *UK opening* Jun 28.
cast Chris Pederson, Bill Coyne, Jennifer Clay, Andrew Pece, Wade Walston, Don Allen, Robert Peyton, Jeff Prettyman, Donna Lamana, Timothy Eric O'Brien, J Dynan Myrtetus, Irene Latter, Mike B the Flea, Maggie Ehrig, Grant Miner, Christina Beck, Dorlinda Griffin, Robert Griffin, Anna Schoeller.

Mixing aggressive shock-tactic setpieces with an apparently tough, impassive gaze at a gang of outsiders – young LA punks, branding themselves The Rejected and colonizing the dream-home slums of the abandoned suburbs – Penelope Spheeris still somehow achieves the unlikely-sounding feat of simultaneously patronising and sentimentalising punk sub-culture. Her kids are invariably victims (of their variously uncaring, broken, incestuous or gay domestic backgrounds, or simply of society), touchingly recreating the most conventional of alternative families and coming across as merely weirdly accoutred, misunderstood latter-day hippies. Only the slim narrative, based on a running dog-eat-dog confrontation with lumpen neighbours rings remotely, if ungrippingly true.

SUCCESS IS THE BEST REVENGE

(De Vere Studio-Gaumont-The Emerald Film Partnership/BFI)
dir-pro Jerzy Skolimowski *scr* Jerzy Skolimowski, Michael Lyndon *ph* Mike Fash, in Technicolor *ed* Barrie Vince *pro des* Voytek *mus* Stanley Myers, Hans Zimmer *r time* 91 mins *UK opening* Nov 25.
cast Michael York, Joanna Szczerbic, Michael Lyndon, Jerry Skol, Michel Piccoli, Anouk Aimée, John Hurt, Ric Young, Claude Le Sache, Malcolm Sinclair, Hilary Drake, Jane Asher, Adam French, Sam Smart, Tim Brown, Maribel Jones, Mike Sarne, Maureen Bennett, Martyn Whitby.

A sort of sequel to 'Moonlighting', in spirit if not in style. The fact that this wonderfully chaotic and exhilarating political fantasy – with all its rage, surrealism and sense of cinema – played in London for about ten minutes is an indication of the extent to which even art-house film-goers have lost their curiosity for the extraordinary.

SUPERGIRL

(Artistry-Cantharus/Warner/Tri-Star)
dir Jeannot Szwarc *pro* Timothy Burrill, Ilya Salkind *exec pro* Pauline Coutelenq *scr* David Odell, based on the comic strip character *ph* Alan Hume in Panavision, colour *ed* Malcolm Cooke *pro des* Richard MacDonald *mus* Jerry Goldsmith *r time* 124 mins *UK opening* Jul 20 *US opening* Nov 21.
cast Faye Dunaway, Helen Slater, Peter O'Toole, Mia Farrow, Brenda Vaccaro, Peter Cook, Simon Ward, Marc McClure, Hart Bochner, Maureen Teefy, David Healy, Sandra Dickinson, Robyn Mandell, Jenifer Landor, Diana Ricardo, Nancy Lippold, Sonya Leite, Linsey Beauchamp, Michelle Taylor, Nancy Wood.

Supergirl

The Superperson cycle plummets into a morass of unfunny camp and ropy special effects as Supergirl travels to earth in pursuit of a magical rock which has fallen into the grasp of megalomaniac superbitch Dunaway. Instead of a gutsy comic-strip heroine, what we get is a soppy individual who gazes gooey-eyed at sunsets and bunny rabbits and succumbs to a surfeit of hammy supporting actors and blatant back-projection.

THE SURE THING: See US section

Suburbia

THE SWING

(Pelemele Film-Roxy Film-Luggi Waldleitner-Project Film in Filmverlag der Autoren-Bayerischer Rundfunk/Artificial Eye)
dir-scr Percy Adlon, based on the novel by Annette Kolb *pro* Eleanore Adlon *ph* Jürgen Martin, in colour *ed* Clara Fabry *art dir* Heidi Luedi *mus* various *r time* 130 mins *UK opening* Dec 26.
cast Rolf Illig, Christine Kaufmann, Anja Jaenicke, Joachim Bernhard, Lena Stolze, Susanne Herlet, Jenny Thelen, Elisabeth Bertram, Günther Strack, Dorothea Mortiz, Ilrich Tukur, Irm Hermann, Anja Buczkowski, Gusti Weishappel.

In several ways, Adlon's version of Annette Kolb's autobiographical novel about her youth in late 19th-century Munich is an attractive film – the period details are picturesque and the tone affectionate. However, particularly in view of its considerable length, the film seems to lack a dramatic structure or shaping attitude. Then, too, the approximate similarity of subject matter cannot help but invoke a comparison with Bergman's 'Fanny and Alexander' – and it is never easy to measure up against a masterpiece.

SWORD OF THE VALIANT: See US section

SYLVESTER: See US section

SYLVIA: See US section

A TASTE OF WATER

(Maya Film Production Association/Cinegate)
dir Orlow Seunke *pro* Jan Musch, Orlow Seunke, Tijs Tinbergen *scr* Orlow Seunke, Dirk Avelt Kooiman *ph* Albert van der Wildt, in colour *ed* Orlow Seunke, Tom Erisman *art dir* Dorus van der Linden *mus* Maarten Koopman *r time* 108 mins *UK opening* Jun 27.
cast Gerard Thoolen, Dorijn Curvers, Joop Admiraal, Hans van Tongeren, Olga Zuiderhoek, Moniek Toebosch, Standa Bareš, Ab Abspoel, René Groothoff, Jean Pierre Plooij, Bram van der Vlugt, Roelant Radier, Elsje Scherjon, Omar El Jout, Hans Veerman, Frans Faassen, Jaap Hoogstra.

This Dutch movie makes an exaggerated show of originality by treating an ostensibly sociological subject – a social worker's attempts to rehabilitate a retarded young girl – in terms not of realism but of wild expressionism. However well-meaning the director's attempt to vitalize his material, the end result is more emetic than humanly revealing.

The Swing

The Terminator

Teachers

TEACHERS

(MGM-UA)
dir Arthur Hiller *pro* Aaron Russo *exec pro* Irwin Russo *scr* W R McKinney *ph* David M Walsh, in Metrocolor *ed* Don Zimmerman *pro des* Richard MacDonald *r time* 106 mins *US opening* Oct 5 *UK opening* Feb 1.
cast Nick Nolte, Jobeth Williams, Judd Hirsch, Ralph Macchio, Allen Garfield, Lee Grant, Richard Mulligan, Royal Dano, William Schallert, Art Metrano, Laura Dern, Crispin Clover, Morgan Freeman, Madeleine Sherwood, Zohra Lampert, Mary Alice, Katharine Balfour, Vivian Bonnell.

A muddled mix of social criticism and sour satire, this profile of an urban high school is dramatically contradictory and incoherent. Still, it flails at so many serious and comic targets that it does randomly hit quite a few, and there are significant pleasures from the large, capable cast.

TERMINAL CHOICE: See US section

THE TERMINATOR

(Orion/Rank)
dir James Cameron *pro* Gale Anne Hurd *exec pro* John Daly, Derek Gibson *scr* James Cameron, Gale Anne Hurd *ph* Adam Greenberg, in colour *ed* Mark Goldblatt *art dir* George Costello *mus* Brad Fiedel *r time* 107 mins *US opening* Oct 26 *UK opening* Jan 11.
cast Arnold Schwarzenegger, Michael Biehn, Linda Hamilton, Paul Winfield, Dick Miller, Shawn Schepps, Bruce M Kerner, Franco Columbu, Bill Paxton, Brad Rearden, Brian Thompson.

Stylish entertainment that finds some original twists in the sci-fi genre, as killer robot Schwarzenegger arrives from the future to kill the mother of a future rebel saviour. The witty script anchors some convincingly chilling action scenes that include some of the best (if far from the most elaborate) chases and duels in a while.

A TEST OF LOVE: See Annie's Coming Out

THIEF OF HEARTS: See US section

THIS IS SPINAL TAP
(Embassy/Mainline)
dir Rob Reiner *pro* Karen Murphy *scr-mus* Christopher Guest, Michael McKean, Harry Shearer, Rob Reiner *ph* Peter Smokler, in CFI colour *ed* Robert Leighton *pro des* Dryan Jones *r time* 82 mins *US opening* prior to Jul 1984 *UK opening* Sep 7.
cast Rob Reiner, Michael McKean, Christopher Guest, Harry Shearer, R J Parnell, David Kaff, Tony Hendra, Bruno Kirby, June Chadwick, Fran Drescher, Joyce Hyser, Vicki Blue.

A very funny documentary lampoon about the rise and fall of a 'heavy metal' rock group. Filled with in-jokes for those in the know about such things, plus more than enough other gags for those that aren't. The take-off of rock video (not surprisingly, all but indistinguishable from the real thing) is alone worth the price of admission.

THOSE GLORY GLORY DAYS
(Enigma-Goldcrest-Channel 4/Fox)
dir Philip Saville *pro* Chris Griffin *exec pro* David Puttnam *scr* Julie Welch *ph* Phil Meheux, in colour *ed* Max Lemon *art dir* Maurice Cain *mus* Trevor Jones *r time* 90 mins *UK opening* Aug 3.
cast Zoe Nathenson, Sara Sugarman, Cathy Murphy, Liz Campion, Amelia Dipple, Elizabeth Springgs, Julia McKenzie, Peter Tilbury, Julia Goodman, Stephen Chase, Bryan Pringle, John Salthouse, Danny Blanchflower, Eva Lohman, Frances Barber, Rachel Meidman, Bob Goody, John Joyce, Lucy Hornack.

Observer soccer scribe Julie Welch reminisces with colleague and former hero Danny Blanchflower over her schoolgirl experience of Tottenham Hotspur's 1960/61 Double-winning season. A solid idea about youthful emotional investment comes across as a tackily whimsical anecdote of giggly adventurism, earthbound fantasy and anachronistic satire, even more cruelly exposed on its brief big-screen outing than it was as part of Channel 4's generally dire 'First Love' series.

Those Glory Glory Days

THREE CROWNS OF THE SAILOR

(Antenne 2-L'Institut National de l'Audiovisuel-Societé du Cinéma du Panthéon/BFI)
dir-scr Râúl Ruiz *ph* Jean Lafaux, Maya Feuillette, José-Luis Vasconcelos *ph* Sacha Vierny, part in colour *ed* Janine Verneau, Valéria Sarmiento, Jacqueline Simoni-Adamus, Pascale Sueur *mus* Jorge Arriagada *r time* 122 mins *UK opening* Nov 23.
cast Jean-Bernard Guillard, Philippe Deplanche, Nadège Clair, Lisa Lyon, Jean Badin, Claude Dereppe, Franck Oger.

A sublime slice of romantic surrealism about mariners and movies, fixing the ancient, obsessively repetitive stories of the former (about love and death in every port) in gorgeously alluring, allusive images that recall the finest dreamers of the latter. Extending, with wryly enigmatic self-consciousness, the Wellesian art-movie tradition of 'Lady From Shanghai' and 'The Immortal Story', Ruiz performs a cinematic tango with its more exotic conventions. More signs than meanings, and all the more refreshing for it.

TIGHTROPE

(Malpaso/Warner)
dir-scr Richard Tuggle *pro* Clint Eastwood, Fritz Manes *ph* Bruce Surtees, in Technicolor *ed* Joel Cox *pro des* Edward Carfagno *mus* Lennie Niehaus *r time* 114 mins *US opening* Aug 17 *UK opening* Nov 2.
cast Clint Eastwood, Geneviève Bujold, Dan Hedaya, Alison Eastwood, Jennifer Beck, Marco St John, Rebecca Perle, Regina Richardson, Randi Brooks, Jamie Rose, Margaret Howell, Rebecca Clemons, Janet MacLachlan, Graham Paul, Bill Holliday, John Wilmot, Margie O'Dair, Joy N Houck Jr, Stuart Baker-Bergen.

Three Crowns of the Sailor

Top Secret!

Clint Eastwood continues to explore interesting variations of his star persona in this intriguing thriller by Richard Tuggle (screenwriter of 'Escape from Alcatraz'). Eastwood plays a detective with kinky tastes tracking a mad killer who taunts him by following in his footsteps through the New Orleans underworld. Reminiscent in theme of the great Otto Preminger Fox melodramas of the forties, 'Tightrope' never quite delivers on its promise despite authentically opaque cinematography by Bruce Surtees, due primarily to excessive caution and inexpressive staging by debut director Tuggle.

TOP SECRET!

(Paramount)
dir-exec pro Jim Abrahams, David Zucker, Jerry Zucker *pro* Jon Davison *scr* Jim Abrahams, David Zucker, Jerry Zucker, Martyn Burke *ph* Christopher Challis, in Metrocolor *ed* Bernard Gribble *art dir* John Fenner, Michael Lamont *mus* Maurice Jarre *r time* 90 mins *US opening* prior to Jul 1984 *UK opening* Sep 28.
cast Val Kilmer, Lucy Gutteridge, Christopher Villiers, Omar Sharif, Peter Cushing, Jeremy Kemp, Billy J Mitchell, Michael Gough, Harry Ditson, Jim Carter.

The writer-director trio who irresistibly lampooned disaster movies in 'Airplane!' here come partly unstuck by trying to send up any number of cinematic conventions: war films, spy stories, even teenage romance. But allowing that the picture tends to fly apart at the seams, it still has terrific energy, a fund of good humour and bad taste, and some cartoon-like invention worthy of Frank Tashlin, much of which (such as the episode of the secret agent compressed along with his car into a cube of scrap metal) defies not only gravity of either kind but also adequate verbal description.

TURK 182: See US section

2010

(MGM-UA)
dir-pro-scr-ph Peter Hyams, based on the novel by Arthur C Clarke, in Metrocolor *ed* James Mitchell, Mia Goldman *pro des* Albert Brenner *mus* David Shire, Richard Strauss, György Ligeti *r time* 116 mins *US opening* Dec 7 *UK opening* Mar 5.
cast Roy Scheider, John Lithgow, Helen Mirren, Bob Balaban, Keir Dullea, Douglas Rain, Madolyn Smith, Dana Elcar, Taliesin Jaffe, James McEachin, Mary Jo Deschanel, Elya Baskin, Savely Kramarov, Oleg Rudnik, Natasha Shneider, Vladimir Skomarovsky, Victor Steinbach, Jan Triska, Larry Carroll.

A belated sequel to the Kubrick monolith that'll now presumably be known to posterity as 'Twenty-0-One', Peter Hyams' space odyssey is inevitably a less involvingly enigmatic experience. The mysteries around Jupiter now attracting a Russo-American mission are played off rather too purposefully against the earthbound drama of a revived Cold War, while a finger pointed at the duplicitous original programmers of HAL 9000 is the only explication offered to the Big Questions left hanging so tantalisingly by Kubrick. An alien intelligence still offers warnings and wonderment to awe-struck astronauts, but merely reveals a liberal-humanist orientation in place of clues about its original. Among the Earth-persons, Helen Mirren as an accent-perfect Soviet cosmonaut appears the best spur to détente.

Above: 2010. Right: Tightrope

Under the Volcano

Unfaithfully Yours

only the bare bones of the book's retelling of the final hours in the life of an alcoholic ex-British consul in a Mexican town prior to World War II. The meat for these bones is provided by Albert Finney's performance – the best in a career that in recent years has seen far from fine work. Jacqueline Bisset and Anthony Andrews aren't up to the demands of their parts, but Finney's power and Huston's directorial eloquence more than make up for them.

UNFAITHFULLY YOURS
(Fox)
dir Howard Zieff *pro* Joe Wizan, Marvin Worth *exec pro* Daniel Melnick *scr* Valerie Curtin, Barry Levinson, Robert Klane, based on the screenplay by Preston Sturges *ph* David M Walsh, in DeLuxe colour *ed* Sheldon Kahn *pro des* Albert Brenner *mus* Bill Conti *r time* 96 mins *US opening* prior to Jul 1984 *UK opening* Sep 7.
cast Dudley Moore, Nastassja Kinski, Armand Assante, Albert Brooks, Cassie Yates, Richard Libertini, Richard B Shull, Jan Triska, Jane Hallaren, Bernard Behrens.

Though nowhere near as effervescent as the Preston Sturges original, this remake is nonetheless polished and mildly diverting. It also gives Dudley Moore his best rôle in some time as a conductor suspicious of his beautiful young wife. Nastassja Kinski has rarely been livelier. Richard Libertini and Albert Brooks add fine support.

UNTIL SEPTEMBER: See US section

UTU
(New Zealand Film Commission/ Miracle)
dir Geoff Murphy *pro* Geoff Murphy, Don Blakeney *exec pro* Don Blakeney, David Carson-Parker, Kerry Robins *scr* Geoff Murphy, Keith Aberdein *ph* Graeme Cowley, in Fujicolor *ed* Michael Horton, Ian John *pro des* Ron Highfield *mus* John Charles *r time* 104 mins *UK opening* Apr 26.
cast Anzac Wallace, Bruno Lawrence, Tim Elliott, Kelly Johnson, Wi Kuki Kaa, Tania Bristowe, Ilona Rodgers, Merata Mita, Faenza Reuben, Tom Poata, Martyn Sanderson, John Bach, Dick Puanaki, Sean Duffy, Ian Watkin, Joe Malcolm, Ian Stewart, Ronnie Smith, Connie Gilbert, George Waaka.

Breakthrough film by Geoff Murphy ('Goodbye Pork Pie'), a realistic and ironic epic about a Maori rebellion in the nineteenth century. Complex in its attitudes, dynamic in its narrative, consistently surprising in its development, 'Utu' surpasses similar efforts like 'The Chant of Jimmie Blacksmith' by many degrees of sophistication and style. One of the best films of the year.

V v

VALLEY GIRL
(Valley-9000 Prods/New Realm)
dir Martha Coolidge *pro-scr* Wayne Crawford, Andrew Lane *exec pro* Thomas Coleman, Michael Rosenblatt *ph* Frederick Elmes, in colour *ed* Eva Gardos *pro des* Marya Della Javier *mus* Scott Wilk, Marc Levinthal *r time* 99 mins *US opening* prior to Jul 1984 *UK opening* Nov 30.
cast Nicolas Cage, Deborah Foreman, Elizabeth Daily, Michael Bowen, Cameron Dye, Heidi Holicker, Michelle Meyrink, Tina Theberge, Lee Purcell, Richard Sanders, Colleen Camp, Frederic Forrest, David Ensor, Joanne Baron, Tony Plana, Tony Markes, Christopher Murphy, Robby Romero.

Genial reworking of the Romeo and Juliet premise to reflect contemporary American teenage argot and conflicting lifestyles. A suburban teenage girl finds romance with an urban Hollywood hunk despite the bigoted opposition of her peer group. Believe it or not, this is what passes for class conflict in the States. An appropriately selected song soundtrack and an encyclopedic compendium of slang and dating attitudes makes this one for a time capsule. It's all a long way from 'The Graduate': here the kids rebel against the indifference of marijuana-smoking parents who are into (yuk!) health food.

U u

UNDER THE VOLCANO
(Ithaca-Conacine Prods/Fox)
dir John Huston *pro* Moritz Borman, Wieland Schulz-Keil *exec pro* Michael Fitzgerald *scr* Guy Gallo, from the novel by Malcolm Lowry *ph* Gabriel Figueroa, in Technicolor *ed* Roberto Silvi *pro des* Gunther Gerzeo *mus* Alex North *r time* 109 mins *US opening* prior to Jul 1984 *UK opening* Aug 31.
cast Albert Finney, Jacqueline Bisset, Anthony Andrews, Ignacio Lopez Tarso, Katy Jarado, James Villiers, Carlos Riquelme, Emilio Fernandez, Gunter Meisner, Rene Ruiz.

The faults of John Huston's adaptation of Malcolm Lowry's classic study of spiritual disintegration are plain, but so are its virtues. Abandoning the novel's stream-of-consciousness structure (which had tested the imaginations of many directors and writers) was perhaps a technical necessity, but a dramatic loss. Huston and scriptwriter Guy Gallo can offer

Above: Valley Girl. Right: Utu

VAMPING: See US section

A VERY MORAL NIGHT

(Dialög Filmstudio-Hungarofilm/
Cannon-Gala)
dir Károly Makk *scr* István Örkény,
Peter Bacsó, based on the short story
'The House with the Red Light' by
Sándor Hunyady *ph* János Tóth, in
Eastman Colour *ed* György Sivó
art dir Tamás P Balassa *mus* Chopin,
Johann Strauss, Jacques Offenbach,
Leo Delibes and others *r time* 99 mins
UK opening Apr 12.
cast Margit Makay, Irén Psota, Carla
Romanelli, Györgyi Tarján, György
Cserhalmi, Edith Leyrer, Mari Kiss,
Ildikó Kishouti, Zsuzsu Mányai, Edith
Soós, Katalin Szécsi.

*Made in 1977, this slight Hungarian
anecdote seems scarcely to merit its
belated importation. Taking place
mainly in a brothel in a small
provincial town at the turn of the
century, the film has a premise of
near-farce – to prevent an unexpected
visitor from discovering the truth about
the place, it has to be passed off as a
boarding rather than a bawdy house –
but executes it in a slow-moving,
sentimental fashion. Visual decoration
and some able performances only just
succeed in holding slumber at bay.*

A VIEW TO A KILL

(MGM-UA)
dir John Glen *pro* Albert R Broccoli,
Michael G Wilson *scr* Richard

A View to a Kill

Maibaum, Michael G Wilson *ph* Alan
Hume, in Panavision, Technicolor *ed*
Peter Davies *pro des* Peter Lamont
art dir John Fenner *mus* John Barry
r time 131 mins *US opening* May 24
UK opening Jun 13.
cast Roger Moore, Christopher
Walken, Tanya Roberts, Grace Jones,
Patrick Macnee, Patrick Bauchau,
David Yip, Fiona Fullerton, Manning

Redwood, Alison Doody, Willoughby
Gray, Desmond Llewelyn, Robert
Brown, Lois Maxwell, Walter Gotell,
Geoffrey Keen, Jean Rougerie, Daniel
Benzali, Bogdan Kominowski,
Papillon Soo Soo.

*Weakly conceived James Bond entry,
far inferior to John Glen's previous
efforts which boasted keenly propulsive*

*narratives and stunning stunts. One
doesn't look for conviction or
consistency in a Bond, but here even
minimal bows in the direction of an
integrated plot are scant. The setpieces
are indifferently executed and seem
arbitrarily shoehorned into the story,
while Christopher Walken makes the
least persuasive nemesis of the entire
series.*

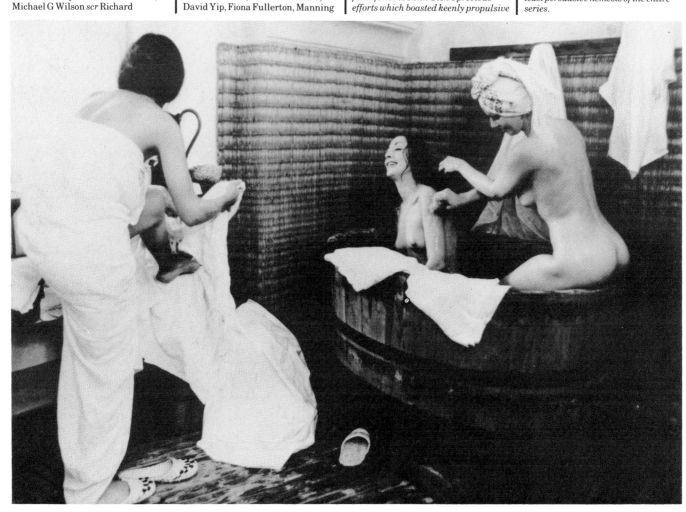

A Very Moral Night

VIGIL
(First Blood-Last Rites-New Zealand
Film Commission/Enterprise)
dir Vincent Ward *pro* John Maynard
exec pro Gary Hannam *scr* Vincent
Ward, Graeme Tetley *ph* Alun
Bollinger, in Eastman Colour *ed*
Simon Reece *pro des* Kai Hawkins
mus Jack Body *r time* 90 mins
UK opening Jan 25.
cast Bill Kerr, Fiona Kay, Gordon
Sheilds, Penelope Stewart, Frank
Whitten, Arthur Sutton, Snow
Turner, Bill Liddy, Maurice Trewern,
Eric Griffin, Emily Haupapa, Debbie
Newton, Bob Morrison, Lloyd Grundy,
Joseph Ritai, Josie Herligy, Sadie
Marriner, Bill Brocklehurst,
Rangitoheriri Teupokopakari.

A kind of Kiwi 'Cold Comfort Farm',
and a real weirdo. Vincent Ward's
enigmatic rural melodrama, set on a
forbidding hill farm, centres on a
young girl with the characteristically
off-putting name of Toss. Though Toss
herself, trudging through the omni-
present mud in ballet costume and
gumboots, is an appealing enough
figure, it is difficult to give much of a
toss for her widowed mother, the randy
handyman, or the ga-ga grandpa who
constitute the rest of the dramatis
personae, or to get at all involved in
their attempts to get their tractor
working – which provides the mainstay
of the 'plot'. Ward supplies striking
visual atmosphere – a cinematic
equivalent of Beckett, even – but it's not
enough to keep boredom at bay.

VISIONQUEST: See US section

WATER
(HandMade/Rank)
dir Dick Clement *pro* Ian La Frenais
exec pro George Harrison, Denis
O'Brien *scr* Dick Clement, Ian La
Frenais, Bill Persky, from a story by
Bill Persky *ph* Douglas Slocombe, in
colour *ed* John Victor Smith *pro des*
Norman Garwood *mus* Mike Moran
r time 97 mins *UK opening* Jan 18.
cast Michael Caine, Valerie Perinne,
Brenda Vaccaro, Leonard Rossiter,
Billy Connolly, Dennis Duggan,
Fulton McKay, Jimmie Walker, Dick
Shawn, Fred Gwynne, Richard
Pearson, Maureen Lipman, Trevor
Laird, Chris Tummings, Kelvin
Omard, Oscar James, Charles Thomas
Murphy, Felicity Dean, William
Hootkins.

With its overabundance of cheerful
stereotypes, its consistently off-the-
mark political satire, its frenetic ill-
timing of the half-dozen good jokes it
contains, 'Water' is the kind of comedy
that cries out for a script editor,
preferably one who isn't producing or
directing the film.

Vigil

Water

Wetherby

WETHERBY

(Greenpoint-Film 4 International-Zenith/Palace)
dir-scr David Hare *pro* Simon Relph
ph Stuart Harris, in Technicolor *ed*
Chris Wimble *pro des* Hayden Griffin
art dir Jamie Leonard *mus* Nick Bicât
r time 102 mins *UK opening* Mar 8.
cast Vanessa Redgrave, Ian Holm,
Judi Dench, Marjorie Yates, Tom
Wilkinson, Joely Richardson, Robert
Hines, Bert King, Paula Tilbrook,
Stephanie Noblett, Richard Marris,
Stuart Wilson, Diane Whitley, Mike
Kelly, Tim McInnerny, Suzanna
Hamilton, Penny Downie, Katy
Behean, Christopher Fulford

*Possessing none of the immediate
impact of his debut telefilm 'Licking
Hitler', playwright David Hare's first
big-screen outing is perhaps rather too
subtly political for its own good.
Attempting to dissect a national
malaise of repression and reticence, it
constructs a taut grid of class lines and
lies to pinpoint a little piece of
Yorkshire that'll forever remain Home
Counties, where spinster Redgrave and
her social circle paddle furiously
beneath a placid surface to avoid
drowning in the pervasive angst that
has already led a stranger in their
midst to exhibitionist suicide. Facial
expressions and flashbacks hint at the
'whys', while an intellectual policeman
searches for the 'wherefores', but the
suggestion that everyone's implicated
in a Thatcherite crime of anti-passion
eventually seems too damply abstract to
excite.*

WHAT MAKES DAVID RUN?

(Productions de la Guéville-7 Films-FR3/Warner)
dir-scr Elie Chouraqui *pro* Xavier
Gelin *exec pro* Danièle Delorme, Yves
Robert *ph* Robert Alazraki, in colour
ed Georges Klotz *set des* Christian
Siret *mus* Michel Legrand *r time* 99
mins *UK opening* Jul 5.

cast Francis Huster, Nicole Garcia,
Charles Aznavour, Magali Noel,
Michel Jonasz, Nathalie Nell, Anouk
Aimée, André Dussolier, Katia
Tchenko, Charles Gérard, Annie Noel,
Maurice Benichou, Geneviève Mnich.

*What makes people make films like
this? A dismal comedy about the* angst
*and ambitions of the frantically movie-
mad son of an upwardly mobile Jewish
family, it concerns his problems both in
his relationship with a patient, loving
but independent girlfriend, and in his
plans to make a semi-autobiographical
film. The shadow of Fellini looms not
only in the structural similarity to '8½',
but also in the collection of wacky*

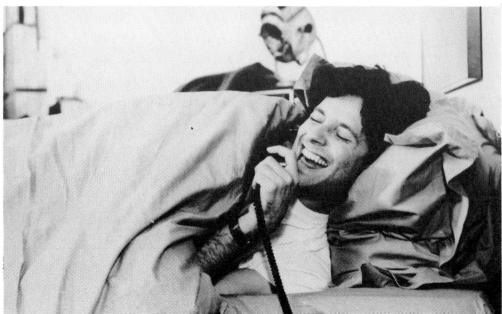

What Makes David Run?

grotesques remembered and imagined by David as he struggles to find scenes for his movie. Overblown in its characterization and nostalgia, inept in its attempt to merge the personal with the political, the film's most damning qualities are its hero – such a self-centred, snivelling bourgeois brat that it is impossible to care about his dilemmas one jot – and the fact that it is simply not funny.

WHERE THE GREEN ANTS DREAM
(ZDF/Artificial Eye/Orion Classics)
dir-scr Werner Herzog *pro* Lucki Stipetić *ph* Jörg Schmidt-Reitwein, in colour *ed* Beate Mainka-Jellinghaus *art dir* Ulrich Bergfelder *mus* Fauré, Ernst Bloch, Klaus-Jochen Wiese, Wagner, Wandjuk Marika *r time* 100 mins *UK opening* Oct 18 *US opening* Feb 8.
cast Bruce Spence, Wandjuk Marika, Roy Marika, Ray Barnett, Norman Kaye, Colleen Clifford, Ralph Cotterill, Nicolas Lathouris, Basil Clarke, Ray Marshall, Dhungala I Marika, Gary Williams, Tony Llewellyn-Jones, Marraru Wunungmurra, Robert Brissenden, Susan Greaves, Michael Glynn.

Werner Herzog reveals an artistic bankruptcy one hopes is only temporary in this pompous, shallow and unoriginal piece of Germanic sentimentality about the mystic superiority of aboriginal peoples. Herzog's hypnotic images no longer impress; they've become his clichés. By contrast, his recent shorter documentaries on mountain climbing ('The Dark Glow of the Mountains') and the Miskito Indians of Nicaragua ('The Ballad of the Little Soldier') reverberate with the passion and truth missing from this artificial, self-inflated exercise.

WHO'S THAT SINGING OVER THERE? See US section

WILD GEESE II
(Thorn EMI)
dir Peter Hunt *pro* Euan Lloyd *exec pro* Chris Chrisafis *scr* Reginald Rose, based on the novel 'The Square Circle' by Daniel Carney *ph* William Reed, in Technicolor *ed* Keith Palmer *pro des* Syd Cain *mus* Roy Budd and others *r time* 125 mins *UK opening* May 24.
cast Scott Glenn, Barbara Carrera, Edward Fox, Laurence Olivier, Robert Webber, Robert Freitag, Kenneth Haigh, Stratford Johns, Derek Thompson, Paul Antrim, John Terry, Ingrid Pitt, Patrick Stewart, Michael Harbour, David Lumsden, Frederick Warder, Malcolm Jamieson, Billy Boyle.

This nominal (virtually unrelated) follow-up to the earlier box-office hit has a plot so asinine – the springing of Hess from Spandau at the behest of a TV talk-show executive in search of a scoop – that it could surely have been filmed almost scene for scene as a satirical farce. The realization is perfunctory and implausible to a degree, and one is merely left pondering what can possibly have induced Olivier to have taken on the demeaning chore of a guest-star spot as Hess. (See Turkeys of the Year.)

Where the Green Ants Dream

Wild Geese II

71

A Woman in Red

THE WILD LIFE: See US section

WINDY CITY: See US section

WINTER KILLS
(Winter Gold Prod/ICA Projects)
dir-scr William Richert, based on the novel by Richard Condon *pro* Fred Caruso *exec pro* Leonard J Goldberg, Robert Sterling *ph* Vilmos Zsigmond, in colour *ed* David Bretherton *pro des* Robert Boyle *art dir* Norman Newbury *mus* Maurice Jarre *r time* 96 mins *UK opening* Mar 8.
cast Jeff Bridges, John Huston, Anthony Perkins, Sterling Hayden, Eli Wallach, Dorothy Malone, Tomas Milian, Belinda Bauer, Ralph Meeker, Toshiro Mifune, Richard Boone, Elizabeth Taylor, Donald Moffat, David Spielberg, Brad Dexter, Michael Toma, Ed Madsen, Irving Selbst, Chris Soldo.

The genesis of 'Winter Kills' is a movie scenario in itself. From a novel by Richard Condon ('The Manchurian Candidate', 'Prizzi's Honour') two producers (one since murdered, the other jailed) prepared a package with hot new director Richert and an extraordinarily starry cast. But the story – the brother of an assassinated US president stumbles across evidence of a major conspiracy – was evidently too close to reality. Money suddenly ran out, Richert eventually finished the film alone in 1978, and its release was mysteriously curtailed. A fascinating revival, directed with great wit and exuberance, and boasting another fearsome cameo from John Huston as the indomitable family autocrat.

WITNESS
(Paramount)
dir Peter Weir *pro* Edward S Feldman *scr* Earl W Wallace, William Kelley, based on a story by William Kelley, Pamela Wallace, Earl W Wallace *ph* John Seale, in Technicolor *ed* Thom Noble *pro des* Stan Jolley *mus* Maurice Jarre and others *r time* 112 mins *US opening* Feb 8 *UK opening* May 24.
cast Harrison Ford, Kelly McGillis, Joseph Sommer, Lukas Haas, Jan Rubes, Alexander Godunov, Danny Glover, Brent Jennings, Patti LuPone, Angus MacInnes, Frederick Rolf, Viggo Mortensen, John Garson, Beverly May, Ed Crowley, Timothy Carhart, Sylvia Kauders, Marian Swan, Maria Bradley.

Peter Weir's first American film is also his finest to date. Part thriller, part

Winter Kills

romance, part anthropological essay, it concerns the events that follow a young boy's watchful presence at a murder. The cop investigating the case discovers that the culprits are corrupt colleagues, and – his own life threatened – he returns to the home of the boy and his mother to hide away. Thus far, the thriller. Romance takes over for a while as he falls in love with the mother, but the film also turns into a touching portrait of the enormous gap between the cop's urban cultural background and that of his hosts, the Amish. Despite a lack of structural unity the film has much to offer in terms of its quietly understated performances (Ford is something of a revelation as the cop), its luminous imagery and its dispassionate view of two worlds geographically close but spiritually worlds apart. Yet another

film, in fact, that demonstrates that the best portraits of contemporary America are often made by non-Americans. (See Films of the Year.)

A WOMAN IN FLAMES
(Robert van Ackeren Filmproduktion-Dieter Geissler Filmproduktion-Pik 7 Film Produktions-und Vertriebs/Gala/Almi Classics)
dir-exec pro Robert van Ackeren *scr* Robert van Ackeren, Catharina Zwerenz *ph* Jürgen Jurges, in colour *ed* Tania Schmidbauer *pro des* Herbert Weinand, Heidrun Brandt *mus* Peer Raben *r time* 105 mins *UK opening* Aug 31 *US opening* Feb 3.
cast Gudrun Landgrebe, Mathieu Carrière, Hanns Zischler.

A middle-class woman abandons her world for that of the fetishist to whose

taste she caters as a Berlin prostitute. Plenty of whips and vibrators (and one memorable hand-held shot which doesn't concern either), but not as instructive as it might have been.

A WOMAN IN RED
(Orion/Rank)
dir Gene Wilder *pro* Victor Drai *exec pro* Jack Frost Sanders *scr* Gene Wilder, based on the script for 'Un éléphant ca trompe énormément' (1976) by Jean-Loup Dabadie, Yves Robert *ph* Fred Schuler, in DeLuxe colour *ed* Christopher Greenbury *pro des* David L Snyder *mus* John Morris *r time* 86 mins *US opening* Aug 15 *UK opening* Oct 12.
cast Gene Wilder, Charles Grodin, Joseph Bologna, Judith Ivey, Michael Huddleston, Kelly Le Brock, Gilda Radner, Kyle T Heffner, Michael

Zorek, Billy Beck, Kyra Stempel, Robin Ignico, Viola Kates Stimpson, Danny Wells, Buddy Silberman, Monica Parker, Ernest Harada, Julann Griffin.

Dispirited Americanized remake of the Yves Robert comedy 'Pardon Mon Affaire', which although light at least manipulated its plot with a sense of structure, character and taste, all of which are conspicuously missing in this vulgar, overdrawn, sniggling movie. Gene Wilder has always been his own worst enemy as a director, somehow managing to approach his material simultaneously with hysteria and indifference. The result is what no one needed: an eighties equivalent of those hypocritical Hollywood sex comedies of the early sixties.

Witness

THE FILMS RELEASED ONLY IN THE US

Reviews by *Myron Meisel*
1 JULY 1984-30 JUNE 1985

**THE ADVENTURES OF
BUCKAROO BANZAI: ACROSS
THE 8TH DIMENSION**
(Sherwood/Fox)
dir W D Richter *pro* Neil Canton, W D
Richter *exec pro* Sidney Beckerman
scr Earl Mach Rauch *ph* Fred J
Koenekamp, in Panavision,
Metrocolor *ed* Richard Marks, George
Bowers *pro des* J Michael Riva *mus*
Bones Howe *r time* 103 mins *US
opening* Aug 10.
cast Peter Weller, John Lithgow, Ellen
Barkin, Jeff Goldblum, Christopher
Lloyd, Lewis Smith, Rosalind Cash,
Robert Ito, Pepe Serna, Ronald Lacey,
Matt Clark, Clancy Brown.

*Aggressively hip, tongue-in-cheek
adventure, loaded with imaginative
high-tech art direction and eccentric
comic invention. None of it works very
well. Peter Weller makes a phlegmatic
superhero (who's also a rock star and a
nuclear physicist) who combats the
wicked Dr Lizardo (John Lithgow).
Confusion and jumble don't slow down
the confidence of W D Richter's
direction. The movie, like the hero,
could use a lot more humility.*

ALAMO BAY
(Delphi III/Tri-Star)
dir Louis Malle *pro* Louis Malle,
Vincent Malle *exec pro* Ross Milloy *scr*
Alice Arlen *ph* Curtis Clark, in colour
ed James Bruce *pro des* Trevor
Williams *mus* Ry Cooder *r time* 98
mins *US opening* Apr 3.
cast Amy Madigan, Ed Harris, Ho
Nguyen, Donald Moffat, Truyen V
Tran, Rudy Young, Cynthia Carle,
Martino Lasalle, William
Frankfather, Lucky Mosley, Bill
Thurman.

*A rich, fascinating subject – the tension
between refugee Vietnamese and local
Texans over depleted commercial
fishing territory – is handled in
politically and emotionally didactic
terms by the normally incisive Louis
Malle. The characters are less
dimensional here in fiction than in the
superb documentary on the same
theme, 'Fire on the Water'. The
Manichean melodrama undermines
credibility and impact rather than
enhances them.*

ALMOST YOU
(Wescom/Fox)
dir Adam Brooks *pro* Mark Lipson
exec pro Charles C Thieriot, Sandy
Climan, Stephen J Levi *scr* Mark
Horowitz, based on a story by Adam
Brooks *ph* Alexander Gruszynski, in
colour *ed* Mark Burns *art dir* Nora
Chavoosian *mus* Jonathan Elias
r time 96 mins *US opening* Mar 29.
cast Brooke Adams, Griffin Dunne,

Karen Young, Marty Watt, Christine
Estabrook, Josh Mostel, Laura Dean,
Dana Delany, Miguel Pinero, Joe
Silver, Joe Leon, Daryl Edwards,
Suzzy Roche.

THE AVIATOR
(MGM – UA)
dir George Miller *pro* Mace Neufeld,
Thomas H Brodek *scr* Marc Norman,
based on the novel 'The Aviator' by
Ernest Gann *ph* David Connell, in
Metrocolor *ed* Duane Hartzell *pro des*
Brenton Swift *mus* Dominic Frontiere
r time 96 mins *US opening* Mar 8.
cast Christopher Reeve, Rosanna
Arquette, Jack Warden, Sam
Wanamaker, Scott Wilson, Tyne Daly,
Marcia Strassman, Will Hare.

*Once again the wrong George Miller (ie
'The Man from Snowy River', not 'Mad
Max') plies a shallowly outdated
drama against a stunning landscape
backdrop. Christopher Reeve plays an
embittered pilot who is brought back to
humanity by a spoiled rich brat
(Rosanna Arquette) when the two of
them must survive injury, cold and
predatory wolves after crashing in the
northern wilderness. A terrible
screenplay repeatedly embarrasses the
leads, who withdraw from their
natural audience rapport, while
Miller's narrative disintegrates by the
final reels.*

THE BEAR
(Embassy)
dir Richard C Sarafian *pro* Larry
Spangler *exec pro* James Hearn *scr*
Michael Kane *ph* Laszlo George, in
DeLuxe colour *ed* Robert Florio *pro
des* George Costello *mus* Bill Conti,
Charles Koppelman, Martin Bandier
r time 112 mins *US opening* Sep 28.
cast Gary Busey, Cynthia Leake,
Harry Dean Stanton, Jon-Erik
Hexum, Carmen Thomas, Cary
Guffey, Steve Greenstein, D'Urville
Martin, Eric Hipple.

BEST DEFENSE
(Paramount)
dir William Huyck *pro* Gloria Katz *scr*
William Huyck, Gloria Katz, based on
the novel 'Easy and Hard Ways Out' by
Robert Grossbach *ph* Don Peterman,
in colour *ed* Sidney Wolinsky *pro des*
Peter Jamison *mus* Patrick Williams
r time 94 mins *US opening* Jul 20.
cast Dudley Moore, Eddie Murphy,
Kate Capshaw, Helen Shaver, George
Dzundza, David Rasche, Mark Arnott,
Peter Michael Goetz, Tom Noonan.

BLAME IT ON THE NIGHT
(Tri-Star)
dir-pro Gene Taft *exec pro* Tony Wade
scr Len Jenkin *ph* Alex Phillips, in

Technicolor *ed* Tony Lombardo *pro des*
Ted Haworth *mus* Ted Whitfield *r time*
85 mins *US opening* Nov 2.
cast Nick Mancuso, Byron Thames,
Leslie Ackerman, Dick Bakalyan,
Leeyan Granger, Rex Ludwick,
Melissa Prophet, Sandy Kenyon,
Merry Clayton, Billy Preston, Ollie E
Brown

*Unrealized father-son reconciliation
drama with a military-school boy
forced to accompany rock-star father on
tour. Miscasting, shallow scripting
and a ridiculous song score sink this,
despite the sensitivity of the players and
validity of the premise.*

BLESS THEIR LITTLE HEARTS
(Independent Feature Project/Billy
Woodberry)
dir-pro-ed Billy Woodberry *scr*
Charles Burnett *ph* Charles Burnett,
Patrick Melly *mus* Archie Shepp,
Little Esther Phillips *r time* 80 mins
US opening Dec 12.
cast Nate Herd, Kaycee Moore,
Angela, Ronald and Kimberly
Burnett, Eugene Cherry, Lawrence
Pierott, Ernest Knight, Ellis Griffin.

BODY DOUBLE
(Columbia)
dir-pro Brian De Palma *exec pro*
Howard Gottfried *scr* Robert J Avrech,
Brian De Palma *ph* Stephen H Burum,
in Metrocolor *ed* Jerry Greenberg, Bill
Pankow *pro des* Ida Random *mus* Pino
Donaggio *r time* 109 mins *US opening*
Oct 26.
cast Craig Wasson, Gregg Henry,
Melanie Griffith, Deborah Shelton,
Guy Boyd, Dennis Franz, David
Haskell.

*Brian De Palma's ransacking of
Hitchcockian motifs gets more
meaningless each time out. Vileness
and voyeurism stamp this indelibly as
a personal work, but the themes are
shallow and the style superficial.
Melanie Griffith's phlegmatic porn star
makes for bright scenes, but even these
are undermined by Craig Wasson's
charmlessness as the hapless actor-
protagonist.*

BREWSTER'S MILLIONS
(Universal)
dir Walter Hill *pro* Lawrence Gordon
exec pro Gene Levy *scr* Herschel
Weingrod, Timothy Harris, based on
the novel by George Barr McCutcheon
ph Ric Waite, in Technicolor *ed*
Freeman Davis, Michel Ripps *pro des*
John Vallone *mus* Ry Cooder *r time* 92
mins *US opening* May 22.
cast Richard Pryor, John Candy,
Lonette McKee, Stephen Collins,
Jerry Orbach, Pat Hingle, Tovah
Feldshuh, Joe Grifasi, Peter Jason,

David White, Jerome Dempsey, Ji-Tu
Cumbuka, Yakov Smirnoff, Hume
Cronyn.

*The classic farce has oft been remade,
most memorably by Allan Dwan in
1945. This attempted modernization
lacks invention or wit, misfiring badly
in its otherwise laudable attempt by
star Richard Pryor and director Walter
Hill to instil a certain wistful romance
and deeper feelings to the clanging
mechanism of having to squander a
fortune to inherit a bigger one. Pryor
once again fails to sustain a comic lead
in a narrative context. As for Hill,
though one can detect his operating
intelligence derailing, this is his sole
impersonal work to date.*

THE CARE BEARS MOVIE
(Nelvana/Samuel Goldwyn)
dir Arna Selznick *pro* Michael Hirsch,
Patrick Loubert, Clive Smith *exec pro*
Carole MacGillvray, Robert Unkel,
Jack Chojnacki, Lou Gioia *scr* Peter
Sauder *mus* John Sebastian *r time* 75
mins *US opening* Mar 29.
voices Mickey Rooney, Georgia Engel,
Harry Dean Stanton.

**CAREFUL, HE MIGHT HEAR
YOU**
(Syme International – NSW Film
Corp/TLC Films)
dir Carl Schultz *pro* Jill Robb *scr*
Michael Jenkins, based on the novel
by Summer Locke Elliott *ph* John
Seale, in Panavision, Eastmancolor *ed*
Richard Francis Bruce *pro des* John
Stoddart *mus* Ray Cook *r time* 116
mins *US opening* Jun 15.
cast Wendy Hughes, Robyn Nevin,
Nicholas Gledhill, John Hargreaves,
Geraldine Turner, Isabelle Anderson,
Peter Whitford, Colleen Clifford, Julie
Nihill.

*Despite the Australian Academy
Awards, this overwrought and
underdramatized soap opera feints at
Sirk territory and comes up with
Tradition of Quality melodrama
instead. A boy in care of a poor but
loving aunt and uncle is stolen by a
wealthy aunt from the city, in whose
custody he suffers and rebels. All
technique in the film is so crashingly
obvious that no one can miss the clumsy
stabs at artistry. One of the worst scores
of recent memory.*

CAT'S EYE
(MGM – UA)
dir Lewis Teague *pro* Martha J
Schumacher *scr* Stephen King *ph* Jack
Cardiff, in JDC Widescreen,
Technicolor *ed* Scott Conrad *pro des*
Giorgio Postiglione *mus* Alan Silvestri
r time 93 mins *US opening* Apr 12.

cast Drew Barrymore, James Woods, Alan King, Kenneth McMillan, Robert Hays, Candy Clark, James Naughton, Tony Munafo, Mary D'Arcy.

CHEECH AND CHONG'S THE CORSICAN BROTHERS
(C&C Brown/Orion)
dir Thomas Chong pro Peter MacGregor-Scott scr Cheech Marin, Thomas Chong ph Harvey Harrison, in DeLuxe ed Tom Avildsen art dir Daniel Badin mus Geo r time 87 mins US opening Jul 27.
cast Cheech Marin, Thomas Chong, Roy Dotrice, Shelby Fiddis, Rikki Marin, Eddy McClurg, Robbi Chong, Rae Dawn Chong, Laurie Maine.

CLOAK AND DAGGER
(Universal)
dir Richard Franklin pro Allan Carr exec pro C O Erickson scr Tom Holland ph Victor J Kemper, in Technicolor ed Andrew London pro des William Tuntke mus Brian May r time 101 mins US opening Aug 10.
cast Henry Thomas, Dabney Coleman, Michael Murphy, Christina Nigra, John McIntire, Jeanette Nolan, Eloy Casados, Tim Rossovich, Bill Forsythe.

Loose reworking of the 1949 'The Window', this thriller appealingly uses a young boy's fantasies about his father to give psychological charm and weight to a nest-of-killer-spies plot. Director Richard Franklin handles the suspense capably, and the cast is uniformly ingratiating. An underrated entertainment.

COCOON
(Fox)
dir Ron Howard pro Richard D Zanuck, David Brown, Lili Fini Zanuck scr Tom Benedek, based on a novel by David Saperstein ph Don Peterman, in colour ed Daniel Hanley, Michael J Hill pro des Jack T Collis mus James Horner r time 117 mins US opening Jun 21.
cast Don Ameche, Wilford Brimley, Hume Cronyn, Brian Dennehy, Jack Gilford, Steve Guttenberg, Maureen Stapleton, Jessica Tandy, Gwen Verdon, Herta Ware, Tahnee Welch, Barret Oliver, Linda Harrison, Tyrone Power Jr, Clint Howard, Charles Lampkin, Mike Nomad, Rance Howard.

Aliens disguised as humans return to earth to rescue their comrades left behind in an earlier visit, but a by-product of their operation is a Fountain of Youth that changes the lives of three couples in a neighbouring retirement community. Director Ron Howard ('Splash') applies a deft touch to this suspect mix of old-fart comedy and Spielbergian benign visitations, aided particularly by a dashing group of elderly players who bring genuine humanity to their rôles. The final reels, in particular, are contrived and phoney, fatal to a movie whose sole virtue is charm. Howard is undeniably talented: but has he anything at all to say artistically?

CODE OF SILENCE
(Orion)
dir Andy Davis pro Raymond Wagner scr Michael Butler, Dennis Shryack,

Mike Gray ph Frank Tidy, in colour ed Peter Parasheles, Christopher Holmes pro des Maher Ahmed mus David Frank r time 101 mins US opening May 3.
cast Chuck Norris, Henry Silva, Bert Remsen, Molly Hagan, Joseph Guzaldo, Mike Genovese, Nathan Davis, Ralph Foody, Allen Hamilton, Ron Henriquez, Ron Dean, Wilbert Bradley.

Director Andrew Davis ('Stony Island') accomplishes the challenging task of building an effective, dynamic action film around Chuck Norris. Basically, he keeps a lot of balls in the air around the phlegmatic hero while making no demands on him, and he adds a sense of complexity with acute sociological observation in the characterizations and use of Chicago locations. First rate in all departments, it might have been a major film with any iconographically potent star in the lead.

CRIMES OF PASSION
(New World)
dir Ken Russell pro Barry Sandler, Donald P Borchers exec pro Larry Thompson scr Barry Sandler ph Dick Bush, in colour ed Brian Tagg pro des Richard Macdonald mus Rick Wakeman r time 101 mins US opening Oct 19.
cast Kathleen Turner, Anthony Perkins, John Laughlin, Annie Potts.

Ken Russell revels in sexual excess yet again, this time without any sense of cultural importance. The result is daft, witty and bracing, enhanced by courageous performances by Kathleen Turner, who as a top designer with a secret night life as a hooker takes more risks than Russell, and Anthony Perkins, who flirts with self-parody as a degenerate religious madman. Silly when serious, it conveys great conviction at its most apparently facetious.

D.A.R.Y.L.
(Paramount)
dir Simon Wincer pro John Heyman scr David Ambrose, Allan Scott, Jeffrey Ellis ph Frank Watts, in Panavision, colour ed Adrian Carr pro des Alan Cassie mus Marvin Hamlisch r time 99 mins US opening Jun 14.
cast Mary Beth Hurt, Michael McKean, Kathryn Walker, Colleen Camp, Josef Sommer, Ron Frazier, Steve Ryan, Barret Oliver, Danny Corkill.

DESPERATELY SEEKING SUSAN
(Orion)
dir Susan Seidelman pro Sarah Pillsbury, Midge Sanford exec pro Michael Peyser scr Leora Barish ph Edward Lachman, in colour ed Andrew Mondshein pro des Santo Loquasto mus Thomas Newman r time 104 mins US opening Mar 29.

cast Rosanna Arquette, Madonna, Aidan Quinn, Mark Blum, Robert Joy, Laurie Metcalf, Anna Levine, Will Patton, Peter Maloney, Steven Wright, John Turturro, Anne Carlisle, Shirley Stoler.

Stylish farce that plausibly revives the old chestnut of amnesia and exchanged identities, this time between a bored young housewife and an amoral drifter. Director Susan Seidelman ('Smithereens') has a keen command of textures and glances that helps bring out the humour from the able cast. The last reel smacks of too much studio-style advice, merely working out the plot instead of climaxing it, but otherwise a delightful and unusual contempo wrinkle on screwball.

DIARY FOR MY CHILDREN (NAPLO GYERMEKEIMNEK)
(Mafilm Studio-Hungarofilm/New Yorker Films)
dir-scr Marta Meszaros ph Miklos Jancso ed Eva Karmento pro des Eva Martin mus Zsolt Dome r time 85 mins US opening Oct 31.
cast Zsuzsa Czinkoczi, Anna Polony, Jan Nowicki, Pal Zolnay, Mari Szemes, Tamas Toth.

An orphan in post-war Hungary rebels against the authority of her party-member aunt. A heartfelt, rigorously styled memoir by Marta Meszaros, keenly photographed and acted, but above all an intellectually and emotionally honest work about Communist society from an Iron Curtain nation. What might be conventional in our cinema assumes extraordinary power in theirs.

THE FAMILY GAME (KAZOKU GEEMU)
(Art Theatre Guild – Toho/Cinevista – Promovision International)
dir-scr Yoshimitsu Morita, based on a book by Yohei Honma pro Shiro Sasaki, Yu Okada ph Yoneo Maeda, in colour ed Akimasa Kawashima art dir Tatsumi Nakazawa r time 106 mins US opening Sep 14.
cast Yusaku Matsuda, Juzo Itami, Saori Yuki, Ichirota Miyagaway, Junichi Tsujita.

Kinema Jumpo winner as the best Japanese film of the year, this mordant attack on traditional family values undertakes some bold formal experiments in colour, composition and structure, but fails to make most of them pay off with pointed satire. Reminiscent of Kon Ichikawa comedies (like 'Kagi'), there seems to be more expressive enthusiasm than sustained vision in the direction of Yoshimitsu Morita.

FANDANGO
(Amblin/Warner)
dir-scr Kevin Reynolds pro Tim Zinnemann exec pro Frank Marshall, Kathleen Kennedy ph Thomas Del Ruth, in Technicolor ed Arthur Schmidt, Stephen Semel art dir Peter Landsdown Smith mus Alan Silvestri r time 91 mins US opening Jan 25.
cast Kevin Costner, Judd Nelson, Sam Robards, Chuck Bush, Brian Cesak, Marvin J McIntyre, Suzy Amis, Glenne Headly, Pepe Serna, Elizabeth Daily, Robyn Rose.

FIRSTBORN
(Paramount)
dir Michael Apted pro Paul Junger Witt, Tony Thomas exec pro Stanley R Jaffe, Sherry Lansing scr Ron Koslow

ph Ralf D Bode, in Technicolor ed Arthur Schmidt pro des Paul Sylbert mus Michael Small r time 103 mins US opening Oct 26.
cast Teri Garr, Peter Weller, Christopher Collet, Corey Haim, Sarah Jessica Parker, Richard Brandon, James Harper, Richard E Szlasa.

Suburban drama of teenage children of divorce coping with mother's psychopathic lover. Authentic dialogue and acute social observation lift this above its conventional story, which relaxes into a familiar thriller climax. The astute editing and character detail of the first half is among the best work director Apted has done.

THE FLAMINGO KID
(ABC Motion Pics/Fox)
dir Garry Marshall pro Michael Phillips scr Neal Marshall, Garry Marshall ph James A Kontner, in DeLuxe colour ed Priscilla Nedd pro des Lawrence Miller r time 100 mins US opening Dec 21.
cast Matt Dillon, Richard Crenna, Hector Elizondo, Jessica Walter, Fisher Stevens, Brian McNamara, Carole R Davis, Martha Gehman, Molly McCarthy, Leon Robinson, Janet Jones, Bronson Pinchot.

Pleasingly old-fashioned comedy-drama of a teenager grappling with materialistic values during a summer job at a country club in the early sixties. The emphasis on recognizable value conflicts is refreshing, and the cast exudes feeling, especially Matt Dillon, Richard Crenna as a sharp operator and Hector Elizondo as Dillon's proud plumber father.

A FLASH OF GREEN
(Spectrafilm)
dir-ed Victor Nunez pro Richard Jordan exec pro Sam Gowan art dir Carlos Asse mus Charles Engstrom r time 131 mins US opening Jun 19.
cast Ed Harris, Blair Brown, Richard Jordan, George Coe, Joan Goodfellow, Jean De Baer, Helen Stenborg, William Mooney, Isa Thomas, John Glover, Bob Murch, Joan MacIntosh, Bob Harris.

Faithful adaptation of a pre-Travis McGee John McDonald novel, concentrating on character and period authenticity in a tale of a cynical reporter's struggle to overcome the moral impact of being manipulated by corrupt interests. Ed Harris gives a strong, thoughtful performance that is continually undermined by spatially incoherent editing and uncertain direction. Victor Nunez ('Gal Young Un') obviously understands the material, but he has serious trouble mounting a narrative in even elementary visual terms.

FLASHPOINT
(HBO Pictures/Tri-Star)
dir William Tannen pro Skip Short scr Dennis Shryack, Michael Butler, based on the book by George La Fountaine ph Peter Moss, in Metrocolor ed David Garfield pro des Paul Greimann mus Tangerine Dream r time 94 mins US opening Aug 31.
cast Kris Kristofferson, Treat

Williams, Rip Torn, Kevin Conway, Kurtwood Smith, Miguel Ferrer, Jean Smart, Guy Boyd, Mark Slade, Robert Blossom, Tess Harper.

FLETCH
(Universal)
dir Michael Ritchie *pro* Alan Greisman, Peter Douglas *scr* Andrew Bergman, based on the novel by Gregory McDonald *ph* Fred Schuler, in Technicolor *ed* Richard A Harris *pro des* Boris Leven *mus* Harold Faltermeyer *r time* 98 mins *US opening* May 31.
cast Chevy Chase, Joe Don Baker, Dana Wheeler-Nicholson, Richard Libertini, Tim Matheson, M Emmet Walsh, George Wendt, Kenneth Mars, Geena Davis, Bill Henderson, William Traylor, George Wyner, Tony Longo, James Avery, Larry Flash Jenkins, Ralph Seymour, Reid Cruickshanks, Bruce French.

Chevy Chase's best solo vehicle to date features the comedian as a sarcastic investigative reporter tracking down corruption and drug rings while using an array of aliases, disguises and wisecracks. The character (and the movie itself) inconsistently adopt a superior, condescending tone to everyone else, and the humour is entirely grounded on the tonic effect of snide put-downs and put-ons, a dubious talent at which Chase excels. No one else in the film matters. Michael Ritchie directs efficiently without apparent personal engagement.

FRIDAY THE 13TH – A NEW BEGINNING
(Paramount)
dir Danny Steinmann *pro* Timothy Silver *exec pro* Frank Mancuso Jr *scr* Martin Kitrosser, David Cohen, Danny Steinmann *ph* Stephen L Posey, in Metrocolor *ed* Bruce Green *pro des* Robert Howland *mus* Harry Manfredini *r time* 92 mins *US opening* Mar 22.
cast John Shepard, Melanie Kinnaman, Shavar Ross, Richard Young, Carol Lacatell, Vernon Washington, Dominic Brascia, Tiffany Helm, Debbisue Vorhees, John Robert Dixon, Ron Sloan.

GARBO TALKS
(MGM – UA)
dir Sidney Lumet *pro* Burtt Harris, Elliott Kastner *scr* Larry Grusin *ph* Andrzej Bartkowiak, in Technicolor *ed* Andrew Mondshein *pro des* Philip Rosenberg *mus* Cy Coleman *r time* 103 mins *US opening* Oct 12.
cast Anne Bancroft, Ron Silver, Carrie Fisher, Catherine Hicks, Steven Hill, Howard Da Silva, Dorothy Loudon, Harvey Fierstein, Hermione Gingold, Richard B Shull, Michael Lombard, Ed Crowley, Alice Spivak, Maurice Sterman, Antonia Rey, Court Miller, Denny Dillon, Karen Shallo, Adolph Green, Betty Comden, Arthur Schlesinger Jr.

Naturally, being a Sidney Lumet movie, everyone else yells. A trifle that might have had charm if one didn't sense a caged forcefulness nervously at bay. Transparent heart-tugging as a son tries to please his eccentric, dying mother, yet the players skilfully inhabit their characters even as they are self-consciously packaged as 'bits'.

THE GOODBYE PEOPLE
(Coney Island Prods/Embassy)
dir-scr Herb Gardner, based on his stage play *pro* David V Picker *ph* John Lindley, in DeLuxe colour *ed* Rick Shaine *pro des* Tony Walton *r time* 104 mins *US opening* Oct 19.
cast Judd Hirsch, Martin Balsam, Pamela Reed, Ron Wilver, Michael Tucker, Gene Saks.

THE GOONIES
(Amblin/Warner)
dir Richard Donner *pro* Richard Donner, Harvey Bernhard *exec pro* Steven Spielberg, Frank Marshall, Kathleen Kennedy *scr* Chris Columbus, based on a story by Steven Spielberg *ph* Nick McLean, in Panavision, Technicolor *ed* Michael Kahn *pro des* J Michael Riva *mus* Dave Grusin *r time* 111 mins *US opening* Jun 7.
cast Sean Astin, Josh Brolin, Jeff Cohen, Corey Feldman, Kerri Green, Martha Plimpton, Ke Huy Quan, John Matuszak, Robert Davi, Joe Pantoliano, Anne Ramsey.

Kiddie rendition of Tom Sawyer pluck and Indy Jones thrills, as a motley group of youngsters foils comic criminals and seeks out pirate treasure in an underground world bedecked with natural disasters and Rube Goldberg booby traps. The sentimentality and manipulation are laid on thickly in the patented Spielberg manner, but the film is so unabashedly aimed at its youthful audience that it would be churlish to expect any adult pleasures or restraint. Director Richard Donner turns in a splendid job, keeping the complicated action coherent and overlapping the babbling dialogue effectively.

GOTCHA
(Universal)
dir Jeff Kanew *pro* Paul G Hensler *exec pro* Michael I Levy *scr* Dan Gordon, based on a story by Paul G Hensler, Dan Gordon *ph* King Baggot, in Technicolor *ed* Michael Stevenson *art dir* Norman Newberry *mus* Bill Conti *r time* 94 mins *US opening* May 3.
cast Anthony Edwards, Linda Fiorentino, Nick Corri, Alex Rocco, Klaus Lowitsch.

GRANDVIEW, USA
(CBS Theatrical/Warner)
dir Randal Kleiser *pro* William Warren Blaylock, Peter W Rea *exec pro* Jonathan Taplin, Andrew Gellis *scr* Ken Hixon *ph* Reynaldo Villalobos, in Astro Color *ed* Robert Gordon *pro des* Jan Scott *mus* Thomas Newman *r time* 97 mins *US opening* Aug 3.
cast Jamie Lee Curtis, C Thomas Howell, Patrick Swayze, Troy Donahue, Jennifer Jason Leigh, William Windom, Carole Cook, Ramon Bieri, John Philbin.

GYMKATA
(MGM – UA)
dir Robert Clouse *pro* Fred Weintraub *scr* Charles Robert Carnes, based on the novel 'The Terrible Game' by Dan Tyler Moore *ph* Godfrey Godar, in Metrocolor *ed* Robert A Ferretti *pro des* Veljko Despotovic *mus* Alfi Kabiljo *r time* 90 mins *US opening* May 3.

cast Kurt Thomas, Tetchie Agbayani, Richard Norton, Edward Bell, John Barrett, Conan Lee, Bob Schott, Buck Kartalian.

Juvenile nonsense that purports to create a new martial art out of gymnastics. Olympic medallist Kurt Thomas plays a CIA recruit who must secure a listening-post on the Soviet border by successfully completing a deadly obstacle course in an Afghan-like kingdom. Robert Clouse does a superb film once every five years or so ('Darker Than Amber', 'Enter The Dragon', 'The Big Brawl'), and even this lame dud has passages of alert direction to no conceivable end.

HEART OF THE STAG
(Southern Light Pics Inc/New World)
dir Michael Firth *pro* Don Reynolds, Michael Firth *scr* Neil Illingworth, based on a story by Michael Firth *ph* James Bartle, in colour *ed* Mike Horton *pro des* Cary Hansen *mus* Leonard Rosenman *r time* 91 min *US opening* Jul 27.
cast Bruno Lawrence, Mary Regan, Terence Cooper, Anne Flannery, Michael Wilson.

HEARTBREAKERS
(Jethro Films/Orion)
dir-scr Bobby Roth *pro* Bob Weis, Bobby Roth *exec pro* Lee Muhl, Harry Cooper, Joseph Franck *ph* Michael Ballhaus, in DeLuxe colour *ed* John Carnochan *mus* Tangerine Dream *r time* 98 mins *US opening* Sep 28.
cast Peter Coyote, Nick Mancuso, Carole Laure, Max Gail, James Laurenson, Carol Wayne, Jamie Rose, Kathryn Harrold, George Morfogen, Jerry Hardin.

Contemporary study of male bonding actually achieves original insights with good characterizations and provocative relationships. Exceptionally strong and individualized work by Peter Coyote and Nick Mancuso, a skilful evocation of the Los Angeles art scene, and a fresh awareness of how sex is lived today create a bracing work that augurs much from writer-director Roth.

HEAVEN HELP US
(HBO Pictures/Tri-Star)
dir Michael Dinner *pro* Dan Wigutow, Mark Carliner *scr* Charles Purpura *ph* Miroslav Ondricek, in Technicolor *ed* Stephen A Rotter *pro des* Michael Molly *mus* James Horner *r time* 104 mins *US opening* Feb 8.
cast Donald Sutherland, John Heard, Andrew McCarthy, Mary Stuart Masterson, Kevin Dillon, Malcolm Danare, Jennie Dundas, Kate Reid, Wallace Shawn, Jay Patterson, George Anders, Dana Barron, John Bentley, Imogene Bliss, Philip Bosco, Donahl Breitman, Nolan Carley.

Creditable debut film for Michael Dinner, a coming-of-age comedy-drama set in a Catholic boys' school in the early sixties. The able script creates sufficient fresh characters and situations to overcome the familiarity of the subject, and the youthful players make uniformly believable and individualized impressions.

HEAVENLY BODIES
(PSO/MGM-UA)
dir Lawrence Dane *pro* Robert Lantos, Stephen J Roth *scr* Lawrence Dane, Ron Base *ph* Thomas Burstyn, in colour *ed* Robert Lambert *pro des* Lindsey Goddard *mus sup* Irwin Mazur, Kevin Benson *r time* 89 mins *US opening* May 31.
cast Cynthia Dale, Richard Rebiere, Walter George Alton, Laura Henry, Stuart Stone.

THE HOLY INNOCENTS
(Ganesh Producciones/Samuel Goldwyn)
dir Mario Camus *pro* Julian Mateos *scr* Antonio Larreta, Manuel Matji, Mario Camus, based on the novel by Miguel Delibes *ph* Hans Burmann, in Eastmancolor *ed* Jose Maria Biurrun *mus* Anton Garcia Abril *r time* 105 mins *US opening* Jun 2.
cast Alfredo Landa, Francisco Rabal, Terele Pavez, Agustin Gonzalez, Juan Diego, Maribel Martin, Belen Ballesteros, Juan Sachez, Agata Lys, Mary Carrillo, Jose Guardiola, Manuel Zarzo.

HOT MOVES
(Spectrum Cinema Prods/Cardinal Pictures)
dir-pro Jim Sotos *exec pro* Ralph Kent Cooke, J Don Harris, Martin Perfit *scr* Larry Anderson, Peter Foldy *ph* Eugene Shugleit, in CFI colour *ed* Drake P Silliman *art dir* George Costello *mus* Louis Forestieri *r time* 86 mins *US opening* Oct 5.
cast Michael Zorek, Adam Silbar, Jeff Fishman, Johnny Timko, Jill Schoelen, Debi Richter, Virgil Frye, Tami Holbrook, Monique Gabrielle, David Christopher.

IMPULSE
(ABC Motion Pictures/Fox)
dir Graham Baker *pro* Tim Zinnemann *scr* Bart Davis, Don Carlos Dunaway *ph* Thomas Del Ruth, in DeLuxe colour *ed* David Holden *pro des* Jack T Collins *mus* Paul Chihara *r time* 88 mins *US opening* Sep 28.
cast Tim Matheson, Meg Tilly, Hume Cronyn, John Karlen, Bill Paxton, Amy Stryker, Claude Earl Jones.

A JOKE OF DESTINY
(Radiovideo Service/Samuel Goldwyn)
dir-scr Lina Wertmuller *pro* Giuseppe Giovannini *ph* Camillo Bazzoni, in colour *ed* Franco Fraticelli *art dir* Enrico Job *mus* Paolo Conte *r time* 105 mins *US opening* Sep 12.
cast Ugo Tognazzi, Piera Degli Espositi, Gastone Moschin, Roberto Herlitzka, Renzo Montagnani, Enzo Jannacci, Valeria Golino, Massimo Wertmuller.

A laboured satirical farce from Lina Wertmuller, redeemed only by a splendidly frenzied comic turn by Ugo Tognazzi as a status-conscious official who must deal with the absurd consequences of his government's inept obsession with security for its officers.

JOY OF SEX
(Paramount)
dir Martha Coolidge *pro* Frank Konigsberg *scr* Kathleen Rowell, J J Salter *ph* Charles Corell, in colour *ed* Allan Jacobs, William Elias, Ned

Humphreys *art dir* Jim Juraka *mus* Bishop Holiday, Scott Lipsker, Harold Payne *r time* 93 mins *US opening* Aug 3.
cast Cameron Dye, Michelle Meyrink, Charles Van Eman, Lisa Langlois, Colleen Camp, Joanne Baron, Danton Stone, Ernie Hudson, David H MacDonald, Darren Dalton, Robert Prescott, Paul Tulley, Christopher Lloyd, Heidi Holicker, Christen Kauffman, Terry Wagner-Otis.

The National Lampoon had its name removed from this quickie teen comedy, made on a TV budget and schedule in an effort to redeem the purchase of the title of Alex Comfort's best-selling manual. There's some effort at charm and sympathy for a teenage girl's perspective, but with no success.

JUST ONE OF THE GUYS
(Summa Entertainment-Triton Ltd/Columbia)
dir Lisa Gottlieb *pro* Andrew Fogelson *exec pro* Jeff Franklin, based on a story by Dennis Feldman *ph* John McPherson, in Metrocolor *ed* Lou Lombardo *pro des* Paul Peters *mus* Tom Scott *r time* 100 mins *US opening* Apr 26
cast Joyce Hyser, Clayton Rohner, Billy Jacoby, William Zabka, Toni Hudson, Sherilyn Fenn, Deborah Goodrich, Leigh McCloskey, Arye Gross, Robert Fieldsteel, Stuart Charno, John Apicella, Kenneth Tigar.

JUST THE WAY YOU ARE
(MGM-UA)
dir Edouard Molinaro *pro* Leo L Fuchs *exec pro* Jerry Zeitman *scr* Allan Burns *ph* Claude Lecomte, in Eastmancolor *ed* Claudio Ventura, Georges Klotz *art dir* Francois de Lamotte *mus* Vladimir Cosma *r time* 94 mins *US opening* Nov 16.
cast Kristy McNicol, Michael Ontkean, Kaki Hunter, Robert Carradine, Lance Guest, Alexandra Paul, Andre Dussolier, Timothy Daly, Patrick Cassidy, Catherine Salviat, Billy Kearns.

KING DAVID
(Paramount)
dir Bruce Beresford *pro* Martin Elfand *scr* Andrew Birkin, James Costigan *ph* Donald McAlpine, in Panavision, colour *ed* William Anderson *pro des* Ken Adam *mus* Carl Davis *r time* 114 mins *US opening* Mar 29.
cast Richard Gere, Edward Woodward, Denis Quilley, Niall Buggy, Jack Klaff, Cherie Lunghi, Alice Krige, Jean-Marc Barr, Ian Sears, Hurd Hatfield, John Castle, Tim Woodward, David De Keyser.

Yeoman attempt to make a Biblical epic in contemporary terms founders on the inability to penetrate the dramatic conflicts of this most human of scriptural sagas. Richard Gere looks stunning in the part, but he seems incapable of suggesting the complexity of the character.

LADYHAWKE
(Warner)
dir Richard Donner *pro* Richard Donner, Lauren Schuler *exec pro* Harvey Bernhard *scr* Edward Khmara, Michael Thomas, Tom

Mankiewicz *ph* Vittorio Storaro, in Technicolor *ed* Stuart Baird *pro des* Wolf Kroeger *mus* Andrew Powell *r time* 124 mins *US opening* Apr 12.
cast Matthew Broderick, Rutger Hauer, Michelle Pfeiffer, Leo McKern, John Wood, Ken Hutchingson, Alfred Molina, Giancarlo Prete, Loris Loddi, Alessandro Serra.

THE LAST DRAGON
(Motown Prods-Delphi III/Tri-Star)
dir Michael Schultz *pro* Rupert Hitzig *exec pro* Berry Gordy *scr* Louis Venosta *ph* James A Contner, in Technicolor *ed* Christopher Holmes *pro des* Peter Larkin *mus* Mischa Segal *r time* 109 mins *US opening* Mar 22.
cast Taimak, Vanity, Chris Murney, Julius J Carry 3rd, Faith Prince, Leo O'Brien, Make Starr, Jom Moody, Glen Eaton.

LAST NIGHT AT THE ALAMO
Alamo Films/Cinecom)
dir Eagle Pennell *pro-ed* Kim Henkel, Eagle Pennell *exec pro* Ed Hugetz *scr* Kim Henkel *ph* Brian Huberman, Eric A Edwards *art dir* Fletcher Mackey *mus* Chuck Pinnell, Wayne Bell *r time* 80 mins *US opening* Jul 3.
cast Sonny Carl Davis, Louis Perryman, Steve Matilla, Tina-Bess Hubbard, Doris Hargrave, J Michael Hammond, Amanda LaMar, Peggy Pinnell, Kim Henkel, David Schied, George Pheneger, Henry Wideman, John Heaner, Ernest Huerta, Pam Feight.

An American independent feature (shot in black and white) that boasts a screenplay of genuine literary quality and a passel of strong performances. A popular Texas watering hole is about to close down, and the regulars gather to carouse for the last time. What might be conventional in a play makes a satisfying alternative in cinema, and all the elements here are meticulously assembled for verisimilitude and emotional sincerity.

LIFEFORCE
(Cannon/Tri-Star)
dir Tobe Hooper *pro* Menahem Golan, Yoram Globus *scr* Dan O'Bannon, Don Jakoby, based on the novel 'The Space Vampires' by Colin Wilson *ph* Alan Hume, in colour *ed* John Grover *pro des* John Graysmark *mus* Henry Mancini *r time* 101 mins *US opening* Jun 21.
cast Steve Railsback, Peter Firth, Frank Finlay, Mathilda May, Patrick Stewart, Michael Gothard, Nicholas Ball, Aubrey Morris, Nancy Paul, John Hallam.

A paradigm of dumb, opportunistic producing with absolutely no sense of the marketplace: one can only hope that Cannon is fibbing about the mega-budget on this tacky sci-fi vampire/zombie movie since it looks as cheapjack as its omnibus exploitation concept. Stupefyingly bad dialogue provides the only amusement, despite indications that Tobe Hooper ('Poltergeist', 'The Texas Chainsaw Massacre') wanted to connect with something deeper in the material. This one plays like the screenwriters pillaged the novel's notions and tossed off a single-draft continuity for quick bucks, and the producers couldn't tell the difference.

THE LITTLE DRUMMER GIRL
(Pan Arts/Warner)
dir George Roy Hill *pro* Robert L Crawford *scr* Patrick Kelly *scr* Loring Mandel, based on the novel by John Le Carré *ph* Wolfgang Treu, in Technicolor *ed* William Reynolds *pro* Henry Bumstead *mus* Dave Grusin *r time* 130 mins *US opening* Oct 19.
cast Diane Keaton, Yorgo Voyagis, Klaus Kinski, Sami Frey, Michael Cristofer, David Suchet, Eli Danker, Thorley Walters, Kerstin De Ahna, Anna Massey, Dana Wheeler-Nicholson, Robert Pereno, Moti Shirin.

Diane Keaton overcomes fundamental miscasting with a brilliantly insecure portrayal of the actress involved in Palestinian terrorism in this adaptation of the Le Carré best-seller. Though much of the book's ironies and subtleties are lost, director George Roy Hill concentrates on fundamentals, and the result is more incredible than might have reasonably been expected.

LITTLE TREASURE
(Vista Films/Tri-Star)
dir-scr Alan Sharp *pro* Herb Jaffe *exec pro* Joanna Lancaster, Richard Wagner *ph* Alex Phillips, in Metrocolor *ed* Garth Craven *pro des* Jose Rodriguez, Granada Estevez, Enrique Estevez *mus* Leo Kottke *r time* 95 mins *US opening* May 1.
Cast Margot Kidder, Ted Danson, Burt Lancaster, Joseph Hacker, Malena Doria, John Pearce, Gladys Holland, Bill Zuckert, James Hall.

LOST IN AMERICA
(Geffen Company/Warner)
dir Albert Brooks *pro* Marty Katz *exec pro* Herb Nanas *scr* Albert Brooks, Monica Johnson *ph* Eric Saarinen, in Technicolor *ed* David Finfer *pro des* Richard Sawyer *mus* Arthur B Rubinstein *r time* 91 mins *US opening* Feb 15.
cast Albert Brooks, Julie Hagerty, Garry Marshall, Art Frankel, Michael Greene, Tom Tarpey, Ernie Brown, Maggie Roswell, Charles Boswell, Donald Gibb.

Albert Brooks continues to be the most innovative comic actor-director in films, Woody Allen's post-'Manhattan' heir. Brooks isn't afraid to explore the obnoxious side of his characters, and here he delves deeply into the self-absorbed pseudo-idealism of the 'yuppie' class. His visual approach isn't nearly as uniquely innovative as it was in 'Real Life' or 'Modern Romance', and the film ends abruptly and unsatisfyingly, circumventing its third act, but what's actually there is choice, timely satire.

LOVELINES
(Tri-Star)
dir Rod Amateau *pro* Hal Taines, Michael Lloyd *scr* Chip Hand, William Hillman *ph* Duke Callaghan, in Metrocolor *ed* David Bretherton, Fred A Chulack *art dir* Robert K Konoshita *mus sup* Michael Lloyd *r time* 93 mins *US opening* Nov 2.
cast Greg Bradford, Mary Beth Evans, Michael Winslow, Don Michael Paul, Tammy Taylor, Stacey Toten, Robert Delapp, Frank Zagarino, Todd Bryant, Jonna Lee, Robin Watkins, Claudia Cowan.

LUST IN THE DUST
(New World)
dir Paul Bartel *pro* Allan Glaser, Tab Hunter *exec pro* James C Katz, Robert Raymond *scr* Philip Taylor *ph* Paul Lohmann, in colour *ed* Alan Toomayan *art dir* Walter Pickette *mus* Peter Matz *r time* 87 mins *US opening* Feb 8.
cast Tab Hunter, Divine, Lainie Kazan, Geoffrey Lewis, Henry Silva, Cesar Romero, Gina Gallego, Nedra Volz, Courtney Gains, Woody Strode, Pedro Gonzalez-Gonzalez, Daniel Firshman, Ernie Shinagawa.

A disappointing Western spoof from Paul Bartel that mostly involves flailing actors chewing the scenery in an effort to maximize the already inflated camp aspects of the comedy. Divine has his/her moments, as always, but the film ends up smothering its vulgarity with sweetness, and vice versa.

MACARTHUR'S CHILDREN
(Orion Classics)
dir Masahiro Shinoda *pro* You-No-Kai, Masato Hara *scr* Takeshi Tamura, based on the novel by Uy Aku *ph* Kazuo Miyagaw, in colour *ed* Sachiko Yamaji *pro des* Yoshinobu Nishioka *mus* Shinichiro Ikebe *r time* 120 mins *US opening* May 17.
cast Takaya Yamauchi, Yoshiyuki Omori, Shiori Sakura, Masako Natsume, Shuji Otaki, Haruko Kato, Ken Watanabe, Shinsuke Shimada, Taketoshi Naito, Chiharu Shukuri, Bill Jensen, Takashi Tsumura, Jyuzo Itami, Hiromi Go, Shima Iwashita.

MARTIN'S DAY
(World Film Services/MGM-UA)
dir Alan Gibson *pro* Richard F Dalton, Roy Krost *scr* Allan Scott, Chris Bryant *ph* Frank Watts, in colour *ed* David de Wilde *pro des* Trevor Williams *mus* Wilfred Josephs *r time* 82 mins *US opening* Feb 22.
cast Richard Harris, Lindsay Wagner, James Coburn, Justin Henry, Karen Black, John Ireland.

MASS APPEAL
(Universal)
dir Glenn Jordan *pro* Lawrence Turman, David Foster *exec pro* Joan B Kroc *scr* Bill C Davis, based on his stage play *ph* Don Peterman, in Technicolor *ed* John Wright *pro des* Philip Jeffries *mus* Bill Conti *r time* 100 mins *US opening* Dec 17.
cast Jack Lemmon, Zeljko Ivanek, Charles Durning, Louise Latham.

Adaptation of an award-winning play about a successful priest (his parish moved to the suburbs for the film), who compromises his values to win congregational support, and his confrontation with a firebrand youth who galvanizes him to moral courage. Pedestrian film-making, but at least there is an emphasis on character. Workmanlike turns by Jack Lemmon and Zeljko Ivanek.

MEATBALLS PART II
(Space Productions/Tri-Star)
dir Ken Wiederhorn *pro* Tony Bishop, Stephen Poe *exec pro* Lisa Barsamian *scr* Bruce Singer, based on a story by Martin Kitrosser, Carol Watson *ph* Donald M Morgan, in Movielab colour

ed George Berndt *pro des* James William Newport *mus* Ken Harrison *r time* 96 mins *US opening* Jul 27.
cast Archie Hahn, John Mengatti, Tammy Taylor, Kim Richards, Ralph Seymour, Richard Mulligan, Hamilton Camp, John Larroquette, Paul Reubens.

MISCHIEF
(Fox)
dir Mel Damski *pro* Sam Manners, Michael Nolin *exec pro-scr* Noel Black *ph* Donald E Thorin, in DeLuxe colour *ed* Nick Brown *pro des* Paul Peters *mus sup* Barry DeVorzon *r time* 93 mins *US opening* Feb 8.
cast Doug McKeon, Catherine Mary Stewart, Kelly Preston, Chris Nash, C W Brown, Jami Gertz, Maggie Blye, Graham P Jarvis, Terry O'Quinn.

MISSING IN ACTION 2 – THE BEGINNING
(Cannon)
dir Lance Hool *pro* Yoram Globus, Menahem Golan *scr* Arthur Silver, Larry Levinson, Steve Bing *ph* Jorge Stahl Jr, in TVC colour *ed* Mark Conte, Marcus Nanton *pro des* Michael Baugh *mus* Brian May *r time* 95 mins *US opening* Mar 1.
cast Chuck Norris, Soon-Teck Oh, Cosie Costa, Steven Williams, David Chung, Joe Michael Terry, John Wesley, Bennett Ohta, Prof Toru Tanaka, Christopher Cary, Pierre Issot.

MOVERS & SHAKERS
(MGM-UA)
dir William Asher *pro* Charles Grodin, William Asher *scr* Charles Grodin *ph* Robbie Greenberg, in Metrocolor *ed* Tom Benko *art dir* Donald L Harris *mus* Ken and Mitzhie Welch *r time* 79 mins *US opening* May 3.
cast Walter Matthau, Charles Grodin, Vincent Gardenia, Tyne Daly, Bill Macy, Gilda Radner, Steve Martin, Penny Marshall, Earl Boen, Michael Lerner, Joe Mantell, William Prince, Nita Talbot, Sandy Ward.

Anaemic, toothless Hollywood satire. Charles Grodin is a nervous screenwriter recruited by production chief Walter Matthau to come up with a concept for using the title of a best-selling sex manual, which Matthau has bought as a favour to his dying friend, producer Vincent Gardenia. There are glimmers of adult emotions provided by the players, but the writing is so sketchy and poorly observed and the direction (by William Asher, who did better with 'Johnny Cool' and Beach Party movies) so uninflected that nothing in it is of comic or dramatic consequence.

MOVING VIOLATIONS
(Fox)
dir Neal Israel *pro* Joe Roth, Harry Ufland *exec pro* Pat Proft, Doug Draizin *scr* Neal Israel, Pat Proft, based on a story by Paul and Sharon Boorstin *ph* Robert Elswit, in DeLuxe colour *ed* Tom Walls *art dir* Virginia Fields *music* Ralph Burns *r time* 90 mins *US opening* Apr 19.
cast John Murray, Jennifer Tilly, James Keach, Brian Backer, Ned Eisenberg, Clara Peller, Wendie Jo Sperber, Nedra Volz, Fred Willard,

Lisa Hart Carroll, Nadine Van Der Velde, Ben Mittleman, Victor Campos, Willard Pugh, Sally Kellerman.

THE MUPPETS TAKE MANHATTAN
(Delphi II/Tri-Star)
dir Frank Oz *pro* David Lazer *exec pro* Jim Henson *scr* Frank Oz, Jay Tarses *ph* Robert Paynter, in Technicolor *ed* Evan Lottman *pro des* Stephen Hendrickson *mus* Ralph Burns *r time* 94 mins *US opening* Jul 13.

The further adventures of the motley band, as they hit the pavement in the Big Apple, trying to sell their college revue to Broadway. The Muppets haven't lost their unflagging pleasantness, but the novelty and bite are long gone. Nice songs and jokes aren't enough to sustain adult interest, and the attempted transformation of Kermit the Frog from a Bing Crosby to a Gene Kelly figure isn't credible. The concluding nuptials of Kermit and Miss Piggy bodes ill for the next sequel.

MY NEW PARTNER (LES RIPOUX)
(Film 7/Orion Classics)
dir-pro Claude Zidi *scr* Claude Zidi, Didier Kaminka, based on an original story by Silmon Mickael *ph* Jean-Jacques Tarbes, in Eastmancolor *ed* Nicole Saulnier *art dir* Françoise De Leu *mus* Francis Lai *r time* 107 mins *US opening* Mar 8.
cast Philippe Noiret, Thierry Lhermitte, Regine, Grace de Capitani, Julien Guiomar, Pierre Frag, Claude Brosset, Albert Simono.

THE NEW KIDS
(Columbia)
dir Sean S Cunningham *pro* Sean S Cunningham, Andrew Fogelson *scr* Stephen Gyllenhaal *ph* Steve Poster, in Metrocolor *ed* Rita Roland *art dir* Pete Smith *mus* Lalo Schifrin *r time* 90 mins *US opening* Jan 18.
cast Shannon Presby, Lori Loughlin, James Spader, John Philbin, David H MacDonald, Vincent Grant, Theron Montgomery, Eddie Jones, Lucy Martin, Eric Stoltz, Paidge Lyn Price, Court Miller.

NIGHT PATROL
(New World)
dir-ed Jackie Kong *pro* Bill Osco *scr* Murray Langston, Bill Levey, Bill Osco, Jackie Kong *ph* Jurg Walthers, Hanania Baer, in colour *art dir* Jay Burkhardt *r time* 82 mins *US opening* Nov 23.
cast Linda Blair, Pat Paulsen, Jaye P Morgan, Jack Riley, Billy Barty, Murray Langston, Pat Morita.

A NIGHTMARE ON ELM STREET
(Media Home Ents-Smart Egg Pics/New Line)
dir-scr Wes Craven *pro* Robert Shaye *exec pro* Stanley Dudelson, Joseph Wolf *ph* Jacques Haitkin, in DeLuxe *ed* Rick Shaine *pro des* Greg Fonseca *mus* Charles Bernstein *r time* 91 mins *US opening* Nov 9.
cast John Saxon, Ronee Blakeley, Heather Langenkamp, Amanda Wyss, Nick Corri, Johnny Depp, Robert Englund, Charles Fleischer, Joseph Whipp, Lin Saye.

Wes Craven's horror film surmounts its conventional boogey-man plot with an above average youth cast and a genuine appreciation for the persistence of dreams in our waking consciousness. Its virtues are matters merely of moments, but they are memorable.

1918
(Cinecom)
dir Ken Harrison *pro* Lillian Foote, Ross Milloy *exec pro* Lewis Allen, Peter Newman *scr* Horton Foote, based on his own play *ph* George Tirl, in colour *ed* Leon Seith *art dir* Michael O'Sullivan *mus* various *r time* 91 mins *US opening* Apr 26.
cast William Converse-Roberts, Hallie Foote, Rochelle Oliver, Matthew Broderick, Jeannie McCarthy, Bill McGhee, L T Felty, Horton Foote Jr, Tom Murrel, Phillip Smith.

The home front down South in World War I, as the influenza epidemic exacts its toll on a young family. Horton Foote ('Tender Mercies', 'To Kill a Mockingbird') adapts his own autobiographical one-act play largely by padding its simple anecdotal action to feature length. The result is nostalgic lyricism so tasteful it sinks into pallid posturing. Good care is taken with the physical production, particularly for a low-budget independent, but there's neither sufficient character development nor narrative incident to sustain interest, and the direction of Ken Harrison lacks shape, design or pulse.

NINJA III – THE DOMINATION
(MGM-US/Cannon)
dir Sam Firstenberg *exec pro* Menahem Golan, Yoram Globus *scr* James R Silke *ph* Hanania Baer, in Metrocolor *ed* Michael Duthie *pro des* Elliot Ellentuck *mus* Udi Haroaz *r time* 95 mins *US opening* Sep 14.
cast Lucinda Dickey, Jordan Bennet, Sho Kosugi, David Chung, T J Castronova.

NO SMALL AFFAIR
(Columbia)
dir Jerry Schatzberg *pro* William Sackheim *exec pro* George Justin *scr* Charles Bolt, Terence Mulcahy *ph* Vilmos Zsigmond, in colour *ed* Priscilla Nedd, Eve Newman, Melvin Shapiro *pro des* Robert Boyle *mus* Rupert Holmes *r time* 102 mins *US opening* Nov 9.
cast Jon Cryer, Demi Moore, George Wendt, Peter Frechette, Elizabeth Daily, Ann Wedgeworth, Jeffrey Tambor, Judy Baldwin, Jennifer Tilly.

Precocious teenager falls in love with an 'older' (ie early twenties) woman and tries to make her a star. Good San Francisco locations and lensing fail to redeem dubious borrowings from 'It Should Happen To You' and other better films. Leads have some charm but Jerry Schatzberg conveys little through his impersonal direction.

NOTHING LASTS FOREVER
(Broadway Pictures/MGM-UA Classics)
dir-scr Tom Schiller *pro* Lorne Michaels *ph* Fred Schuler, in Technicolor *ed* Kathleen Dougherty,

Margot Francis *art dir* Woods MacKintosh *mus* Cheryl Hardwick *r time* 82 mins *US opening* Aug 29.
cast Zach Galligan, Apollonia va Ravenstein, Lauren Tom, Dan Aykroyd, Imogene Coca, Anita Ellis, Eddie Fisher, Sam Jaffe, Paul Rogers, Mort Sahl, Jan Triska, Rosemary De Angelis, Clarice Taylor, Bill Murray.

OH, GOD! YOU DEVIL
(Warner)
dir Paul Bogart *pro* Robert M Sherman *exec pro* Irving Fein *scr* Andrew Bergman *ph* King Baggot, in Technicolor *ed* Andy Zall *pro des* Peter Wooley *mus* David Shire *r time* 96 mins *US opening* Nov 9.
cast George Burns, Ted Wass, Ron Silver, Roxanne Hart, Eugene Roche, Robert Desiderio.

OXFORD BLUES
(Winkast/MGM-UA)
dir-scr Robert Boris *pro* Cassian Elwes, Elliott Kastner *ph* John Stanier, in Technicolor *ed* Patrick Moore *pro des* Terry Pritchard *mus* John DuPrez *r time* 93 mins *US opening* Aug 24.
cast Rob Lowe, Ally Sheedy, Amanda Pays, Julian Sands, Julian Firth, Alan Howard, Gail Strickland, Michael Gough, Aubrey Morris.

PALE RIDER
(Warner)
dir-pro Clint Eastwood *exec pro* Fritz Manes *scr* Michael Butler, Dennis Shryack *ph* Bruce Surtees, in Panavision, Technicolor *ed* Joel Cox *pro des* Edwart Carfagno *mus* Lennie Niehaus *r time* 115 mins *US opening* Jun 28.
cast Clint Eastwood, Michael Moriarty, Carrie Snodgress, Christopher Penn, Richard Dysart, Sydney Penny, Richard Kiel, Doug McGrath, John Russell.

Clint Eastwood makes a valiant attempt to resurrect the traditional western on his mighty box-office shoulders, adapting the classical situation from 'Shane' to his satisfying persona. He's more persuasive than Alan Ladd, but the rest of the plot elements fare less well: the development of the civilized characters (here gold miners instead of farmers) is unconvincing and uncompelling. His direction of action remains solid, enhanced by fresh landscapes and Bruce Surtees' patented backlighting. Eastwood remains a fascinating talent open to challenges, and one wishes this endeavour had worked out better.

THE PARTY ANIMAL
(International Film Marketing)
dir-scr David Beaird *pro* Bryan England, Mark Israel *exec pro* C Fox *ph* Bryan England, in DeLuxe colour *ed* Susan Jenkins *pro des* Ron Siegal *r time* 78 mins *US opening* Aug 24.
cast Mathew Causey, Tim Carhart, Robin Harlan, Suzanne Ashley, Jerry Jones, Frank Galati, Luci Roucis.

PERFECT
(Delphi III/Columbia)
dir-pro James Bridges *exec pro* Kim Kurumanda *scr* Aaron Latham, James Bridges *ph* Gordon Willis, in Panavision, Technicolor *ed* Jeff

Gourson *pro des* Michael Haller *mus* Ralph Burns *r time* 120 mins *US opening* Jun 7.
cast John Travolta, Jamie Lee Curtis, Anne De Salvo, Marilu Henner, Laraine Newman, Mathew Reed, Jann Wenner, Charlene Jones.

Much maligned by journalists, this portrait of a 'Rolling Stone' reporter accurately captures much of the questionable tactics and deluded editing that are typical of this end of the profession. But the film's glories lie more in its dramatic visual plan, which subtly organizes the space around the characters to express their social relations and internal malaise in an inventive pop progression from Antonioni. Director James Bridges and cinematographer Gordon Willis have devised a startlingly original new approach to the 'scope frame. All performances are excellent, especially Marilu Henner's inspired improvisations, Laraine Newman's modernist patterns, Jamie Lee Curtis' star-calibre sex appeal, and John Travolta doing his best work to date.

LA PETITE SIRENE (THE LITTLE SIREN)
(Apple Films-FR3-J Roitfel Prods-Les Lyons-Stephan Films/World Artists Releasing)
dir-pro-scr Roger Andrieux, based on the novel 'Les Petites Sirènes' by Yves Dangerfield *ph* Robert Alazraki, in colour *ed* Kenout Peltier *art dir* Jean-Baptiste Poirot *mus* Alain Jomy *r time* 104 mins *US opening* Aug 3.
cast Laura Alexis, Philippe Leotard, Evelyne Dress, Marie Dubois.

An adult mechanic, beset by a fourteen-year-old girl with a crush on him, gradually finds himself drawn into a sexual relationship with her. The film avoids falling into distastefulness by its careful observation of behaviour amidst a refusal to compromise the emotions involved for either humour or pathos.

POLICE ACADEMY 2: THEIR FIRST ASSIGNMENT
(Ladd Co/Warner)
dir Jerry Paris *pro* Paul Malansky *exec pro* John Goldwyn *scr* Barry Blaustein, David Sheffield, based on characters created by Neal Israel, Pat Proft *ph* James Crabe, in Technicolor *ed* Bob Wyman *pro des* Trevor Williams *mus* Robert Folk *r time* 87 mins *US opening* Mar 29.
cast Steve Guttenberg, Bubba Smith, David Graf, Michael Winslow, Bruce Mahler, Marion Ramsey, Colleen Camp, Howard Hesseman, Art Metrano, George Gaynes.

PRIME RISK
(Mikas I/Almi)
dir-scr Michael Farkas *pro* Herman Grigsby *exec pro* Bernard Farkas *ph* Mac Ahlberg, in colour *ed* Bruce Green *art dir* Christopher Henry *mus* Phil Marshall *r time* 100 mins *US opening* Apr 12.
cast Toni Hudson, Lee Montgomery, Samuel Bottoms, Clue Gulager, Keenan Wynn, Lois Hall, Rick Rakowski, John Lykes, James O'Connell.

PRIZZI'S HONOR
(ABC Motion Pictures/Fox)
dir John Huston *pro* John Foreman *scr* Richard Condon, Janet Roach *ph* Andrzej Bartkowiak, in colour *ed* Rudi Fehr, Kaja Fehr *pro des* Dennis Washington *mus* Alex North *r time* 129 mins *US opening* Jun 14.
cast Jack Nicholson, Kathleen Turner, Robert Loggia, William Hickey, John Randolph, Lee Richardson, Anjelica Huston, Michael Lombard, Lawrence Tierney, Joseph Ruskin, Ann Selepegno.

John Huston's black comedy variations on 'Godfather' themes are frequently clever, boldly acted, and sport a rigorously applied visual approach. Like 'Beat the Devil', though, its wit is never quite amusing enough nor its focus on romantic entanglements persuasive enough, to accord it status as a major work. Jack Nicholson gives yet another courageous performance as a pro hit man who is heir apparent to the Mob, while Kathleen Turner as his wife and rival assassin continues to establish herself as the pre-eminent star of her generation, but their passion for one another is more postulated than communicated. The deliberately slow pace magnifies small flaws. Huston tackles another difficult assignment here, once again proving better on defence than offence.

PUMPING IRON II: THE WOMEN
(Cinecom)
dir-pro George Butler *exec pro* Bernard Heng, Lawrence Chong *scr* Charles Gaines, George Butler, based on their book 'Pumping Iron II: The Unprecedented Woman' *ph* Dyanna Taylor, in colour *ed* Paul Barnes, Susan Crutcher, Jane Kurson *mus* David McHugh, Michael Montes *r time* 107 mins *US opening* May 3.
cast Lori Bowen, Carla Dunlap, Bev Francis, Rachel McLish, Kris Alexander, Lydia Cheng, Steve Michalik, Steve Weinberger, Randy Rice, Tina Plakinger.

THE PURPLE ROSE OF CAIRO
(Orion)
dir-scr Woody Allen *pro* Robert Greenhut *exec pro* Charles H Joffe *ph* Gordon Willis, in colour *ed* Susan E Morse *pro des* Stuart Wurtzel *mus* Dick Hyman *r time* 82 mins *US opening* Mar 1.
cast Mia Farrow, Jeff Daniels, Danny Aiello, Irving Metzman, Stephanie Farrow, David Kieserman, Elaine Grollman, Victoria Zussin, Mark Hammond, Wade Barnes, Joseph G Graham, Don Quigley, Maurice Brenner, Paul Herman, Rick Petrucelli, Peter Castellotti, Milton Seaman, Mimi Weddell, Tom Degidon, Mary Hedahl.

Woody Allen for the third time in a row offers up an unambitious anecdote in lieu of a fully developed, complex work. The film deals with an onscreen character who leaves the plot to romance a dream-starved member of the audience, wreaking havoc in both the fictional and the real world. Mia Farrow plays the Allen character here, and in many ways she is emotionally richer in the rôle than he. Allen imparts a sweetness and charm to his conceit, but there's nothing remotely profound in his rather tenuous comedy here.

RAMBO: FIRST BLOOD, PART II
(Tri-Star)
dir George Pan Cosmatos *pro* Buzz Feitshans *exec pro* John Goldwyn *scr* Sylvester Stallone, James Cameron *ph* Jack Cardiff, in Panavision, Technicolor *ed* Mark Goldblatt, Mark Helfrich *pro des* Bill Kenny *mus* Jerry Goldsmith *r time* 96 mins *US opening* May 22.
cast Sylvester Stallone, Richard Crenna, Julie Nickson, Charles Napier, Steven Berkoff, Martin Kove, Andy Wood, George Kee Cheung, William Ghent, Vojo Goric, Dana Lee, Baoan Coleman, Steve Williams, Don Collins, Chris Grant, John Sterlini, Alain Hocquenghem, William Rothlein, Tony Munafo, Tom Gehrke.

Rabidly jingoistic, auto-erotic power fantasy in which Stallone becomes the focus and release for the collective frustrations of the American people. Rambo is released from prison to go on a one-man mission to locate missing American soldiers imprisoned in Vietnam. The relentless lack of even fundamental credibility actually contributed to its popularity. Under the circumstances, George Pan Cosmatos ('Of Unknown Origin', 'The Cassandra Crossing') actually directs as if the material warranted serious consideration, abetted by excellent lighting by Jack Cardiff.

THE RAZOR'S EDGE
(Columbia)
dir John Byrum *pro* Robert P Marcucci, Harry Benn *exec pro* Rob Cohen *scr* John Byrum, Bill Murray, based on the novel by W Somerset Maugham *ph* Peter Hannan, in colour *ed* Peter Boyle *pro des* Philip Harrison *mus* Jack Nitzsche *r time* 128 mins *US opening* Oct 19.
cast Bill Murray, Theresa Russell, Catherine Hicks, Denholm Elliott, James Keach, Peter Vaughan, Brian Doyle-Murray, Stephen Davies, Saeed Jaffrey, Faith Brook, Andre Maranne.

Bill Murray cannot plausibly carry the rôle of a Maugham seeker, and John Byrum's adaptation neither captures the period flavour of the original nor establishes any contemporary relevance. Sole survivor: Theresa Russell's lost soul, a star turn as valid for our age as Anne Baxter's Oscar winning incarnation was for 1946. (See Turkeys of the Year.)

RAZORBACK
(McElroy & McElroy/Warner)
dir Russell Mulcahy *pro* Hal McElroy *scr* Everett De Roche, based on the novel by Peter Brennan *ph* Dean Semler, in Panavision, colour *ed* Bill Anderson *pro des* Bryce Walmsley *mus* Iva Davies *r time* 94 mins *US opening* Nov 16.
cast Gregory Harrison, Arkie Whiteley, Bill Kerr, Chris Haywood, David Argue, Judy Morris, John Howard, John Ewart, Don Smith, Mervyn Drake, Redmond Phillips, Alan Beecher, Peter Schwartz, Beth Child, Peter Boswell, Brian Adams, Jinx Lootens, Don Lane.

RED SONJA
(MGM-UA)
dir Richard Fleischer *pro* Christian Ferry *exec pro* A Michael Lieberman *scr* Clive Exton, George MacDonald

Fraser, based on stories by Robert E Howard *ph* Giuseppe Rotunno, in Metrocolor *ed* Frank J Urioste *pro des* Danilo Donati *mus* Ennio Morricone *r time* 89 mins *US opening* Jun 28.
cast Brigitte Nielsen, Arnold Schwarzenegger, Sandahl Bergman, Paul Smith, Ernie Reyes Jr, Ronald Lacey, Pat Roach, Terry Richards, Janet Agren.

RETURN TO OZ
(Walt Disney/Buena Vista)
dir Walter Murch *pro* Paul Maslansky *exec pro* Gary Kurtz *scr* Walter Murch, Gill Dennis, based on 'The Land of Oz', Ozma of Oz' by L Frank Baum *ph* David Watkin, in Technicolor *ed* Leslie Hodgson *pro des* Norman Reynolds *mus* David Shire *r time* 110 mins *US opening* Jun 21.
cast Nicol Williamson, Jean Marsh, Fairuza Balk, Piper Laurie, Matt Clark, Michael Sundin, Tim Rose, Sean Barrett, Mak Wilson, Denise Bryer, Brian Henson, Stewart Larange, Lyle Conway, Steve Norrington, Justin Case, John Alexander, Deep Roy, Emma Ridley, Sophie Ward, Fiona Victory, Pons Maar.

A glum, charmless sequel to 'The Wizard of Oz', more faithful to the spirit of the L Frank Baum originals perhaps, but lacking the enriching character relationships and magic of the musical classic. The first half hour plunges a depressed Dorothy into frightening electroshock therapy by a threatening quack, until she escapes to a devasted, lifeless Oz she must reanimate. Highly variable effects-work promoted by cost-cutting undermine the spell, which rarely aims at being bewitching anyway. The puppet characters and clay animated villains are not sufficiently imaginative to overcome their essential lifelessness.

THE RIVER RAT
(Sundance Institute-Larson Rickman/Paramount)
dir-scr Tom Rickman *pro* Bob Larson *exec pro* Michael Apted *ph* Jan Kiesser, in Technicolor *ed* Dennis Virkler *pro des* John J Lloyd *mus* Mike Post *r time* 93 mins *US opening* Sep 21.
cast Tommy Lee Jones, Martha Plimpton, Brian Dennehy, Shawn Smith, Nancy Lea Owen, Norman Bennett, Tony Frank, Angie Bolling.

Writer Tom Rickman's directorial debut isn't visually inspired, but his storytelling has a Twain-like tall-tale expansiveness that is quite appealing. Tommy Lee Jones is released after years in prison and must prove his love to his sceptical tomboy daughter as they raft downriver to escape a crooked warden. Respectable family fare that could have been much better.

ROADHOUSE 66
(Atlantic)
dir John Mark Robinson *pro* Scott M Rosenfelt, Mark Levinson *exec pro* Thomas Coleman, Michael Rosenblatt *scr* Galen Lee, George Simpson *ph* Tom Ackerman, in colour *ed* Jay Lash Cassidy *pro des* Chester Kaczenski *mus* Gary Scott *r time* 90 mins

US opening Aug 31.
cast Willem Dafoe, Judge Reinhold, Kaaren Lee, Kate Vernon, Stephen Elliott, Alan Autry, Kevyn Major Howard, Peter Van Norden, Erica Yohn.

RUSTLER'S RHAPSODY
(Paramount)
dir-scr Hugh Wilson pro David Giler exec pro Jose Vicuna ph Jose Luis Alcaine, in colour ed John Victor Smith pro des Gil Parrondo mus Steve Dorff r time 88 mins US opening May 10.
cast Tom Berenger, G W Bailey, Marilu Henner, Andy Griffith, Fernando Rey, Sela Ward, Patrick Wayne, Brant Van Hoffman, Christopher Malcolm, Jim Carter, Billy J Mitchell.

Often clever, though rarely funny spoof of 'B' westerns that approaches its satire with an amiable genre self-consciousness that encompasses a wide range of conventions. Director Hugh Wilson displays affection in his approach, restraint in his treatment and skill in his timing, all of which makes one wish to enjoy the film more. What's onscreen can hardly be faulted, but on the other hand, it's just barely entertaining.

ST ELMO'S FIRE
(Delphi IV/Columbia)
dir Joel Schumacher pro Lauren Shuler exec pro Ned Tanen, Bernard Schwartz scr Joel Schumacher, Carl Kurlander ph Stephen H Burum, in Panavision, Metrocolor ed Richard Marks art dir William Sandell mus David Foster r time 108 mins US opening Jun 28.
cast Rob Lowe, Demi Moore, Andrew McCarthy, Judd Nelson, Ally Sheedy, Emilio Estevez, Mare Winningham, Martin Balsam, Jon Cutler, Joyce Van Patten, Andie MacDowell, Jenny Wright, Blake Clark.

At times this youth-audience knockoff on 'The Big Chill' verges into unintentionally funny parody, but it's meant to be deeply felt and might have been, too, if a well-designed outline setting up the characters and situations promisingly had been developed with any attention to the truth instead of carelessly careening through sloppy plotting and maudlin interactions. Not really bad, it's still something of a monstrosity to behold.

SAM'S SON
(Worldvision Enterprises/Invictus Entertainment)
dir-scr Michael Landon pro Kent McCray ph Ted Voightlander, in colour ed John Loeffler art dir George Renne mus David Rose r time 104 mins US opening Aug 17.
cast Eli Wallach, Anne Jackson, Timothy Patrick Murphy, Hallie Todd, Alan Hayes, Jonna Lee, Michael Landon, Howard Witt, William Boyett, John Walcutt, David Lloyd Nelson, William H Bassett, Harvey Gold, James Karen.

SECRET ADMIRER
(Orion)
dir David Greenwalt pro Steve Roth exec pro C O Erickson scr Jim Kouf, David Greenwalt ph Victor J Kemper, in Technicolor ed Dennis Virkler

pro des William J Cassidy mus Jan Hammer r time 98 mins US opening Jun 14.
cast C Thomas Howell, Lori Loughlin, Kelly Preston, Dee Wallace Stone, Cliff De Young, Leigh Taylor-Young, Fred Ward, Casey Siemaszko, Scott McGinnis, Geoffrey Blake, Rodney Pearson, Courtney Gains, Jeffrey Jay Cohen, Cory Haim.

SILENT NIGHT, DEADLY NIGHT
(Tri-Star/Aquarius)
dir Charles E Sellier pro Ira Richard Barmak exec pro Scott J Schneid, Dennis Whitehead scr Michael Hickey, based on a story by Paul Caimi ph Henning Schellerup, in Metrocolor ed Michael Spence pro des Dian Perryman mus Petty Botkin r time 79 mins US opening Nov 9.
cast Lilyan Chauvan, Gilmer McCormick, Toni Nero, Robert Brian Wilson, Britt Leach, Nancy Borgenicht, H E D Redford, Danny Wagner.

SKYLINE (LA LINEA DEL CIELO)
(La Salamandra PC/Kino International)
dir-scr Fernando Colomo ph Angel Luis Fernandez, in Eastmancolor ed Miguel Angel Santamaria r time 83 mins US opening Jul 18.
cast Antonio Resines, Beatriz Perez-Porro, Jaime Nos, Roy Hoffman, Irene Stillman, Whit Stillman, Patricia Cisarano.

Fernando Colomo's winsome comedy makes gentle cross-cultural observations as a Spanish photographer with art-world aspirations tries to make it in New York City. No revelations or insights, but honest comedy done with a fresh eye, enhanced by an understated portrayal by Antonio Resines in the lead rôle.

THE SLUGGER'S WIFE
(Delphi II/Columbia)
dir Hal Ashby pro Ray Stark exec pro Margaret Booth scr Neil Simon ph Caleb Deschanel, in Metrocolor ed George Villasenor, Don Brochu pro des Michael Riva mus Patrick Williams r time 105 mins US opening Mar 29.
cast Michael O'Keefe, Rebecca DeMornay, Martin Ritt, Randy Quaid, Cleavant Derricks, Lisa Langlois, Loudon Wainwright III.

SNOWDROP FESTIVAL
(Czechoslovak Film Prods/I.F.E.X.)
dir Jiri Menzel scr Bohumil Hrabal ph Jiri Macak, in colour mus Jiri Sust r time 85 mins US opening Nov 14.
cast Rudolf Hrusinsky, Jaromir Hanzlik, Jiri Schmitzer, Petr Cepek, Zdena Hadrobolcova, Joseph Somr, Libuse Safrankova, Miloslav Stibich, Eugen Jegorov, Borik Prochazka.

Yet another winsome rural comedy from Jiri Menzel, centring on a rivalry between neighbouring villages that erupts over a banquet of wild pig. Menzel's skills at this type of humour have worn dull from overuse: as a first film, it would show promise, but it's a pale imitation of his prior work.

SONGWRITER
(Tri-Star)
dir Alan Rudolph pro Sydney Pollack exec pro Mike Moder scr Bud Shrake ph Matthew Leonetti, in Metrocolor ed Stuart Pappe pro des Joel Schiller mus Larry Cansler r time 94 mins US opening Oct 12.
cast Willie Nelson, Kris Kristofferson, Melinda Dillon, Rip Torn, Lesley Ann Warren, Mickey Raphael, Rhonda Dotson, Richard C Sarafian.

Tangy musical comedy about the country music business, a hipster's view of cornpone. Alan Rudolph weaves a tart mosaic of Bud Schrake's colourful dialogue, Willie Nelson's canny cool, Rip Torn's diabolic degeneracy, Lesley Ann Warren's tremulous emotionality, authentic songs and lots of good feeling.

STICK
(Universal)
dir Burt Reynolds pro Jennings Lang scr Elmore Leonard, Joseph C Stinson, based on the novel by Elmore Leonard ph Nick McLean, in Technicolor ed William Gordean pro des James Shanahan mus Barry De Vorzon r time 109 mins US opening Apr 26.
cast Burt Reynolds, Candice Bergen, George Segal, Charles Durning, Jose Perez, Richard Lawson, Castulo Guerra, Dar Robinson, Alex Rocco, David Reynoso, Sachi Parker, Tricia Leigh Fisher, Tim Rossovich, Deanna Lund.

STRAIGHT THROUGH THE HEART (MITTEN INS HERZ)
(Westdeutscher Rundfunk-Al Olga Film Production/New Line)
dir Doris Doerrie pro Denyse Noever scr Jelena Kristl ph Michael Goebel, in colour ed Thomas Wigand r time 90 mins US opening Feb 8.
cast Beate Jensen, Sepp Bierbichler, Gabriele Litty, Jens Mueller-Rastede, Joachim Hoepner.

A startlingly original work that surpasses most of the more highly touted and less effective German feminist films. Beate Jensen is brilliant as an alienated youth affecting punk styles who is drawn into shamming pregnancy to preserve an odd relationship with an older bourgeois man. Without contrivance, the film evolves harrowingly from social comedy into psychological tragedy.

THE SURE THING
(Monument/Embassy)
dir Rob Reiner pro Roger Birnbaum exec pro Henry Winkler scr Steven L Bloom ph Robert Elswit, in colour ed Robert Leighton pro des Lilly Kilvert mus Tom Scott r time 94 mins US opening Mar 1.
cast John Cusack, Daphne Zuniga, Anthony Edwards, Boyd Gaines, Tim Robbins, Lisa Jane Persky, Viveca Lindfors, Nicollette Sheridan, Larry Hankin.

Rob Reiner follows 'This Is Spinal Tap' with a more conventional variant on 'It Happened One Night' with two spatting college freshmen falling in love as they hitch across the country. The plot material is often suspect, but the humour is genuine and the players

achieve a consistent behavioral charm that renders the spurious pandering elements inoffensive. This may be as close to a creditable comedy as contemporary commercial requirements allow.

SWORD OF THE VALIANT
(Cannon)
dir Stephen Weeks pro Menahem Golan, Yoram Globus exec pro Michael Kagan, Philip M Breen scr Stephen Weeks, Philip M Breen, Howard C Pen ph Freddie A Young, Peter Hurst, in Fujicolor ed Richard Marden, Barry Peters pro des Maurice Fowler, Derek Nice mus Ron Geesin r time 101 mins US opening Dec 7.
cast Miles O'Keeffe, Cyrielle Claire, Leigh Lawson, Sean Connery, Trevor Howard, Peter Cushing, Ronald Lacey, Lila Kedrova, John Rhys-Davies, Douglas Wilmer, Brian Coburn, Emma Sutton, Bruce Liddington, Wilfrid Brambell.

SYLVESTER
(Rastar/Columbia)
dir Tim Hunter pro Martin Jurow scr Carol Sobieski ph Hiro Narita, in Metrocolor ed Howard Smith, Suzanne Pettit, David Garfield pro des James W Newport mus Lee Holdridge r time 102 mins US opening Mar 15.
cast Richard Farnsworth, Melissa Gilbert, Michael Schoeffling, Constance Towers, Pete Kowanko, Yankton Hatten, Shane Serwin, Chris Pedersen.

SYLVIA
(Southern Light-Cinepro/MGM-UA Classics)
dir Michael Firth pro Don Reynolds, Michael Firth scr Michele Quill, F Fairfax, Michael Firth, based on the books by Sylvia Aston-Warner ph Ian Paul, in colour ed Michael Horton set des Gary Hansen mus Leonard Rosenman r time 98 mins US opening May 31.
cast Eleanor David, Nigel Terry, Tom Wilkinson, Mary Regan, Martyn Sanderson, Terence Cooper, David Letch, Sarah Pierse.

TERMINAL CHOICE
(Madger Film Prods/Almi)
dir Sheldon Larry pro Gary Madger exec pro Jean Ubaud, Maqbook Hameed scr Jeal Bell, based on a story by Peter Lawrence ph Zale Magder, in colour ed Murray Magder pro des David Jaquest mus Brian Bennett r time 97 mins US opening May 10.
cast Joe Spano, Diane Venora, David McCallum, Robert Joy, Don Francks, Nicholas Campbell, Ellen Barkin, Chapelle Jaffe, Clare Coulter.

THIEF OF HEARTS
(Paramount)
dir-scr Douglas Day Stewart pro Don Simpson, Jerry Bruckheimer ph Andrew Laszlo, in Metrocolor ed Tom Rolf art dir Edward Richardson mus Harold Faltermeyer r time 100 mins US opening Oct 19.
cast Steven Bauer, Barbara Williams, John Getz, David Caruso, Christine Ebersole, George Wendt.

TURK 182
(Fox)
dir Bob Clark pro Ted Field, Rene DuPont exec pro Peter Samuelson,

Robert Cort *scr* James Gregory Kingston, Ddenis, John Hamill, based on a story by James Gregory Kingston *ph* Reginald H Morris, in colour *ed* Stan Cole *pro des* Harry Pottle *mus* Paul Zaza *r time* 98 mins *US opening* Feb 15.
cast Timothy Hutton, Robert Urich, Kim Cattrall, Robert Culp, Darren McGavin, Steve Keats, Peter Boyle, Paul Sorvino, Thomas Quinn, Norman Parker, Dick O'Neill.

Trumped up rabble-rouser that opens with some fair sketches of blue collar life but degenerates into terminal nonsense as Timothy Hutton becomes a New York Kilroy dogging a corrupt mayor with his graffiti to protest treatment of his older brother, a crippled former firefighter. The shamelessness of the Rocky-like attempt to orchestrate audience cheers guarantees all loss of sympathy for such transparent manipulation. Bob Clark ('Porky's') possesses unerring instinct for exploiting the least compelling aspects of his material.

UNTIL SEPTEMBER
(MGM-UA)
dir Richard Marquand *pro* Michael Gruskoff *scr* Janice Lee Graham *ph*

Philippe Welt, in Metrocolor *ed* Sean Barton *pro des* Hilton McConnico *mus* John Barry *r time* 95 mins *US opening* Sep 21.
cast Karen Allen, Thierry Lhermitte, Christopher Cazenove, Marie Catherine Conti, Hutton Cobb, Michael Mellinger, Nitza Saul, Rochelle Robertson, Raphaelle Spencer, Johanna Pavlis.

VAMPING
(Atlantic)
dir Frederick King Keller *pro* Howard Kling *exec pro* Nathan Boxer, Patrick Duffy, Frederick King Keller *scr* Michael Healy, Robert Seidman *ph* Skip Roessel, in colour *ed* Darren Kloomok *pro des* Howard Kling, Karen Morse, Stratton Rawson *mus* Ken Kaufman *r time* 107 mins *US opening* Jul 27.
cast Patrick Duffy, Catherine Hyland, Rod Arrants, Fred A Keller, David Booze, Jed Cooper, Steve Gilborn.

VISIONQUEST
(Warner)
dir Harold Becker *pro* Jon Peters, Peter Guber *exec pro* Stan Weston, Adam Fields *scr* Daryl Ponicsan,

based on a novel by Terry Davis *ph* Owen Roizman, in Technicolor *ed* Maury Winetrobe *pro des* Bill Malley *mus* Tangerine Dream *r time* 105 mins *US opening* Feb 15.
cast Matthew Modine, Linda Fiorentino, Michael Schoeffling, Ronny Cox, Harold Sylvester, Charles Hallahan, J C Quinn, Daphne Zuniga, Frank Jasper.

WHO'S THAT SINGING OVER THERE? (KO TO TAMO PEVA)
(Centar Film-Yugoslavia Film/ International Home Cinema)
dir Slobodan Sijan *scr* Dusan Kovacevic *ph* Bozidar Nikolic, in Eastmancolor *mus* Vojislav Kostic *r time* 84 mins
US opening Nov 23.
cast Pavle Vujisic, Dragan Nikolic, Aleksander Bercek, Neda Aneric, Slavko Stimac, Bora Stepanovic, Tasko Nacic.

Slobodan Sijan emerges as a major international talent in this sophisticated allegory of a bus rolling through the wartime countryside. Sijan deftly manipulates peasant and military types through satire to pathos

to horror, positioning his work as a Yugoslav variation on Buñuel. A Los Angeles arthouse success.

THE WILD LIFE
(Universal)
dir Art Linson *pro* Art Linson, Cameron Crowe *scr* Cameron Crowe *ph* James Glennon, in Technicolor *ed* Michael Jablow *pro des* William Sandell *mus* Edward Van Halen *r time* 96 mins *US opening* Sep 28.
cast Christopher Penn, Ilan Mitchell-Smith, Eric Stoltz, Jenny Wright, Lea Thompson, Brin Berliner, Rick Moranis, Hart Brochner, Susan Blackstone, Cari Anne Warder, Robert Ridgely, Michael Bowen, Angel Salazar, Randy Quaid.

WINDY CITY
(CBS Theatrical/Warner)
dir-scr Armyan Bernstein *pro* Alan Greisman *ph* Reynaldo Villalobos, Technicolor *ed* Clifford Jones *pro des* Bill Kenney *mus* Jack Nitzsche *r time* 102 mins *US opening* Sep 21
cast John Shea, Kate Capshaw, Josh Mostel, Jim Borrelli, Jeffrey DeMunn, Eric Pierpoint, Lewis J Stadlen, James Sutorius.

NOTEWORTHY DOCUMENTARIES

The following includes only feature-length documentaries, only noteworthy works of general cinematic interest, and only films that played theatrical engagements in both New York and Los Angeles in 1984-85. It represents about one-third of the feature docs that actually played. Those of exceptional quality or interest are indicated with an asterisk.

*STREETWISE
dir Martin Bell

*KADDISH
dir Steve Brand

*SEVENTEEN
dirs Joel deMott and Jeff Kreines

*GEORGE STEVENS: A FILM-MAKER'S ODYSSEY
dir George Stevens Jr

*TOKYO-GA
dir Wim Wenders

*THE DARK GLOW OF THE MOUNTAINS
dir Werner Herzog

*BALLAD OF THE LITTLE SOLDIER
dir Werner Herzog

*SUNLESS
dir Chris Marker

*COMEDIENNE
dir Katherine Matheson

*MUSICAL PASSAGE
dir Jim Brown

*THE TIMES OF HARVEY MILK
dir Robert Epstein
(Oscar winner)

THE GOOD FIGHT
dir Noel Bruckner, Mary Dore, Sam Sills

SEEING RED
dir James Klein, Julia Richert (Oscar nominee)

*IMPROPER CONDUCT
dir Nestor Almendros, Orlando Jimenez-Leal

*IN HEAVEN THERE IS NO BEER?
dir Les Blank

*CHAMBRE 666
dir Wim Wenders

BEFORE STONEWALL
dir Greta Schiller, Robert Rosenberg

MARLENE
dir Maximilian Schell (Oscar nominee)

HE MAKES ME FEEL LIKE DANCIN'
dir Emile Areolino (Oscar winner)

RAOUL WALLENBERG: BURIED ALIVE
dir David Harel

THE SECRET AGENT
dir Jackie Ochs

BURROUGHS
dir Howard Brookner

*CHICKEN RANCH
dir Nick Broomfield, Sandi Sissel

*IN THE NAME OF THE PEOPLE
dir Frank Christopher (Oscar nominee)

BITTER CANE
dir Jacques Arcelin

"I'M ALMOST NOT CRAZY ..." JOHN CASSAVETES – THE MAN AND HIS WORK
dir Michael Ventura

MISSISSIPPI BLUES
dir Bertrand Tavernier, Robert Parrish

THE SILENT PIONEERS
dir Lucy Winer

THAT'S DANCING
dir Jack Haley Jr

SANFORD MEISNER – THE THEATER'S BEST-KEPT SECRET
dir Sydney Pollack

THE US YEAR

The year came in like *Ghostbusters* and ended with Sylvester Stallone finding a pot of gold at the end of the *Rambo*. Remakes, sequels, genre pictures and star vehicles: the studios found that predictability meant profitability from the record summer of 1984 right through the year.

Mixing genres became Hollywood's newest high concept. Eddie Murphy's *Beverly Hills Cop,* the Christmas hit that continued drawing until May, was a comedy disguised as a police picture. *Ghostbusters,* in which Bill Murray played his patented gross-out slob, was a special-effects piece with a lot of jokes. Ditto *Gremlins,* in which Joe Dante's little furry friends almost totalled small-town America.

Earthbound adventure films usually scored better than interplanetary action. The call of the unknown was too strange to make significant hits out of David Lynch's *Dune,* Peter Hyams' *2001* or John Carpenter's *Starman* (though Jeff Bridges was Oscar-nominated for his portrayal of the disorientated extraterrestrial).

'Serious' movies had to settle upfront for second-class box office, booking minimal exposure until word of mouth could convince conservative ticket-buyers. *Amadeus, A Passage to India, A Soldier's Story* and *Places in the Heart* thus won success the hard way. *Amadeus* cleaned up on Oscar night, just as had an earlier Saul Zaentz-Milos Forman collaboration, *One Flew Over the Cuckoo's Nest.*

Places provided its star Sally Field with a platform for the most squirm-making Academy Award acceptances speech in years: "You really like me! You really like me!" Other rich Hollywood stars who played poor farm girls received neither financial

rewards nor the Academy's kudos: Jessica Lange in *Country* and Sissy Spacek in *The River.* The horseshoe was on the other foot when Harrison Ford played a poor farm boy in *Witness.* Perhaps his name and the gun he had in his hand for the non-farm half of the movie made a difference.

Stars were well advised to stick close to their images. Sylvester Stallone concealed his pie-plate pectorals behind a fringed shirt in *Rhinestone,* most critics' nomination for Most Pathetic movie of the year. Richard Gere danced in his diapers in *King David,* a movie that showed why Biblical stories are best avoided by Hollywood. Robert De Niro had a brief encounter with Meryl Streep in *Falling in Love,* but few accepted him as a Romeo. John Travolta unwisely let Jamie Lee Curtis do the dancing in *Perfect,* a dud despite – or because of – *Rolling Stone* magazine's total immersion in the screenplay.

Bill Murray got serious for *The Razor's Edge* and, though he played his part perfectly adequately, no one wanted to see him get serious. Nick Nolte's tough-guy stock declined after he wore a coat and tie in *Teachers* and allowed himself to get under Katharine Hepburn's thumb in *Grace Quigley.*

Many big stars sat the year out: Jane Fonda, Warren Beatty, Al Pacino, Sean Connery. Some young performers recently admitted to the million-dollar-a-picture ranks became over-choosy and disappeared from view: Kevin Bacon, Debra Winger, Tom Cruise.

Among star directors, Francis Coppola exceeded his own money-wasting record with the $50 million *The Cotton Club.* Brian De Palma borrowed Hitchcock's 'grammar' once again for his

sexy, violent *Body Double,* which many felt was a double negative. David Lean was at last allowed back into movie houses with *A Passage to India,* a moderate hit. Peter Bogdanovich came back with *Mask,* a sort of *Elephant Man* in the sunshine. John Huston had a banner year directing Albert Finney as a drunk in *Under the Volcano* and Jack Nicholson as a hood in *Prizzi's Honour.*

Great energy was lavished on chronicling every aspect of American high-school life. The result of this audience-pleasing effort was a couple of moderate hits and many, many flops. The *Porky's* cycle of teenpix may not be over yet, but the studios will doubtless be more careful after this year's experience.

The Karate Kid, in which a world-class wimp becomes an unbeatable warrior, was a big summer hit. *VisionQuest,* in which a gangly kid becomes an unbeatable wrestler, wasn't. Nor was *Sylvester,* in which a cowgirl becomes an unbeatable three-day-eventer.

Similarly, *Bachelor Party* satiated the audience for getting-laid pictures. *Revenge of the Nerds, The Wild Life, Grandview USA, The Joy of Sex, No Small Affair* and even *Porky's Revenge* held less interest for fickle youth. *The Breakfast Club* profited from taking its audience slightly more seriously, and *The Sure Thing* was praised as a kids' *It Happened One Night. Heaven Help Us* pleasantly introduced Matt Dillon's brother Kevin, but Matt's film *The Flamingo Kid* was a bigger hit. C Thomas Howell's *Secret Admirer* was the only school-set picture to reach for the school's-out audience.

Attempts to cast gadget movies with teenagers were failures: *The Last Starfighter* and *Electric Dreams.* Younger children fared better, though,

in *Goonies* and *Return to Oz.*

Returning to Oz was Australian Mel Gibson after three misses in America: *The Bounty, The River* and *Mrs Soffel.* Among other interlopers scorned in the year of the American Olympics hysteria were British directors whose films had animals in their titles: Alan Parker's *Birdy* and John Schlesinger's *The Falcon and the Snowman.* Irishman Neil Jordan's *The Company of Wolves* was given a 1,000-screen release but remained largely unseen.

Nor did Americans abroad impress audiences at home: *Oxford Blues* (England), *Until September* (France) and *American Dreamer* (France again) were unappreciated romances made more cheaply in Europe because of the strong dollar.

'America First' wasn't Hollywood's only foreign policy, but that consideration remained paramount in every aspect of movie-making. *The Killing Fields* did well, but it could only have been produced because it told the story of Cambodia's tragedy through an American's eyes. *The Little Drummer Girl* attacked America's ally Israel and failed, despite having American Diane Keaton in the lead. *Best Defense* criticized the Pentagon's weapons madness but the casting of Limey Dudley Moore vitiated the movie's box-office chances. *Protocol* made fun of the State Department by putting Goldie Hawn in charge of greeting foreigners, which might have seemed funnier if Jerry Lewis were President. Among other failures were *Top Secret!* and *Gotcha!,* spy comedies that made light of things dear to Reagan's heart.

Red Dawn led the American counter-attack, showing how a few Colorado kids could hold off the Cuban hordes. Rescuing the putative prisoners of war in Vietnam seemed a foolproof scenario. *Uncommon Valor* had established this new sub-genre the previous year, and *Missing in Action, Missing in Action 2* and *Rambo: First Blood Part II* all made big bucks ploughing the same furrow.

Macho action movies were usually a sure bet. Chuck Norris' two *Missing* pictures, plus *Code of Silence,* established him as a mainstream star after years labouring in Bruce Lee's shadow in the chop-socky trenches. In *Terminator* Arnold Schwarzenegger proved he could draw just as well in sunglasses as in his Conan wig.

Clint Eastwood varied his image a few millimeters, playing a kinky cop in *Tightrope,* a parody of Dirty Harry in *City Heat* and an imitation of Shane in *Pale Rider.* Clint's *City Heat* co-star Burt Reynolds had a less successful year, bombing in *Cannonball Run II* and *Stick.*

'Relationship' pictures were box-office poison. Audiences, as usual, had seen more relationships on television than they could stomach. *Mass Appeal,* financed by McDonalds humburger heiress Joan Kroc, drew few to see the squabbling between Jack Lemmon and his curate. *Turk 182!,* focusing on Timothy Hutton's relationship with his brother, was another Hutton flop. Neil Simon's *The Slugger's Wife* struck out. *Fandango* was one Steven Spielberg presentation that grossed low.

America's standin' tall moviegoers shunned female-orientated action pictures like *Supergirl, Baby* and *Sheena.* Men decided not to take their girlfriends to lovey-dovey pictures like *Dreamscape* and *Thief of Hearts.* Lack of sufficient gunplay doomed 'soft' films of all kinds, such as Sidney Lumet's *Garbo Talks. E.T.* kids Drew Barrymore and Henry Thomas became croppers with *Irreconcilable Differences* and *Cloak and Dagger.*

Nevertheless, some film-makers who worked independently of the studios were happy to settle for the modest profits available in the growing 'domestic art film' market. *Choose Me* and *Maria's Lovers* were interesting romances no major would have financed, so they found their niches among the *cognoscenti* who don't see their movies in malls. Equally popular away from the multiplexes was the unclassifiable *Paris, Texas. Blood Simple* proved that a stylish James M Cain-ish picture will always have an audience. Out-and-out weirdness *(Stranger Than Paradise* and *The Brother from Another Planet)* also scored on this circuit.

The studios' efforts to be sophisticated sometimes paid off. Geffen's backing for Albert Brooks produced a profit, with the Yuppie satire *Lost in America.* The same company also benefited from Woody Allen's *The Purple Rose of Cairo.* Among mainstream comics, Richard Pryor's *Brewster's Millions* didn't draw well enough to make back its high cost. Chevy Chase found a character he can repeat in *Fletch.* Steve Martin recovered from a string of failures by letting Lily Tomlin share his body in *All of Me. The Woman in Red,* Gene Wilder's re-make of the French farce *Pardon Mon Affaire,* was his return to wide popularity. John Landis' *Into the Night,* however, was too poker-faced to be a hit.

We may not see any more put-on movies for a while. Fox blew some big bucks spoofing action pictures in *Buckeroo Banzai* and gangster pictures in *Johnny Dangerously.* Other parodies that closed on Saturday night were two mock Westerns, *Lust in the Dust* and *Rustler's Rhapsody.*

Musical tie-ins to movies remained an important area of downside protection on moviemakers' balance-sheets. *Purple Rain,* was in the black even before it opened because of Prince's popularity in the record shops. When it did open it became the biggest hit musical in years. Paul McCartney's *Give My Regards to Broad Street* was the biggest failure in years. Jonathan Demme's *Stop Making Sense* proved that well made concert films still have an audience. *Desperately Seeking Susan* capitalized on Madonna's monopoly of the pop charts. Willie Nelson's *Songwriter* proved again that country music fans won't go to see movies without car chases. *Amadeus* somehow succeeded despite lengthy passages of Mozart.

Boardrooms were busy buying and selling. 'Killer bee' Rupert Murdoch bought half of Fox and $2 billion worth of TV stations after just missing acquiring Warner Bros. Warner's fate remains uncertain, as pleasure boat-maker Chris-Craft sought control and the company considered selling its TV interests to stay independent.

Disney paid dearly for its independence from corporate predators, winding up poorer and under new management anyway. Columbia owner and Tri-Star co-owner Coca-Cola changed its soft-drink formula. But Coke remained entranced by Hollywood, buying TV programme-maker Embassy, also a mini-major film-maker.

MCA, Universal's owner, was attracting such raiders as Phillips Petroleum. MGM-UA shuffled executives – Frank Yablans out, Alan Ladd Jr in – and majority stockholder Kirk Kerkorian was reportedly seeking to sell the studio's Culver City lot. Paramount, which lost executive whiz Barry Diller to Fox, says it's in the market for some TV stations. While CBS and ABC have been dealing with takeover bids, their film-making activities have been in abeyance.

BART MILLS

US TOP 12
BEVERLY HILLS COP
GHOSTBUSTERS
RAMBO: FIRST BLOOD PART II
GREMLINS
PURPLE RAIN
THE KARATE KID
WITNESS
AMADEUS
INDIANA JONES AND
THE TEMPLE OF DOOM
TIGHTROPE
A VIEW TO A KILL
POLICE ACADEMY 2
THE TERMINATOR

US FLOPS
ALAMO BAY
THE AVIATOR
SYLVESTER
GIVE MY REGARDS
TO BROAD STREET
THE SLUGGER'S WIFE
MASS APPEAL
THE JOY OF SEX
GARBO TALKS
BIRDY
CHEECH & CHONG'S
THE CORSICAN BROTHERS
GRANDVIEW USA

THE UK YEAR

Disasters and British film rubbed pretty close during the twelve months in question. *The Killing Fields* intrigued audiences as a picture about revolution in Cambodia but it also figured as the headline over any account of carnage – whether in Lebanon's Bekaa Valley where the wine comes sweeter thanks to rivers of blood, or in Belgium's Heysel Stadium, where British football fans will never be forgotten. And the banner which journalists longed to write over accounts of the collapse of the Johnson Matthey Bank was: "Film Mogul Brings Down Bank Of England". It didn't happen, of course, but Pakistani shipping magnate Mahmud Sipra had drawn heavily on his credit line to finance *The Jigsaw Man* and purchase Ireland's Ardmore Studios as well as other enterprises.

Since the musical is said to flourish in times of economic hardship and social difficulty, you could tell what the film financiers thought of the current state of Britain. Marching bands went through their paces in industrial Birmingham for *Knights and Emeralds.* Snooker players sang their way to a final showdown in *Billy the Kid and the Green Baize Vampire* on sets at Twickenham Studios. And Julien Temple brought together a flock of rock stars and dancers for the musical *Absolute Beginners,* set in London during the fifties.

But, despite these harbingers of doom and the fact that a fair number of local films turned into turkeys at the box office, the industry itself stayed in a buoyant mood throughout the year. None of the casualties ever added up to disaster for any company, apart from Mr Sipra's outfit, and there seemed to be plenty of optimism to go around.

Helping things along were the decent performances by such films as *Another Country, The Killing Fields, A Private Function, The Company of Wolves* and *Nineteen Eighty-Four.*

Two British-made films competed for Academy Awards and came away with rather little. By a lucky chance *Amadeus,* which garnered the real prizes, was written by an Englishman. It helped to keep alive the myth that Brits have a magic touch currently when it comes to winning Oscars. Any pride that was damaged could find compensation in David Hare's seizure of half the top prize at Berlin for *Wetherby*. And neither Nicolas Roeg's *Insignificance* nor Alan Parker's *Birdy* went unmentioned at the final ceremony of the Cannes Film Festival.

Journalists writing about the film industry tend to overwork terms like irony and paradox, but how else to describe a government policy which removes incentives to local film production while simultaneously backing British Film Year to celebrate the industry's achievements? The final stages of the Films Bill, which takes away state responsibility for the film sector, was hard fought. Final arguments were forlornly marshalled in favour of the Eady levy principle, the National Film Finance Corporation and tax breaks. Everyone from Bond producer Cubby Broccoli, supposedly much thinned by weeks on a health farm, to the lowliest of aspiring film directors put their thumbprint on the campaigning document. Come May, however, and the battle was lost on all fronts.

Left in the wake of this rout was the privatized successor to the NFFC. Typically, there was squabbling over whether it should be regarded as son or

daughter. And everyone screeched in horror when the body was inelegantly christened the British Screen Finance Consortium. But there was nothing really ugly about the proposals to run the organization, put forward by the relevant executives from Rank, Thorn EMI, Channel Four and the British Videogramme Association.

Plenty of cold water was also on hand to douse the more doom-laden rhetoric of the campaigners for subsidy. That wasn't really surprising since executives at Thorn EMI, Goldcrest and other places have to prove to investors that film-making can be a profitable activity. But it did really appear as if there hadn't been a better time to raise money for film-making. The banks were falling over themselves to get into movies. Geoff Reeve got Cayzer merchant bank to come in on his production programme following the release of *The Shooting Party*. County Bank came in on Quintet's *The Chain* and then took a major stake in the company. Sales agent Terry Glinwood tapped a reportedly open-ended line of credit from Hill Samuel. And various chunks of capital were poured into the coffers at Goldcrest and Thorn EMI.

With the financial stakes increasing apace, it did seem that time was up for the bumblers, whingers and amateurs. Production companies which had been winging it on their reputation as fledglings cast off the veneer of innocence and tried to look like serious competitors in the international marketplace.

Goldcrest celebrated its first year of slightly profitable activity with an expansive production programme that guaranteed red balance sheets in 1985. Cynics said that it was madness for a

British company to get tied up in £60,000,000 worth of film projects. But Robert De Niro, Al Pacino and Nastassja Kinski were there to sugar the pill for investors by joining the ranks of either the Jesuit warriors for Christ in Roland Joffé's *The Mission* or the armies of Hugh Hudson's *Revolution.*

Goldcrest held hands with Virgin Films for *Absolute Beginners,* which got going in the late spring of 1985 after falling at the starting blocks the previous summer. The subsidiary of Richard Branson's entertainments empire, which also became airborne during the year in question, had its work cut out getting *Nineteen Eighty-Four* onto the screens before New Year's Eve and within anything close to the original budget figure. Several other projects got discarded along the way and there was no peace after completion. Director Michael Radford got wide exposure for his disagreement with the financing company over a soundtrack by the Eurythmics.

Still securing 'new company' kudos is Zenith Productions, feature subsidiary of Central Television. In its first year of operation, the outfit could claim credit for Berlin prizewinner *Wetherby* and Cannes competitor *Insignificance.* Upcoming is a production programme calculated to appeal to the tabloid brigade with films on the fatal romance between punk rocker Sid Vicious and Nancy Spungen as well as the career of brothel-keeper Cynthia Payne.

Zenith production head Margaret Matheson used to run Central TV's drama department. Another female executive who came into features from television had a harder time keeping her head above water. The first fruits of Verity Lambert's time at Thorn EMI – Bill Forsyth's *Comfort and Joy,* Mike Hodges's *Morons from Outer Space* and Michael Hoffman's *Restless Natives* – all received a critical drubbing. At presstime, Lambert was due to be retired into independent production, alongside another batch of producers, within the Thorn EMI orbit.

If the burgeoning of the film musical is one indicator of our times, the quest for quasi-historic British heroes to challenge the long supremacy of James Bond was another. After nine years of trying, producer Kent Walwin finally got *Biggles* into his bi-plane over the barren wastes of London's dockland region. And even while one bunch of Bosch were being shot to pieces. Timothy Burrill announced his intention to revive Bulldog Drummond, last impersonated by Richard Johnson in 1968.

Biggles was one of a group of pictures brought out of storage and dusted down for production. Dylan Thomas's *The Doctor and the Devils,* a tale of bodysnatching and harlotry written over thirty years ago for Rank Films, finally went before the cameras at Shepperton with Freddie Francis directing. Derek Jarman got the green light from the British Film Institute Production Board to make *Caravaggio,* about whose non-production he has already written a book. Another long-cherished project which moved to the starting blocks was Bill Douglas's *Comrades,* his first since the autobiographical trilogy completed in 1979.

British film-makers took rather more interest in their recent past than hitherto. Ruth Ellis, the peroxide blonde with upper-class aspirations that turned murderous, was resurrected in *Dance with a Stranger.* Also set in the fifties were Roeg's *Insignificance* and Temple's *Absolute Beginners.* Michael Palin went back a decade with his Lady Macbeth Maggie Smith to explore the more basic sides of life in *A Private Function.* Plunging deeper into British history was Trevor Nunn who had all RSC hands on deck and called out the sixteenth-

century nylon for his account of the very short Tudor reign of *Lady Jane* Grey.

While Bill Forsyth was setting up a barnyard picture in Canada, Scottish film-making was all cheap imitations of *Gregory's Girl.* The central focus of activity outside London was the North and Midlands. Liverpool writer Alan Bleasdale knocked out *No Surrender* –

about the Protestant v Catholic battle in a Liverpool nightclub one New Year's eve – between his smash TV series *Boys from the Blackstuff* and a stage musical about Elvis Presley. Also Liverpudlian is romantic comedy *Letter to Brezhnev,* an account of two ladies out on the town with some Russian sailors. It was under Birmingham's Spaghetti Junction that Ian Emes made *Knights and Emeralds.*

None of the major companies underwent executive reshuffles, but the quangos were hot potatoes. Those trying to recruit someone with exceptional managerial, financial and creative expertise to run the British Screen Finance Consortium kept on having to

raise the price. And when Peter Sainsbury quit the British Film Institute Production Board, film academic Colin McCabe had to be cajoled into taking on the difficult task.

Some people left the country, but not enough to cause concern. Clive Parsons, whose dissatisfaction with the quality of British screenplays is common

It's unlikely that the theatrical revenue for 'The Company of Wolves', the most successful British film of the year, would even have paid for the set.

knowledge, left for Los Angeles to run Kings Road Productions after completing *Comfort and Joy* in Glasgow. Jonathan Lynn also went to the West Coast, seeking to resolve the problems involved in making a film based on the game of *Cluedo.* And David Puttnam announced that he would go to Harvard as a fellow in moral philosophy to escape the eggheads who keep criticizing him and his films.

One couldn't have blamed anybody else who decided to get away from the depressing cinema admissions figures. Only around 54,000,000 cinema tickets were sold in 1984 – a reduction of 12,000,000 on the previous year. Although there was useful money available from cinemas for the big American

films such as *Ghostbusters* and *Beverly Hills Cop,* it's unlikely that the theatrical revenue for *The Company of Wolves,* the most successful British film of the year, would even have paid for the set.

But ritual incantations about the mystery of cinema's decline in the UK did start to be replaced by talk of reform and five-year plans. All the circuits spent some money on refurbishment. Managers were retrained and urged to go out into local communities to sell the cinema experience. It was claimed that ticket price cuts and the increased publicity generated by British Film Year helped to drag cinema attendances back to the 1981 level for the first six months of 1985.

What hope there is for the future lies in plans to build new cinemas on out-of-town sites where the pundits say that audiences want their entertainment. American Multi-Cinema, the McDonalds of the American cinema business, unveiled plans for a ten-plex in Milton Keynes due to open in the autumn of 1985. CIC Theatres and Thorn EMI also have new state-of-the-art houses on the drawing board.

A fresh influx of American pictures also kept confidence up at the studios, where building went on apace. Elstree opened a new office block. The replacement 007 stage at Pinewood was finished on schedule over the ashes and cinders of the previous construction. And the Lee Brothers cooked up plans for Shepperton Studios, which they acquired in August, involving new stages and offices, a swimming pool and tennis courts as part of their 'film village' concept.

Looked at objectively, the British film industry seems to have notched up too few real success to justify this flow of cash and confidence. After all, much is uncertain about the future for audiovisual media. But an industry that has been sluggish and declining for so long is bound to get a bit overexcited when things start looking up and perhaps that ebullience, tempered with strong doses of wisdom, will turn out to be the sector's greatest asset.

JAMES PARK

FILMS OF THE YEAR
CARMEN

Nowhere in George Orwell's *Nineteen Eighty-Four* does it mention that in and around the year of the title the world would be driven mad by an epidemic of *Carmens*.

Dazed by Godard, flamenco'd by Saura, and battered by Brook, most of us contemplated a 2½-hour version of Bizet's opera by Francesco Rosi with all the pleasurable excitement of someone tied to a railway line while the 9.55 from Seville approaches. Even the all-star cast of singers – Placido Domingo, Ruggero Raimondi, Julia Migenes-Johnson – did not allay dread. Domingo came fresh from Zeffirelli's disastrous movie bash at *La Traviata*, Raimondi seems of late to have given up vocalising for appearing in weird French films (by Losey, Resnais) and Migenes-Johnson has usurped British television screens with a

series of chocolate-box anthologies of best-loved arias.

But the hell with forebodings. Rosi's *Carmen* is a triumph. As befits the director of *Salvatore Giuliano*, *The Mattei Affair* and *Christ Stopped at Eboli*, the film is scorched, passionate, *al fresco* and full of brilliantly labyrinthine movement: not only of cast and crowds within individual scenes but of perspective and panorama within the sweep of the opera's travels. Where in the theatre we usually endure creaking canvas rocks, backcloth moons and Seville squares you couldn't swing a cat in, Rosi swings his camera round the whole of Southern Spain.

What's more, Rosi comes closer than Godard, Saura or Brook to explaining why we've gone dotty about *Carmen* in this decade. The

reason is, of course, that Merimée's story and Bizet's opera are radicalism made romantic. The heroine is a working-class girl who flamboyantly thumbs her nose at authority. Not only does she give her captors the slip, after being arrested for a bit of cat-fighting in the cigarette factory, but she even dishes out humiliation to her officer-lover by landing *him* in the slammer. Carmen is a proletarian feminist before her time: she's the opera's scalding – and sexy – contrast to both drippy, domesticated Micaela and upright, boobyish Don José. And when she's punished for her independence of mind in Act Four by being stabbed to death, it's not José we're rooting for.

And if Julia Migenes-Johnson isn't the most sexy and swashbuckling broad ever to hit a high C, who is? Not for Rosi an ageing *mezzo* wheeled out of La Scala to bang out Bizet under a burning sun. Migenes-Johnson has luscious looks, cascading hair, hydraulic hips; she has the true measure of Carmen's seductive wilfulness. She can also, of course, sing; her natural soprano giving a brightness to the gypsy's tunes, which your usual *mezzo* tends to purr out from the chest like a cat trapped under the sofa.

And then there is the *sans-pareil* Domingo! People have complained of his solid acting. Tush tush! Tsk Tsk! When someone complained to Rosi that Domingo's performance was "wooden", Rosi came back smartly, "But naturally. Don José is a wooden character." Of course he is. He's a toy soldier standing to attention in the nursery when a big horrible cat comes in. He doesn't at first realize his fate because the cat comes disguised as a slinky young

woman and throws a rose at him. It's only later that the poor fool realizes he is the *plat du jour*. Domingo's blind, bland rectitude is the perfect foil for Johnson's liquefactious guile, and when he opens his mouth he lets out sounds like you've never heard before. The voice is molten gold, streaming across the Andalucian firmament. Was Caruso better than this? I don't believe it.

Rosi has also taken the astounding – one would have thought suicidal – decision not to stylize. Not for him the frozen baroque gestures or plotted symmetries of Losey's *Don Giovanni*. Instead we're plunged into red-hot *verismo*. In the children's chorus, we don't see a platoon of housetrained teenyboppers lined up to trill out Bizet's melody. Instead the chorus is laid over a long-shot scene of rampaging ragamuffins hurtling after Don José, who's riding into town – dust round his hooves and sunlight smacking his helmet – with his regiment. And when Don José investigates Carmen's misdoings, we follow him right into the cigarette factory for a blast of 1870's industrial realism: the sweatshop slatterns poring over giant tongues of raw tobacco, a rank and steamy sunlight pouring through the high windows, straw scattered on the floor.

Yet for all its realism, the movie is never less than musical. Rosi finds visual rhythms and *rubati* to match the score. The 'La fumée' chorus is a delicate tracery of coiling arm movements, intertwining arabesques among the singers and filigree crane-shots through the leaves of a tree. Escamillo's show-stopper ('To-re-a-dor') is done as a blazing royal progress by the matador, on foot through the nocturnal gypsy fires

surrounding Lillas Pastia's bar. Ruggero Raimondi's finery picks him out as a greater fire among the smaller, and Rosi adds further sparkle by having the love-singed Carmen scatter light at him from a piece of broken mirror held before a fire.

Rosi's triumph, though, is his cinematisation of Act Three. He ushers us into the vast, beautiful, frowning gorges during the entr'acte music, and cameraman Pasqualino de Santis gives an added scowl to the skies by using a dark filter. We're in a twisting Gothic landscape out of Salvator Rosa or Caspar David Friedrich. It's the opera's witching hour – when Bizet casts his spell and turns it from comedy to tragedy. And even Micaela's big number, 'Seule en ce lieu sauvage', is staged by Rosi not as a stand-up-and-warble setpiece but as a giddying alternation of vast long shot and moon-pale, tremulous close-up.

It's not Rosi's fault, it's Bizet's, that the climax is a bit of a let-down. Here we are back in Seville for more tunes and sunlight, followed by a quick murder. It's all too perfunctory. (Has anyone made a study of how the last acts of operas are nearly *always* the worst'?) And it is probably a miscalculation – though we're all for originality – to have Carmen already sitting in her seat for the bullfight when José appears lurking unshaven at the back of the stalls. To have her pals whisper to her "You're not safe here", when she's clearly safer here, sandwiched between the paying customers, than she would be anywhere else in Spain, invites charges of daftness. She then has to *get up* and *go out* of the arena in order to be stabbed to death.

Yet this is a mere hiccup in the hurricane. At movie's end, when Carmen gets her undeserved come-uppance with a sharp instrument, both music and movie have howled into overdrive again. And look at cameraman de Santis's antics with the dark filter again! He's made a sky charred and *enragé* – it even seems to burn black the tops of the buildings – and Domingo and Migenes-Johnson go into the final dance of death like two Strindberg characters told to sing for their suffering.

Corridas of power, indeed. Terrific!

For years and decades we've been told by disbelievers that you can't put opera on the screen. Too 'artificial', too 'hothouse', too 'theatrical', they say. They will *just* about allow the picture-book stylizations of a Syberberg's *Parsifal*, because that's playing the game the opera's way. But how can you have people going around singing in real locations?

Rosi has answered them. Opera, like any other art, is about real passions, real people and real places. That it takes that reality and super-heightens and super-decorates it does not mean that reality disappears. It's a thread deep inside all the embellishments and flourishes and encrustations. All the film director has to do is find that thread and pull like crazy. If the opera doesn't fall apart (as only a bad one will), it'll reform itself into a new and thrilling and equal shape for the cinema.

HARLAN KENNEDY

THE COMPANY OF WOLVES

Wolves are the most feared of animals, and the fear has crept into legend, into myth, into the fabric of dreams. *The Company of Wolves* is a dream-film, a fantasy.

Of course, fantasy belongs to the make-up of many of the arts, in the novel and the poem, in theatre and painting. And the cinema lives on it. But there is a fantasy which is not simply the product of an exploring imagination. It has its home next door to reality. In the errant mind the real event of daily life can become veiled in the fanciful. One thinks as time goes on of incidents not as they actually occurred but adorned with details which deceiving memory has added. Go back after twenty years to a well-recalled landscape. Somehow it doesn't look the same as it looked in the mind's eye; the very shape and size have altered. The fantasy-creator in ourselves has imprinted a false image. Imperceptibly fantasy impinges on the everyday.

The work of art, moving in the mysterious area between fact and the creative, is faced with a difficult problem: to present the shifting relationship between the ordinary and the extraordinary, the mundane and the magical. The cinema has no difficulty with conventional magic. With its resources of cutting and trick camerawork it can easily persuade us that the old hag turns into the fairy godmother or that the pumpkin is really a fine coach. But to present the two aspects, the mundane and the magical in relationship to one another and to the human figure – that is the crux.

The Company of Wolves is based on a short story – no more than twelve pages of it – by Angela Carter. It is directed by Neil Jordan, who collaborated with the author in writing the screenplay. And the film has the bewitching air of half-reality which breathes from the pages of the story. A young girl, an adolescent, dreams. Her life belongs to the country of dream, but she still lives in a village, in a family, in the normal world. At the beginning of the film her dream is nightmarish, an experience of terror. But she dreams on, she will not awaken. And the audience in the cinema sees her sometimes as the child of the village, sometimes as the figure of legend. The achievement of the film is that one finds it almost impossible to separate the two images.

The girl is seen in the company of her grandmother, an old woman in the traditional dress of fairy-tale; the parents are just returning. The girl goes with the old woman to a village gathering. It is a wedding, and the grandmother uses the opportunity for a warning. She tells a story of another wedding: the bridegroom was what was called a travelling man. He came and went, nobody knew much about him. On the wedding night there was wolf-howling in the darkness outside. The bridegroom got up and went out into the night – and he did not come back. Never marry, says the old woman, a man with eyebrows which meet, for that signifies a werewolf.

At this moment the idea of the werewolf, the human being who changes bodily into a savage and dangerous animal, begins to dominate Neil Jordan's film. It is a film of its period. The figure of the man-wolf has been frequent during the last few years in the fantasies of the transatlantic and European cinema. There was the tale of the two Americans hiking in England, *An American Werewolf in London*. They hear strange sounds as they walk on the moors, and sure enough one of them is wolf-bitten; according to the conventions of werewolf legend he is himself turned into a man-wolf. That was part-comedy, part-drama. There was a very different outcome to the tale, one of a group of Pirandello stories, in the Italian *Kaos*: the isolated farm, the man driven half mad by the full moon and howling outside all night while his wife goes to bed with the lover she has always wanted – but she has no pleasure since her partner is too deeply affected by the plight of her wretched husband. Werewolf cinema doesn't go in for happy endings. *The Company of Wolves* is different. For now the wolf himself moves into the foreground. He is no longer the terror of an old wives' tale; he is pleasing, seductive.

The girl has an admirer, a village boy who wants to take her for a walk in the woods after church. She is not interested in this normal human companionship. She

runs away, leaving the boy to search for her. And in this search he makes a terrifying discovery. He finds the carcass of a farm animal. it has been wolf-mauled; and he runs back to the village to spread the news that there is a wolf on the prowl. A hunt is organized. There is an interlude of reality. But the hunt has no success.

Soon we are back, not in the fantasy of legend but in the stuff of fairy-tale. The children of western Europe have for centuries been brought up on monstrous tales of murder and mutilation. One of them is the tale of Red Riding Hood, and at this point the film confronts its audience with the familiar threat: the child sent on a fatal errand. The girl – Rosaleen is her appropriate name – is safe at home with her parents. But she is to take a basket of gifts to her grandmother. She has to go through the forest and she is warned to keep to the paths. The old story stirs into life.

On her way she meets a young man, much handsomer, much more beguiling than the village boy whose company she had scorned. She is taken by the stranger's looks and manners, and foolishly, as one thinks, she stops to talk to him. She doesn't notice that his eyebrows almost touch one another. He will meet her, he says, at the cottage.

The climax has the expected beginning. The girl reaches the cottage. There is no grandmother there. But the wolf is there, beautiful, feral. And now the werewolf legend and the fairy-tale are both reversed. The girl looks older now, a woman rather than a child; and she holds the wolf in her arms, caresses him, strokes his terrible head. She has been accepted into the company of wolves.

When Angela Carter's story ends it is Christmas Day. There is a blizzard, but it will end, and as the clock strikes the moon shines on the snow and the paw-prints of the werewolf; it is His birthday, the day of reconciliation. And in Neil Jordan's film too there is reconciliation. The movie has its passages of violence. But the violence of the old fairy-

tale so familiar to thousands of children has been subdued, the nature of the wolf has been subdued; human imagination and the corridors of dream have tamed him.

Not the kind of film which used to be associated with the British cinema. One used to think that this country, though it could produce fine work, lacked the adventurousness which can mark the cinema of many European countries. One no longer feels that. Like the United States, Britain has welcomed the creative talents of many people from near and far. Neil Jordan has worked in Ireland; his first film, *Angel*, was set in that country and was a notable study of what might be called the infection of Irish violence. Something of the Irish adherence to legend is clear in his new movie. But his cast is mainly British. It is led by Angela Lansbury, a distinguished actress who has had successes on both sides of the Atlantic. The girl who plays Rosaleen, the dreaming heart of the narrative, is a discovery from England; Sarah Patterson was only thirteen when she was picked for the difficult rôle of the

child who alters as the tale unfolds and ends it as a maturing character three years older. The cast includes names from both stage and film: David Warner, Graham Crowden (well remembered from his work in Lindsay Anderson's films), and Stephen Rea, who played the central figure of *Angel*. It is a team which works together to create the atmosphere of fantasy which rules the film. Behind them one recognizes the work of creative technicians: sensitive camerawork and design, and the extraordinary effects of magic and make-up which nowadays one is apt to take for granted.

But when all is said and done one comes back to the first creative mind, the author, and to her adaptation for the screen, and to the translation of the idea into visual terms by the director. *The Company of Wolves* is a film which repeatedly surprises, sometimes shocks and always enchants. One emerges from its web of dream still uncertain which event, which relationship is fact and which fantasy.

DILYS POWELL

PARIS, TEXAS/REPO MAN

It has become almost a truism to say that many of the best films dealing with America's more unfamiliar byways have been made by non-American directors. It seems that a director with an outsider's view can frequently present a more lucid portrait of the Land of Golden Opportunity than can a home-grown film-maker. As long ago as the twenties and thirties, the Swede Victor Sjöström and the German Fritz Lang were dissecting the American Dream in movies like *The Wind* and *Fury*. In the fifties Douglas Sirk brought a recognizably European sensibility to Hollywood melodrama, transforming rags-to-riches weepies into scathing critiques of a society divided by money, racism and class. In more recent years, directors as diverse as Antonioni (*Zabriskie Point*), John Boorman (*Point Blank* and *Deliverance*), Jacques Demy (*The Model Shop*) and Peter Yates (*Breaking Away*) have all chipped in with less than glowing portraits of Stateside life, pointing to

violence, rampant capitalism, class differences, alienation and a loss of faith in the Dream as inescapably American phenomena.

Hardly surprising then that two of the year's most interesting films should have been made by two non-Americans. Wim Wenders' *Paris, Texas* continues to reveal the director's fascination with America displayed in earlier films like *Kings of the Road, The American Friend* and *The State of Things*. Except for the final scenes of the last, those movies were made across the Atlantic, back in Europe. But *Paris, Texas* – for all that it is an international co-production between France and West Germany – is a bona fide American work, shot by a stranger in paradise. And the geographical move seems to have resulted in a parallel shift in the German director's attitude towards the Promised Land.

In *Kings of the Road*, one of Wenders' central characters complained that America had colonised the European

unconscious. Fascinated by American music, movies, and motors, Wenders nevertheless saw the American influence in post-war Europe as a baleful economic and cultural stranglehold. That view was reiterated in *The American Friend* (innocent German picture-framer corrupted by psychopathic American businessman) and in *The State of Things* (ambitious European film-artist betrayed by duplicitous American financiers). The new film, however, presents us with a more serene contemplation of American life and landscape. Europe is notable for its absence, and America has become a repository of Myth, Solitude and Loss.

Although set in modern times, the film begins with an image familiar from countless Westerns: a lone man, sunbaked and haggard, stumbles wearily through the harsh Texas desert to arrive, exhausted and mute, at an isolated shack. He refuses to explain whence he came; only

when his brother Walt comes to drive him back to Los Angeles does it become apparent that the man, Travis, has been missing, presumed dead, for four years. Having 'lost' his family, he has been in the wilderness ever since.

In Los Angeles he stays with Walt and his wife Anne, who have become surrogate parents to Travis' son Hunter. Only slowly does the boy accept that this taciturn, troubled man, rather than Walt, is his true father. But when Travis reveals that he wants to see his wife Jane once more, and discovers that she is living in Houston, the travelling starts off once more, with father and son driving off to find her working in a peep-show parlour. There, from behind a one-way mirror, Travis finally opens up and explains to Jane his story: a tale of marital jealousy, drinking and violence, of a night when the family's trailer home had caught fire, and Jane had disappeared with her child into the darkness, leaving Travis physically and emotionally burned.

Wenders' intimate epic has been widely praised for the fact that at last he has given a significant, well-rounded and sympathetic part to a woman, also for the fact that, for the first time in his films, there is a tender admission of love betweeen a man and a woman. Touching though Jane and Travis' reunion scene may be, however, the director still lacks the courage – or commitment – to allow his estranged couple to do anything more than talk of love while separated by glass. Jane is not even allowed to see her husband. After their lengthy discussion through a glass darkly, Travis ensures that mother and child are reunited – in his absence – and leaves the two of them once more. Hardly progressive sexual politics! A woman's rôle is to raise her child, a man's simply to do what a man's gotta do. At the end of the film, in true Western style, Travis rides off into the night, leaving the town for the desert.

The closing scenes, and the long peep-show parlour parley between Travis and Jane, are the least successful moments in an otherwise fascinating movie. The declaration of love seems forced, awkward, while the film – which for so long has relied on images alone to convey mood and emotions – takes a turn towards talkiness, making too explicit the reasons for Travis' strange behaviour. Where the film does score highly is in the first half, detailing the man's tentative, clumsy and often painful reintegration into a society he has abandoned. As played by Harry Dean Stanton, Travis' anguish, obsession and sheer confusion is made plain without words. His raddled features, bruised eyes, and strangely loping walk suggest nothing less than a stranger in a strange land. And yet he is an American, in America. As craggy as the desert that has been his home for so long, he seems out of place in the concrete canyons of Los Angeles: unable to sleep nights, he sits in the gardens under the stars, watching cars racing along the freeway, planes taking off from a nearby airport. Further images of wandering.

Therein lies Wenders' vision of America: a land of mythical odysseys, of transience, huge distances, rootlessness and eternal searching. Many of the film's characters are either foreign immigrants or Americans dreaming of being somewhere else. The title tells all, referring to a dusty, disused desert backlot bought by Travis' father, the spot where Travis may have been conceived. For Travis, like his parents who longed to visit France, the little bit of land is a substitute, the locus of a dream of impossible romance. America is haunted by the spectre of Europe, the days of opening up the Western frontier are no more, and laconic men wander lost,

vainly searching for a home, hope and true love.

A different, less mythical view of contemporary America is apparent in *Repo Man*, a first feature by expatriate Alex Cox. The film shares in common with *Paris, Texas* star Harry Dean Stanton and cameraman Robby Muller, and yet Cox's concerns could hardly be more different from Wenders'.

One of the most original and inventive independent movies to emerge in years, *Repo Man* is part comedy, part sci-fi, part thriller and part socio-political satire. Young dissillusioned punk Otto is pressured by seedy, scowling car-repossessor Bud (Stanton) into joining him in risking life and limb by recovering limos from purchasers who have been unable to keep up their payments. The work becomes more complicated and hectic when he becomes involved in a search for a '64 Chevy Malibu, driven by a lobotomised nuclear scientist and bearing a lethal cargo in its boot. During his Candide-style adventures, Otto encounters a variety of weird eccentrics: CIA clones, UFO freaks, acid-casualties, vengeful punks, not to mention repo man's arch enemies, the Rodriguez Brothers, a pair of manic motorists straight out of the pages of a Richard Brautigan novel.

Repo Man engages and excites throughout its tireless invention and its wry observations of the quality of life in Los Angeles' seedier districts. This is Reaganite America at its most absurd, its most consumerist. Otto's dippy hippy parents send off all their money to lunatic TV evangelist Reverend Larry; Bud has nothing but contempt for the unfortunates who are too poor to pay for their cars, and despises virtually all humanity: "An ordinary person avoids tense situations – Repo Man spends his life getting into tense situations." Everyone is either on the make or putting their faith in some ludicrous superior power. Even anti-establishment Otto has his head turned by the smell of money. Cox sees his film as political, and has described his repo man as "cowboy enforcers of the capitalist system". Yet another Western in disguise?

Despite the director's stress on the injustices and absurdities of rampantly capitalist America, despite his attention to the sort of characters and poverty-ridden places rarely shown in the movies, it would be wrong to exaggerate the serious nature of the film. Much of the humour is delightfully wacky: an ageing hippy

drones on about "the more you drive the less intelligent you are" (a riposte to road movies?); a grumpy and violent security guard spends his spare time knitting; vicious anarchic punks want to settle down and get married. Other moments revolve around witty parodies of other movies: the sinister traffic cop who stops the scientist's Chevy is straight out of *Psycho*; the nuclear whatsit that wastes anyone who opens the Chevy's boot recalls *Kiss Me Deadly*; and most mischievously, the absurd, unexpected, and uplifting ending in which Otto and the car-hating hippy are transported heavenwards in the glowing Chevy makes a mockery of the climax of *Close Encounters*. None of these parodies is gratuitous, however; they are all seamlessly woven into the fabric of the movie as a whole.

It is indeed Cox's remarkable success in gathering all the different strands – sci-fi, politics, *film-noir*, comedy, movie-references, a punk soundtrack – into a bizarre but coherent unity that makes his directorial debut so massively invigorating. He may have been aided by Muller's crisp, evocative camerawork and by a collection of excellent performances from a largely unknown cast. But it is finally his script, which forever twists and turns into strange side-alleys, and his assured direction, which somehow manages to keep the whole thing moving in logical, comprehensible progression, that make him a talent to watch in the future. Wenders may have produced a more lyrically sensuous and elegaic picture of the New West, but Alex Cox's punky portrait of the byways of modern American life simply sparkles with energy, insight and pure imagination.

GEOFF ANDREW

NINETEEN EIGHTY-FOUR

"The Film of the Year", ran the ad copy – for once not hyperbolic, merely accurate. Putting George Orwell's classic speculative fantasy on screen at the very moment the actual 1984 rolled by was an irresistible idea. True, we aren't really living in the totalitarian state the disgruntled ex-socialist prophesied would come to pass if certain socio-political notions were carried to their logical extreme. Yet no viewer of Michael Radford's film can hope to resist the temptation to draw parallels between the actual *now* and the fictional one that Orwell from his gloomy post-war perch concocted – particularly if that spectator is a citizen of Thatcher's England or Reagan's America.

In a way *Nineteen Eighty-Four* was always a film. Long before Radford – or his less engaging 1956 predecessor Michael Anderson – got hold of it, this cautionary tale of social tyranny has been seen less as a simple story than a blueprint for visualisation. Once read, Orwell's novel is invariably *seen*. No teacher who ever assigned it to a class (it became a cornerstone of standard curricula with astonishing swiftness) ever feared it would go over student's heads. The particulars of Orwell's politics may need explaining, but the novel's vivid language ensured its narrative core was thoroughly understood.

Still, like all works of popular culture with 'lives of their own', this easily comprehended core differed in emphasis from Orwell's. What Orwell wrote was a story about Winston Smith, a drone-like worker in the 'Ministry of Truth' whose growing awareness of the system that surrounds him soon leads to his doom. What fired the popular imagination, however, was

that system itself, spectrally embodied by its all-powerful all-seeing leader 'Big Brother'. In this cultural matrix Smith was simply a means to an end. We crawl inside his skin to see all the better what stands just outside it. As a result, initial revulsion for many often changes to a darkly humorous brand of affection. What is 'Big Brother' after all if not 'image' in politics at its most thoroughgoing. 'Strong leadership' – every society's most frequently raised demand – could not find a better champion. As for his famous inversions – "War is Peace", "Freedom is Slavery" – we hear them every night on the television news mouthed by world leaders less immediately omnipotent than he. Truly 'Big Brother' is

someone we have all in one way or another come to 'love'. It's Winston Smith that's the problem. What does this sad, colourless little man have to say to us – especially in the here and now of the real 1984? For that we must do what Radford has done – cut through decades of social absorption and return to the work at its root – not the imaginary 1984 but the real 1948 in which it was written.

It is this past, not the actual present or imagined future, that is the key to Radford's treatment. The décor (by Allan Cameron) is that of post-war Europe – smouldering ruins pockmarked with a few relatively unscarred structures. The colour (Roger Deakins is the cinematographer) suggests a

faded rotogravure illustration. Looking as if it were left out in the rain too long, then dried slowly in the sun, the film is almost sensuous with decay. Yet we cannot luxuriate in it as with such recent anti-utopian fantasies as *Blade Runner* or *The Road Warrior (Mad Max II)*. Politics is far too pressing a concern – made all the stronger by Radford's insistence that we use the film as a palimpsest. We see Orwell's 1984 through our own, whatever fantasies we may have once harboured about Orwell's, *and* his (real) 1948. Adding to these levels of simultaneous perception is the lingering suspicion that the whole thing could be taking place in an alternative universe, much like Phillip K Dick's *The Man in the High Castle*.

This dizzying contextual inventiveness has unfortunately given some critics the easy way out. In *Sight and Sound* Jill Forbes, who considers Orwell's tome "a classic of juvenile literature", praised Radford's efforts for producing "a British film shot in distinctively English locations" – as if the whole affair were a slightly more eccentric Ealing production. There is undoubtedly no small degree of cleverness involved in a production offering viewers such sights as Alexandra Palace, Battersea Power Station and Senate House made strange by spacio-temporal alteration. But we remain cinematic tourists on holiday at our own risk. A film interrogating an individual's relationship to the state – at the most absolute gut-level imaginable – is not to be sniffed at in this here and now.

It is doubtless due to this blatant sobriety that *Nineteen Eighty-Four* was received so coolly in the US, where its nostalgic charms counted for very little. Unlimited optimism ruled the roost in post-war America; Orwell's less than sanguine vision of the future came as a rude shock. Today anti-utopias are common. But Radford's film is quite devoid of the larky fun of Kubrik's *Clockwork Orange* – when its hero is crushed by the state he remains that way. Likewise the much-vaunted 'new patriotism' can take little pleasure in Radford's film. In the US Orwell's book was immediately seized upon as a propaganda tool – virtually taught in the schools as What Would Happen If The Russians Took Over during the Cold War of the fifties. Today, however, as Winston Smith watches a film praising the glorious heritage of 'Oceania' during a 'Ten Minute Hate' one can only think of a Republican Party election commercial. 'Hates' of more than ten minutes duration are today being directed against the government of Nicaragua, and the 'evil empire' of the

Soviet Union. Meanwhile – just as in Orwell – former enemies like China are treated as friends and allies as if no previous hostilities had ever existed. And now in the wake of Reagan's visit to Bitburg even the Nazis...

No, there's no avoiding *Nineteen Eighty-Four* as rendered by Radford. Even the "juvenile literature" aspect cited by Forbes proves to have teeth in it. Smith's love for Julia, forbidden by the state, has doubtless represented the essence of *verboten* sexual longings in many an adolescent mind. But what is this 'love' but lust – a mindless indulgence in a fetish object only too glad to make herself available as such. Perfect is Radford's seizing on Smith's obsession with the dress and lipstick of the prostitute he meets in the forbidden zone. All the better when this dress and lipstick return on Julia – Suzanna Hamilton just barely repressing a sense of gleeful triumph as she puts them on, making her eventual betrayal all the clearer, especially to those attentive to Lang

(particularly *House by the River*) and Rivette (particularly *Merry Go Round*). And John Hurt's Smith is likewise perfect. What better casting? Already beaten, he is there ready to be beaten again. So let us not speak of suspense. Let us simply gaze at the workings of a well-oiled machine turning over and over as it devours its human components with an almost graceful, cold, deadly logic.

We know where it's all leading of course. To that horrible room where a ghastly contraption with live rats will be strapped to Smith's face. Yet Radford refuses us the luxury of revulsion. What Burton's O'Brien (an almost perpetually disappointing actor giving his cinematic farewell on a note of unimaginable glory) is saying in his crisply deliberate voice is clear. The state wants you, and will take you anyway it can. Simple, mindless obedience, moreover, is not enough. One must know that one will be punished for any transgression. And it is from this punishment that love

will proceed.

Easy to see where all this springs from. Orwell is clearly a public school boy who never quite got over his canings. Learning to "love Big Brother" is consequently a homoerotic nightmare (another connection to adolescent sexual distress). But as Burton's O'Brien peers at Hurt's Winston Smith on the torture rack, another image comes to mind – out of Borowczk's *Jeux des Anges*, or one of Bacon's screaming Popes. Here is horror so extreme that it almost eradicates any notion of horror. Yet we're quite beyond Kubrick's haughty anti-humanism here, as one's thoughts turn to similar visions – Pasolini's *Salo*, Russell's *The Devils*, Beth B and Scott B's *Black Box*. And beyond cinema, to life itself. Need we list the countries where torture is a daily affair, where the individual and the state are locked as one in a vice-like grip. Yes, it's *Nineteen Eighty-Four* all right – just in time for 1984.

David Ehrenstein

AMADEUS

It's now official: *Amadeus* has won the Oscar for Best Picture of the Year, which everyone knows from past experience must certify it as middlebrow art for a nation in which all classes regard themselves as middle class. Milos Forman acknowledged the irony of this turn of events when accepting the Los Angeles Film Critics direction award: "You know, Mozart didn't get any critical prizes during his lifetime. They went to Salieri. I hope receiving such recognition doesn't imply I am a Salieri."

Peter Shaffer's award-winning play was a successful entertainment that promised to turn into an inferior movie, one of those overstuffed, costumed composer biopics with lots of tony music snippets. Milos Forman's film instead converts Shaffer's clever conceit into a profoundly moving and scintillating work of art that vastly overshadows its antecedent.

Admiration for the film *Amadeus* puts one in suspect company, but then the debates over its quality seem mostly beside the point, which assuredly is not whether the masses are 'at least' being exposed to Mozart or whether Mozart's glory and genius is being defamed. The answer to both questions is "of course", followed by "so what?" Mozart's music will take care of his reputation quite nicely for the rest of human history, thank you. He's as fair game for artistic licence as any other eminence. Few leapt to the defence of the hapless historical figures of *Ragtime* (which now looks like a tentative preliminary exploration by Forman of themes more fully realized in *Amadeus*), who arguably have our contemporary ears far less securely than Mozart. Some were sincerely offended by the portrayal of Mozart as a braying, scatalogical vulgarian, considering it slanderous, particularly in light of the splendour of his art. This attitude precisely corresponds to the perceptions of Salieri. Naturally, none of these people recognize this irony: Salieris never do.

Otherwise, sophisticated viewers would doubtless discern a device familiar from literature: the unreliable narrator. The story is related by a dying Salieri, committed to an insane asylum, as a defiant 'confession' to a young priest. He assures Salieri that "all men are equal in God's eyes", a proposition the reptilian composer snorts at. Forman devotes a lot of time to setting up this narrative situation, emphasizing that what we are seeing is Salieri's version of events, coloured not only by his envious subjectivity but also by many years' remove. Salieri relishes his rôle of madman and the rumoured poisoner of Mozart. He's designing a place in history for himself with this priest, as well as playing a mocking game with his lost religious faith.

Nearly all the objections to *Amadeus* as faulty history, scabrous invention or even scurrilous philosophy can be dismissed as dramatically invalid when the film is analysed from the viewpoint of Salieri's narration. Part of the fun, and the profundity, of the film derive from sharing the little cosmic jokes with Salieri. This narrative technique, common as it is in modern literature, rarely works well in films, because movies do not lend themselves either to expressing the consciousness of individual characters or to lying: the concrete reality of images generally conveys too great a presumption of reliability, as Hitchcock discovered in his experiment with a prevaricating flashback in *Stage Fright*.

Salieri signals his unreliability right off, sketching in his background as a basis of class envy that precedes the sexual and professional jealousies that will surface later. In a detail virtually thrown away for comic effect, Salieri invokes the doctrine of God's silence by recalling how ardently he had prayed not for inspiration or genius, but for fame and greatness. In 'answer' to his prayer, his father, a barrier to his musical career, drops dead. Indeed, that is what he was really praying for. So young Salieri embarks on his path to success by the 'murder' of his own father, just as by this confession he is attempting to seal his niche in history by establishing his 'murder' of Mozart.

Salieri's Mozart is, in fact, a projected fantasy image of himself, just as Mozart embodies all Salieri's unattainable dreams and ambitions. Typical of Forman's sly expressive details: just before Salieri first sees Mozart, the cut is from an insert of him reaching for one of his beloved sweets.

Salieri believes that he, perhaps more than anyone else, appreciates the sublime beauty of Mozart's creations. Yet he cannot reconcile the man as he perceives him with the music. Salieri subscribes to the silly notion that confuses a man's character with his talent, finding it insupportable that such an infantile creature should be chosen as a divine instrument. To revenge himself on God, he will destroy Mozart: scheming to have him lose official favour, reducing him to poverty and obscurity, and ultimately oppressing the hapless genius into an early grave.

Shaffer's essential theme here isn't markedly different from his earlier stage success,

Equus, in which another older man of great sensibility and passive passion envies with deep dissatisfaction the creative spirit and active passion of a younger man utterly unlike himself, but over whom he exercises a measure of control. While Shaffer is a skilful playwright of wit and intelligence, he is not by any means a great or profound artist. One might call his works, so popular in his day and so unlikely to endure, the equivalent of Salieri's workmanlike compositions. In Milos Forman's formidable hands, however, *Amadeus* is transformed into a rich meditation on the adversary relation between the artist and society. Society is mediocre, by definition, tending to shun the artist as extraordinary and therefore deviant, even as it lionizes culture and dotes on celebrity.

In the play, the subject is Salieri, and the focus is on his rage, ironies and ruminations. In the film Mozart is not a supporting character to Salieri's sardonic self-flagellation but the actual subject of the story. This externalizes the dramatic tension by balancing the antagonism. More important, it concentrates on the more interesting tale of Mozart's achievements and failures, which, in turn, make Salieri's own damnation more piercing and meaningful. Provocatively, Salieri becomes the classical voyeur to Mozart's exhibitionist.

Mozart is not the *idiot savant* portrayed in the play, babbling out music straight from the soul of the deity. Instead, he is intensely conscious of his music, its integrity and its craft (only Salieris believe that clean first drafts represent an absence of labour). His impassioned defence of *The Marriage of Figaro* argues that 'elevated' themes are not of the essence of profound art; it makes a splendid speech, and he risks the Emperor's censure by challenging even his most amiably offered criticisms. Further, Salieri's association of the Commendatore with Leopold Mozart may not be deep criticism, but it confirms that *Don Giovanni* represents acute personal expression by Mozart.

Amadeus further establishes that Milos Forman is the Lubitsch of our age, extending the canon from *Loves of a Blonde* through *Taking Off* and *Hair*. No other director today examines the varieties of social behaviour so keenly. Salieri and society reject Mozart for his manners, and Forman has always been interested in the relation between normal and deviant conduct. His realization of the eighteenth century world is economical but utterly convincing, but more importantly, he provides a contemporary perspective on the period, avoiding the fallacious goal of mere recreation by instilling the immediacy of modern concerns into his meticulous *mise-en-scène*. Mozart's music is splendidly selected and deployed to enhance the drama, while Forman's subtle choice of angles, cutting, tempo and cunning with his players draws out sublime emotional nuances.

Amadeus has a few niggling flaws. The burlesque of *Don Giovanni* for the groundlings, while it works conceptually in the structure of the piece, makes no sense when the opera had so few performances and none for the masses. More crucially, Mozart's fall from courtly grace, a critical dramatic inflection point, is never specifically dramatized, when a single short scene could have accomplished the goal.

Otherwise, Forman's work bristles with creative inspiration and sound judgements. The decision to use non-star players like F Murray Abraham and Tom Hulce was essential: on the one hand, the aura of mediocre envy of Salieri would have been negated by the privileged relationship a recognizable star has with an audience; and Mozart would not be as poignant in his unconscious self-destruction if we did not feel towards him as a callow, unknown youth. It's superior that Abraham hasn't the stature of a Scofield, and that Hulce captures the ecstatic dudgeon of a brash, brilliant Mozart, making him a dynamic artist rather than merely an obscene hedonist (it improves the calibre of Salieri's imagination, and the ironies of his revenge). Worthy, too, is the shrewdly obtuse characterization of Jeffrey Jones as the Emperor, a dilettante who understands his rôle perfectly as an embodiment of power. (Throughout, Forman's command of political context is refreshingly sophisticated.)

Best of all is the utterly fabricated climax of Salieri taking Mozart's dictation of the *Requiem* from his deathbed. The technical talk invigorates despite the circumstances, and the revelry in the details of inspiration and dutiful collaboration make this perhaps the only time the unalloyed joy of the work of creation has been conveyed dramatically on film. The cross-cutting here evokes a complex symphony of emotions itself. Salieri is plotting to take credit for the composition at Mozart's funeral, but though foiled in that, he nevertheless partakes of Mozart's profundity in his rôle as scrivener and ensures the world of Mozart's final gift. Besides, it is likely just a fantasy of Salieri's anyway, and far more interesting as his invention than as merely that of the authors. In 'murdering' Mozart, Salieri becomes kin to him, a surrogate father killing his child in expiation for having once 'killed' his own father for the musical career exposed by Mozart's genius to have been a valueless lie.

Oscar aside, *Amadeus* was, with *Once Upon a Time in America* and *Choose Me*, the best English-language film of the year. Not to misunderstand, though: it remains somewhat less than a masterpiece. After all, it may be a little too middlebrow.

MYRON MEISEL

ONCE UPON A TIME IN AMERICA

The leading actor in Leone's dreaming epic is not James Woods; nor is it Elizabeth McGovern; nor, for all the excellence of his performance, is it Robert De Niro. The main character in the film is time. The theme is one that has always fascinated Leone. One could point to some of the more obvious symbols in his earlier films like the handless clocks that litter the landscape of *Once Upon a Time in the West*, or the musical fob-watch in *For a Few Dollars More* that was a continuous reminder of rape and revenge and was used to time the final shootout.

In *Once Upon a Time in America* the item which first brings the young Noodles (De Niro) and Max (James Woods) together in their life of crime is a stolen pocket-watch, and it passes between them throughout the film as a kind of talisman. Moreover, the all important keys that can open the left-luggage locker where the gang store their loot are hidden in a grandfather clock. Quite literally, Leone is saying, the key to the mystery is in the clock.

His fascination with time, however, goes far deeper than these surface devices; and here it is necessary to be a little dogged about the film's plotting. In strictly chronological terms, it divides into three phases: 1923, when the adolescent gang – consisting of Noodles, Max, Cockeye, Dominic and Patsy – is formed on the Lower East side of Manhattan; 1933, when after several successful years of illicit trading in hooch the end of prohibition spells an end to the gang's activities, as a result of which Max plans to pull an ambitious bank raid, and Noodles, anxious to avoid their destruction in this mad scheme, betrays them to the police, and they are all slaughtered in the rain; and 1968, when Noodles, after living anonymously in Buffalo

in a self-imposed exile for thirty-five years, returns to New York, summoned by a strange letter which seems to hold a solution to the mysteries he has been pondering while in exile.

He discovers that in fact Max had engineered Noodles into betraying the gang, faked his own death, has stolen Noodles' one true love (Elizabeth McGovern), had a son by her and begun a new life as a successful politician called Secretary Bailey. These are the bare facts with which Noodles is presented, but he can only make true sense of them by a contemplation of his past; and this is exactly what the film recreates. From the

starting point of 1968, it shifts teasingly backwards and forwards in time, in much the same way that human memory does. Time for any of us is rarely chronological; events advance or recede according to their importance. The final despairing weight of history, which bows Noodles' shoulders as an old man, can only make full and immediate tragic sense if the audience is allowed the same to-and-fro connections and flashbacks which Noodles makes in hindsight and which are one of cinema's greatest strengths.

Since this chronological switchback is the main *raison d'être* of the film, it seems all the more ironic that the film

was savagely cut for American audiences, and rearranged into chronological sequence. As Leone himself said in interview at the time: "Vincent Canby of the *New York Times* said the film looks like a trailer. I'm sure he's right, but probably not for reasons that he understands." In fact, this rearrangement must have proved much more difficult than it sounds for Leone pulls off some startling cinematic coups by the audacious use of jump cut. The day after Noodles has supposedly betrayed the gang, and is being pursued by hitmen from the gang's remnants, he goes to Grand Central Station, buys a ticket on the first journey out (to Buffalo as it happens) and leaves through a massive doorway which is surrounded by a collage of advertisements of the period (1933). The camera holds on the frame of the door, while the strains of Paul McCartney's 'Yesterday' can be faintly heard on the soundtrack. Noodles' face, some thirty-five years older then reappears in the glass of the door and the camera pulls back to reveal the same doorway, but now decorated with a huge green apple surrounding it. The time is now 1968 and pop art has arrived within seconds.

Later, after he has returned to the left-luggage locker and retrieved a suitcase full of money and a note saying that this is advance payment for his next and last task, a task whose nature he has yet to learn, he is seen scurrying along under a dark New York elevated highway, clearly fearful that he is being followed. Suddenly a hand swoops to relieve him of the money, but as the film cuts to show us the thief, the hand is revealed as belonging to Max, and the scene is back in the 1930s when Max arrived to greet Noodles upon his release from jail. Noodles' suspicions of being followed were correct, but what is dogging his footsteps is not some modern mugger but his own history, which is only slowly unravelling for him.

This postponement of immediate answers is also clearly the film's design upon its audience as well as Noodles' main suspense. And it is a theme which Leone plainly signals right at the outset. Noodles is first seen on the night after his betrayal of the gang to a police sergeant on the telephone. He has escaped to a Chinese opium den and taken flight in a drug induced reverie. On the film's soundtrack a telephone begins to ring. It continues through several more scenes, scenes which he is clearly remembering in his fantasy, but the jangling will not desist even when he is seen to lift the receiver. The audience is gradually made aware that this insistent ringing is part of De Niro's recurrent nightmare, a ghost from what he believes was his single act of betrayal when he phoned the police. The nightmare invades his whole life, infects him with a terrible guilt, and reduces him to the point where not even the film's final extraordinary revelations can move him to action. When Leone was asked why he had chosen to concentrate on a Jewish gang rather than the more usual Mafia, he replied: "Because I think they were more dangerous. In reality the Italians exported a load of peasants, and later re-imported the Mafia gangsters. But the Jews were more subtle. They sat behind desks. They made telephone calls. And, as we all know, a telephone call can be more deadly than a gun."

More deadly, but also much more effective as a warning to the audience not to take the film on a realistic level. Noteworthy, too, is one of the credited scriptwriters – Enrico Medioli, specifically imported by Leone because he had written a screenplay of *A la Recherche du Temps Perdu* for Visconti, just one of the many possible Proust films that never got made.

Of course the film is a great celebration of all that was wonderful about the old Hollywood gangster movies.

There is no European director, *pace* Wenders, who is more in love with the conventions of Hollywood genres than Leone. Apparently the script for *Once Upon a Time in the West*, partly written by Bertolucci, consisted entirely of quotes from both dialogue and incident in Hollywood Westerns. But while he pays direct homage in . . . *America* with quotes from everything from the original *Scarface* to *The Great Gatsby*, he is still acting as a commentator on the genre, sometimes picking it apart at the seams, sometimes showing up the glaring faults.

The notorious rape scene, in which an enraged Noodles, driven to distraction at the prospect of losing his beloved Deborah (Elizabeth McGovern) for ever, savagely rapes her in the back of the car taking her to the station, is dwelt on at such unconscionable length and with such insistent nastiness that it would seem unimaginable that anyone might derive prurient pleasure from it. In this scene, and in many others, Leone is saying, "Look: you used to think that gangsters were heroes. They are not. They are men who get rich by extortion and murder. They are violent. And they are so emotionally stunted that they cannot relate to a woman as far above their station as Deborah undoubtedly is by any other mode than violence."

But perhaps the greatest

departure from the genre lies in the portrayal of Noodles by De Niro. We have become used to screen gangsters who are men of near superhuman abilities (see the recent De Palma *Scarface*, a man who could emerge from *mountains* of cocaine with a regularity that would fell an ox). Their goals are much the same as anyone else's – money and beautiful women and power – but their route to these goals tends not to be circumscribed by the tedious scruples that bother the majority of men still stuck in the rut of legality. Noodles, however, is resoundingly ordinary. Deborah tells him as an adolescent that she will never love him because he will never be anything more than a "two bit punk", and indeed this proves true; when he hires an enormous beachside restaurant complete with orchestra in order to woo her, the effect is one of sumptuous vulgarity; he doesn't even know what wine to order.

Thirty-five years in Buffalo doing nothing except going to bed early is likely to take its toll on anyone, but in the sections set in 1968, De Niro turns in a portrait of disillusioned old age of incredible authenticity. Leone reported: "We would finish the day's shooting and he would stagger back to his trailer without any spring in his step. He wouldn't go out in the evenings. He was always cold like an old man and wanted extra clothes. You can

watch the film solely for his performance and it is a different experience every time."

The weight of time and the guilt of betrayal have taken their toll on Noodles. When he finally confronts Max in his new incarnation as the successful politician, the final task required of him is that he shoot Max who is facing political scandal. Noodles cannot even bring himself to be revenged on the man who stole his life. Too worn out and demoralized to accede to Max's demands he wanders outside to watch some revellers pass by in a series of thirties convertibles. The immediate memory recalled is from *The Great Gatsby* with its ghosts of wealth, gaiety and enormous waste. 'God Bless America' can be heard faintly on the soundtrack. And then Noodles witnesses Max throw himself into the back of a passing garbage–grinder truck, or so it appears. It would be hard to imagine a more bizarre or disgusting end to an empire.

Noodles, who once had everything, is reduced to a rag of a man, bent and broken by time. He has nothing left to him but his memories of the opium den where he had once taken refuge on the night of the betrayal. The film's final image is of his opium-sodden smile at some shadows on the wall caused by the Chinese puppet show in the den. It may not be much, but it is everything that is cinema.
CHRIS PEACHMENT

BEVERLY HILLS COP/ WITNESS

Beverly Hills Cop and *Witness* have been amply acknowledged as two of the most successful films of the year in the United States. Indeed, the Eddie Murphy picture has emerged as a monster, having become both the highest-grossing comedy of all-time and the biggest money-earner in screen history not to have Steven Spielberg's or George Lucas' names attached to it. *Witness*, while nowhere near that level, nevertheless represents a stunning commercial breakthrough for Peter Weir, the Australian director heretofore associated with critically respected but only modestly profitable pictures.

What has not been remarked upon is that these two films are, in blueprint form if not in treatment, virtually the same movie. Released domestically less than two months apart and by the same company, Paramount, both concern big-city policemen whose unorthodox methods of investigating murder cases lead them to territory so different from their home turf that they seem like aliens in a foreign country, if not another world. With the major difference that *Witness* involves a tentative romance, while *Beverly Hills Cop* features no love interest whatsoever, the dramatic progression of both films is practically the same, and both end with the inevitable shoot-out between the good guys and bad guys.

That the films' striking fundamental similarity has gone largely undetected stands as a tribute to the artistic success of both films on their own terms. With such functionally identical leading men and plot lines, it is hard to imagine the two films emerging with any more distinct personalities than they do. One, after all, is a raucous comedy that most people consider a one-man show, while the other depends greatly upon texture and finely graded performances for its impact. For two pictures that basically start and finish at the same respective points, the differences in the ways they affect audiences are enormous. At the same time, both satisfy to greater degrees than the vast majority of Hollywood studio-produced entertainments in recent years.

At the heart of the two films is the outrageous, almost implausible contrast between the policemen and the extreme environments in which they find themselves. Within the context of the mainstream commercial cinema, greater-than-usual care has been devoted to what might be called ethnological authenticity of the primary, exotic settings. In both cases, the skill with which these backgrounds are presented are decisive factors in the films' successes.

For decades, Beverly Hills has widely been exploited by films and television for its glamorous image, and audiences for pictures from *A Star is Born* to *Shampoo* have been drawn, at least in part, by the prospect of seeing the most celebrated of American suburbs laid out before their eyes. *Beverly Hills Cop* is rare among these films for having virtually nothing to do with show business, and is certainly better for it. What it capitalizes upon instead is the contrast between the community's white, rich and

uptight ruling class and the wide range of weird outsiders and foreigners, of whom Eddie Murphy's Detroit cop is by far the lowest on the totem pole. The reigning establishment is duly represented by the straight-arrow members of the local police force, but otherwise, Beverly Hills is populated by people who, in their own ways, are at least as strange as Murphy. The principal villain is English (Steven Berkoff), a man even more accustomed to violence than Murphy and clearly given to offbeat tastes, while the most noticeable cameo is Bronson Pinchot's priceless, Peter Sellers-like impersonation of the young art gallery employee of indeterminate origin whose own line of jive one-ups Murphy's.

Working familiar genre terrain, the film-makers have managed to pick the right symbols of affluence, heightening their reality just so for the desired satirical effect – the art gallery with its *outré* centrepiece exhibit, the stuffy hotel willing to back down from Murphy at the mention of Michael Jackson's name, the posh restaurant whose *maître d'* is similarly bamboozled by Murphy. Accurately enough, the Beverly Hills portrayed in the film is one characterized first and foremost by a status-oriented attitude, and the main source of humour stems from Murphy's brazen assault on a society possessed of one of the most refined caste systems in the world.

Whereas the inhabitants of Beverly Hills might be fully expected to have telephones in their automobiles, the citizens in *Witness* possess neither phones nor cars. Rarely in an American-set film has such a rigorously exclusive minority community been so extensively depicted as has

the Amish one here, and the film-makers have managed, in graceful and unlaborious fashion, to get across the fundamentals of a religious group of which few Americans had probably ever heard before seeing the film. Weir has handled the Amish with much respect, and generates such a feeling of warmth that one can only fault him and the writers for idealizing them; even atheists might admit to sensing something resembling nostalgic, sentimentalized emotions in the face of a community so simple, upstanding and pure, especially when contrasted to the dirty, nasty world lurking around its edges. They must be doing something right, one feels, if they have so successfully kept the evil influences of modern society at bay for so long.

One of the brimming ironies stemming from a comparison of the two pictures, one that sends curious, mixed signals in this conservative American era, is that the simple, religious virtues of the Amish have been painted so much more favourably and benevolently than have the more popular secular charms of BevHills. In the Reagan Age of shameless wealth and unembarrassed

materialism, no location could better embody what is revered today than Beverly Hills; nevertheless, everyone gets a great kick out of seeing its smarmy residents and officials cut down to size by someone as hip and streetwise as Murphy. The actor's personality is so strong that prevailing standards must bend to him; he's always right, and the audience gets off watching him prove it.

Witness inordinately simplifies Amish life, making it appealing by stressing the importance of the work ethic, and glosses over off-putting elements, such as religious orthodoxy and the inferior status of women. But the film is made sufficiently complex, if not realistic, by the fact that neither policeman Harrison Ford nor the Amish are always right. Each side has things to learn from the other and any viewer who believes in peaceful coexistence can probably take a measure of satisfaction in the melancholy conclusion.

The reticence of the romance at the heart of *Witness* plays a major part in the film's effectiveness, and the danger of a sexual relationship for Ford and Kelly McGillis infuses their barn tryst with an eroticism

seldom seen in American films these days. By contrast, the most sexual Eddie Murphy becomes in *Beverly Hills Cop* is when he hilariously poses as Berkoff's gay lover. Blacks, especially of the comic variety, may be acceptable as movie stars, but sex – so much a part of the stage acts of both Murphy and Richard Pryor – is taboo. The recent breakdance pictures represented models of racial harmony, but even the physically precocious young stars of these films were denied their natural sexual interests. *Beverly Hills Cop* is a buddy-buddy picture in which one of them – Murphy's white best friend – is dead. By the same token, in *Witness*, Ford's closest ally on the police force is black, and his death prompts a crucial dramatic move in the story.

The two pictures even bear a resemblance in the manner in which their respective directors were chosen. It was former Paramount production head Robert Evans who, having selected Roman Polanski to make *Chinatown* after the latter's *Macbeth*, articulated the theory of deliberately hiring talented directors when they're cold from a flop, rather than riding high after a

success, in order to get the commercial best out of them. Martin Brest could not have been colder after being fired from *WarGames*, but his ease with Murphy's improvisational comic brilliance is perfectly in line with his taste for Ray Sharkey's inspired jabbering in *Hot Tomorrows*. Not dissimilarly, Peter Weir stood in a momentary limbo after *The Mosquito Coast* failed to gel last year and took on his first American-based production at a moment's notice. At the same time, his lush, almost suffocatingly intense portraits of the Pennsylvania landscape often parallel his humid, threatening evocations of Australian tropics in *The Last Wave*.

Finally, both films are genre pieces that triumph by parading successfully as something else: *Beverly Hills Cop* as an insolent, terribly hip stand-up comedy routine; *Witness* as an achingly tender cross-cultural love story. Neither is necessarily easy to pull off, and their commercial acceptance stands as a sign of how cleverly the disguises have been worn.

TODD MCCARTHY

A PASSAGE TO INDIA

David Lean has always been a master of transition, of the shift from one scene to another, done with such skill that the change seems inevitable and becomes an integral part of the narrative. Perhaps he was attracted to E M Forster's *A Passage to India* because it is, in hindsight, essentially a novel about transition: about the start of the shift from the British Raj to Indian independence, of the end of an era of separate states and the beginning of a nation and, on a personal level, of a change in attitudes. Aziz becomes a hater of all things English, Mrs Moore moves from the serenity of faith to a belief in an indifferent universe, Adela Quested from unquestioned certainties to understood doubts.

Forster abandoned novels after *A Passage to India*. Lean has returned to film-making with the story after an absence of fourteen years, and returned triumphantly. If he failed to win an Oscar, there were nevertheless enough other awards, not to mention

success at the box office, to satisfy his pride – so wounded, he claimed, by the New York critics' personal attacks on him at the time of *Ryan's Daughter* that he no longer wanted to make films.

Lean's directorial approach is an old-fashioned one, though none the worse for that. He is primarily a story-teller and he uses all the old narrative tricks to keep our attention. His style was established a long time ago. In *The Bridge on the River Kwai*, for instance, the camera pans to the blazing disc of the sun in the sky and then moves back to earth – and to a scene miles away, with William Holden sweating through the jungle. That is a perfect transition from one scene to another, as well as a cinematic technique no longer in favour among younger directors who prefer more abrupt jumps. Such style is part of the charm of *A Passage to India* which is, at least, a display of almost forgotten skills and, at best, a distinguished and gripping narrative. Even if it is never

quite E M Forster's novel, it is still an object lesson in film-making, in making money – and images – count.

Take just one moment. The train carrying Mrs Moore, Adela Quested and representatives of the Raj passes over a high bridge. As it trundles across with the wheels making – to quote Forster – "a pomper, pomper, pomper sound", the noise is echoed by a hacking cough and there is a cut to beneath the bridge, where a group of wretched Indians lie huddled and pain-wracked. Then the sound is echoed again by the thumping of a bass drum and Lean, who is his own editor, cuts to a military band and the glittering regimental ceremony of welcome for the Collector.

It is the repeated variations on the sound that binds the scenes together, but the images play against each other too, resonating as they do so. The train, with its British passengers high and uncaring above the Indian Poor, and the contrast in light – the train resplendent in the

rays of the setting sun, the beggars crouching in darkness, the sudden glare of bright sunshine for the procession – deftly combine to provide an instant apprehension of the social and racial complexities, of the distance between the English and the Indians.

Forster's book is not an easy one to film. The hesitancies and indecisions of the text do not translate well and many of the characters, particularly the British with their desire to flog every native in sight and call in the army at the first hint of trouble, are crude caricatures. Lean was attacked by Christopher Hitchens in the *Times Literary Supplement* for "his boring stereotype of the British as teak-headed fools", which suggests that Hitchens has never read Forster. Lean's film is more balanced in depicting the English than Forster's novel. He allows them their humanity and achieves a greater reality than Forster's coarse, unthinking blimps.

The film has roused the anger of many close to Forster, notably Santha Rama Rau, who turned the book into an effective play by the device of ignoring the last third of the book and concentrating on the court-room drama. There are mistakes in social or religious nuance, such as Godbole, the high-caste Brahmin, paddling with Adela Quested and the Muslim Aziz. Lean's India is much less dirty than Forster's. There are no flies in the film – not even that central mass, hanging from the light flex in Aziz's squalid bedroom that occasionally arouses his shame.

The novel is a literary confidence trick. To the question of what did happen in the Marabar caves, Forster gave the answer that he didn't know. In a letter to William

Plomer, he wrote that he tried "to show that India is an unexplainable muddle by introducing an unexplained muddle". But it is one thing to leave something unexplained, and another not to be able to explain it – particularly in a novel where the writer, God-like, is able to articulate the thoughts as well as the words and actions of his characters.

Forster's failure to know is a failure of nerve, a liberal cop-out – a suburban timidity that fits well with the book's place of origin (Weybridge, 1924). It also suggests, and a reading of the book confirms, that Forster was never really engaged by his creations – "the characters are not sufficiently interesting for the atmosphere," he wrote in a contemporary letter. His early stories, collected in *The Celestial Omnibus*, are literally and literarily full of Panic and Pandemonium – of the presence of the great goat-footed god of the Greeks – and such pagan whimsy (characteristic of other Edwardian homosexual writers) seems to have carried over to the Marabar Caves in Adela's encounter with something alien and inhuman.

Lean's filming of this central scene stays very close to Forster. Indeed, his film has a greater fidelity to Forster's novel than Santha Rama Rau's play, for he keeps in proportion the court scenes – the novel deals with them in less than one chapter out of thirty-seven – and provides a wider context to grapple with the complexities of the story. He fails, though, with Mrs Moore, despite Peggy Ashcroft's Oscar-winning performance in the rôle. To quote Forster again, "Mrs Moore does not signify." Lean has not provided the dialogue with which she can explain what happens to her at the Marabar Caves, which is something far more terrible than happens to Adela. Instead, he relies on Ashcroft's powers of expression, and great though these are they cannot convey, without some words, the despair – "nothing has value" – that consumes her soul and her desire to live.

Lean gets good performances from all the cast, with James Fox outstanding as Fielding. Alec Guinness's performance has met with jibes about Peter Sellers' impersonations, but he seems to me to capture perfectly that air of saintliness and silliness that is found in Forster. Guinness is, as Godbole should be, both mystic and clown. Victor Banerjee's Aziz has an appropriate hectic charm.

Lean's best invention is Judy Davis – too attractive to be entirely convincing as Adela – riding her bicycle to a ruined temple, where she is frightened by monkeys scrambling among erotic sculpture – a correlation of her own inner fears that marks her retreat from sexual stirrings, and is a forerunner of her headlong flight from the caves.

Lean, possibly limited by his budget (the film cost $16 million), has not gone for the blockbuster treatment of his more recent films. *A Passage to India* is more intimate than epic in its style, and all the more effective for its concentration of the various pairings of the central relationships – Adela and Ronnie, Mrs Moore and Aziz, Aziz and Fielding, Fielding and Adela – as they try, and fail, to connect with one another. His main concession to the felt wishes of audiences is to sweeten the ending, providing a greater reconciliation between Aziz and Fielding than the novel does, which empasizes the impossibility of an equal relationship between the two men. Yet Forster's "not yet" was written before India gained her independence. In this post-imperialist age, a belief in the possibility of equality between the two men is a justifiable alteration.

The film is finely directed, beautifully photographed, gives James Fox his best rôle since he returned to film acting, is faithful to Forster in all that matters and shows that Lean has lost none of his impeccable skills. He is making films again, and good ones. What more can one ask? Only, perhaps, that he makes some more.

JOHN WALKER

101

THE KILLING FIELDS

Weighing up the relative merits of 1984's Oscar-nominated Best Films, Sheila Benson, the *Los Angeles Times* critic, hazarded that, forty years hence, *The Killing Fields* will be adjudged the most considerable of a distinguished quintet. While *Amadeus* went on to trawl the bulk of ephemeral honours, *The Killing Fields* nosed ahead of both *A Passage to India* and *Places in the Heart* for the crumbs. Not such crumbs either, with the film's three Academy Awards usefully pointing up its cornerstone trio of essential strengths – construction/pace, look and performance.

The movie's initial miracle is that it's British. This isn't by way of being a mindlessly chauvinistic observation, rather a stark statement of fact: £10 million expended by a British financier on, for the most part, British creative and technical talent telling a, superficially, obscure story from the Third World with American reverberations. There was no real precedent. It was simply – though matters like these are rarely simple – a question of backing talent and letting it get on with it.

David Puttnam had first gleaned the hint of a movie from a single column wrap-up piece in *Time* which told of the emotional reunion of *New York Times* reporter Sydney Schanberg with his former stringer, Cambodian Dith Pran, in Thailand. After the Khmer Rouge takeover and the evacuation of Phnom Penh by the Americans (and all Western journalists) in 1975, Pran was left behind to suffer terrible privations for the next four-and-a-half years under the Red yoke. Schanberg, devastated at having to leave Pran to his fate, returned home to collect glittering prizes for his Cambodian coverage, which he knew would not have been possible without Pran's help. The personal story had a happy ending even if the backcloth was of a genocide of some three million people in a revolution "more radical and brutal", wrote Schanberg, "than any other in modern history."

Puttnam approached Schanberg about the possibility of a film on the subject only to be told that the journalist was about to turn the whole story into a major *New York Times* magazine piece – entitled *The Death and Life of Dith Pran* – which was then likely to be up for grabs to the highest bidder. It was published in January 1980, and Puttnam, who had secured $200,000 from a company called International Film Investors (which used to be in partnership with Goldcrest, the film's eventual backers), put in his bid. On the day he started shooting *Chariots of Fire*, he acquired the rights to a project which, then, still had the same working title as the article.

Early on, from IFI, there was some pressure on Puttnam to develop the film as a package (Sidney Lumet as director, Paddy Chayevsky as writer and Dustin Hoffman as star), which was strenuously resisted by the independently minded producer. The first thing was to get a workable screenplay and for this he turned to 'unknown' Bruce Robinson, a handsome, if stodgy, British actor in films like *The Brute* and Truffaut's *L'Histoire d'Adele H,* but probably best-known publicly as a one-time lover of Lesley-Anne Down. In fact, away from the gossip columns, Robinson had become a full-time writer, completing three unproduced screenplays for Puttnam before being assigned the Schanberg-Pran story. For Puttnam, Robinson always had one unshakable quality about all his writing – *passion*, a very un-British trait, the producer regularly asserts, in connection with indigenous big-screen adaptation.

Directorially the choice, two years further on, rested between the tried Louis Malle and the television-experienced, if cinema-untested, Roland Joffé. Puttnam, following his tradition of boosting first-time helmers (Alan Parker, Ridley Scott and Hugh Hudson) settled on Joffé, not for any altruistic motive but because he felt the director would be able to "sublimate his ego completely to the issue in hand." With Malle, there might have been the danger of the piece becoming "Louis's film".

As for casting, they eventually settled on an anonymous star Sam Waterston, as Schanberg, and, most remarkably, a doctor called Haing S Ngor to play Pran. (With hindsight, the selection of Ngor seems all the more inspired in view of his own amazing story which would make an astonishing movie in its own right. Like Pran, he too was a Cambodian 'intellectual' who after suffering terribly under the Khmer Rouge finally managed to make his escape, but not before his closest family was decimated. Joffé first met him when Ngor was working in Los Angeles as an assistant supervisor for the Indo-Chinese Employment Programme.) Thailand was selected to double for Cambodia, and in May 1983, the movie began shooting.

The result is a film which, despite its long gestation, has kept its principal ingredient, passion, unswervingly intact. For whatever faults there are in the screenplay – and there

are quite a few – *The Killing Fields* continuously burns with a heat and energy that defies you to underestimate it.

Of course, a movie's a movie and real life's often quite another thing, so one never quite knows how much licence is implicit when a film contends it's a true story. It's worth pointing out that Robinson's screenplay has

safe and well. Later, before he went to Thailand, Pran visited the Killing Fields – as a tourist. Not quite the stuff of movies, of which this movie is never less than chock-full.

Wondrously designed by Roy Walker and vividly photographed by Chris Menges, every frame is packed with incident and emotion, whether on a huge

'Imagine' which blares intrusively at the finale over an already emotion-packed reunion between the two men.

This helps underscore the critical contention that *The Killing Fields* is, above all, a producer's film which, in itself, goes part of the way towards explaining the intriguing theory that the movie could be viewed as a

idealism but his innate understanding of the basic needs of the mass cinema audience. Americans will, after all, take only so much self-flagellation, yet their toleration of intelligent Red-bashing seems limitless.

This makes *The Killing Fields* appear both naive and simplistic which may, to a certain extent, be true. But

opted for a slightly different version of events in dealing with Pran's last days in Cambodia.

The film tells us that having finally managed to slip away from his Khmer Rouge overlords, Pran gets over the border into Thailand by way of a horrifying trek through the Killing Fields of the title. History *actually* relates that, after the Vietnamese subsequently invaded Cambodia and the Khmer Rouge were driven back to the hills and forests – there was no love lost between these rival Communist factions – Pran became mayor of his home town of Siem Reap. At this time some foreign journalists visited the town and Pran was able to get a message out via one of them to Schanberg saying he was

canvas of battle or picking out a single child trying to block its ears to the horror all around. Less convincing is the depiction of the press, somehow at its least attractive but, arguably, at its most effective in war. Schanberg comes over as a bit of a prig and, perhaps intentionally, a shade unsympathetic. (In this aspect, *The Killing Fields* is decidedly inferior to, say, Roger Spottiswoode's *Under Fire* which wears a valid cloak of cynicism that might have well suited Joffé's film.)

Its success is not one of subtlety but as an epic pitched on a relentless visual and emotional level. Which perhaps excuses the film's two other excesses – a patchwork score by Mike Oldfield, and the use of John Lennon's

reworking of *Chariots of Fire*. Two men of different faiths winning their respective 'races' against all odds. It's a matter of record that Bruce Robinson's original extreme anti-American stance was toned down in the development of the screenplay; Roland Joffé's well-known left wing sympathies, which found expression in television work like *The Spongers* and *United Kingdom*, were clearly sublimated here along with his ego. So while we initially survey the detritus of American imperialism, it's nothing in comparison to the ensuing Red holocaust which makes the world of George Orwell's *Nineteen Eighty-Four* seem positively cushy. This emphasis has much to do not only with Puttnam's own

then, the film is much more to do with people caught up in events than events themselves. So while we may not care hugely for Schanberg the man, we are made to feel his guilt acutely. And thanks to Ngor's outstanding performance (for which Roland Joffé must surely take vast credit), Pran becomes a figure of truly heroic dimensions.

It is, to return to my original thesis, a British film triumph, all the more triumphant because cool, detached understatement – the norm in indigenous film-making – has been substituted by white hot commitment. The change, though startling, makes for a riveting, refreshing and extremely bold movie.

QUENTIN FALK

GHOSTBUSTERS

Without America, there could have been no *Ghostbusters*, just as without America there could be no Ronald Reagan. You win some and you lose some.

Ghostbusters is in that great Hollywood tradition of moronic inspiration which gave the world an eyesore that became a cynosure (the Hollywood sign), a 100-foot-high monument made of rubbish that became the city's most famous sculpture (the Watts Towers), and of course the Three Stooges.

Hollywood is where all the greatest morons find their fullest scope. Yes, this town has no shame. In *Ghostbusters*, the best silly movie in years, there isn't a shred of sense, not a single redeeming thread of thought. It's two hours of heaven for 12-year-olds.

The film crosses a gang comedy with a horror spoof, so that if the earthbound gags ever flag, the supernatural can have a whirl. It's the most spectacular and expensive comedy since Spielberg's *1941*, but unlike that turkey *Ghostbusters* never makes the mistake of letting the special effects experts become jokebusters.

It's true that the film's ending is a bit too long on flashy gee-whizzery and a bit short on laughs, but most of the time when the disembodied presences appear on screen, they're there for laughs. Most memorable among the manifestations are the fiend that materializes from the puschcart hamper with a bunch of hot dogs in its mouth, and the taxi driver who wears a standard cabbie's hat – but underneath the hat he turns out to have a decomposing skull instead of a face.

Generally, though, the actors provide the movie's best moments. Bill Murray,

Harold Ramis and Dan Aykroyd are Venkman, Spengler and Stantz, respectable professors of the paranormal at New York University. But their research grant runs out and they are forced to take their diabolical expertise into the marketplace. Demonstrating that Reaganism's stress on free enterprise isn't misplaced, these cloistered academics thrive in the real world of business. More than most, they know how to make the invisible hand of capitalism shell out.

It turns out that just at that time New York is being plagued with enough ectoplasmic appearances to populate a summerful of poltergeist movies. But our intrepid 'paranormal investigators' remain unspooked. They battle these little devils to a standstill until they must face the ultimate incorporeality, a King Kong-sized spirit from the vasty deep, the Stay-Puft Marshmallow Man.

Let's honour Bill Murray now as the world's funniest living white comedian, instead of waiting until he's decrepit as we did with Charlie Chaplin. It is Murray who makes the $30 million cost of *Ghostbusters* pay off. The film's idea and even its title are lifted from earlier laff riots (the Bowery Boys' 1946 *Spook Busters* and 1957 *Spook Chasers*). But Murray's comedy is fully mid-eighties in its cool egocentrism.

An early sequence shows off Murray's flippant wit at its best. Tackling their first demon-destroying job, our three heroes see how formidable these phantoms really are. One of these ghoulish greedy-guts whistles down a hotel corridor, leaving piles of destruction and pools of exteriorised protoplasm in its slipstream. Murray staggers out of the scummy wreckage and cries in outrage and astonishment, "He slimed me!" The phrase became 1984's contribution to the list of most-often-repeated movie lines, along with *Sudden Impact*'s "Go ahead, punk, make my day."

Murray is a rumpled semi-competent who always makes his adversaries say uncle because of his supreme self-confidence. Nothing that goes wrong is his fault because he invariably has a blame-shifting explanation. He gets his own way because getting his own way is all he ever thinks about. He's a grown-up 12-year-old who's so cute he's forgiven everything.

Later in the film Murray and his pals are called on the carpet. On hand is their nemesis, the city inspector William Atherton. Aykroyd says it was all the fault of this "dickless wonder". Atherton claims that isn't true. "Well, is it true?" Murray is asked. "Yes, it's true," Murray says. "This man has no dick."

That's a classic nonsense put-down, made fresh by Murray's impudent scatology. A similar air of precocious pubescence hangs over Murray's pursuit of statuesque ice-maiden Sigourney Weaver, in whose fridge reside the Beasties from Beyond. At one point, Murray is present in Weaver's *Rosemary's Baby*-ish flat when Weaver becomes possessed and begins coming on to him. Thinking quickly, he says, "I have a rule not to become involved with possessed people . . . actually, it's more of a guideline."

This gag is virtually spoken to the camera. Murray has created his own one-on-one relationship with the audience. He speaks almost directly to them, functioning as a stand-in for them on the screen. He's in the movie and commenting on it at the same time. That's why Murray became a star in *Meatballs* in spite of the fact that it was such a predictable vehicle: the star of the movie seemed like he was sitting in the same row as the hecklers throwing popcorn at the screen.

When Murray suppresses his subversive personality and becomes part of the movie he's in – when he becomes an actor, not a comedian – he

disappears. In *Tootsie*, he dutifully served his function as a necessary element in the dramatis personae and then left the screen and the audience's memory simultaneously. Nor does his range include straight leading man parts, as *The Razor's Edge* showed. Murray appeared in *Ghostbusters*, incidentally, only because Columbia agreed to finance

identified as the late John Belushi's sidekick, are also adept gag-timers in their own right. They ought to be able to play these jokes right – they wrote them.

Aykroyd produced the complex original screenplay, building a fantastic superstructure on the simple premise of the title. The Aykroyd-Ramis final draft left plenty of room for

other elements have dominated. One of his most valuable skills is remaining silent, just standing there looking quizzical while the audience work up their anticipation for the payoff they know he'll deliver.

The wise director paces Murray through the movie, avoiding too great an involvement in the plot. *Ghostbusters*' director, the

The Razor's Edge.

It's the on-the-sidelines aspect of Murray's humour that causes him to work best as a member of an anarchic ensemble. Previous group triumphs have included *Caddyshack*, which co-starred Chevy Chase and Rodney Dangerfield, and *Stripes*, which co-starred Ramis and John Candy. The cornier the set-up, the more Murray will shine: just play the old gags and then focus on Murray's reaction.

In *Ghostbusters*, as in his other films, Murray doesn't hog the camera. Rick Moranis has some good bits as Weaver's neighbour and lovesick lapdog. Ramis, who remains better known as a director (*Caddyshack* and *National Lampoon's Vacation*), and Aykroyd, still

Murray's improvisations. If comedy ever received respect at Academy Award time, their mantelpieces would be full. They must, unfortunately, be content with being multi-millionaires beloved by millions. As for Aykroyd's and Ramis' function as actors in *Ghostbusters*, however, it's mainly to fill out the perimeter of the frame and give the screen something to do while the audience picks themselves up out of the aisles after Murray's jokes.

No stand-up comedian, Murray needs something strong to react against. Unlike Richard Pryor or Eddie Murphy, Murray isn't comfortable basing routines on his own personality. His biggest laughs are one-liners coming at the ends of scenes

Czech-born Canadian Ivan Reitman, is experienced at organizing Murray-vehicle gang comedies. In fact, Reitman could be called the godfather of the aggressive style of non-Jewish undergraduate comedy that has dominated movies since the success of *Animal House* (1978), which he produced. Reitman was the man *National Lampoon* publisher Matty Simmons hired to translate the Lampoon's literary humour into other media. Comics whose careers Reitman fostered in his radio and stage shows later starred on TV's *Saturday Night Live* and now star in Reitman's movies. For discovering Murray, if for nothing else, Reitman deserves immortality.

BART MILLS

STARMAN

A few years ago, in the wake of the extraneous *Escape from New York* and the malodorous *The Thing,* it might have seemed appropriate to ask: Whatever happened to John Carpenter?

When Carpenter sprang into prominence with *Assault on Precinct 13,* he seemed like a film-maker who had the instinctive skill to create equivalents of the unparalleled programme pictures of Hollywood's past that amounted to more than reductive pastiche or self-conscious homage. *Precinct 13* may be enriched for *cognoscenti* by its allusions to Hawks and *Rio Bravo,* but its effectiveness does not depend on them; intra-mural knowingness is subsumed into executive know-how.

At that time, Carpenter confided that he wanted to

make a horror film, "a really scary one", and with *Halloween* he succeeded, probably beyond anyone's and certainly beyond the box-office's expectations, in creating a cinematic machine for saying boo. All the same, *Halloween* is hardly surfeited with story-telling substance, and in the later light of *Escape from New York* and *The Thing,* one began to fear that Carpenter had come to identify modernist genre cinema with no more than sensationalism and special effects.

In *The Thing* (which, symbolically enough, was not so much a remake as an anti-remake of the old Hawks picture of the same name), the high-tech metamorphoses are certainly horrific enough to make anyone shut their eyes, except that the enervation of

the surrounding narrative is such that the viewer's eyes may well have already closed in slumber.

Consequently one approached *Christine* with low expectations, which the film promptly caused one to revise upwards. *Christine* may be at base a formula picture, one of the sundry Stephen King adaptations about demonic persons or objects which virtually constitute a sub-genre unto themselves. But it is formulaic in the most fruitful sense; whilst Carpenter does not seek (as fashionable jargon has it) to subvert or transcend his material, he brings to it the qualities of pacing and observation which makes the film more than the illustration of a script or the demonstration of a gimmick.

Christine is a special effects

movie; but if the set-piece sequences are its commercial *raison d'etre,* it is the framework surrounding them – the evocation of a California small town, the judicious balance between realism and caricature in the incidental characterizations – which holds the film together. The movie evinces that brand of total craftsmanship which makes the line between *auteur* and *metteur-en-scene* seem thin indeed. And if the 'impersonal' element of the movie (though in some respects it revisits the terrain of *Halloween* with more pointedness and wit) brings Carpenter closer to the model of a Michael Curtiz than a Howard Hawks, one can only rejoin, heretical though the view might once have been, that some of Curtiz's pictures have stood the test of time a good deal better than some of Hawks'.

It seems appropriate in two ways to approach *Starman* by way of its director's antecedent history. For one thing, Carpenter clearly wishes to annex himself to the Hollywood tradition in which a film-maker's creative personality emerges from within a succession of disparate and/or convention-bound projects ("If I had three wishes," he once said, "one of them would be, send me back to the 1940s studio system"). And for another, *Starman* intimates, albeit perhaps unconsciously, a turning point: its deeper interest lies in how it diverges from what Carpenter has done before.

The flying saucer shots with which *Starman* opens might suggest, a bit discouragingly for some of us, that we are in for another excursion into space opera; there might seem to be a rattling of the familiar box of tricks in the hocus-pocus attaching to the arrival on American soil of an extraterrestrial visitor on what proves to be a fact-finding mission, and in his on-camera transformation into the shape of Jeff Bridges, whose premature demise has left Karen Allen a desolate widow. But the movie comes down to earth in more than the literal sense. As Bridges coerces the understandably disconcerted Allen into driving him halfway across America to a rendezvous point, *Starman* abandons high-tech sorcery and flying saucery and turns toward its audience the human face of sci-fi.

In a way, what ensues is a suspense story, with the tried-and-true premise of the race against time by parties whom an opposing faction, in this case suspicious American officialdom, is out to stop. But the film also has a generic component of more recent vintage: rather as *Christine* enlisted the conventions of teenage melodrama, *Starman* resembles the road movies of the early seventies, though it incorporates an element of more traditional romantic comedy in a form which predominantly illustrated male bonding relationships. (Or possibly, thinking back to *It Happened One Night,* it would be more appropriate to say that this element is re-incorporated.)

As *Starman* hits the road, as the comic misunderstandings pile up

(the interloper has only limited English and is quite unacquainted with the etiquette of the rest room) and Allen's suspicions turn to sympathy and fondness for the humane non-human, what one senses is a loosening up on Carpenter's part – not, certainly, in technique but in style.

A new subjectivity is at work, a concern with character and its interplay for their own sake rather than as counters in a plot. If it is something of a surprise to find a Carpenter movie boasting a PG certificate, it is hardly less of one, though certainly gratifying, to realize that a player in one has received an Oscar nomination – and Jeff Bridges' performance is beautifully accomplished, full of humorous detail, touching without ingratiating; Karen Allen, too, has an affecting quality of the commonsensical and uncosmetic.

The film, however, keeps very much on the move, and no less important than the foreground action is the shifting background against which it is played out – lacklustre diners, a bustling motel, sweeping vistas of landscape and highway. Moreover, if Carpenter is greatly aided by the Panavision camerawork of Donald M Morgan, graphic and modulated in a way that never calls attention to itself,

the contribution of the screenwriters, Bruce A Evans and Raymond Gideon, should not be disregarded, either for the sentimental delicacy of the love scenes or the robust humorous invention of the Las Vegas episode, wherein the starman's superior intelligence enables him to make slot-machines disburse their jackpots at the merest

touch. Nor does the movie succumb to predictability in terms of plot construction: the conclusion strikes an upbeat note without resorting to the glibly happy ending that might have seemed on the cards.

In the traditional, studio-era sense, *Starman* strikes one as a collaborative venture, though still as a film 'by' John Carpenter. And, though in hard fact virtually any mainstream movie is now going to carry a dauntingly high budget, it does not feel like a prestige or 'event' movie: it has a sense of proportion, of belonging to a continuum, and perhaps it is that above all which makes it so encouraging.

Of course, and quite properly, *Starman* is tailored to the demands of a predominantly youthful contemporary audience. It has spectacle and stunts and surprises. But these aren't an end in themselves, they are made to serve another purpose – telling a story in the way that only the cinema can. And that is an achievement which these days makes one feel ready to stand up and cheer.

TIM PULLEINE

TURKEYS OF THE YEAR
WILD GEESE II

A quick burrow among airport bookstalls, moments before risking your life in the air, will confirm the fact that most of the books on offer are constructed of interchangeable elements; rather like the different grades of Meccano, except that none of the books gets harder as you go up the scale. Titles like *The Matabele Transfer*, *The Bongoland Conspiracy*, *The Lumumba Complaint* suggest acres of comforting violence. And Nazis; there are always the men in jodhpurs and boots dreaming of Poland. There is nothing wrong with any of this, of course. Indeed, there is a great deal of pleasure to be had from mentally constructing movies along the same lines. It's a game called 'Quiet Days in Cliché'.

So settle back in your seat and let the mind wander over every movie cliché you have ever sat through in those dreadful hours between noon and teatime when the tube has only shoot-outs to offer. I suggest the scenario would come out like this:

1. Violence is taken for granted in this genre, but if it is a British film then it must appeal to the twin indissoluble elements of the British image of themselves: snobbery and sentimentality. For the first you import Edward Fox, with his drawl that suits any member of the upper classes from General Sir Brian Horrocks to Edward VIII, and his perfect manners. For the second, you kick off with a *hommage* to a dead actor, say Richard Burton if he happened to star in a previous film on the same subject and was

about to in this one. For the tough bits you'll need an American who looks like Clint Eastwood with acne and can talk with his mouth closed, say Scott Glenn. Now you are off and running.

2. Introduce them both. Have Glenn walk down Carnaby Street. This will remind old men in the audience of the sixties, and flatter Americans for their good sense of geography.

3. The job. Something impossible, but with Nazis in it. Springing Hess from Spandau prison is the first thing that comes to mind, but a good reason is hard to make up, so leave that very hazy. No one will notice. Brief Fox on the job with a video potted history of Hess just to fill in the dimmer members of the audience who don't know their history. For the brighter ones tired of exposition have Fox say midway through: "I'm well acquainted with all of this." Finish the video just in case. *Then* Fox can say: "This is the most insane piece of work I've ever been offered." That way people will know he's going to take it.

4. Team up the two psychos. This means the older one acting as rear cover to the younger one. He can limp around in the shadows, occasionally shooting shifty-looking Arabs who are stalking up behind Glenn. When he does this, he can give a toothy smile and a thumbs up.

5. Briefing and the gathering of the team. This is dull but necessary. Grunt over maps. Stick pins in wall. Put mercenaries through gruelling exercises.

6. Case the target. A good bit this. Jog around Spandau in a track suit looking as inconspicuous as any lone jogger in an electric blue track suit would do. Give beady looks at barred windows. Check stopwatch. Have musicians bang the bass wires of a piano with a sledgehammer for the soundtrack every time there is a close up of the prison.

7. Love interest. Barbara Carrera is hot this year. Have her as the secretary to some top brass. Scott Glenn must be terribly rude to her at first. At the first sign of danger she can give way to hysterical sobs; he can take her in his arms, murmur "it's all right" and then engage in some slo-mo thrashing between the sheets.

8. Warm up plot. Bring on more Nazis. Have Scott Glenn kidnapped in back of car by indeterminate villains. Have him say: "What do you want?" Would it be *too* much of a cliché to have them reply: "We will ask the questions, Mr Haddad. Welcome to Berlin"? Of course it wouldn't.

9. Torture him in back of car with a plastic bag over his head. This gives him a good excuse for some backseat violence and an improbable roll out of the car at high speed. Stick him in hospital with bruises like a rainbow on his body and something fetching in the scar department stuck to his cheekbone. This will please the German duelling factions at least.

10. He needs a past? Something in Beirut, wife and child murdered perhaps. "Death ate its way into me." That's enough psychological motivation, it holds up the action.

11. Bring on the 'characters'. Stratford John must weigh in at about thirty stone these days. He's old enough to have seen *The Maltese Falcon*, so have him model himself on Sydney Greenstreet. Have him chuckle "By jove, sir, I like your style", sweat a lot, not shave, and have a heart of gold.

12. Other characters: there must be at least two Russians. One is the hard man, balding but sinewy, in a brown military

uniform with red stars on it. He is firm but a soldier of the old school, ie decent. The second Russian is in a shiny blue suit with four buttons on the jacket, all of them done up. He eats without a knife and fork, is superior to the military man, and despatches people who fail with terrifying violence. There must also be a deserter from the IRA in the mercenaries. This will enable a kindly drill sergeant to shoot off his kneecaps at close range in revenge for all that has happened in Ulster, which will definitely reassure the English in the audience.

13. Weaponry. This must be copious, and make nice crunchy noises while being cocked. Silencers are very sexy; that dull 'phut' and the look of surprise on the victim's face. Flick knives are good value too, but they must always be drawn out of the pocket, held up delicately and vertically along the side of the cheek before they are flicked open. This looks chic.

14. Capture Hess. Storming Spandau just not on. Therefore cunning scheme of drugs, armoured convoy to hospital, faked accident, switch Hess with dead body lookalike, run off with Hess. A child could do it, but preferably one that looked like Scott Glenn.

15. Hess should be played by ageing grand old actor with tremendous charm. Preferably a Lord. He can put on the tired-old-man-who-has-seen-it-all act, piping and trebling that he would rather be back in his cosy cell. Have the mercenaries protest: "The knowledge you have could change the course of world history." Not even Hess could reply to that.

16. Let him go back inside. It's the only way out of a dead end plot. Have Fox bid goodbye at the gates in customary polite form: "Lovely party. Thanks most awfully."

Now open your eyes, the reverie of cliché is over. A ridiculous game, of course; nobody would ever be so stupid as to make a movie along those lines.

CHRIS PEACHMENT

RED DAWN

Sometimes the most far-fetched movie fantasies are the ones that were meant to look the most realistic. John Milius marshalled the most up-to-date military equipment for *Red Dawn* and based his scenario on the most up-to-the-minute headlines, yet the result was an utterly unbelievable wish-movie that only a dimwit survivalist could find convincing.

If John Milius lived in Central Asia, he might have directed a documentary about the Russian invasion of Afghanistan. Instead, being American, and a red-blooded American at that, Milius made a movie about a Russian invasion of Colorado.

In Milius' fevered imaginings, Communist troops from South of the Border parachute into the unsuspecting towns of the soft underbelly of America, killing or rounding up the inhabitants. Only a few Americans, mostly youngsters, escape. The teenagers head for the hills, vowing to repulse the invaders or die in the attempt.

Milius, the writer of *Apocalypse Now* and director of *Conan the Barbarian,* explained his implausible premise: "Suppose all of Central America fell and the Communist regimes formed an alliance. They could field a significant force. Cuba has an army of half a million, including reserves. Nicaragua aims to create a standing army of 300,000.

"If Mexico has a revolution – and it's close – we'll see a vast influx of refugees to the American Southwest. Among them could be agents who could prepare the way for an armed incursion."

In Milius' movie the American guerrillas are led by Patrick Swayze and include C Thomas Howell and Powers Boothe (as a downed fighter pilot). Milius uses kids as his protagonists because in a sense *Red Dawn* is a fulfilment of his own childhood dreams of zapping the Russkies.

Milius is known for being Hollywood's most macho moviemaker. When Clint Eastwood wanted Dirty Harry to get really tough, he had Milius write him *Magnum Force.* In *The*

Wind and the Lion, Milius made gun-toting Teddy Roosevelt an unlikely cinema hero. And he made the keynote to *Conan* a quotation from Friedrich Nietzsche: "That which does not kill us makes us stronger."

In a sense, then, Milius was doing a favour for those who could watch *Red Dawn* and live. For a start, the movie is an optical endurance test, for it seems to have been photographed in natural light when the sun was behind a cloud. As for our ears, they must endure some of the most crashingly wooden lines ever uttered on screen. The script actually includes this dialogue: "The Russians are coming. The Russians are coming."

audience that Swayze's little band of mountain marauders isn't the only resistance to the invasion. And yes, Boothe lets us know that the Big One has been dropped, though far over the horizon.

Red Dawn shares with Hollywood's more liberal movies, like the peace-mongering *War Games,* a distrust of America's military establishment. After all, the Confederacy rose up from the grassroots and stood off Washington's War Department for four years. In *Red Dawn* as in *War Games,* it takes the aroused Common Man to save the country when the generals and politicians fall down.

Milius believes America's

are killed. Our way of life is shattered for ever."

Red Dawn raises the question of whether Americans would indeed fight to defend their country. The withdrawals from Vietnam, the débâcle of the hostage rescue attempt in Iran, the unexpected difficulties encountered by the US force that 'liberated' Grenada, the Marines who died as sitting ducks in Lebanon – all of these suggest weakened American fighting ability.

But whose proud stripes and bright stars are so gallantly streaming in the twilight's last gleaming of Ric Waite's cinematography? It's Milius waving his flag: "I'm of the firm

Red Dawn recalls the numerous 'lost platoon' war movies of bygone days, with the addition of women to the other allsorts on the troop roster. There is a turncoat, a doubter, a stalwart and a psycho. Howell's transformation from a mild and ordinary high school kid into a bloodthirsty maniac is is off-puttingly demonstrated when the poor young actor is required to drink blood and say with a smile, "It wasn't that bad." Richard Widmark, where are you when we need you?

Unfortunately, Milius is a better director of typewriter keys than actors. Powers Boothe, the one actor of stature in the cast, is wasted as a sort of news-reader. His main function is to tell the

nuclear policy is a key to its national character. "We invented the atomic bomb and we're the only people who have used it in war. At the same time, we're the only nation in history that had a chance to rule the world and turned it down – in 1946, before the Russians had the bomb. America has an overriding sense of morality. We're straight-shooters. This, coupled with our righteous ferocity, would make us good fighters if we were invaded."

Milius sees *Red Dawn* as a cautionary tale – a projection of what might happen if America lets down its guard. "The movie isn't pro-war," he says. "It shows the cost of war. It isn't a fun and neat hey-let's go-fight-the-Russians movie. Most of the kids

belief that if we were invaded, the Russians would meet resistance from civilians far stronger than anything the Afghan freedom fighters have dreamed up. I think the Americans would be very, very good at guerrilla warfare, even though we've never had to do it before.

"It's in our nature. The ferocity of the American people has always been underestimated. During the Civil War, every European country sent observers, and they all went back horrified at our ferocity. 'Leave these people alone,' they advised. 'Thank God they're an ocean away.'"

BART MILLS

THE KEY

Tinto Brass once said: "To me, power is criminal and popular pornography is better than bourgeois art." That was before he went on to create an entirely new genre: unpopular pornography, a unique category into which can be fitted his most recent movie *The Key*.

The Key is a bourgeois production, dedicated to the belief that sex is to be endured rather than enjoyed and that what is really thrilling is power, at least when it is exemplified by fascism. The bad sight of the year was the ineffably middle-class Frank Finlay, grey hair curling around the edges of his bra and panties, suspenders and stockings, having a heart attack while making love to his wife, in what you might call the movie's climactic scene. Brass's achievement, by means of a sniggering voyeurism and perfunctory attitude to sex, was to make eroticism boring. Even by the standards of Brass, who begins at the bottom – or, at least, at Stefania Sandrelli's – *The Key* is a botched and unlovely exercise. It illustrates that old saw, where there's muck, there's brass; and where there's cinematic muck, there's Tinto Brass.

What seems to turn him on is not eroticism, but fascism. Or maybe he has discovered that there is an audience for the pornography of domination, for sex and swastika. The only moments in which *The Key* comes alive is when its political background, the rise of Mussolini, is sketched in. His first feature, *Salon Kitty*, with its setting of a Nazi brothel, was almost taken seriously by critics and enjoyed a scandalous success in Europe. Before that, Brass was an unknown experimental director. He has managed to make the transition from the underground to the sewer with no improvement in his rudimentary technique, which consists of pointing the camera vaguely towards the action and hoping for the worst.

After *Salon Kitty* came Penthouse's *Caligula* in 1976. Great actors – Gielgud, O'Toole and others – flocked to appear in it, for reasons that remain obscure. Law suits fortunately kept him away from the camera for a couple of years, after which he made *The Action*, a film that probably not even he saw. *The Key* marks his return to directing for an international audience.

Brass's persuasive powers must be great. Even after the horrendous fucked-up fiasco of *Caligula,* he was able to engage for *The Key* Frank Finlay, an actor who does not lack for work and who was once a leading member of Britain's National Theatre, taking over from Paul Scofield as Salieri in the original stage production of Peter Shaffer's *Amadeus*. Perhaps after playing one mediocrity, he wanted to work with another.

Brass, once described by PierNico Solinas, a fellow toiler on *Caligula,* as "looking like a sumo wrestler gone to seed", is never less than gross on film. He is gradually working his way through the major perversions. *The Key* toys with transvestism, necrophilia and urolagnia. It is a story of one man's obsession – with making as much money from gullible audiences as possible.

Finlay plays a professor of art, an expert on Klimt, who is frustrated, after years of marriage, by his wife's prudery. She will not let him see her naked and lies back and thinks of Italy when they make love. Her prudery takes unusual forms: after an opening scene in a night-club, which must be the most inept exposition on film, full of characters telling each other what they, but not the audience, already know, the movie shows her peeing into a Venetian canal. These first moments illustrate Brass's theory of soft-core porn: surround it with culture and you can get away with anything.

Finlay deals with his frustrations by confiding them to his diary. He then locks it away in a drawer and leaves the key where his wife, whose prudery does not apparently constrain her curiosity, can find it. Meanwhile their daughter, who is even more prudish, brings home her new boyfriend. Mum finds him attractive, though it's impossible to see why. He turns out to be the sort of lover who not only keeps his socks and suspenders on after stripping, but also wears floral underpants – in the forties, yet. But that is getting ahead of the story. Mum first spills wine down the front of the boy's trousers so that she can wipe it off and then rushes away to collapse while peeing, though this time she chooses the bathroom rather than the canal.

Boyfriend and Finlay carry her dripping into the bedroom where the boy, who has, of course, medical skills, gives her an injection in a plump and sagging buttock and is, of course, entranced by what he sees. Exit the young lovers. Finlay, on heat from his wife's flirtations with the boy, seizes his chance to see her naked and strips and screws her while she remains semi-conscious. And so it goes.

She finds the diary and responds to her husband's pervervid fantasies by having an affair with the boy, and in turn starts a diary of her own, which she leaves where he can find it. Better films have been made on slimmer pretexts, but not worse ones. Brass's attention never seems concentrated on the film. It's not just that the characters lack any depth; they don't even have shallows. Sex is something no one enjoys; it's seen as a side-effect of what really matters: manipulating the lives of others. the result is anaphrodisiac, as one dreary encounter follows another. The direction and photography are dire: even Venice is reduced to no more than a dirty postcard.

Brass has never been noted as an actor's director; here, though, he is consistent in obtaining poor performances from everyone. Finlay walks through the film like a man fearful of treading on something nasty on the pavement, his face fixed in a rictus of embarrassment. If bottoms could express emotion, then no doubt Stefania Sandrelli's would be showing a similar expression, rather than the flaccidity that Brass focuses upon.

O'Toole used to call Brass Tinto Zinc. But he is far less precious than that and needs flushing away down the nearest canal. Gore Vidal had the last word to say on the subject, in a criticism aimed at *Caligula* but as relevant to any of Brass's films. "It's not an ugly film, nor a pornographic film, simply a ridiculous film. The person who's directing it isn't a good or a bad director, he's simply a ridiculous director."

John Walker

BOLERO

The Dereks' *very* personal interpretation of Edgar Rice Burrough's classic jungle fantasy *Tarzan the Ape Man* provided an occasion for derision the likes of which has seldom been seen. Adding injury to insult, in the Dereks' view, were the actions of the film's distributors MGM-UA. In order to placate the objections of the Burroughs estate – who had found Bo's jungle jigglings not at all to their liking – six seconds of *Tarzan* footage were excised. These six seconds may not seem like much (the 112 minutes to which they were originally attached weren't much either) but to the Dereks every moment of Bo was golden.

Determined that their next venture wouldn't suffer a similar fate, John and Bo elected to go the independent route. *Tarzan* had, after all, done reasonably well at the wickets – certainly far better than anyone had expected. And John-produced images of Bo were still selling posters, calendars, photo-essay books and the like. Enter those dashing Israeli entrepreneur-adventurers Menahem Golan and Yoram Globus. On the look out for titles to swell the roster of their Cannon Group Productions, they joined up with the Dereks who, if nothing else, were certain to provide something eminently. . .exploitable.

And so *Bolero*, "an adventure in ecstasy", was born. The story (in the loosest sense of the term) of a lady and a bullfighter, it offered the promise of Bo against Spanish backgrounds. All was going swimmingly at first – then trouble struck the production. Bo's leading man Fabio Testi, who had raised temperatures in Monte Hellman's deliciously libidinal western *China 9 Liberty 37,* had – according to various press reports – developed a cold sore on his lip. These reports went on to detail that this sight upset his co-star in no uncertain terms. Whatever the cause of distress, Testi was quickly off the production, replaced by a young newcomer Andrea Occhipinti. Problems of a different sort arose with this leading man, however, as the dailies revealed that the

slim Occhipinti looked a shade on the skimpy side when juxtaposed with the Valkyrie-like Bo. Time out for weight work-outs quickly remedied this situation . . . somewhat.

Everything was copasetic with the Dereks once again as they brought their latest epic to a conclusion. But clouds quickly loomed on the horizon as Cannon in the interim had entered into a distribution agreement with (gasp! shudder!) MGM-UA! Looking at what John and Bo had wrought, the company declared *Bolero* X-worthy – a situation they claimed they could not tolerate. Refusing to release *Bolero* MGM-UA had in effect consigned the production to a distribution limbo. Unless Cannon, or the Dereks, would do it themselves this was a film destined to stay on the shelf. Cannon released it with a self-applied X rating.

Judging from the results, however (yes, we must finally deal with the film itself, painful as the prospect may be), MGM-UA was perhaps being gallant. Yes, *Bolero* has plenty of Bo in the altogether, coupling with her co-star Occhipinti with an enthusiasm and an aura of authenticity that perhaps only a movieola viewing could technically substantiate. But when it comes to the sexual goods *Bolero* is no more deserving of an X than *Bambi*. Sex may be the subject, but when it comes to

actual arousal, *Bolero* is about as erotic as an instructional documentary on tractor repair.

One of the joys of bad film scholarship is trying to divine the film-makers intentions from their actual results. Looking at an Edward D Wood Jr classic like *Plan 9 from Outer Space* or *Bride of the Monster,* it's easy to see the desire to make a perfectly ordinary programmer buried beneath a corpus of technical ineptitude. Not so with the Dereks. There's no telling what was behind this lame-brained lust story. And John's photographic expertise only adds to the confusion. He's a really first-rate cinematographer. When images look this good, the fact that nothing of any consequence is going on inside them only makes matters worse. You begin to think it's *you,* not them, as one limp aimless scene follows another in a story

ostensibly set in the roaring twenties – though featuring costumes that seem to have been left over from one of Sam Katzman's sixties-era acid freak-out exploitation epics.

Bo is a rich playgirl, just out of school, longing for adventure, and mad for her favourite movie star Rudolph Valentino. Hot to experience what she calls "extasy" – she insists it's spelled with an X (so much for her education) – she and her best girlfriend (Ana Obregon) set out for Arabia to lose their virginity

(a perpetual theme with the Dereks). "Let's go wallow in it!" says Bo. Indeed. Once there our heroine meets with a young sheik who offers to take the 'gift' of Bo's innocence – only to fall asleep while trying. The audience at this point might be moved to join him. But Bo is quickly off to Spain where she sets her sights on a bullfighter (the aforementioned Occhipinti). Bo's a determined girl. Conquering his initial reticence to deal with her (the minutes fly by like hours, with sub-plots detailing his previous mistress, Bo's efforts to buy his horses and wine vineyards and such) she presents herself to him in her customary costume – her birthday suit.

The pace quickens as Bo and her beau finally get down to the business the customers shelled out their ever-inflated dollars to see. Elmer Bernstein's score thunders and thrusts on the soundtracks as the leads do likewise. Occhipinti (shy? embarrassed? both?) chooses not to regard the camera's direction as he goes about his duties. Bo, meanwhile, clings to him in a manner suggesting a ship-wreck victim hugging a life-preserver. They heave, they pant, and then they (and maestro Bernstein) subside. Is it all over? Can we go home now? Oh no, there's more.

Occhipinti gets gored by a bull in his nether regions. Not surprisingly he lapses into a deep sulk. "That *thing* is going to work again – I guarantee it!" says our heroine fiercely – pointing to his loins. "Maak Muuu haaar agggga!" he screams into his pillow – meaning, of course, "Make me hard again." And, wouldn't you know it, Bo knows just what to do to do so. In no time at all they're clutching and heaving again – but with a difference. Clouds of white smoke suddenly flood the set and a big neon sign spelling out the word "EXTASY" appears over their heads.

"I told you there was an X in it," says Bo in triumph. There's a zero in *Bolero,* too. Two of them in fact. One for John, and one for his ever-huggin' Bo.
DAVID EHRENSTEIN

THE RAZOR'S EDGE

The remake of *The Razor's Edge* represents Bill Murray's reward and the public's punishment for the success of the star's comedies. Given to Murray as a sop for agreeing to appear in *Ghostbusters* (hardly a bad deal for the studio), the picture is a self-serving travesty of W Somerset Maugham's still quite wonderful novel. It also stands as a case study of the extent to which the crafts of literary adaptation and narrative story-telling have declined in the New Hollywood.

Neither the 1944 novel nor Edmund Goulding's Fox film two years later have become overburdened with reputations as sanctified classics, so the decision by Murray, one of contemporary comedy's drollest goofballs, to embark upon a new version was greeted more with quizzicality than outrage. The problems of a young man trying to find himself after the traumas of World War I seemed pretty far afield for this Meatball and Ghostbuster, and buffs could be seen scratching heads over the idea of Murray trying on any rôle once played by Tyrone Power.

With no existing evidence to go on, one could imagine that Murray really was a smart, serious guy after all, and that director John Byrum would summon up the inspiration to match the pretension he exhibited in his first two films, *Inserts* and *Heart Beat*.

Alas, one's worst fears, rather than naive hopes, for the project were confirmed. Whereas screenwriter Lamar Trotti made a largely remarkable attempt to represent Maugham accurately in the 1946 film, it turns out that Murray and Byrum, who wrote the new script together, were less interested in truly adapting the novel than in fashioning a vanity production to spotlight their left-over hippie-era fascination for mystical spirituality, Himalaya-style. Tailoring the material as a star vehicle, the scenarists unsurprisingly focused upon the part of the story featuring Larry Darrell, a young Midwesterner (like Murray) who perturbs his closest friends by rejecting the conventional, comfortable life that could be his in favour of attempting to uncover the mysteries of life through a string of journeys, quests and menial jobs.

What made the novel work so well is that it did not endorse or idealize Darrell's search in the slightest. Rather, it found the perfect counterpoint to him in the

person of Elliot Templeton, the effete, snobbish, ultra-civilized uncle of Darrell's one-time girlfriend, a man who seeks the meaning of life in the way a table is set or how one dresses for a ball – in other words, through style and social standing. Templeton's concerns may seem superficial, but to him they are just as meaningful as Darrell's insights are to the latter. One man may choose the spiritual, another the temporal, but, in Maugham's view, it all comes down to about the same thing in the end. By judiciously balancing the activities and points of view of these two men, Maugham, who thrusts himself prominently into the book as both story-teller and friend to the major characters, was able to judge them both critically and appreciatively.

In the old Fox version, Clifton Webb's Templeton was a sterling creation, really a perfect representation of the character. As fine an actor as Denholm Elliott is, he had little chance of equalling Webb going in, but was made to seem almost ludicrous by the way the film-makers reduced and faintly ridiculed the character. Murray and Byrum clearly had no understanding of, sympathy for or interest in Templeton, and in the process of minimizing his importance they fatally ruptured the structure of the piece. More understandably, they also eliminated the Maugham character, whom Trotti and Goulding had dared, and got away with, including in their version.

Tyrone Power was far from profound as Darrell, but his looks and something about his politeness in society, which bespoke much about his upbringing, made him the sort of fellow people would ask about and discuss during his long absences. If one decides to be generous and accept him in the rôle, Murray's performance is far from a disaster; the flaky humour the actor bestows upon the character is not unwelcome, even if it's unexpected, and he gets across enough of Darrell's restlessness to make the viewer understand the character.

Nevertheless, the picture just lurches along from scene to scene and year to year making nothing but a bland impression until Theresa Russell has her turn at bat. Seen briefly early in the film as a member of the Chicago socialite crowd, she reappears in drastically reduced circumstances as a drunken Parisian whore whom Darrell tries to save through love. Looking startlingly like Louise Brooks here with her short, brown hair-do, Russell also resembles the great silent actress in her bracing ability to inject massive doses of electricity and carnality into motion pictures whenever she appears in them. Academy voters always had a soft spot for fallen women and alcoholics, so Anne Baxter had little trouble winning an Oscar for her rendition of Sophie forty years ago. Russell's work is even more convincing, but stands as the only definitive element in otherwise unauthentic surroundings. In this regard, not one setting in the film looks like the United States, even though a number of important scenes are set there, and rarely has so little Parisian atmosphere come through in a picture to have locationed there.

Fortunately, perhaps, for everyone's sanity, *The Razor's Edge* flopped at the box office, despite the draw of Murray's name. Had it been a smash, other young actors might have got it into their heads to undertake radical changes of pace, and we might have ended up next year with Sylvester Stallone in *The Fountainhead*, Brooke Shields in *Queen Christina*, or Eddie Murphy, Matt Dillon and Bo Derek in *Design for Living*. Actually, the way things are going, we still might.

Todd McCarthy

112

THE NATURAL

It can't only be me: virtually every movie, no matter how good (or bad), seems significantly too long. Most could benefit decisively from a snip of five minutes or more (which represents a great deal of footage); others drag on and on with extraneous material that detracts from whatever tenuous narrative structure the feckless director has jerry-built.

There are a lot of reasons for this sorry trend. Some of it derives from an initially worthy reaction to the zoom/cut gyrations of the late sixties and early seventies. Longer takes became fashionable instead, so that the same conventional dialogue-dominated scene which in the thirties would have covered actors' waste motions (like crossing a room) by use of cross-cutting, today is played out with every extraneous beat intact. The result is that what used to be a 90-minute film will now run at least ten per cent longer. Indeed, the *average* length of a major Hollywood release is edging close to a full two hours, and rare is the 'important' film that does not exceed that formerly forbidding barrier.

But that's just a question of style. More irksome, and more common, are the instances where film-makers never form a clear notion, while shooting, of just what their movie is actually about. Instead, they make scenes, or pursue images, without any coherent sense of their place in a whole. As a consquence, the same film-makers fall in love with their footage instead of concentrating on telling a story to an audience. (Audiences, in turn, are continually demonstrating that they aren't necessarily concerned with seeing a coherent story.) Perversely, these directors are often most emotionally attached to the weakest pieces of material, or at least show a tunnel-visioned predilection for the isolated impact of a scene or shot.

One of the most sorry examples of this syndrome is Barry Levinson's trashing of Bernard Malamud's *The Natural*. For the first hour, it's hard to discern what the film is about, other than

baseball and portents, but there are a lot of enjoyable character actors around creating an expectation that *something* is going to happen, and the movie is interestingly photographed (Caleb Deschanel) and scored (Randy Newman). Besides, Levinson's debut work, *Diner*, was first-rate. It was also his own vision. In its second hour, one realizes that *The Natural* hasn't any ideas developing whatsoever, and what's worse, it's flailing about onscreen with confusing, contradictory, pointless scenes. There's no point of view here, let alone a vision. Forget moral issues: by the time the film staggers to a pumped-up climax, the absence of any meaning at all has become so transparent that it's hard to work up resentment at such patent manipulation, especially when the strain to extract our interest fails from ineptitude.

There's some sadness to this disaster, since the corrosively dark novel afforded some interesting source material, with a chance for Robert Redford to reach for a new dimension in his first acting rôle in four years. Malamud's work isn't so classic as to be sacrosanct, so there is no harm in the film-makers departing from its themes, provided they developed ones of their own. Instead, they've simply cribbed a plot premise and appropriated an aura of ambiguous mysticism to conjure up a vehicle for the vacuous star iconography of Redford.

He plays an aspiring big leaguer whose career is derailed by a cruel, arbitrary fate, only to re-emerge mysteriously sixteen years later as the sport's oldest rookie, a miracle player to transform a sorry team into a pennant contender. It's obvious now that Redford may well be incapable of honest acting. On reflection, he hasn't given an interesting performance since 1972, with *The Candidate* and *Jeremiah Johnson*. But worse, Redford seems to demand that every project be distorted to whitewash his character into some variant of the white knight or suffering Jesus, incessantly

insinuating a self-congratulatory air of phoney righteousness just when some shading or ambiguity might actually create a dramatically incisive character. Here it's even more offensive than it had been in *Brubaker*. In *The Natural,* he's certainly symbolic: but of what? He's so intent on being a glossy pseudo-mythic figure that he blands out into mere opacity. He's well cast here, but he distorts the entire scenario with his unyielding adherence to being well cast.

Given Redford's starpower and poor artistic judgement, there was little chance of a noteworthy film. Still, there's no excuse for Levinson's dithering mess. Running an unconscionable 138 minutes, it could easily – *easily!* –

lose forty of them and gain focus and impact in the process. Rushed into release, the film frankly looks like a first cut that was never properly finished. Many features might run that long at some point in post-production, but few stay that length after critical editing work. It's painfully obvious *The Natural* was locked prematurely. Such indifference to form bespeaks a lack of respect for the public.

Needless to add, the film was a considerable hit, confirming not only Redford's continuing appeal but also that audiences today are willing to respond to cues to emotion, like behaviorally trained rats, more than to the ministrations of the story-teller. Malamud's misanthropic fable could never have drawn this size an audience, but the foolish supernaturalism in the movie vies with howlingly bald good/bad oppositions (characters even wear black and white as appropriate) before wrenching to a synthetic *Rocky*-like triumph.

In this shallow context, stalwart turns by Wilford Brimley, Joe Don Baker and Richard Farnsworth can't sustain much interest, while the conscientious Robert Duvall is shockingly ill-served by an enigmatic character who changes to suit the purposes of different scenes. Glenn Close secured an embarrassing Oscar nomination for a part that calls for her to stand about beaming stupidly as an avatar of womanly goodness. Oddly, the most interesting performance is turned by Darren McGavin, who shrewdly eschewed screen credit, as an eccentric fixer.

There are worse films than *The Natural*, naturally, but few that have left me more depressed by wasted talent and loss of craft. Redford has such a keen appreciation for the exercise of his power and represents such special commercial casting potential that it's a shame he hasn't greater concern for the integrity of material. He owes that obligation to his art, if not himself.

MYRON MEISEL

SCREAM FOR HELP

Michael Winner has this astounding ability to surpass himself. Just when you think he has hit rock bottom, he dives into even further depths of catchpenny dementia. But even he will surely never surpass *Scream for Help?* This is the film that makes *Death Wish* seem like *La Règle du Jeu* and *Death Wish II* like the complete works of Shakespeare.

Yet, as they say, it could all have been so

First Mum's car is tampered with and she ends up with a leg in plaster. Then Christie's best friend is killed by a hit-and-run driver after witnessing stepfather Paul (David Brooks) *in flagrante* with his mistress Brenda. Then Christie herself narrowly escapes with her life after Polaroid-snapping Paul, again *in flagrante* with Brenda (when does the poor man get a break?). Oh and goodness me, I forgot the man who came to read the electricity

history to have spent twenty-five prolific years in the business and to be slam-banging away in much the same where-shall-I-put-the-camera-now vein at the end of his career (though let's not count on that) as at the beginning.

The real scream in *Scream for Help* is its determination to whip up dramatic energy at *every* minute of the story, even when nothing much is happening. And there are moments, even in the crowded life of this family, when

manages to neutralize both Paul and Brenda (Brenda gets the fusebox treatment and ends up sizzling on the cellar floor) while at the same time keeping up Mum's morale. Not that Mum can't keep it up herself, since whenever she's called upon to demonstrate rapid movement she can get that plaster leg locomoting like crazy.

The trouble is, of course, that as soon as we realize that this mother-daughter duo can beat all comers, however well-armed or numerically superior, the suspenseful urgencies of "Can they survive?" are swapped for the more academic "How will they survive?" And in most examples of the American splatter genre, the repetitive ride through violence and terror ends up creating such a blasé response in the audience that unless the story constantly ups the ante in terms of exotic weaponry there are heads nodding off in the stalls. Even our young heroine's final *coup de couteau*, when she's confronted in her bedroom by the last surviving villain and pulls on him a kitchen knife kept under her pillow (whatever happened to the days when young girls slept with teddy bears?), is greeted by us with "Ah yes (yawn), another impalement."

The wonder is that this 90-minute spell of homicidal lunacy goes about its business with such a straight face. Which is why, if one looks at it through a different mental lens as black comedy rather than a murder thriller, it starts to look better. Who could resist the opening? Young Christie sits by a boating lake, in the last golden rays of an afternoon sun, tells the camera sweetly and directly who she is and where she lives, and then says (equally sweetly and directly), "I think my stepfather is trying to murder my mother."

Michael Winner once said of one of his films, with memorable understatement, "It isn't your Luis Buñuel." The only saving grace of *Scream for Help* is that from time to time – and no doubt quite inadvertently – it almost *is* your Luis Buñuel.
HARLAN KENNEDY

different. . .(shimmering dissolve and flashback). The original screenplay by Tom Holland (of *Psycho II*) has the kind of story premise that would fuel a grand black comedy – New York teenager Christie (Rachael Kelly) thinks her stepfather's trying to kill her mother but no one except the audience believes her. And this perverse scepticism is uproariously maintained, by Christie's friends, by the police and by her mother Karen (Marie Masters), even in the face of a series of 'accidents' that would have convinced the most trusting or idiotic of intended victims. It is as if the Duke of Clarence, when chin-high in the butt of malmsey, had stubbornly believed he was only being shown round the wine cellar by the two nice gents from Château Rothschild.

meter in scene one in Christie's house and ended up as an overdone shish kebab smoking gently on the cellar floor.

Imagine what Hitchcock or Buñuel could have done. Hitchcock could have had Cary Grant as Stepdad, complete with phosporescent glass of milk and dashing smile, ministering to an ever-nuttier Ingrid Bergman, while Margaret O'Brien looked on as the frightful prying child with specs and teeth-brace. And as for Buñuel, what a time he could have had with that leg-in-plaster! Catherine Deneuve as Mum, Fernando Rey as Stepdad and more sexual fetishism than you could shake a fist at.

But the only thing you want to shake a fist at in *Scream for Help* is Michael Winner. He must be the only film-maker in movie

Daughter isn't snapping Stepfather in mid-coitus and Mum isn't crashing her car or falling down stairs (another speciality). But even here Winner makes whoopee with his zoom lens and composers Howard Blake and Johnny Pearson besiege our ears with the alternate shrill and growls of their jazz score.

And when the final act comes along – Mum and Daughter held prisoner in their own home by Paul, Brenda and Brenda's husband, who are wondering how best to murder them – it's open season for Winneresque hyperbole. The tactical ingenuities of our heroine, who musters her brainwaves with the aplomb of Montgomery mustering his troops at Alamein, passeth all understanding. She

LASSITER

The old film industry chestnut that no one *sets out* to make a rotten movie is so regularly roasted that one really does begin to suspect that there has to be something more than just ghastly coincidence lurking behind such regular creative ineptitude.

How else can one explain a film like *Lassiter* which is so desperately and consistently wrong that it goes beyond the realm of mere incompetence into an altogether more culpable area of Cruelty to Tom Selleck and Violence Against the Moviegoer?

Mr Selleck is a huge, immensely personable man, who, fortunately, hasn't (I think) begun to believe constant PR claims that he is the "new Clark Gable". The continuing success of his *Magnum PI* television series has to do with the fact he looks good in colourful Hawaiian shirts, has a pleasant, if rather light voice which is fine for the show's generally joky voice-over narration, and is confined to a format where an audience can drift in and out between the ads without losing too much the thread of an always action-packed story-line. The man, with his bushy moustache, clearly has charm.

Small-screen Selleck suspends my one overriding and nagging concern that he, superficially perhaps, has the appearance and demeanour of a good-natured hard-core porn movie stud. Rather, in fact, like a bumper version of the equally likeable Harry Reems.

Confined to mindless plots in the picturesque environs of Maui, Kaui and Oahu, Mr Selleck is just about perfect. Which is also not to say he could not, or should not, be allowed to *try* to make a successful transition to the big screen which is, after all, in dire need of new, or even slightly soiled, Clark Gables.

What has rapidly to be understood is a fact which is still continually misunderstood by generations of post-war movie moguls: that the millions who boost television ratings have little or nothing to do with cinema queues. Checking in with six-pack and potato chips on a packed sofa at the beginning of a long evening's TV viewing is an altogether more passive process than the active, and often aggravating, business of going out to the cinema. But try telling that to entrepreneurs who tried, and failed, to crank up post-*Kojak* Savalas and *aprés-Six Million Dollar Man* Majors. There was always, I feel, a certain irony when Mr Majors eventually slid gratefully back into telly-land with something called *The Fall Guy*.

The point is, Selleck *per se* isn't big box office. His first film excursion, *High Road to China*, was, despite what you might hear from others, a rollicking good yarn, taking into account the basis of his popularity but extending his range and considerably broadening the canvas. The fact that it flopped had less to do with Selleck's limitations than with the lack of conviction shown by its American distributor.

Now, instead of correctly analysing the error, the same financiers of Selleck's second film, *Lassiter*, seemed to come up with the idea that perhaps, first-time round, their target audience was wrong. That can surely be the only explanation for a 'restricted' certificate, and a particularly gratuitous sequence early on when Lauren Hutton, as a sort of Countess de Sade, wastes her lover in mid-screw. In this, the audience for any kind of Tom Selleck picture – and this, after all, is a 'vehicle' – is rapidly alienated.

In 1939 London, Lassiter, an American jewel thief who plies his trade there, is framed by the British police and FBI into attempting to lift from the German Embassy a hoard of uncut gems which are destined to help finance the Hun's imminent war effort. "Cross me," spits Bob Hoskins as a Scotland Yard Inspector "and you'll do twenty hard years." And in equally melodramatic vein, a wildly over-the-top Hoskins also has to say things like: "I'm a copper. I don't forgive. I don't forget. He's a thief but not here. . .on my patch."

Selleck is surrounded by a gaggle of picaresque characters – from the utterly banal, his dancer girlfriend (flatly played by Mid-Atlantic's very own Jane Seymour) to the completely bizarre, Lauren Hutton. Apart from her lurid opening gambit, we know Miss Hutton's definitely odd when she says, "I like men with scars."

I think Mr Selleck finally realized he had strolled into the wrong film when Miss Hutton bites his lower lip during an embrace and savours the big man's blood. Almost normal in comparison, if as strangely cast, is Lassiter's close friend, and getaway driver, Smoke, played by Ed Lauter. Inevitably he's given one of those pieces of dialogue that help explain the appearance of an American Equity member in a rôle that could have so easily been enacted by a stalwart Brit in the mould of Sam Kydd: "I came here because I found it's my kind of town. Cops don't carry guns!"

And what of the star himself? Apart from looking pretty bemused throughout, he has a certain style, whether in tuxedo, tweeds or trilby. The poster declared "The *Magnum* man hits the big screen with a vengeance." In this case the big screen seems to have fought back on unequal terms. Mr Selleck is opposed in his quest by art direction that drips, nay swamps, with period detail, a script (by David Taylor) that makes his TV stint look like a Magnum Opus, and direction (by Roger Young) that's leaden, except that lead tends to be valuable. On producer 'Big Al' Ruddy's roll-call this one ranks very much on the same scale as *Matilda*, which was about a boxing kangaroo.

I have, however, left the worst for last. The final indignity. Peter Skellern as himself warbling, presciently, 'Let's Call The Whole Thing Off.'

QUENTIN FALK

DUNE

Glancing at a group of stills of *Dune*, one finds oneself wondering why they so accurately recreate the feeling of the film itself. As a rule stills serve simply as a reminder. They reproduce, of course, the smooth features of the stars; they offer a kind of portrait gallery. There may even be a beautifully composed scene. One is grateful for that; but it doesn't revive the speed, the movement, the intense life which delighted on the screen. A still, after all, is still. Why, then, the sense of recreation of the movie as one turns over that handful of shiny photographs of *Dune*?

Perhaps another look at the film itself will help to explain the curious feeling of familiarity as one looks through those photographs. Before you begin your second visit you are warned: you will see a world, says the publicity, "unlike any you have seen before". A future world, of course: the cinema revels in presenting the landscape and the architecture which will confront some future generation, and

Dune (the title, by the way, is the name of a planet) is set ten thousand years away in the unknown. It is a dismal planet. The cinema doesn't as a rule offer encouraging forecasts, and this time the place is badly silted up with sand. Apart from discouraging glimpses of what presumably are other planets the sky gives little cheer; it doesn't provide much light. Never mind, resourceful human nature has preserved some of the amenities of today. The palace inhabited by the leading figures of the story has what might be electric light, and one guesses at other luxuries.

An introduction delivered by one of the female members of the cast puts you wise to the general situation. One really ought to pay heed. But with a world "unlike any you have seen before" waiting to be revealed one is inclined to listen only casually. Anyway, one soon develops some sort of idea. The people of the planet Dune, at any rate the lot who live in the handsomely equipped palace – what happens to outsiders is left vague and one suspects that they

are all conscripted into the armed forces – are called Atreides. But most of the names of people are much fancier, for the writer of the original novel, Frank Herbert, is said to have created a new mythology. (The air today is full of new mythologies; the public demands new heroes. I admit that the only current names I have been able to master have been those of the rabbits in *Watership Down*, and those I have already forgotten. But young audiences adopt the novelties with ease.)

In *Dune's* mythology one superior being, treated with reverence by even the highest ranks, seems to live in a kind of telephone booth which is wheeled in when authority is needed; he appears to consist of a mouth and not much more. We also meet a party of women in sweeping skirts who have had their heads shaved. The absence of hair does not diminish their manner of command; perhaps they are elders or prophets. And there is a figure who floats about at ceiling level: a malevolent figure who eliminates a frightened young man, presumably a rebellious type. Can the floating eminence be Freddy Jones? One is glad to be able to recognize him. One has a natural desire to know which side one is on in this enigmatic setting, and Mr Jones usually plays estimable characters. Not this time. Meanwhile, the people on ground level move very slowly, dead-march time. And now and then somebody says, emphatically, "Spice!"

The monosyllable temporarily adds to mystification. But really it is the key to all the goings on, and now you must settle down to the puzzle. There is plenty of time; the film runs two hours and a quarter; and sooner or later (well, perhaps later) you find that the slow marches have a reason. The house of Atreides is preparing for war. Its members are going to war over the Spice concession. Spice it is which enables its possessors to travel and get around. Probably, though I can't be sure, it helps them to float at ceiling level. Anyway *Dune* depends on Spice.

And now, for a few moments,

things grow more lucid. Battle is joined – you are used to that – with the other group who inhabit Dune. The opening of hostilities is rather obscured by blowing sand. The desert itself has a habit of rearing. But the explosions are familiar; and by the time we get to the statutory single combat one begins to feel almost at home. The House of Atreides lot, led by the handsome son of the family (Kyl MacLachlan), are obviously the ones to cheer; at last one really knows which side one is on. But there is one more shadow. In this final break in the series of non-events one looks for emotion, but the hero (who seems to vanquish merely by thinking of it) never stirs a muscle. He has clearly been directed to play marble-faced.

Dune is rich in talent. The screenwriter and director is the gifted David Lynch. The cast is illuminated by distinguished names: Max von Sydow is there, and José Ferrer, and Silvana Mangano appears as a Reverend Mother. Everything looks in favour; but the spectator emerges not merely bewildered by the new mythology, but stunned by a kind of nothingness. Perhaps he would do better if he were familiar with the novel, if he knew who was who and why as he went along, without having to look it all up in a synopsis.

As for me, still flummoxed, I turn back to those stills. The faces look back at me. But now, after my second visit to the film, they are no longer meaningless. They reproduce *Dune*; they are a precise image of its two and a quarter hours of absurdity. Stills are by nature static. They present the embracing couple struggling to hold the intimate pose or the walking figure caught before he has got both feet on the ground. *Dune* doesn't go in much for embraces, but it gives you plenty of walkers and marchers, all slow, as if animated between naps. The stills present a frozen world. They are the frozen image of a frozen movie.

DILYS POWELL

116

GIVE MY REGARDS TO BROAD STREET

Back in the early sixties, when the Beatles where just jukebox heroes rather than a pop-cultural phenomenon, *the* movie to talk about at parties, assuming you could make yourself heard above the strains of 'Can't Buy Me Love', was unquestionably that sumptuous exercise in mid-life stocktaking, Fellini's *8½*.

Twenty years on, with the surviving ex-Beatles secure in millionaire middle-age, it would doubtless be unfair to blame Paul McCartney's *Give My Regards to Broad Street* on Fellini, though *8½* seems unmistakably to be the model for this peculiar reverie of creative crisis. (Not, anyway, that the model is an exploded one, as Woody Allen's underrated *Stardust Memories* quite recently proved). It's just that in the context of McCartney's script, as realized by former commercials director Peter Webb, it is gut reaction rather than residual snobbery which almost prompts one to enclose words like creative in supercilious quotation marks.

Closer to home, what this stiff-jointed youth movie, from which anyone under the age of forty seems largely to have been banished, perhaps resembles is a conflation of the two features which Richard Lester made with the Beatles in the mid-sixties – though it would be unfair to blame *Broad Street* on Lester either, especially as he reputedly turned down flat an approach to direct it.

On the one hand, it might be trying to emulate *A Hard Day's Night* in offering a kind of fictionalised documentary on the lives of its participants, with McCartney, his wife Linda, and erstwhile oppo Ringo Starr playing 'themselves' (though not, one may feel, without a degree of difficulty) as they go through an impossibly crowded schedule of interviews, filming and recording engagements. On the others, in distant echo of *Help!* there is an attempt to use tongue-in-cheek elements of a mystery thriller, involving in this case a missing master-tape and a sinister (as well as utterly implausible) takeover bid for Paul's company, to provide an underpinning of plot.

Unfortunately, however, the components don't seem amenable to renovation. The one or two sequences which manage to raise a smile, such as the sub-*Goon Show* satire of a BBC visit, are those which hark back most unashamedly to the Beatles era. Of course, in *A Hard Day's Night* we accepted that we were watching sanitised cut-outs of what were then called the Fab Four; but the illusion created by the movie had sufficient spontaneity to carry us along. In *Broad Street,* spontaneity is, to put it mildly, in short supply. In the foreground, everything seems glossily manufactured, whether it is Linda and guests posing with raised champagne glasses by the domestic hearth, as if waiting to be incorporated into a wallpaper advert, or the introduction of Ringo's wife Barbara Bach in the guise of one of those movie journalists who is never seen to make a note or a recording or do a stroke of work of any kind; and in the background, everything is as predictable as the disruption of lunch in the Elstree studio cafeteria by an actor in a monster-suit.

As for the thriller sub-plot, it not only fails to lead anywhere – except quite arbitrarily to Broad Street station, where (ha ha) the custodian of the tape proves to have got locked in what he has taken for the gents – but never even really manages to get started. But the idea behind it is in a way revealing. The tape is thought to have been nicked by an old lag to whom Paul has given employment (the flashback to the job offer – "If you're fibbing and you do one thing wrong, you'll be out" – suggests that the superstar screenwriter may have been overdosing on back numbers of the *Gem* and *Magnet)* and this is but one manifestation of what one might term the pitch the movie is making: selling us a portrait of the rock mogul as a good-hearted ordinary bloke, unsullied by the pressures of wealth and fame. Indeed, the fact that the action is ultimately revealed as a fantasy triggered by these very pressures turns the film into a kind of ritual affirmation, which can end with

McCartney climbing out of his limo more chirpily down to earth than ever.

There may be a gesture towards sentimental self-appraisal in the sequence of McCartney's meeting with an enigmatic father-figure called Jim, ensconced in a room above a dockside pub and played in a demeaning farewell screen appearance by the late Sir Ralph Richardson. (Even sliding downstairs on a tray in *Greystoke* would have been a better *envoi* than this.) Jim dispenses such apothegms as "If you didn't run round so much, you might get a clearer view of the world" – advice which McCartney as screenwriter has failed to take to heart – and when his visitor says that he must be off, replies discouragingly, "You've been off for years." But on leaving him, Paul can do no more than drive interminably around the streets of London to the strains of 'The Long And Winding Road', with self-appraisal turning into renewed self-endorsement.

Of course, as the title might suggest, *Give My Regards to Broad Street* is intended to be, in McCartney's words, "an old-fashioned musical, nothing heavy." And it's fair to say that one of the production numbers,

'Ballroom Dancing', is staged and edited with enough expertise to let one disregard its complete lack of integration into the narrative design. The same cannot, though, be said for most of the other musical episodes, which reach a nadir of bathos in the peculiar Pre-Raphaelite picnic sequence which (for no conceivable reason) is cued by the sound of 'Eleanor Rigby' – even if 'Eleanor Rigby' itself is a good deal more of a song than some of the more recent items on the soundtrack.

It is tempting to say that *Broad Street* resembles a blockbuster home movie, but it would be misleading, because the film lacks that dimension which might render such a description non-pejorative: its artlessness just doesn't feel genuine. In this respect, it could hardly be further removed from *8½*, an artful film if ever there was one, but one which succeeded in creating the illusion of looking into a corridor of mirrors. *Give My Regards to Broad Street* creates only the illusion of a mirror held up by McCartney and his mates, unblushingly giving their regards to themselves.

TIM PULLEINE

FACES OF THE YEAR
KELLY McGILLIS

In the run-up to the release of *Witness* (and after it for that matter) it was hardly surprising that the lion's share of popular press coverage should have been devoted to Harrison Ford's switch from rough'n'tough heart-throb to 'sensitive' serious actor (with the movie's barn-building episode even providing the publicists with a peg to remind us that in less pecunious times Ford had earned his living as a carpenter). But however understandable the focusing of attention on the bankable Ford, who receives sole billing above this title, it would be unfortunate if the qualities of his leading lady were too readily overlooked. Unfortunate, but in the event surely unlikely.

In fact, *Witness* was not Kelly McGillis' first film appearance. She appeared a year before in *Reuben, Reuben,* and even to say that McGillis was the best thing about it might seem like a half-hearted compliment. This was very much a standard *ingénue* rôle, but it would be true to say that – apart from looking pretty in a college-girl sort of way, especially when got up for jogging – she brought an appealing touch of astringency to it and the one scene from the picture which at this remove comes readily to mind is that in which she comes coolly to the aid of Tom Conti's sozzled Celtic bard aboard a train.

When she made *Reuben, Reuben,* the California-born McGillis was still a drama student at the Juilliard School in New York, though she had appeared in summer stock and in Central Park productions of Shakespeare. She was subsequently chosen for the rôle in *Witness* from "hundreds" of contenders, according to the producers, who said they wanted "a good actress who didn't look like a model" – though it might be fair comment that in *Reuben, Reuben* that was rather what she did look like.

The difference, of course, is that in the earlier film McGillis was playing someone of roughly her own age. The Amish woman she plays in *Witness* is, one supposes, meant to be around thirty; the widowed mother, anyway, of a

boy of about ten. This was, then, a character rôle – and it seems that part of the preparation for it required McGillis to be force fed with a calorie-laden diet to give her something of the homely build associated with farmers' wives but not with models. (More usually, though for obvious reasons the fact tends to go unrecorded, actresses have to undergo the reverse process.)

McGillis also readied herself for the part by briefly working as an unpaid helper on an Amish farm, planting potatoes and helping with the milking as well as boning up on speech patterns; the sojourn was – mercifully, perhaps – cut short when her photograph appeared in a local paper and blew her cover.

But if the farm widow is a character rôle, it is not one in the attention-getting (and Oscar-winning) sense associated with alcoholism and the condemned cell. True, we see McGillis before we see Ford, but her part in the movie – and his, to some extent – is subordinated to the overall narrative design.

Yet this very absence of build-up serves as an apt test for a performer, and it is one that McGillis passes with flying colours. The portrait that she sketches for us is one that belongs to the deceptively difficult terrain of ordinary life. Albeit that this woman's existence is suddenly disrupted by violence and danger, she nonetheless inhabits the realm of the everyday, of cooking, mending, looking after a child and a home. (Quite how romantically diffused the movie's evocation of Amish life may be is another matter.)

Besides being a thriller, though, *Witness* is a love story, but one in which the attraction between widow and fugitive cop remains unconsummated and all but unspoken, something that in itself certainly constitutes a novelty on the contemporary screen. Discretion is the keynote: we may, along with Ford, get to glimpse McGillis *au naturel* but the effect remains reticent, chaste. Director and actress between them create a sense of delicacy of respect for feelings,

something more rarely achieved than eroticism.

Possibly, though, the film's single most memorable scene is one that occurs a little earlier. This is the episode where, as Ford works on repairing his car, the radio suddenly comes alive with the nostalgic strains of Sam Cooke's 'Wonderful World' and he is carried away to the extent of coaxing McGillis into a decorously improvised dance. Despite – or more likely because of – the predictable clinch being forestalled, the mutual feeling is conveyed to palpable effect.

Watching McGillis in *Witness,* one is nagged by a stray sense of recollection. Then, perhaps prompted by the neo-western

overtones of the climax, memory comes to the rescue. Surely it is not just the black, stylized severity of the Amish get-up which summons up the image of the young Grace Kelly as the Quaker wife in *High Noon,* the film which made her a star?

Come to think of it there was even an embryonic hint of Grace Kelly's later ambiguous coolness and *hauteur* about the youthful heroine of *Reuben, Reuben.* To identify Kelly McGillis as a potential successor to Grace Kelly might well seem, at this stage, to be expecting too much. But at the very least it will be interesting to find out.

TIM PULLEINE

F MURRAY ABRAHAM

Who remembers F Murray Abraham as a cocaine-smuggling hood called Omar in Brian De Palma's *Scarface*? He was the nasty piece of work, you may just recall, who got unceremoniously dumped from a high-circling helicopter about a third of the way through the picture.

The name – and certainly the exit – was rather more memorable than the rôle, even if the venerable Pauline Kael was moved to describe the actor's performance as "whirlwind". Anyway, you could have knocked down the entire film community with a feather when Abraham (the 'F' stands for Fahrid), probably best know to the American public for his Fruit of the Loom underpants TV ads, and Tom Hulce won the leading rôles in Milos Forman's film of Peter Shaffer's remarkable stage play, *Amadeus*.

Yet, when the Oscars for 1984 were handed out Abraham – who had, to all intents and purposes, been an unknown eighteen months earlier – was regarded by those-in-the-know as a certainty for Best Actor. He duly obliged, and we all felt we had known F

Murray Abraham for ever.

To say those lead rôles in *Amadeus* had been coveted was an understatement. The play, which originally opened in London in 1979 winning two Best Play awards, went on to take five Tonys on Broadway and play full houses; a *succes d'estime* as well as of the box office, the best of all possible worlds. Could there be any other choice than Paul Scofield for Salieri, the bitterly jealous court composer who 'murders' Mozart?

Scofield had created the rôle on stage quite brilliantly, but age – Salieri would have to gain forty years in the course of the movie – and bankability were likely to be factors, which is why Jack Nicholson and Donald Sutherland were variously mooted. Very soon though, Forman made it clear that major stars in the rôles would, he felt, work against credibility, particularly in the case of Salieri, which Forman described as "the most flowery stage rôle of the last decade. But that wouldn't do on screen. I felt in the movie all the intensity of Salieri's obsession had to be reflected in the actor's face.

Murray had that quality from the very first reading."

So where had the 45-year-old actor with the Magoo-like nose and pockmarked skin come from even to be in contention? A Texan from El Paso of Italian and Syrian parents, he first made his name with stage work on and off Broadway. He was a Cyrano and a Richard III as well as appearing in both the theatre and film versions of *The Ritz*.

But when he tested for the part of Salieri, he says: "I felt I was just going through the paces. I was sure they would never cast an American actor, at least one who was a non-star. In this day and age of the bottom line, it seemed inconceivable. After all, I knew who wanted the part. Who *didn't*?

"I think it is the best part written in the last three decades. Even *after* I got the part and congratulatory calls started coming in, I thought it would be snatched away from me at the last minute."

To prepare for the rôle Abraham learned how to play the piano for the first time, and also to read and conduct music while commuting between Prague and California where he was completing his rather different assignment on *Scarface*. He too came, as Tom Hulce did with Mozart, to admire the man he was portraying. "Salieri is so human in his responses. And he's not a coward. What do you do when you are a mediocre composer confronted with genius? Many people would simply quit. But Salieri didn't destroy his work or kill himself. He said no to fate. He was a courageous, crazy man."

Intriguingly, during the long sojourn in Czechoslovakia, Abraham and Hulce began to build up a rivalry and suspicion rather akin to the situation in the movie, starting during the rehearsal period. Apparently Hulce had a very close rapport with actress Meg Tilly, originally cast as Mozart's wife Constanze before breaking her ankle and having to be replaced by Elizabeth Berridge. Abraham recalls: "Tom and Meg were very close. They had these secret jokes and were always laughing

together. I was pushed out and I got resentful. I began to have very nasty feelings that were exactly like Salieri's feelings towards Mozart. When that correspondence between a film and real life occurs, it's a director's dream."

Judging by his finished performance, it's probably fair to say that the actor must himself have been pretty much a director's dream, whether reminiscing to the asylum priest under the weight of Dick Smith's extraordinary old-age make-up or smouldering with envy and resentment in his younger court composer guise.

Abraham, with an intensity that never spills over into artifice, makes us understand perfectly the dichotomy that's central to *Amadeus* – how could such God-given genius have been committed to such an oafish brat like Mozart. He registers clearly his disapproval of the young man, yet, in one particularly marvellous scene, where Constanze blithely hands over some of Mozart's work for Salieri's perusal, he quite movingly expresses his (and our) wonderment at such instinctive brilliance.

The climax of the film, Shaffer's one major invention for the screenplay, is a fascinating deathbed scene where Salieri collaborates with Mozart in taking down dictation for, and prompting, the dying composer's *Requiem*. The idea is that Salieri will eventually take credit for the piece to be played at Mozart's funeral thus hoping to snatch a piece of divinity for himself. There's a terrifying, almost vulpine, urgency on Abraham's face as we not only get to learn a little about the tortured process of composition but also, somehow, are persuaded to aid and abet in Mozart's 'murder'.

And how we all rally to Salieri with his final, chilling cry of: "Mediocrities everywhere – now and to come, I absolve you all." Whether Abraham can emerge from the *tour de force* of this first major rôle remains to be seen.

QUENTIN FALK

TIM McINNERNY

Early in *Wetherby* the character played by Tim McInnerny dismisses himself from the action. But Mr McInnerny is far from done for, and that face, interestingly almost immobile, will be around to haunt us. For the film which David Hare has written and directed is a film that looks back, reconstructs, recapitulates.

Tim McInnerny is not the central performer in this tale of memory and suppressed emotion. The central figure is a teacher played by that powerful and beautiful actress Vanessa Redgrave. She is the woman in whose presence – let's not try to conceal the crisis, for unless it is recognized discussion of the point of the film becomes impossible – the strange young man blows his brains out. This is not a film in which the dramatic shock comes at the end of act two, leaving act three to clear up the debris. Here it comes at the start, and in that respect *Wetherby* has the shape of a thriller; it goes on to investigate the past. And the life it investigates is the life of the teacher, witness to the suicide. The young man, perpetrator of the terrible act, is as I say by no means at the centre of the film. Nevertheless he is placed as the cause of recollection and investigation. And by force of performance he holds that position. He makes himself a central figure.

This is a political film, political not only in the comments of the teacher's dinner-guests – one of whom suddenly explodes in anti-Thatcher rage; she acts, he says, out of revenge, it's as if she were taking revenge for some deep damage. The film is fundamentally political, an exasperated reaction to the society we live in, the society which has formed us. David Hare sees England exemplified in the middle-class society of Wetherby: a society governed by concealment. People never let themselves go. Sometimes, he hints, there isn't anything to let go. Long restraint has destroyed the capacity for violent reaction; people have become dull. Life is lived under cover; whether by nature or by self-discipline, people avoid betraying themselves, they avoid surrendering to the extremes of emotion – and to the actions which surrender might bring.

But there is an exception: that strange young man. Not a central figure; nevertheless his madness, and his suicide is the action of a madman, throws into contrast the ineffectual sanity of the others. He is the irritant which provokes the rest of the world to reveal itself.

David Hare is a man of the theatre, a playwright with an international reputation. *Wetherby* marks his serious beginnings in the cinema. It is a bold beginning. Always keeping the undertone of political feeling, it darts between past and present; only little by little does the spectator arrange the fragments, and always at the heart of events there is the figure of the teacher; the savage suicide brings back half-forgotten memories of her romantic relationship in her past. As a young woman she is played by Redgrave's own real-life daughter (Joely Richardson). One sees her as the girl separated from the boy she cares for: social convention is the barrier until fate takes a hand. And while around her figures of the present revolve – the policeman finally led to the truth about the suicide, the girl who shrinks from close human relationship, all the acquaintances who attend the dinner party, prelude to the act of self-destruction – one character reacts against the general passivity. He is the outsider. He demands some response, some

active answer to his own existence. It is denied; and irrational but positive, he puts a gun in his mouth and pulls the trigger.

Thus Tim McInnerny's performance, though it cannot be taken as the dramatic centre of *Wetherby*, still gives the film the point on which it balances. The character McInnerny plays begins in mystery. He is not invited to the dinner party which opens the action and his hostess supposes that he has been brought by one of her friends; he is a gate-crasher, and his first appearance is an anti-conventional act. He is obsessed by the unresponsive girl; he breaks into her bedroom, only to be furiously ejected. At the library he is again refused: no, he is told, he can't take the books out, he can merely look at them. When in the final revelation the audience learns the truth about the relationship between hostess and uninvited guest, about their absence from the table and their secret sexual encounter, one more rebuff is added to the catalogue. The suicide, which for the audience is his introduction, is his mad passionate reaction to a past which is now to be recounted.

Not much of a rôle, one might say, in which to make a debut, for Tim McInnerny, like the director, is a newcomer to the feature cinema. And yet, with little speech and action almost inexplicable until too late for the audience to reflect, his image persists. It would be unfair to overemphasize the contribution of this young player. And yet he is somehow dominant: he dominates by immobility, by the look on a face which seems not to move, not to speak. Faintly elongated on the screen, it is a face which obeys the rules laid down for film players: feel, think, do nothing. One is grateful for the perceptiveness of casting which gave Tim McInnerny a chance; one looks forward to another opportunity. It would be a disappointment if inappropriate rôles or insensitive direction were to stifle this promising talent.

DILYS POWELL

HAING S NGOR

When Dr Haing S Ngor won the Academy Award as Best Supporting Actor for his performance as Dith Pran in *The Killing Fields*, a small measure of confusion arose as to whether or not the Cambodian was the first person honoured with an Oscar for his very first screen appearance. The question surfaced since Ngor's obvious predecessor in this rarified area of achievement, Harold Russell, seems to have participated in a documentary film prior to having portrayed the paraplegic soldier in *The Best Years of Our Lives*. Be that as it may, the two men clearly belong to a tiny, unusual and disparate group of individuals who have come from fields quite outside acting and proceeded to make deep impressions in their first and, in many cases, only film.

Like Russell, Ngor was the natural, perfect choice for his rôle in *The Killing Fields*. Despite his 'supporting' designation, Ngor is really the constant centre of the film, even when he's not seen, and it seems rather likely that he is actually on screen longer than Sam Waterston, even if he has less to say. Unlike Russell, however, Ngor wears most of his scars inside, not outside. Like the man he plays, Ngor was rounded up, put to work, questioned and tortured, and saw most of his family, as well as his girlfriend, die as a result of Khmer Rouge abominations. Just as Dith Pran did, Ngor managed to escape when the Vietnamese imposed themselves on Cambodia, and both men now live in America.

The simplicity, directness and emotional effectiveness of Ngor's work without question stems from the fact that he himself lived through much of what he is seen experiencing in the film.

The child of a poor family that later became wealthy from the lumber business, Ngor received a French medical degree and was a practising gynaecologist and surgeon when Khmer Rouge troops entered the cities and began rounding up citizens for relocation in the countryside. Like Dith Pran, Ngor masqueraded as a taxi driver,

knowing that either proof or admission of his true previous practice of Western medicine would mean an instant death sentence.

Between 1975 and 1979, Ngor was denounced three times, and on one of these occasions was strung up for five days and four nights and had his legs severely burned before being untied and allowed to live. Early on during his rural detention he was forced to plough fields with his hands for up to twenty hours a day, and to supplement his usual diet of two meagre bowls of rice he began his own small vegetable garden; for this infraction, guards cut off part of the little finger of his right hand. In May of 1979 he was finally able to escape through treacherous mine fields to Thailand, where he worked as a doctor in a refugee camp before being allowed to move to the US eighteen months later.

By 1982, Ngor had completed a course of study at Los Angeles City College and was planning to

enroll in UCLA Medical School (his French degree being of no use in his adopted country) when word began circulating locally that Cambodians were being sought to appear in a major film. Occupied with a $400-per-week position as a job counsellor on the Indo-Chinese Employment Programme at the Chinatown Service Centre, Ngor gave the picture little thought, saying that he considered himself neither

handsome nor young enough for a rôle. Fate intervened, however, in the person of a casting director who attended a Cambodian wedding in Oxnard, up the coast from Los Angeles, at which Ngor was also present. He says he accepted the part because he felt that the film would be "one hundred per cent good for my country", but he insists that he had no idea how important his part was until after he arrived for filming in Thailand.

While proved right in thinking that *The Killing Fields* would successfully re-focus attention on the tragedy that was, and is, Cambodia Ngor went on record that he felt the finished film did not go far enough in depicting the outright horror and brutality of what he and Dith Pran lived through. "Not bad enough, not suffering enough, not starvation enough," insisted the man who should know. "Never show how inhuman Khmer Rouge really is. I told this to Roland (Joffé, the director), but he said if it were too

real, people would not believe it."

Ngor toured and lectured extensively, more on behalf of his country, one felt, than of the film; he never failed to bring audiences up short with either detailed or brief descriptions of what he had lived through, and who among his listeners could possibly offer a personal history to compare, in its excruciating misery, with his? Not long after winning both the British and American Academy

Awards, Ngor was back at work at the Chinatown Service Centre and living in a small apartment in Los Angeles with his fifteen-year-old niece. A younger brother lives a few miles away, and in February 1984 he had the pleasure of being reunited, in Nice, with another niece and her family, whom he had not seen in ten years. Ngor maintains that he still plans to enroll at UCLA, but would like to improve his English before doing so. He also admits that he covets the idea of playing further film rôles.

Unless he started playing Oriental villains in thrillers and exploitation pictures (he's already been offered some), it is hard to imagine that Ngor will find many rôles to choose from. Certainly, his predecessors in the area of talented amateur actors have generally been remarkable one-shots rather than full-bloomers. Few of Rossellini's or Bresson's non-professionals have moved on to anything resembling acting careers. Aside from Harold Russell, probably the most notable example of an out-of-the-blue casting risk paying off was that of attorney Joseph Welch, who had represented the Army during the McCarthy Senate hearings and thereby become something of a national hero, as the judge in Otto Preminger's *Anatomy of a Murder*. Celebrated acting teacher Lee Strasberg had never acted in a film before when Francis Coppola convinced him to take on the rôle of the Jewish gangland kingpin in *The Godfather Part II*, and he was so good that it led to a booming late career as senior thespian, as unexpected as, if not the equal of, the third act of John Houseman's life. Truman Capote and Norman Mailer have 'acted' in fictional films, and any number of film directors have, from time to time, been talked into appearing in front of the cameras. But, however charming, amusing or appropriate any of these turns might have been, Ngor's heartfelt performance seems the least like a stunt. He's been where none of us ever want to be and lived to tell of it, eloquently.
TODD MCCARTHY

MIRANDA RICHARDSON

Miranda Richardson's performance in *Dance with a Stranger* is one of the most astonishing screen debuts for years, marking the arrival of a major talent. She should be cherished by the still renascent British film industry, for her qualities are special enough to be easily ruined, especially by the expert homogenizers of Hollywood who can render young actresses indistinguishable from one another.

She almost transcends acting in the film – the experience is more like being transported in a time machine back to the fifties. Here, trapped by a merciless observation, is a tart (though how Ruth Ellis hated that word) of the period: hair peroxide blonde, appearance impeccably neat, as pretty as a china doll and as fragile. Above all, it is the voice that convinces, with its attempt at gentility – high-pitched and full of subtly misplaced vowel sounds. It has the slightly strangled tones of a BBC announcer of the period (a time when radio newsreaders were possibly still wearing dinner jackets at the microphone), but

the words themselves and the grammar are wrong. And, as with Eliza Dolittle, at moments of stress the accent slips and a Cockney wail sounds through. The actions, too, are of someone trying to be 'ladylike' without ever having observed the real thing at close quarters.

Miranda Richardson, twenty-four and thus a child of the sixties, seemingly effortlessly conveys the essence of an earlier time. Born in Lancashire and trained at the Bristol Old Vic theatre school, she acted on the stage in Bristol (where a young Peter O'Toole first made his reputation) and elsewhere, and then on television, in some less than memorable series, before gaining her first screen rôle in *Dance with a Stranger*.

The film is based on the life and death of Ruth Ellis, the last woman to be hanged in Britain. It's an odd movie, often reminiscent of its shabby settings of cheap British films of the period. Shelagh Delaney's script completely ignores the trial in which Ruth Ellis, who shot her upper-class lover David Blakely after he abandoned her, was

hastened to the gibbet by the prejudices of class and sex. Possibly the reason was that these aspects were covered in J Lee Thompson's *Yield to the Night* (US title: *Blonde Sinner*), made in 1956 soon after Ruth Ellis's death. It was set in the death cell, was more a plea for the end of capital punishment and, incidentally, proved that Diana Dors could act although she never again had such a good rôle. *Dance with a Stranger*, in contrast, virtually ends with the murder itself.

Instead, Delaney and director Mike Newell concentrate on the two obsessional relationships in Ellis's life. There was her passionate affair with David Blakely, a racing driver portrayed by Rupert Everett as an irresolute, drunken charmer irresistibly drawn to Ruth Ellis, as she was to him, however badly he treated her.

And there was the dog-like devotion she inspired in Desmond Cussen (the ever-dependable Ian Holm) who supported her and her son for little emotional reward, becoming a cuckolded spectator to her grand passion. Although the intertwining of these two relationships is the entire concern of the film, there is little attempt to explain either. Both have to be taken on trust, accepted as given so that the audience can watch the working-out of the inevitable tragedy.

Miranda Richardson's likeness to Marilyn Monroe in her portrayal of Ellis is startling. There is the same sense of overwhelming vulnerability, the same feeling of a person out of control, skidding violently around the corners of life. She is someone on the edge of disintegration. The film catches with brutal accuracy the genteel squalor of the drinking clubs at the time – "with a knocking shop upstairs" – in which small-time crooks and wealthy vulgarians mingled with the upper middle-class slumming for excitement.

She shows Ellis's desperate desire for middle-class respectability, her hopes of raising enough money from running the club and from rich

boyfriends to finance buying a house or at least sending her son to boarding school. Her brightness has an air of vacuous vivacity about it; her expression, until Blakely stumbles into her life, is forever calculating.

The most affecting scene is one in which Blakely decides he must marry her rather than the nice girl his mother found for him, and drives her to the village where his mother lives. He goes ahead into a pub to prepare his mother for the meeting. She waits outside in the car. In the country setting, she, neat in her red scarf and white coat, looks out of place, an essentially urban creature. Then out of the pub comes a little group of the elderly upper-class, walking their dogs, thumping their walking sticks and talking inconsequentially – dialogue that is literally miles away from the brittle chatter of her habitat.

And as she stands and watches them disappear down a lane, you can see, simply in the expression on her face, the gradual and shocking realization of the unbridgeable social gap that divides her from Blakely. It marks the beginning of her breakdown.

As Ruth becomes more unstable, so Miranda Richardson brilliantly conveys her loss of reason until the final hideous moments when, drunk, angry and incoherent she stumbles down the road to finish her affair – although the murder does nothing but confirm her love. Her acting impresses by its maturity and the depth of emotion it can convey.

Miranda Richardson has already made two further films; *The Innocent* and *The Underworld*. The latter is one of those cautionary apocalyptic stories of a misshapen future. According to the rumours that filtered back from a closed set, she plays a mutant, ugly and deformed – as far removed as possible from the cheap glamour of *Dance with a Stranger*. It sounds like a fate worse than death, though it will take more than horrific make-up to disguise her blazing abilities.
JOHN WALKER

EMILIO ESTEVEZ

'Washed up at twenty-one' is Hollywood's newest tragic syndrome. Scores of gang movies are produced each year, each starring groups of fresh faces repeating stale jokes. The youthful cast imagine themselves driving Mercedes and bathing in asses' milk for ever. But all too soon, they're over the hill. One or two close-ups, two or three immersions in shaving cream, three or four screen credits, and it's goodbye making movies, hello selling stereos.

Only the lucky, the talented and the clever endure. Emilio Estevez had the luck to be born Martin Sheen's son (the second of three), the talent to survive Francis Coppola's *The Outsiders* ("What remains in the picture of my performance I'm pleased with") and the cleverness to write and produce a movie for himself *(That Was Then, This Is Now)*. Estevez, twenty-two, could well become the biggest Hollywood star whose name ends with a 'z' since Desi Arnaz.

Unlike most ethnically surnamed performers, Estevez chose the less mainstream label over his real name, Sheen. Actually, Estevez was his father's real name, so the son's choice was a rebuke as well as a declaration of independence. "Every time my name appears without his, I'm better off," he says in the firm, positive manner so reminiscent of his father.

"I like my old man a lot, and I'm not going to work with him again for a long time. We work well together. He played my father in a TV movie, *In the Custody of Strangers*, and it was fine. There have never been any problems between us, apart from that fight we had in the Philippines on the set of *Apocalypse Now* which Marlon Brando broke up and which I don't want to talk about.

"I just don't want the association between Dad's name and mine to be heavy. When I was starting out, every time my name was in print, so were his credits. I wanted to avoid that by using the Estevez name. 'Emilio Estevez' was a hurdle I put up for myself, and I got over it and kept on running."

Estevez can now rest on his own laurels. He achieved product identification unaided as one of the stars of *The Breakfast Club*, playing a tongue-tied, muscle-bound wrestler who learns to loosen up. In *Repo Man* he was a nice suburban kid whose car-thieving ways land him in deep radioactive trouble. In *St Elmo's Fire* he plays a law student with a dangerous romantic obsession. And he plays the villain in his own production of *That Was Then, This Is Now*.

One of Estevez' strengths is that he is a hard actor to pigeonhole. Unlike the instantly-castable here-today-gone-tomorrows, he doesn't semaphore one-word characteristics off the screen. Without being a chameleon-like character actor, he has proved himself capable of coming out of many different boxes.

One consistent Estevez quality is reserve. His characters seem to be trying to act older than they are. They're quiet, but they're quick learners. In *Repo Man*, he listens agog as Harry Dean Stanton tells him how to steal cars legally, and soon he's in there hot-wiring with the best of them. In *The Breakfast Club*, his strong silence throughout the first half of the movie turns out to be a pose covering up great fear.

Estevez creates good moments for himself because his characters don't explain themselves with a glance. The long smoulder sets up effective change-of-gear scenes. It's a talent that most of the great American dramatic stars have had. Or maybe in Estevez' case, it's cleverness.

"There never was any doubt in my mind what I was going to do When I was young, I knew I was going to be like my daddy. Whenever I said that, it was usually dismissed as kid's talk. I got older and then the rest of the world found out what I'd known all along."

Estevez has already worked out a programme for avoiding premature departure from the scene. "The idea is never to think you're more important or more interesting than the guy who pushes the camera dolly. If you get lost in the image of yourself, you become how other people see you, and that's when you fall prey to the drugs, the booze, the women and the I-wonder-what-happened-to-what's-his-name."

When he was eighteen, Estevez read S E Hinton's *That Was Then, This Is Now* and wrote the first of many drafts of his screenplay. "It didn't seem like anything I couldn't do. I found out, though, that writing is a lonely job, unless you're a drinker, in which case you always have a friend within reach."

Estevez had acquired the rights to the book "through my Dad's production company. I knew Susie Hinton wouldn't be too hot to give her book to some kid. Having Dad's name attached made it more legitimate, but beyond that he had nothing to do with it. He never even read my script – which was disheartening."

Trying to sell the project to the studios was even more disheartening, especially after the failure of Coppola's second Hinton movie, *Rumble Fish*. For someone Estevez' age, and the age of most moviegoers, the seventies are a fairly distant period, and Estevez found a seventies subject like *That Was Then* hard to market. The story, too, was just as downbeat as *Rumble Fish*. Estevez' character is "a real villain, a kid with no conscience and no morals."

Eventually, though, Estevez sold himself, the property and his screenplay to a group of investors in Minnesota, and the film ws shot in the autumn of 1984. The project enabled Estevez to stand out from all the other camera fodder. "Actors are often thought of as talking props. Every time you break out of that mould, you strike fear in the hearts of those who hold the producers' jobs, and I don't care. That just makes me stronger, because I plan on being more than a talking prop for the rest of my life."

BART MILLS

TIM ROTH

Tim Roth acts with his teeth. Look at him terrifying the cameras as the punk yobbo Trevor in the David Leland-written, Alan Clarke-directed television film *Made in Britain;* the shaven head, the tattooed swastika on the forehead, the pelican nose, but above all the faceful of astounding teeth like icebergs waiting for a *Titanic*.

And then look at him in *The Hit*. He's grown some hair – pale, carrot-hued and bristle-cut, so that he resembles some weird crested bird-youth – and he looks younger. His perversely boyish eyes make Myron an innocent from the start, as he motors hit-man John Hurt, captive Terence Stamp and hostage Laura Del Sol all across Spain towards a date with destiny. ("This country goes on for ever and ever, dunnit?") The big Roth nose, alert with daft quizzicality, seeks out information like a gnu let loose in a library. ("'Ow come they got so many castles, then?") But again it's the teeth that make the Roth charisma. The lips are bared in a shark's-tooth grin as he seeks eternal reassurances from his boss ("Everyfing all right, Mr Braddock?") or starts canoodling with Señorita Del Sol in the back seat ("Ah fink she's tiken a fancy to me"). And every time the mouth gapes or grins that mad, jagged landscape of molars lunges out towards the camera. If Roth ever appeared in a 3D film, we'd all run screaming from the cinema.

Was it ever thus, I hear you ask? Was he always an actor who liked to get his teeth into a rôle? Yes. Let us not forget that the first starring rôle for this now 23-year-old actor was in a school play as. . .Dracula! Those startling incisors, long, white and honed to a perfect point, like sentinel stalactites holding back the macabre curtain of his grin, were first deployed at the Dick Sheppard Comprehensive School in Tulse Hill. It was here that young Tim first decided that he had no particular ambition to become an actor.

So it was off to the Camberwell Art School to study sculpture. Was it here – and we become

speculative at this point – that Roth first learned the plastic possibilities of the human face and body? We are hesitant in saying yes, for a mere six months after signing on at the school he became impatient and threw in the chisel. At last the lights of the histrionic profession were beckoning! He trod the boards at the Cockpit Youth Theatre, the Royal Court Youth Theatre and the Oval Theatre; and when Philip Prowse of the famed Glasgow Citizens Theatre whisked him out of anonymity for a six-week run in Genet's *The Screens*, Roth was on the way to celebrity.

Today you can't watch Roth in *Made in Britain* or *The Hit* without wondering if he isn't *the* British actor of his generation. I don't mean 'actor' *à la* Gielgud or Olivier; one cannot see Roth purling blank verse at the

Barbican or braying sequipedelian soliloquies at Stratford. No, it's as an animated image of eighties nuttiness and disquiet – of dole-age anomy of Thatcher-era shell-shock and of the Dadaist aggro of Punk – that Roth triumphs.

Made in Britain made him, and Mike Leigh's *Meantime* refined, sharpened and perfected him: a numbskull anti-hero with the blazing light of doom and dottiness behind his eyes. In the first of these two telefilms Roth is a totem of almost mindless malignity. With his conk, his teeth and his cropped skull, he looks like Nosferatu. He smashes windows, steals cars, betrays friends. The tattooed imprints on his skin – though they're emblems (a snake, a swastika) not numbers – also seem to rhyme him with concentration camp victims. He's sinned against as

well as sinning. And he's *totally* the victim, even the holy fool, in *Meantime*: as Colin, that dumb rolled-up ball of grievance, like a human hedgehog, whose only late cry of articulate despair is to shave his skull. And not all the dancing, flibbertigibbet logorrhea of his attentive elder brother (Phil Daniels) can coax him into verbalising his melancholy.

Roth warms to Colin even less than we do: "a dim, asthmatic, smelly, horrible wally," he once told an interviewer. For the rôle, Mike Leigh ordered him not to wash his hair for fourteen weeks. This is the kind of command Roth has been getting used to. When making *Made in Britain* he wasn't allowed to bath for four weeks. Both TV characters are dumb, dirty, mutinous, eremetic; the human effluent of a post-affluent society.

It takes a rare actor to give this portfolio of foul qualities a defiant charisma. Yet he does. You can't take your eyes off Trevor; you can't help agonizing for Colin. And Roth gets his reward in *The Hit*, where inside the stock-in-trade numbskull scuzziness a lighter, more cocksure loopiness is trying to get out. Myron in this movie is just as much a walking waste-product as Trevor or Colin, but the Spanish sun has brought out a dormant frisk and swagger. Roth picks up the hint and runs with it, outstripping not only John Hurt, immured in dyspeptic menace throughout the pic, but even Terence Stamp whose grinning Myshkin innocence as the captive is cheerful but one-note.

Roth has the priceless actor's gift of being riveting in reaction as well as action. Watch him as he listens open-mouthed, and with a pixillated squint of awe and bewilderment, to Stamp's roadside speech about Life and Death. The speech ends, the listener's jaw still gapes, the eyes still stare and finally Roth, without changing expression, summons up his considered philosophical response: "You're barmy."

HARLAN KENNEDY.

LESLEY ANN WARREN

Lesley Ann Warren has always been a hidden artistic resource, obviously brimming with talent yet obscured by alternating extremes of typecasting that always seemed to peg her at a level below her full potential. She's been the recipient of enough lucky breaks to fill several careers, but it's often been the sort of fortune that turned on her: stillborn opportunities or promises kept that would have been better forgotten. She's emerged every time with her ability and her dignity intact.

However, after her Oscar-nominated turn as the blonde floozie with feelings and furies in *Victor/Victoria*, Warren shrewdly sought out two dissimilar rôles that persuasively showcase her as one of cinema's best performers: as a promiscuous but vulnerable bar-owner in Alan Rudolph's *Choose Me*, and as an aspiring country singer who eventually finds security in the gospel in his *Songwriter*. She's brilliant in both, and the challenge is now to the artists of the film industry to create the parts worthy of her.

Warren blossomed early. Trained as a dancer, aged fourteen she landed the lead in the national company of the musical *Bye Bye Birdie*, only to have her parents veto the job. Thereafter she originated the second female lead in *110 in the Shade* (a musical based on *The Rainmaker)*, in which she was spotted by director Charles S Dubin and tapped to play Cinderella in a 1965 television special. The fairy-tale image tarnished her for life. Walt Disney brought her to Hollywood as the ingenue in his last production, *The Happiest Millionaire* (1967), amidst hype as "the next Julie Andrews".

The film was not a success, but it's interesting to see how thoroughly Warren's mannerisms were already in place: the pout, the bite of the lower lip, the body seething with unrequited passions. There's something lascivious about her that makes her character's motivations seem more sincere than the film's fraudulent values. Warren was unhappy, suffering a

mini-breakdown at nineteen, doing another Disney *(The One and Only Genuine Original Family Band)* and marrying entrepreneur-hairdresser Jon Peters at twenty.

Though part of the same generation as Barbara Hershey, Karen Black or Carrie Snodgress, Warren was not considered for their rôles. Except for one all-star disaster *(Harry and Walter Go to New York)*, she wouldn't do another feature until 1981.

Instead, her stage work included Paul Sills' adaptation of Ovid's *Metamorphoses*, Scarlett O'Hara in the Harold Rome-Horton Foote musical of *Gone with the Wind*, and the Actors' Studio *Threepenny Opera*. After a single year replacing Barbara Bain on *Mission Impossible*, she became a queen of the MOW (television movie-of-the-week), largely by exploiting her turnabout from the Cinderella image in a series of prostitute and victim rôles: the mini-series *79 Park Avenue* (for which she won a Golden Glove); *Betrayal*, in which she was seduced by her manipulative psychiatrist (Rip Torn); *Portrait of a Stripper*, *Portrait of a Showgirl*, *Love Hate Love*.

Her work was much better than the titles suggest. Her victims fought back hard, however unsuccessfully as Hollywood ideology required. Warren raised the stakes in every rôle with a recklessness rare in television. She was painfully self-aware, but rarely capable of self-control. She stimulated an urge to tenderness in the viewer, because she made it plausible that such virtue would be its own reward.

When Blake Edwards paged her to play James Garner's moll Norma in *Victor/Victoria*, the character was neither blonde nor sported an accent. Norma's platinum wig and Brooklynese were products of a meticulously crafted background bio Warren devised, an effort rarely expended on caricatures. It has been observed that in this comedy of gender impersonation, Warren's bimbo mimics a drag-queen conception of feminine heterosexuality, and the

technical achievement is enhanced by suggesting such complex effects with such a limited behavioral vocabulary.

But such inspirations are their own dead-end: repetition would be meaningless. Warren marked time with a bad movie that was nevertheless underrated, John Avildsen's *A Night in Heaven*, in which Warren adapted her MOW longings for the big screen. The wind-up doll was ready to choose her own path.

She did so, daringly, with *Choose Me*. Rudolph's work had been distinctive but frustratingly inconclusive to date. Aesthetically, *Choose Me* accomplishes everything Rudolph had been attempting for years: a rhythmically complex, sexually sophisticated farce in which comedy shed light on contemporary romantic ideals. Every element of the film seems perfect, but the lynchpin of it all is Warren's emotionally complex creation, which provides the sentimental authenticity that makes the satire and eccentricities credible.

The rôle is like a compendium of all her past parts in microcosm: the bad luck with men, the overcoming of tough economic odds to achieve hard-won independence, the inarticulate yearning for romantic fulfilment, the rawness of her sexual needs. (Like all born stars, she can become her own icon; in addition, she can act.) She isn't funny like Geneviève Bujold's deluding

dispenser of sexual advice to radio listeners; Warren hasn't the liberty of sharing the jokes with the audience. She shares something deeper, and she has the technique to communicate delicate shadings of reaction and desire.

Songwriter is a simpler, less challenging part, with more room for actorly amusement, as Warren plays her chanteuse in loose conspiracy with Willie Nelson, Rip Torn and Kris Kristofferson. She makes stage fright palpable and, armed with pungent Bud Schrake dialogue, she fully creates a background and psychology with minimal strokes.

Lesley Ann Warren has changed little throughout it all, merely using her preternatural empathy with both the spunky indomitability and the masochistic vulnerability of women characters to more pointed, worthwhile ends. I suspect she's got talents yet to be tapped. She's certainly earned the chance to have less good luck and more solid work. She's fresher and more original (and daring) than most of the stars in her age-bracket, and if movie audiences ever get a chance to sample her wares, she might become just as bankable. There's no justice in the world, as any Lesley Ann Warren character learned long before puberty, but here's hoping just the same.

MYRON MEISEL

KIDS FROM 'AMERICA'

When a film is an all-of-a-piece entity like Sergio Leone's *Once Upon a Time in America,* one is reluctant to think about the component parts involved. So smoothly have the elements of casting, costume, music, cinematography and decor been combined with the narrative of this gangster epic, that they all seem to be somehow, magically there – a perfect, impregnable, circular whole. Still, getting down to cases should never be avoided, especially as far as one pivotal aspect of Leone's grand-scaled saga is concerned – the casting of younger performers to play the principals as children.

Ordinarily something relatively simple would be required – juveniles capable of a few scenes worth of work stylistically imitative of the stars who would portray their characters when older. Gangster films of yore like *Manhattan Melodrama* and *Angels with Dirty Faces* were rife with such scenes, filled with telling moments underscoring key events and character flaws that the film

would go on to show made them 'go bad'. Leone's film, however, is cut from a different cloth. He has not the slightest trace of interest in facile psychologising – or any character psychology of the 'causal' sort for that matter. As children his protagonists are as fully formed as they are later as adults. Consequently the childhood scenes do not so much foreshadow later events as introduce behaviour patterns the film continues to expand upon. Moreover, as Leone's complex back-and-forth time structure insists that the past and present act in the narrative as one, these kids are of necessity *already* their adult selves. Luckily for Leone, in every case the younger players prove worthy of their adult counterparts.

As the young Noodles, Scott Schutzman may not facially resemble Robert DeNiro, but his physical movements are the same – particularly the sad weariness of his walk. Still a teenager, he is already the melancholy old man he will become. The terse determination with which he

spits out a key line – "My old man's crying and the old lady's praying. What have I got to go home for?" – speaks volumes about the who/what/why of his character without methodically spelling things out.

Rusty Jacobs as compatriot/antagonist Max (later to be stunningly embodied by James Woods) is just as impressive. Our first sight of him – riding a cart piled high with belongings, as if already a duke in his own domain – radiates with knowing subtlety. The smirk that crosses his face as he bests his supposed pal at every turn has yet to turn into a snarl, but we can feel it rising.

Jennifer Connelly as the young Deborah is the most spectacular of all – so much so that for many she totally wipes Elizabeth McGovern, who plays her as an adult, right off the screen. There's a precedent for this of course – Jean Simmons in *Great Expectations*. And it is that film, rather than *Dead End,* that is clearly on Leone's mind as this creamily glowing nymphet dances in a storage room filled with dusty sacks of provisions before the watchful eye of Schutzman's Noodles, peering at her through a hole in the wall of a lavatory. From this primal scene a life-long obsession – with its accompanying full-flown neurosis – is born.

And then there are the other

children. Noah Moazezi is heartbreaking as little Domenick – scaring himself with his own reflection in the mirror in one scene, dying with off-hand bravery in another. Brian Bloom's portrayal of young Patsy is no less memorable, particularly in the now-famous Charlotte Russe scene. Attempting to buy the favours of a young tart (Julie Cohen as Peggy – another stellar juvenile) he sits on a stairway waiting for her – only to reward himself with the pastry instead.

This scene, an unsettlingly delicate mixture of childhood treats with adult obsessions, marks Leone's film (along with *Moonfleet* and *Night of the Hunter,* but against *The 400 Blows* and *Paris Texas)* as one regarding nascent experience with a dryly jaundiced eye. It also underscores the fact that the director – previously noted for his action skills – is largely responsible for the performances we see here. Still, each young actor deserves a bow. At a time when Hollywood puts youth above all else, talents such as these shouldn't go unnoticed. Unfortunately, it is doubtful whether any of these young talents will work with an artist as sensitive, sympathetic and profound as Sergio Leone in the near future.

DAVID EHRENSTEIN

JOHN MALKOVICH

For someone who is about to become a leading man of the cinema, John Malkovich is no oil painting. At thirty he is already bald, a fact perhaps unfairly emphasized by a dome-like forehead. His chin is certainly a strong feature, in a face that otherwise notably lacks them. There is not much distance between his eyes, and they, in turn, seem to be buried very deep at the back of longish tunnels. He has no voice to speak of.

Moreover, he seems to treat the medium with disdain. "I don't understand film that much and I don't think they are . . . much fun to act in. It's real difficult to get used to films and what they entail, and how long they drag on. It's too technical a medium and it's unfair to actors. They spend four or five hours setting up lights, yet would never dream of rehearsing a scene for four or five hours, or shooting for four or five hours once the scene is perfectly lit. The acting part which people watch is given the least attention. I find that infuriating."

This is, of course, no more than the traditional complaint that actors still in love with theatre bring to this thin and bloodless medium; but for someone supposedly given little attention during the shooting process, he has certainly managed to capture enough attention in the two rôles in which he has appeared to date.

In his first appearance in *The Killing Fields*, there is a scene in which he is keeled over on a bed with a pair of sanitary towels over his eyes. In his second rôle in *Places in the Heart*, he is blind. It is, of course, a reviewer's conceit to suggest that this might have anything to do with those criminal's eyes; but in the stills used to publicize *The Killing Fields* they certainly have an unnerving power, like some beast crouching deep inside its lair and watching your approach to the mouth of the cave. It is as if the two films needed to curb their murderous look.

Born and raised in the small, southern Illinois town of Benton (a nice coincidence, given that Robert Benton was the director of *Places in the Heart*), his grandmother was publisher of the *Benton Evening News*, his mother a secretary and his father, now dead, director of the State Conservation Department and editor of his own conservation magazine. ("We were the only people there who could read.") He acquired a reputation for eccentricity early in adolescence, when he starved himself on nothing but Jello for three months, emerging considerably thinner than his previous fat self, and then adopted a taste for outrageous clothing. It was not until college that he acquired the habit of acting, and then not always successfully. A fellow actor, Tom Irwin, said of him: "He always was a great poseur. And he had this enormous head. We used to call him Tweetybird."

The prestigious Steppenwolf company in Chicago, which he helped found, became Malkovich's base for seven years, during which time he also drove a school bus to help make ends meet. Apparently the children would stand at the back of the bus and wave their fists at him and yell: "Hasn't it gotten through to you why no one sits in the front of the bus. You're weird, you're weird. You're the freak." Apparently he loved this. "John is really attracted by juvenile behaviour," says Irwin.

In the 1984 Broadway revival of *Death of a Salesman* he played Biff to Dustin Hoffman's Willy Loman, apparently on Robert Duvall's recommendation after Duvall had seen him in Sam Shepard's *True West*. A friend described the performance as being like "the person Kubrick did in *A Clockwork Orange;* you can't tell whether he'll kill you or write the Ninth Symphony." David Puttnam's casting director saw him in this production and arranged his appearance in *The Killing Fields*.

The rôle of war photographer is one which has a strong modern pedigree. From the various (illiterate) memoirs of the Vietnam 'war-junkies', few of whom survived, to the cooler, more telling scenarios from Briton Don McCullin, they seem to epitomize a kind of washed-out romanticism, last seen perhaps among the Hemingway expatriates of the twenties, but embodied in a state of speed-induced frenzy. Dennis Hopper set the tone in *Apocalypse Now*, suggesting that he would have made a better Kurtz than Brando's hippo-like preacher. In *The Killing Fields,* Malkovich's Al Rockoff has all the requisite zest and manic energy, springing to life only when his street becomes the scene of hideous death from bombing. But there is also a moment when he has the sense to modulate the performance to something approaching humanity; when he accompanies Sam Waterston's Schanberg to a Cambodian hospital, his wiry body goes slack with horror at the carnage, and for the first time he does not set his camera clicking.

There is also the episode of trying to forge a passport for Dith Pran when imprisoned in the French Embassy, a scene which owes its extraordinary power and suspense entirely to Malkovich's ability to bounce off walls.

His part as Mr Will, the blind lodger taken in by small-holding cotton-farmer Sally Fields in *Places in the Heart*, is one that might have tempted other actors into all sorts of groping mannerisms. Malkovich not only avoids the obvious moves, but manages to take a smallish rôle and show us the man's journey from a very spiky kind of self-reliance, clearly based on deep hurt, to a touching inclusion within the eccentric family fold. Moreover it is done with great, unforced dignity.

There is a moment when he comes blundering into the kitchen to complain that Sally Fields's children have been breaking his book-for-the-blind records. The row is only stopped when his hand accidentally touches the water in which Fields is having a bath. The sudden perplexity of a blind man, suddenly confronted by what he knows must be a naked woman, is a miracle of conflicting emotions made apparent. To have one's fury cut off in mid-stream, to be confronted by a naked woman, to remember what that confrontation was once like, to be reminded of all you have lost since going blind, to be embarrassed by her presence, to be embarrassed by your embarrassment because there are clearly no grounds for embarrassment since she is invisible – all of these things would normally be the stuff of literature. To indicate them dramatically all at once is a fine piece of acting. To have invented the whole scene yourself is nothing short of genius; according to Robert Benton, the whole episode was due to Malkovich's improvisation.

CHRIS PEACHMENT

M EMMET WALSH

If, as received wisdom has it, the thirties were the heyday of the movie character actor, the explanation may be twofold. Films then were more traditionally and formulaically structured, but there were also simply more of them. Thus, an archetypal supporting player like the pugnacious Frank McHugh, the unforgettably dyspeptic editor in *Mystery of the Wax Museum,* appeared that same year, 1933, in no fewer than fourteen other films.

Over the intervening decades, not only has the number of movies been progressively reduced, but the dividing line between leading player and support has tended to blur, with translation from the latter status to the former becoming both easier and more rapid – witness, for recent instance, the cases of Bruce Dern and (pre-eminently) Harry Dean Stanton. Both these players are distinctively tall and gangling, and perhaps there is general truth in the proposition that whereas those in the dwindling species of old-time star possess an indefinable (metaphysical) presence in front of the camera, character players are frequently marked by a clearly definable (essentially physical) sense of shape.

M Emmet Walsh, whose indelibly seedy embodiment of a crooked private eye in *Blood Simple* confirms his place in the front rank of current character actors, is – by contrast to Dern or Stanton – fleshy and corpulent. He is not fat after the epicene manner of Sydney Greenstreet or Laird Cregar, but burly, in the tradition of such fifties stalwarts as Ted De Corsia or Emile Meyer. The latter may be recalled as the warden in *Riot in Cell Block 11* or (best of all) the sadistic cop in *Sweet Smell of Success;* and Walsh, too, has hitherto made most impact on the screen in the guise of ambiguous authority figures, at once smug and bullying – Dustin Hoffman's parole officer in *Straight Time,* the police chief who in coerces Harrison Ford back into action in *Blade Runner.*

In fact, Walsh's credits go back

a good few years, as far as *Little Big Man,* though, to be truthful, memory fails to retrieve his appearance as 'shotgun guard' in that movie. More recent pictures in which he has tangentially featured include *Ordinary People* (he was the swimming coach) and *Reds,* and he has, in the phraseology of the hand-out biography, "numerous TV

movies-of-the-week to his credit, and has guest-starred on many top series," ranging from *Mary Hartman* to *The Waltons.*

But while Walsh has evidently been through the acting mill, there is something about him, in common with many of the best character players, that is reassuringly unactorish. Indeed, there seems, however illogically, to be some confirmation of this in the discovery that he graduated from college with a degree not in dramatic arts but in business administration. Moreover, the fact that one has been unable to find out his date of birth seems obscurely appropriate, too: he is one of those performers who somehow belongs to a perpetual

middle-age.

Writing in *Film Comment* about *Blood Simple,* Hal Hinson appropriately describes Walsh's characterization as "a redneck variation on all the bad cops and corrupt gumshoes in the hard-boiled genre." The effectiveness of the performance is that at one and the same time it offers in plot terms a ready-made shorthand

notation, and in human terms, something more. The studied drawl and the gross cackling laughter are perhaps, persuasive as they are, the expected props of this sort of shady specimen; but they are supplemented by a grotesque brand of defeated dignity – summoned up (for it is a rôle in which conception and execution are seamlessly melded) in the jaunty straw hat which the double-dealing tec keeps at the ready throughout, even using it to fan himself as he surveys the body of the man he has just shot dead.

With his bulging midriff and watery blue eyes, Walsh's investigator-cum-assassin-for-hire becomes a palpable presence on the screen. More than any

other element in the film, he contrives to anchor *Blood Simple* in a milieu where the suggestion that a bar might offer discounts to alcoholics seems to be made only half in jest, and to prevent it becoming only an exercise in post-*noir* style. (Incidentally, Hinson seems off the mark in describing the character as "the kind of half-witted vermin who likes to

torture puppies in his spare time": his corruption is surely rooted in pragmatism rather than perversion and he appears to have his wits very much about him.)

Since *Blood Simple,* Walsh has, sad to say, been seen as the statutory good ole boy sidekick to Chuck Norris in the execrable *Missing in Action* – a demonstration if ever there was one that more, as far as higher billing goes, can sometimes mean less in other respects. These days, though a good character actor is hard to find, it sometimes seems that finding a good character part is harder still.

TIM PULLEINE

QUOTES OF THE YEAR

"I'd prefer not to die by accident. I hope when death comes, it will tug my sleeve gently, touch my eyes with its fingers and close them."
John Huston

"According to tradition, I'm on the road to a self-inflicted death. . . But I don't do drugs of any kind (never did). I'm afraid of guns (always was). And I'm a damn good driver (always will be). So, the only way I'm gonna go is via a plane crash, cancer or a bar-room brawl. I don't drink, so why would I be in a bar-room? I sincerely hope I don't get cancer. And if I ever go down in a plane, I want to speak into the black box so I can be the only one in history to be taped telling the pilot: You're an incompetent swine and I hate you!"
Eddie Murphy

"Chaplin v Keaton? I despise Chaplin. I think he was a faggot. He drives me up the wall. He's so *prissy*. So English – I mean that in the worst sense. I just want to reach into the screen and punch the little fucker. Keaton's just brilliant, one of the funniest people ever on the screen."
Tony Hendra, 'Spinal Tap' star

"The big studios make films like fast food."
Francis Coppola

◆◆◆◆◆◆

"Hollywood is simply geared to cheat you left, right and bloody centre."
John Hurt

◆◆◆◆◆◆

"One of the nicest things ever said to me was by the head of Equity, the actors' union, who told me. 'I need you to be successful: It's important to me and my members.' That's the only British person in my life I can remember saying such a straightforward thing to me."
David Puttnam

"David (Puttnam) said nobody had spoken to him since he won an Oscar for *Chariots of Fire*. Lindsay Anderson said, 'I'm very glad for you, David. You like that kind of thing.' The English, wallowing in failure, bitterly resent success."
John Boorman's diary for July 1982, published 1985

"You read a script and you're really depressed for the rest of the day. You go to a meeting and there are all these people wearing tennis shoes – you know, the latest tennis shoes. And you're depressed that humanity has reached this level."
Coppola art director Dean Tavoularis, on Hollywood

"The moment I told him to stop interfering, he declared war on me, inventing absurd stories, doing everything to make me look like the one responsible for all the problems."
Francis Coppola, on 'Cotton Club' producer Robert Evans

"It's his vision of the movie, not mine."
Robert Evans, on Coppola's 'Cotton Club'

"I saw *The Cotton Club* and I told Coppola: 'After this disaster, there's only one thing for you to do. Commit suicide'."
Kenneth Anger

"America only makes children's pictures."
John Hurt

"Robert Redford is the centre of America – blond, blue-eyed, tall and thin."
Barry Levinson

"It's the director who puts his neck on the line. There are only a few producers who actually hold a film together and I'm not one of them."
Alan Marshall

◆ ◆ ◆ ◆ ◆ ◆ ◆
"I spend most of the time in bed, or losing at tennis, or just being normal."
Sting
◆ ◆ ◆ ◆ ◆ ◆ ◆

"Movies full time? I don't know. I'd have to stay in Los Angeles and with the sexual freedom out there, you can catch stuff that'll make your thing fall off!"
Eddie Murphy

"I want to make a film about LA, this multi-racial society made up of dozens of different minority groups – and all bound together by one unifying factor. Greed."
Bob Swaim, 'La Balance' director on his 'Gold' project

"In England, the critics write about your films – they never think of *talking* about them with you."
Bill Forsyth

"I can write. I think that I edit quite well. I know I could direct – but I'd be mediocre."
David Puttman

"The only thing that stands between this film and greatness is – me."
'2010' writer-producer-director-cameraman Peter Hyams

"What acting really is, is pretending – while you're pretending you're not pretending."
Ted Danson of 'Cheers'

"Acting? It's very sensual. When you're working for a good director, you become subjective and submissive within the security of the boundaries he is creating. So, in his hands, you become his concubine. All that you're seeking at the best of times is his pleasure."
Donald Sutherland

"Acting is hard. Very hard work. You work hard for very many years to learn a technique which you then have the audacity to forget."
William Hurt

◆ ◆ ◆ ◆ ◆
"When I was about eight years old, I happened to mention to my father that I wanted to be an actress and he gave me a wallop in the face."
Greta Scacchi
◆ ◆ ◆ ◆ ◆

"Too much money can be bad for a film."
Richard Goodwin, producer, 'A Passage to India'

"One worm in *Dune* cost more than twice the entire budget of *Paris, Texas.*"
Dean Stockwell

"I'm not crazy about science fiction and I'd never read *Dune.* When Dino's office called me, I thought they said: *June.*"
David Lynch

"David Lynch is the main reason I agreed to do *Dune.* He's very urbane and charming. . .in many ways a quite formal man. And yet, that's just the surface. Underneath, he's a seething mass of angst."
Sting

"Sidney Lumet had seen me in Mel's film and called me. 'Annie, I've a part for you but you're too young and beautiful and sexy.' I said, Sidney, in *To Be or Not To Be,* I wore lifts, I was photographed very lovingly and I was sleeping with the producer."
Anne Bancroft

"If one of them had to play a prophet, he didn't feel the need to go off and sit on a hillside for six months. He just turned up and played a prophet."
Bruce Beresford, on his actors in 'King David'

"You've got to donate yourself to the character. You can't say: 'Jeeze, will I look as sharp as I have in some films?' "
Clint Eastwood

"Naturalism is appearing to be perfectly natural. Of course, you're not: if you were, nothing much would happen. You have to have a very strong degree of energy to appear to be acting natural."
Rex Harrison

"Lady Booze is a very cruel mistress. . .but if we lived a normal, comfortable, middle-class existence, it would be quite impossible to summon the range of emotions required of us as actors."
John Hurt

"In Hollywood, you're a veteran if you have a job of more than six weeks tenure with one company."
Jack Valenti, president of the Motion Picture Association of America

"Movies are the repository of myth. Therein lies their power. An alternative history, that of the human psyche, is contained and unfolded in the old stories and tales. Film carries on this tradition."
John Boorman

"Since the Oscar, I haven't had any big offers although I've had some Hollywood lunches."
Robert Epstein, director of Best Documentary Feature, 'The Times of Harvey Milk'

Brazil will be like Terry Gilliam's Monty Python cartoons which, in turn, are exactly like him – the tangible shape of his dreams."
Jonathan Pryce

◆ ◆ ◆ ◆ ◆

"I got into the habit of going to an art house in Glasgow and seeing films by Godard and Malle. I combed my hair like Maurice Ronet."
Bill Forsyth

◆ ◆ ◆ ◆ ◆

"Movies are fun. But they're not a cure for cancer."
Clint Eastwood

◆ ◆ ◆ ◆ ◆ ◆ ◆

"If I played Hamlet, they'd call it a horror film."
Peter Cushing

"We've had to fight stereotyping for years. It used to be that you didn't work in Hollywood until a circus movie came around. Or, come Christmas time, you'd get a job in a commercial playing an elf."
Dwarf actor Billy Barty

"The content of my films is a secondary issue. I don't start with an idea about content. I start with a *visual image*. I may be one of the few practitioners doing that today. . . I like interesting visual spaces, architecture. I like photographing women because they're aesthetically interesting."
Brian De Palma

"Pictures are not wine. We don't believe in laying them down to gather dust."
Menahem Golan

The moguls we loved to hate were the picture-makers. Today they make more deals than movies. They give you a 'positive maybe'."
Andre De Toth

"A lot of people know what they're doing. I don't know until the next day."
John Cassavetes

"Hollywood doesn't want to make the same pictures I do and I'm too old to change."
Robert Altman

"He is wonderfully subversive, and wickedly funny. Half of what he says, I am sure, is designed to mislead young film-makers."
John Boorman, on Jean-Luc Godard

"Coca-Cola is deeply committed to this (film) business. We like it. We are here to stay. The closeness to consumers is what appeals to us."
Donald Keough, president Coca-Cola, owners of Columbia Pictures

"Am I the sort of person who wants to be in control? No, I'm not. You have to separate me from the stage character. He *has* to be in control or there's no gig. There's anarchy, there's nothing."
Sting

"It's the only hotel I've ever been in where the maids steal the towels that the guests have swiped from other places."
Paul Mazursky, on the Maria Cristina Hotel during the San Sebastian festival

"Sex is not like a hula-hoop. It's not a fad. It's here to stay."
Marilyn Chambers

"At 18, I was the oldest virgin in Chelsea."
Jane Birkin

"There was a bit of male nudity in *Lassiter* and that was handled well. It did not stick out."
Tom Selleck

"I don't see filmed nudity as something scary. . .or obscene. It's not something I am afraid of. I think nudity is easier if there are two of you. . ."
Greta Scacchi

"Most porn films I've ever seen are a wonderful argument in favour of blindness."
Al Goldstein

"The only scripts I've been sent have been so highly pornographic – highly pornographic! – that I'd like to see the films but not be in them."
Rex Harrison

"The stuff that is shot and sold as porn is meant to get you aroused and to climax. I don't think my movies have people coming in their seats."
Brian De Palma

"After a director is fired, it's like he's got AIDS. Nobody will touch him. Nobody wants to come too close."
Director Martin Brest, sacked from 'WarGames', coming back with 'Beverly Hills Cop'

◆ ◆ ◆ ◆ ◆
"I find it really disappointing that a lot of American actors will go to great lengths to gain weight or lose weight or dye their hair – and use the same voice!"
Kathleen Turner
◆ ◆ ◆ ◆ ◆

"Most of us go through life searching for the unobtainable and if we do get it, we find it's unacceptable."
John Huston

"If he heard his best friend was dying while he was on the set, I doubt if he'd take it in. Once he's started work on a film, there's really nothing else in his life."
Ronald Neame, on David Lean

"I had fun with David Lynch and the other actors but it certainly wasn't playing Hamlet."
Sting, on 'Dune'

"If this is going to be an article on women directors, I refuse to be part of it."
French director Diane Kurys

"*Ma chère* Cher – sorry you have to share."
John Boorman, presenting the shared Best Actress award at Cannes

"We tried foam appliances that fit over Daryl Hannah's breasts, which made them look like breasts without nipples. But at the last minute, everyone decided that we'd never get the audience *not* to look at her breasts *especially* if they didn't have nipples."
'Splash' make-up effects man Robert Short

"I'm very irritating to some people. It fascinates me, though, because I'm so sweet really."
Katharine Hepburn

"My first movie was *Going in Style* with George Burns as a pensioner robbing a bank. He called up the studio after we first met and said: 'You told me he was young but you didn't tell me he was *that* young. I have *ties* older than him!'"
Director Martin Brest

"Captain Bligh was a wonderful man. A wonderful, dull man, and a superb navigator. Christian was knocked out by the exotica of the South Seas and Bligh couldn't help but disapprove. I was raised a Quaker. I know about these things."
David Lean, on his 'Bounty' plans

"Don't ask me what the film's about because I don't know. It's wonderful and interesting but impossible to describe."
Tony Curtis, on 'Insignificance'

"I was converted to Catholicism fairly early in my career – at 29. Until then I was wandering in a mist. There was a blinding light or something and suddenly I knew how to do. . .everything. But I didn't stay in the Catholic faith very long. I left it because I couldn't live up to it."
Ken Russell

"I have a very bland face. It's not shopworn, lived in. We have this thing in my family that no one seems to age. My father at 55 looks like my brother."
Christopher Reeve

◆◆◆◆ ◆ ◆

"I wouldn't mind betting that of my half dozen closest friends in Britain who were able to vote in the Academy Awards, four of them didn't vote for *The Killing Fields*. As much as they are fond of me, they can't deal with the notion of my being rampantly successful."
David Puttnam

◆ ◆ ◆ ◆ ◆ ◆

"The very worst moment is the first half-hour of the day's work. . .sometimes I'll tell the camera operator: would you please tell those guys to fuck off and come back in twenty minutes. I can't think with all of them looking at me."
Bill Forsyth

"On *Deathwatch*, Harry Dean Stanton got his part very quickly. He said: 'I'll play my character as a cross between Hugh Hefner and David Frost'."
Bertrand Tavernier

"Paul Henreid told me a story about Michael Curtiz making *Casablanca*. Curtiz suddenly decided he needed a poodle for a scene. The prop man and assistant directors ran in all directions, searching and making calls. Meanwhile, Curtiz and Bogart played chess. . .Eventually, an animal wrangler arrived with a selection of poodles for the director to choose from. 'Not a poodle!' he screamed. 'A poodel! With water!' "
John Boorman

"The difference between Richard Pryor and Eddie Murphy is that Richie is really, genuinely black—a black comedian speaking to black people that the white people happen to overhear. Whereas Eddie is playing the street black for the white audience. He's not a street black at all. He comes from a middle-class family on Long Island. He hasn't really got anything to say. He's just got a posture."
Tony Hendra, 'Spinal Tap' star

"I always think of Eddie Murphy as being more Jewish than black."
'Beverly Hills Cop' director Martin Brest

"If you're young, like me, and driving a great and new car, people say 'Where'd he steal that?' and the cops say 'Pull over!' then they say: 'Wow! It's Eddie Murphy!!! Can I have an autograph?' It bothers me that I'm treated nasty until they know who I am."
Eddie Murphy

"Close to 17,00 stores are selling and renting video cassettes in the United States. The X-rated biz has become a home and hearth industry. We finally took sex out of the theatres and put it back in the bedrooms where it belongs."
David F Friedman, Adult Film Association of America

"If I'm attracted to something I shouldn't refuse to use it just because Hitchcock was attracted to it, too."
Brian De Palma

◆ ◆ ◆ ◆ ◆ ◆

"It's very good to get through them while you're still young, and then talk about how great or bad they were for the rest of your life."
Carrie Fisher, on drugs

◆ ◆ ◆ ◆ ◆ ◆

◆ ◆ ◆ ◆ ◆ ◆

"When Mel told his Jewish mother he was marrying an Italian girl, she said, 'Bring her over. I'll be in the kitchen – with my head in the oven.' "
Anne Bancroft

◆ ◆ ◆ ◆ ◆ ◆

"I was not among those who believed that *Mishima* was going to get made. In fact, I don't think there was anyone among those who thought it was going to be made! It wasn't until New Year's Day 1984, when my daughter was born in Tokyo, that I really felt the film would get made. Being born on New Year's Day is a very important omen in Japanese society, because until recently it used to be the national birthday and everyone's birthday was January 1. . . Three or four days later George Lucas decided he would back the film."
Paul Schrader

"How do I keep fit? I lay down a lot."
Robert Mitchum

"I haven't had an easy ride, but at least it has been a ride."
Nicolas Roeg

"'Make my day' came from the screenwriter, Joe Stinson. Only thing I did is I reprised it at the end – that's my contribution. I saw the line as a goodie, so I said let's throw it in right here."
Clint Eastwood

"I'm less confident now. I'm terrified of doing something wrong."
Eddie Murphy, after 'Beverly Hills Cop'

"Without music I'd just keel over and die."
Ken Russell

"Because I dislike being quoted I find I lie almost constantly when talking about my work."
Terry Gilliam

◆ ◆ ◆

"It ain't *Dirty Harry*, is it?"
Gary Busey, on 'Insignificance'

"Because I first appeared in *Behind the Green Door* when I was 19, everyone thinks I'm stuffed away in some geriatric ward now. My body is my business and I work on it every day."
Marilyn Chambers (35)

"I remember complaining to Bob Rafelson about all the interviews scheduled for us. He said, 'It's easy. All you have to do is change your story every time.' And he would. In one I read he said he'd been a Jesuit priest!"
Jessica Lange

"I think you'd have to be around for a year before you saw his ugly side, assuming he has one."
Norman Mailer, on Clint Eastwood

◆ ◆ ◆

"I only go to America if I'm invited. I certainly wouldn't go there to grub for work."
John Hurt

◆ ◆ ◆

"The first two *Supermans* cost $120 million but those who wound up making money were the distributors, not I. I was losing my money until *Superman III* and *Supergirl*, with which I reduced my losses. *Santa Claus* will be the decisive film."
Alexander Salkind

"Anything funny will make me laugh. I hear jokes that are racist and insult me as a black man, but if they're funny – I laugh."
Eddie Murphy

"My ideal state would be to do an action picture and then a comedy and for every other action picture, a Western."
Walter Hill

"If there's any secret to my success – and I've never sat down and tried to be analytical about it – I think it's that the audience rides along with me."
Clint Eastwood

"He's very laid-back. If you don't bother him, he will never bother you. In that sense, he's like the characters he plays in his films."
Norman Mailer, on Clint Eastwood

"They are all so jealous in Hollywood. It's not enough to have a hit. Your best friend should also have a failure."
Peter Bogdanovich

Private Parts – the comedy that keeps getting bigger."
(Cannes sales hype)

"The first time I hardly felt it because it was all so new. . . But now I feel it. You like me! You like me!"
Sally Field, not on sex but collecting her second Oscar

"In high school I used to play rôles differently each act. What if he limps? He didn't limp in the first act – and he lisped in the third!"
William Hurt

"Good rock'n'roll is a very high testosterone outlet. Movies are very oestrogen – they take you in, give you a house, make you dinner while you warm your feet by their fire. But rock'n'roll grabs your ear, wrestles it to the ground and slaps a big wet kiss on it."
Carrie Fisher

"As I get older, the parts will probably be better. That's happened to Michael Caine and he's become more rumpled."
Christopher Reeve

"You just listen to lectures all day long. And watch movies like *I'll Quit Tomorrow!*"
Robert Mitchum, on life in the Betty Ford Clinic

"We Icelanders are fed up with Vikings."
Director Hrafn Gunnlaugsson

"Rambo is a war machine that can't be turned off."
Sylvester Stallone, on his 'First Blood' character

◆ ◆ ◆ ◆ ◆ ◆

"I've never won anything here. I feel like some mediocre British pole-vaulter at the Olympics coming in 49th."
Alan Parker, before winning the Grand Prix du Jury for 'Birdy' at Cannes.

◆ ◆ ◆ ◆ ◆ ◆

"Women's rôles – forget it. You're either the prostitute or now there's this rash of this contemporary women who's like the city DA who's divorced, who has these two fabulous kids and can take care of them, and also has a great sex life – that superwoman kind of thing."
Amy Madigan

"What I am is the new dream girl – one who has both body and intelligence."
Sybil Danning

"I don't have a fond memory of Mae West. She did her own thing to the detriment of everyone around her. I don't admire superficiality."
Cary Grant

"People want to fuck movie stars and hug television stars."
Ted Danson of 'Cheers'

Q: "How many husbands have you had?"
Zsa Zsa Gabor: "You mean, apart from my own?"

Joan Rivers: "You've had a lot of lovers. Who was the *best* lover you've ever had?"
Joan Collins: "Your husband!"

"OK, now listen. I'd love to have dinner with you but if you think we're going to make love, let me tell you right now we're not. So if you still would like to have dinner with me, fine; but I understand if you say no."
Kathleen Turner, on first dates.

"Part of him is Swiss and, therefore, he is partly a banker."
John Boorman, on Jean-Luc Godard

"Bertolucci is more of a gangster than a movie director. He is one of my enemies."
Maria Schneider

"Sexy? I'm a sexual animal. At times. But I'm also interested in a speck of dust. I don't stare at women's legs all the time."
William Hurt

"Actors like to work with me because I'm a good public – I like to be astonished."
Bernard Tavernier

"A film must be alive. When this happens, it smashes, devours, pulverises any synopsis, plot, story. It speaks, talks and explains itself. It constantly changes itself, its characters weave in and out of the screen. Their performance is different at each screening."
Spanish director Francisco Regueiro

"Playwrights have to take all kinds of garbage from ignorant people who write for the press, when we could be making a nice living writing for movies or television where the critics don't mean anything."
Arthur Miller

"I don't cater to the public; why should I cater to the critics?"
Brian De Palma

"I'm a great believer in exposing to the public how much they are brainwashed every day. My message is: Get your brains washed out. Don't listen to critics and TV commercials. They both lie. One because they're inadequate, the other because they want your money. So, my message is: Keep watching Ken Russell."
Ken Russell

◆ ◆ ◆ ◆ ◆ ◆

"Champagne and caviar? Let's face it, anything you have to acquire a taste for was not meant to be eaten."
Eddie Murphy

◆ ◆ ◆ ◆ ◆ ◆

◆◆◆◆◆◆◆

**"No one caught on that *Ryan's Daughter* was actually an adaptation of *Madame Bovary*."
David Lean**

◆◆◆◆◆◆◆

"I'm Czech, German and Irish, so I'm all mixed up."
Jim Jarmusch, director, 'Stranger Than Paradise'

"I don't like to be out of control. I don't see scary films. I certainly wouldn't go see my films."
Brian De Palma

"Bo Derek was practically unknown at the time she was on Malta for a small rôle in *Orca* (1977). One day, someone pinched her bottom. Straight away, she and John decided to leave. It took an emergency court order to prevent their departure."
Maltese producer Lino Cassar

"I'm over-age and my sign is the dollar. I was born under the sign of the buck and my favourite colour is green."
Arthur Morowitz, boss of America's Video Shack retail store.

"Whenever I think about the budgetary problems, I think about the problems of Errol Flynn . . . reconciling net income with gross habits."
British Foreign Office minister Malcolm Rifkind

"I'm not out to win prizes – that's for horses."
Werner Herzog

"I never really felt threatened. I got a knife-proof vest for crowd scenes, but ultimately I didn't use it. The threats were directed at the Japanese. A foreigner in Japan is like a drunk or a baby – they can't be blamed because they don't know what they're doing."
Paul Schrader, on shooting 'Mishima'

"I wanted to make a biblical movie in which people spoke as they do in normal conversation. Of course, it's not easy. Try saying 'Absalom, my son, my son' as if the line isn't in a glass case."
Bruce Beresford, director of 'King David'

"Women especially are nice to me. I'm not a threat to them like Marilyn Monroe must have been. People sensed that she was naughty, but you never knew how naughty. Me, you know *exactly* how naughty I am."
Marilyn Chambers

"I don't like entertainment."
John Cassavetes

"The only entertainer in the world I'd switch places with right now is Prince. But just for one night – he's only 5ft 3ins!"
Eddie Murphy

THE INCREDIBLE SHRINKING SCREEN

By Harlan Kennedy

Once, life was simple. Movies were shown in movie-theatres. Like the wandering story-teller, the latest Hollywood epic would come to your town, lure you into its mesmeric circle and hold you spellbound in a darkened palace – without breaks for commercials, making tea or answering the telephone, and with the mass devotion of a thousand other gazers to help you concentrate.

The quasi-religious heyday lasted intact until the fifties. It was then that television became a market force, we had two 'delivery systems' (that's the modern buzz-word for media) instead of one, and suddenly battle was joined. And the battle was technology's answer to David and Goliath. TV had all the advantages of being pint-sized, lissom and versatile. It could squeeze in through your front door, it could glow and grin in your sitting-room for hours on end, it could hurl fresh aesthetic sling-shots (including feature films) at the touch of a button as you flicked between channels.

So there they were, entrenched on either side of an invisible wall built by history and fortified by media philosophies.

All cinema could think of as an answer in those early years was to grow bigger and bigger. Cinemascope, Cinerama, Circlorama, 3-D, you name it, it came out and wrapped itself around you. But this high noon of elephantiasis didn't succeed in snatching audiences away from the cathode ray. And ever since then the cinema has shown insidious signs of believing that there's as much advantage in joining television as in trying to beat it.

Most movie trends since the fifties have been TV-imitative. Television's topical immediacy? Cinema could

'A Passage to India': wrap-around gigantism...

match it with hi-fi sci-fi parables *(Fail Safe, The Manchurian Candidate)* made from the hints dropped by real headlines. Television's programme continuity? Cinema could match it with sequelitis *(Godfathers, Rockys, Airports, Halloweens)* and with several mini-genres like the teenage horror flick, the comic-strip space romp, the breakdance musical. The narrative hard drug of television's multi-million-dollar soap operas? The cinema could hit back (and win Oscars) with *Terms of Endearment.*

Today the battle panorama has become more crowded than ever. Not only are we witnessing the bizarre sight of much modern cinema imitating TV in its pursuit of seriality and soap-op intimacy, but instead of two 'delivery systems' we now have five – cinema, television, video, cable and satellite – and no doubt more to come.

The alarming thing about this overcrowded hi-tech canvas is that all the crowds are going the same way. Four of the five delivery systems use television as their outlet, and the staple products of the fifth system – movies – is also

the major supply product to at least two of the other four (video and cable).

So whither the feature film? For this is one-way traffic with a vengeance. When movie pundits cry, as they often do with painful screech, "The cinema is dying!", they usually refer to dwindling audiences and closing movie-houses. But there are clear and alarming signs in the mid-eighties that the death of the Cinema is happening *independently* of the death of cinemas. The long reach of video, cable and network TV, with their major market importance in terms of film-viewing, is shaping the way movies are made – ever more compact and televisual in both style and structure – even when those movies are 'primarily' intended for the big screen. For although delivery systems have multiplied, the public itself still has a simple choice between two viewing facilities: the telly and the movie-theatre. And the first, boasting an ever larger audience and expanding range of product, is starting mercilessly to dictate the aesthetics of the second.

For all the proliferating technology, in short, we're still watching a slogging match between small screen and large. The only difference is that it's more one-sided than before, and its extremes have become more hyperbolic. Feature films are dividing more sharply than ever before into opposite poles of wrap-around gigantism (the rare beleaguered blockbusters and spectacles that still stalk the land) and TV-fitted homeliness. *Greystoke, A Passage to India, Legend* at one extreme: *Terms of Endearment, Falling in Love, Mask* at the other.

Yet few commentators have troubled to explore *why* there should be a battle between the two in the first place; what it is in their aesthetic genes that makes them congenital enemies. Reading most critics who wax philosophic on the subject of cinema versus television, you get the impression that both media were the products of parthenogenesis: fatherless kids forever unaccountably scrapping in the back gardens of twentieth-century art and technology.

But the truth is that cinema and television were born of completely constrasting parentage, and their impacts as media differ *according* to that contrast. When this different ancestry is examined, the rivalry is seen to have a clearer contour and more comprehensible cause.

Cinema sprang from a visual lineage – painting and photography (indeed the very thrust of most semiological movie studies is based on this fact) – and it gathered sound only as a later ancillary. Television sprang from a verbal lineage. It was the offspring of sound radio: a raconteur in the home, a mystery guest magically formed of airwaves, who stood in your hearth and babbled messages of news or entertainment. TV was thus the heir to a purely aural medium, whose strengths and preferences had already been formed when the addition of vision came along.

Indeed, television's early programming was a carbon copy of existing radio fare – quiz shows, chat shows, news, classic serials, soap operas. And so strong was the radio-inherited verbal emphasis that TV's visual style set itself early on into the seldom-varying *ad hoc* pragmatism of head-and-shoulders framing.

Most TV programmes were made, and still are, so that they can be looked away from. The husband can hoover the carpet, the wife can mend a fuse, and the essential information – headlines in a news programme, plot points in a soap opera – will still come through from television from the sound alone.

Today, as pressure from the encroaching video future intensifies, that TV style – emphasizing the verbal, de-emphasizing the visual – is spreading out to movies. Though there is still a

stalwart quota of spectacles at one extreme, the middle ground in cinema has fallen away almost completely. We are left with an odd, extremist opposition between the last-ditch Large (the movies of folklore and fantasy, of costumed and colourful derring-do) and the ever-proliferating Small (the domestic dramas and quasi-soaps).

Made-for-TV movies have established a set of small-screen tropes and techniques that have crept out into theatrical movies and colonized all but the most determinedly spectacular. Deep-focus effects are seldom achievable on the television screen, so many of these films aim at making a virtue of foreshortened perspective and the telephoto lens. Intricate background detail and lighting go for little on the tube, so these films often use backgrounds as no more than a filler to denote location or time-of-day.

The worst expressive shrinkage of all is to be found in the way these movies group their characters or compose their actions within the frame. Three decades have been spent *failing* to find a solution to the discrepancy between screen ratios in cinema and TV. We've all

suffered through the most extreme example of this: Cinemascope movies in which a nose on the left talks to a nose on the right with a vast intervening expanse of Arizona desert or Kansas prairie.

You can identify a Cinemascope film immediately on the box. First of all, it calls itself 'inemascop' and makes a token but unsuccessful attempt to squeeze in the full width of the credit titles by concertina'ing the frame. Thus any characters who happen to be walking or riding through a credits sequence look as if they have just come from a session on the rack. Horsemen resemble elongated versions of Don Quixote, and even well-fed actors like Bud Spencer or Orson Welles can emerge looking like martyrs out of El Greco.

Meanwhile you can play the fascinating game of trying to guess what movie you're watching from the delicately lopped titles. Has anyone seen LIZABETH TAYLO and OCK HUDSO in IAN? A fine film, this. It was once called GIANT. And who could forget AN HEFLI and LENN FOR in 10 TO YUM (alias 3.10 TO YUMA?)

Once past the squeezy

hurdles of the credit titles, wide-screen films on television can get even worse. By 'panning and scanning' to fit a 2.3:1 image onto a 1.3:1 format, the TV technicians ensure that you see only about half the original movie-frame at a time. In this process the old film literally becomes a new film. There are new cuts: two people talking in a car, a favourite screen-filling Scope set-up, becomes on television two people talking in alternative head shots. And there are new camera 'pans', as the TV scanner whirs queasily between character left, character middle and character right in what was once an all-embracing wide-screen group shot.

And of course there are those tantalising mystery-shots, when person A (on screen) is addressing his remarks to person B (offscreen) and we haven't the foggiest idea who person B is. (A recent TV transmission of *The Godfather Part II* had John Cazale talking on one side of the screen, across a big picture-window overlooking Lake Tahoe, to a nose and a pair of feet on the other. Only a trained chiropodist or nasologist could have identified these as Al Pacino's.)

This kind of viewer agony is at its most extreme in telly versions of *early* wide-screen films (of the fifties or early sixties). Those were the years, when directors like Minnelli or Cukor or Nicholas Ray used every elastic inch of the Cinemascope screen and the spectre of TV and video sales had not yet come to haunt film-making as a major market force.

Today a director who uses every inch of the wide screen, to pack in aesthetic impact or narrative information, knows he's committing virtual hara-kiri. The movie will be incomprehensible when it reaches the small screen, which is where it might well have to make most of its money. So directors trim their panoramas accordingly. You'll seldom see a noses-only confrontation in a movie made today that's travelled from big screen to small; film-makers are more careful to bunch their vital characters together. And often, if you

...and 'Falling in Love': TV-fitted homeliness.

'Starman': Carpenter never takes the action to the edges of the screen.

interaction of the characters, no radical variations of dimension, perspective or viewpoint.

Nor are these constrictions merely aesthetic. The medium is the message, and the style in which a movie is made helps form its content. If the style favours intimacy – the close-up or talking-heads two-shot rather than the sweeping crowd scene or lush landscape – then the *subjects* or *stories* favoured will be those which can be pushed forward by dialogue rather than image, by the close interplay of a small group of characters, by settings domestic or local rather than epic.

In other words the subjects that have clustered gravitationally towards the made-for-TV movie – the small-town problem pic (Tony Richardson's *A Death In Canaan*), the courtroom drama (Lamont Johnson's *Fear on Trial*) or the sleek, narrow-corridor action film (Steve Spielberg's *Duel*) – are increasingly the subjects being turned out by a cinema ever more conscious of its products' eventual destination.

Peter Bogdanovich's *Mask*, for instance, is a television problem-pic in big-screen clothing, complete with the stereotypical characterization that has

catch that big-screen movie while it's still in the cinema, you'll be amazed how much inessential space the film surrounds its central knot of action with. That's the built-in throwaway stuff that the TV scanner can 'scan out'.

The problem of incompatible screen ratios may be at its worst with wide-screen movies; but even films made in a narrower format – 1·85:1, say, as opposed to Scope's 2·35:1 – suffer substantial lopping when translated to the television screen. The latter's 1·33:1 ratio corresponds only to the narrowest cinema format, rarely used today, the Academy ratio.

Fear of small-screen shrinkage ensures that even the best-looking big-screen movies today seldom use the full width of the frame. John Carpenter's lean and gleaming *Starman* revels in the devouring spaces of Wisconsin prairie or butte-flanked highway or Arizona meteor crater. But whenever there's vital narrative information to impart in the visuals – in a fight, a car chase or a conversation in which talker's and reactor's faces must both be seen – Carpenter never takes the action to the edges of the screen. In over-the-shoulder duologues between Karen Allen and Jeff Bridges – which in the fifties would have gained visual dynamism by each head being placed at the extremity of the screen – the talkers are pushed in towards the centre, with sizeable portions of scan-out

footage on either side.

With expressive possibilities cramped by the near-rectilinear format of the TV screen, and with no television executives yet taking a brave plunge and showing wide-screen films unchopped (ie with a bland band large enough to admit the full image strip), TV is thus virtually dictating movie styles. And the style influences the content. What television movies and their cinema ilk – from *The Chain* to *The Breakfast Club*, *Parker* to *Mask* – gravitate towards is a two-dimensional visual style in which there is no competing 'background' to distract from the foreground

'Mask': a television problem-pic in big-screen clothing.

'The Chain': overgrown British sitcom.

become a made-for-TV speciality; the Smug-and-Blinkered Authority Figure (the headmaster), the Hellraising-but-Lovable Bohemians (the Hell's Angels), the Nice Girl Who Can Save Your Soul (the hero's blind girlfriend). And Jack Gold's *The Chain* is an overgrown British sitcom *entirely* peopled with the kind of next-door fun-figures who crowd up British peak-hour televiewing; the Oleaginous Tightfist (Nigel Hawthorne), the Lady Snob (Judy Parfitt), the Philosophical Cockney (Warren Mitchell).

Scarcely less influential on modern movie styles than the television format and screen-size is the TV attention span. Television plays, films and soaps are almost *built* to be interrupted: not just by the restless viewer who wants to make coffee or put the cat out while a programme is running, but by the sudden machine-gun bursts of consumer evangelism known as 'commercial breaks'. So programmes need to feature characters who are swiftly identifiable (ie 'types') and also to be made in neat and tidy dramatic arcs, rising from plateau to peak, conversation scenes to cliffhangers. The *'longeur'*, the non-sequitur or *any* disorienting structural unorthodoxy can prove fatal.

In works like this, and in feature films that take their cue from them, dramatic surprises are carefully, predictably spaced and visual surprises are virtually non-existent. The viewer is never shaken out of the comforting knowledge of being in a familiarised fictional parish where the people and events behave according to their types, and where there are no radical or violent changes of pace, place or perspective.

The modern-day rearguard 'epic', by contrast, thrives on precisely that rollercoaster kinesis. As one backlash-against-TV blockbuster upscreens another – from *Return of the Jedi* to *Indiana Jones and the Temple of Doom*, from *Gremlins* to *Ghostbusters* – the cinema of spectacle and *grand guignol* is moving into an area where high-speed sense-extremism is its own reward, its own justification.

Qualities of enriching background detail pass unrecognized in 'Eureka'…

No surprise that critics complain there are no human beings in these films. There aren't: just capering caricatures and comic-strip heroes. These movies are reflex cinema: compensation films that seize on all the visual delights and wonders cast aside by television, on its demure march to a pin-size humanism, and blow them big-screen size.

Extreme oppositions are one thing. Schizophrenia is another. The alarming thing about today's sundered cinema is that there is almost no equivalent of the rich middle-ground harmonisings of the real and surreal, the humanist and expressionist, that existed in the fifties and sixties and before, with directors like Hitchcock, Peckinpah, Sirk, Minnelli, Penn and Kubrick. And when a dense-textured non-epic movie *does* come along – like Roeg's *Eureka* or Babenco's *Kiss of the Spider Woman* or Von Triers's *The Element of Crime* – critical powers have become so atrophied that the films' qualities of enriching background detail or emblematic effect pass unrecognized or uncomprehended. It's judged on little more than genre efficiency – is it a good murder thriller/prison drama/who-dunnit? – and the hell with any novel injections of thought or imagination.

Technology, of course,

which has been the feature film's enemy in recent years, could yet come to its rescue. Televisions with a wide-screen facility are on the way, we're told, in America, which also promise the higher sharpness and definition of a multi-thousand-line screen. If there are new image spaces to fill and new visual capabilities to be catered for, then the industry's story-tellers and image-makers will be mobilised to answer technology's challenge. And an aesthetic that has been in retreat for the last decade or so will at last push itself into

forward gear again.

If we're luckier still, of course, *cinemagoers* will push themselves into forward gear again and get back into the cinemas. In large enough numbers to ensure that the wide screen goes on wearing its wall-to-wall smile, however many fresh recruits are gathered by the glowing enemy in the sitting-room. After all, the largest movie screen in the world opened in Paris this summer. If the cinema is tired of trying to join television, let's urge its return to the good old days of trying to beat it.

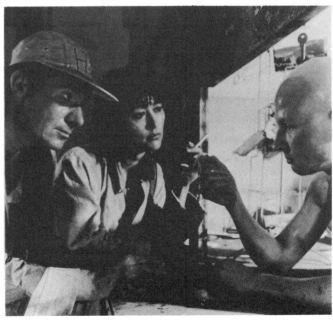

…and in 'The Element of Crime'.

FESTERING FESTIVALS

By Tony Crawley

First, just check the schedule and take a deep breath. A *very* deep breath:

Los Angeles, New Delhi, San Francisco, Brussels, Park City (Utah), Melbourne, Luxembourg, Rotterdam, Gothenburg, Miami, Brooklyn, Padua, Monte Carlo, Budapest, Porto, Ouagadougou (Upper Volta), Berlin, Quebec, Tampere (Finland), Palma de Mallorca, Antwerp, Rivertown (Minnesota), Santarem (Portugal), Tampa, Zaragoza (Spain), Madrid, Dallas, Vienna, Hong Kong, San José, Durban, Kansas City, Cleveland, Sorrento, Istanbul, Salsomaggiore (Italy), Las Vegas, Oberhausen, Houston, Oakland, Athens (Ohio), Chicago, Vancouver, Seattle, Atlanta, Cracow, Selb (West Germany), Vermont, Tokyo, Osnabruck, Varna, Reykjavik, Pesaro (Italy), Cartagena (Colombia), Barcelona, Munich, Moscow, Turin, Gerona (Spain), Gijon (ditto), Wellington, Ogden (Utah), Nairobi, Auckland, Taormina, Boston, Odense, Locarno, Edinburgh, Hiroshima, Vevey (Chaplin's Swiss home, so comedies only), Montreal, Venice, Cork, Rimini, Ghent, Toronto, San Sebastian (just!), London, Sydney, Florence. . .

And that as any weary, cross-eyed *festivalier* will have observed, is not counting. . .the French lot! France is where I live and I could live on (and sometimes off) just the French fests, without recourse to crossing borders, much less catching planes and winding up, perchance, in Beirut – where, believe it or not, a horror festival was about to be staged just three or four years ago. As if the place didn't have enough real blood in the streets.

This French year, I've had

Avoriaz horrors, Chamrousse comedies, women's films in Creteil, Paris enthographics, Epinay shorts, Cognac thrillers, and Biarritz industrials; even in little Marly-le-Roi, which is exactly where I live, we've had a three-day animation festival. Not bad, that, for a town without a cinema.

But, even that is not all. Cabourg, being so closely associated with Proust, has begun a festival of romantic films. Annecy, of course, remains the bi-annual king of the animation events, although Antibes and Juan Les Pins have lately joined forces to try and steal some of its considerable thunder. Saint Tropez managed,

Cannes: a collision of tempers and egos.

somehow, to arrange a second video-clip circus, although the first one last year wound up bankrupt (not unlike poor San Sebastian, still not sure if it will reach thirty-three next year). And then, Paris closes the year down with a horror fest staged in the largest of the 422 cinemas in and around town, with the audience, in the best *Rocky Horror* style, participating every which way from make-up to yells, hisses, cheers or boos. The more blood spilt, the better chance of winning.

The Quimper event this year was devoted to a week of British cinema, the one at Deauville is always all-American, the one at Nice is all Italian – while Pesaro's, in Italy, is always Indian. Luxembourg invites German films and two German weeks are for South East Asia and 'borderland' movies. Such events are not all named after the host town. Madrid's horror show is, or rather was until this year, dubbed Imagfic. Porto's similar deal is, inevitably, Fantasporto. The Kansas City do is hyped as Show-A-Rama. One Berlin event calls itself: Show Tech. Cattolica (has to be Italy, right?) is the setting for Mystfest. And Philadelphia prefers to call its festival, Philafilm.

It is not merely the film-makers/pushers/buyers/sellers/gawpers and the ever-attendant media armies that suffer battle fatigue on all these fronts. After presiding over the 1985 Cannes jury for two rainy weeks in May, Milos Forman was just too whacked to join the first Tokyo jury ten days later. Understandable. Being on the jury is a doubtful honour, as I recall from such a stint in Brussels, because you are

obliged to see *all* the films.

Then again, it's a wonder anyone survives the Cannes campaign. No matter the competition – inside France or out – Cannes remains the *grandpére,* the biggest – if not the best – event on the elastic international film festival calendar. (Just how Durban has been on it for seven years is one mystfest I've not been able to solve.)

Cannes is special. It is the only place where, within a frenetic forty-eight hours – and no 48 hours can ever have been as fevered as 48 hours at Cannes in mid-circus – you have the choice of anything up to thirty-five films opening within the same hour (some festivals are lucky if they have thirty-five films showing over a week). Should you so desire, and you then locate and placate the publicist involved, you can get to interview John Huston, Mel Gibson, Pamela Sue Martin, Gerard Depardieu, Akira Kurosawa, David Bowie ("fifteen minutes only, remember?"), Hanna Schygulla, Marcello Mastroianni, Wim Wenders, Marco Ferreri and. . .C Gordon Liddy.

Not that any of it matters. Can you name this year's Best Film at Cannes? The Best Actor and Actress at Cannes *last* year? Do you recall that Cannes winners have included such thespians as Murray Melvin, Marlon Brando, Rita Tushingham, Terence Stamp, Kitty Winn, Joanne Woodward, Orson Welles, Jack Nicholson, Vanessa Redgrave (twice) and the guy who's still never got an Oscar, Paul Newman? Of course not.

Yet it all seems so damned important at the time. Around 5,500 media men, women and machines, second only to the Olympics' score, cover Cannes every year. Front-page news on all

French papers and magazines. Top of the TV News. Satellite coverage to America. But, in the end, just another festival. And there are four others daring to compete at the same time – in Switzerland, Canada and two in America.

Mussolini, of all people, started film festivals at Venice in 1933. Goebbels was really responsible for Cannes. In 1936, Hitler's propaganda minister was an honoured guest of the film-mad Duce at the third Venice happening. Naturally, a German movie had to win. Any German movie! Luis Trenker's *Kaiser of California* was chosen to have the top Golden Lion award – rather than Jean Renoir's classic, *La Grande Illusion,* promptly banned for its pacifism in the Axis countries. Rightly miffed, the French stalked out of Venice and set about starting their own event – for 1 September 1939. Goebbels and his master had other ideas, which shows how little film people were in touch with reality (and still are – look at Manila!).

Cannes finally opened on 20 September 1946. It was all so much easier then. A prize for every film turning up, a Press Corps of a mere 700, and 5,000 other movie visitors. Those figures have been tripled by now, covering producers, directors, scenarists, and of course distributors of everything from the current Soviet exports like *The Invisible Man,* Egypt's *Love Atop the Pyramids,* Japan's re-tread of *Godzilla,* and Hollywood's *Bloodsuckers from Outer Space.*

Charlton Heston summed up the scene for himself and

Charlton Heston: "In terms of relating to film as art, (festivals) are nonsense."

later for posterity when publishing his diaries. "Film festivals serve as a useful marketplace for independent film-makers trying to get some sort of distribution, but this is their only valuable function. In terms of relating to film as an art, they're nonsense."

The festivities that begin and end the Cannes event are the most nonsensical. A matter of anything Oscar can do we can do even more boringly. The French, watching it all on TV at home, don't realize this as they're never allowed to see the full or edited Oscarcast.

For the big 35th birthday bash opening in 1982, special 35th anniversay trophies were presented, for services rendered, to a formidable bunch of film directors. They included Antonioni; as well they might. Two weeks later, when he was almost forgotten in the jury's eventual list of winners, he was presented on closing night with an extra award. They called it a. . .35th anniversary award.

Last year, I think it was – no, it was 1983 (they tend to blur, you know) – the Cannes organizers decided to similarly honour actors with career-awards on opening night. Once again, they got themselves a good line-up. De Niro was there – in a beret, over the head he'd shaved for Leone. Loren was resplendent in red. Dirk Bogarde came down from the hills above Cannes. Schygulla was anything but shy. Depardieu was big, Ingrid Thulin slim and Fernando Rey bearded.

In short: anyone who could take time off and make the trip got a present.

Bette Davis could not attend. She was poorly. Could she send someone in her stead? No, she couldn't. So, what to do. Cannes had an award going spare. Another winner had to be found. And who, for instance, could pick up an award initially allocated for Bette Davis. Would you believe. . .Liza Minnelli?

But then, the whole Cannes thing is too vast an enterprise to run totally smoothly. By the time the various international winners are dutifully chosen (juries always manage to include some film or performance

Robert Mitchum with Simone Silva: her state of undress was the 'scandale' of 1954.

from the Eastern Bloc), so many egos and tempers have collided along the Croisette that the trophy holders are almost ritually booed by what little Press is still left in town.

Biggest guffaws that I remember were in 1980 when Anouk Aimée and Michel Piccoli won the acting nod for an Italian film, Marco Bellocchio's *Salto nel Vuoto/Leap into the Void.* The film was screened in Italian with Piccoli and Anouk dubbed by Vittorio Caprioli and Livia Giamalmo. The jury insisted it had seen the French-lingo print. Funny. No one else had.

Naturally, no jury on God's earth, never mind festival director Gilles Jacob's earth, is going to please the media multitudes, much less the dizzying assemblage of film-makers and hypers. . . whether concerned with the festival's competition, or the myriad of sidebar events, topped by the Market, where distribution companies from all over the globe come to sell their new wares. Or, as is increasingly noticeable, last year's unsold commodities.

Not everyone goes to Cannes to see films, not even to sell films. National debts are guzzled, chomped, digested and vomited at all the brunches, lunches, dinners, parties, barbecues, banquets that interfere with film-going. It's a freeloader's paradise, a veritable convention for thieves and hookers. One must fight to get into the films and fight to get out.

The Press hordes, the French battalions in particular, make Fellini's paparazzi in *La Dolce Vita* (the 1960 winner) look like a choirboy's outing. To watch them at work – whether damn near rioting to get into a screening or surrounding either Jack Nicholson or a nude nonenity on the beach (better still, Nicholson with a nude. . .anything to match Bob Mitchum and Simone Silva's *scandale* of 1954) – is akin to watching John Landis yelling Action! on *Animal House Hits the Riviera.* With everyone playing Belushi.

Two weeks in Cannes is no way to give up smoking.

And it's much the same the whole world over. It's known as the excitement of a festival. Whether the chosen genres being spotlighted are art, industry, new cinema, old cinema, aviation, animation, agrarianism, alpinism, space, even Celtic films. Or, as staged in the other Venice (California) last year, The International Gypsy Film Festival.

At French events, the Press goes mad (hourly) and raves on about the majesty of the Seventh Art. It sounds fine but it just isn't true. All festivals, Cannes in particular, are about the eighth art. Hyping. It doesn't matter a damn if oversell ruins the chance of a prize – just so long as fifty more photo calls, thirty extra interviews, twenty tellies, twenty-five radios and the inevitable documentary film team can be squeezed in before the star/director/whomever flops to the floor hyperventilating like a Sony at fast speed.

Ultimately, as Mussolini's finance minister, Giuseppe Volpi, realized in 1933 (actually, he first cottoned on to the idea in 1930), it's the host town which benefits the most. In common with all French festivals (and given the global impact of Cannes, not just French), the home town uses the event to increase income from tourists by extending The Season. Deauville tags its festival on the end of the summer. Cannes started that way and eventually switched to the beginning – if only to beat Venice – settling on the middle weeks of May. Sorrento has lately followed suit, changing dates from Autumn to Spring without caring about clashing with Italy's other event, Salso.

A film festival, therefore, has patently less to do with the furtherance of cinema – no matter what debates it stages – than with the invaded township making sure it wins the largest slice of the available financial action. Why else would they be mounted in such far away places with strange sounding names as Ouagadougou in the Upper Volta – or isn't that now Burkina Faso?

Pushing for that extra revenue, and maybe helping

Glenda Jackson: failed to win even a celebrity tennis match in Tokyo.

put the town on the map, is the reason why San José has suddenly taken a liking to fantasy films, why Osnabruck adores experimentalists and why Varna opens its Bulgarian doors twice during the summer; in June to all the usual festival vulgarians deeply committed to health, humanitarian and scientific films, and then to animation lovers a view months later. It's why Turin has developed this appetite for sports films, why Quebec positively cherishes 8mm, Vermont favours documentaries – or it does with a little help from Marlboro – and Gijón, in Spain, welcomes children's movies.

Then, there are the unmentionables. The Manila farce for one, finally shuttered and for good, one hopes. I have nothing against Filipino films, of course (it was Cannes which introduced us to Lino Brocka, not Manila); but the fact that Hollywood and the world's media – including far too many Fleet Street freeloaders – accepted invitations to enjoy the largesse of President Marcos' ego tells its own story. Going to Manila is

like attending a film festival in Ethiopia. Likewise, Durban, which managed to notch up its seventh festival this year, with as many as sixty-three films, including a tribute to British Film Year. So much for cultural boycotts.

Tokyo got into the act in June with the biggest prize on the circuit for its sole competition category – best film by a new director – in which the winner was promised $1,500 million

Kirk Douglas, Cannes jury president in 1980: mistaken for Douglas Sirk?

towards another movie. Tokyo, running at the same time as the rather better other Tokyo festival (known,

in somewhat Orwellian style, as the Asia Oceania Festival), did not quite match its publicity and could only attract stars by running a celebrity tennis tournament, arranged by the wife of Claude Lelouch. She missed out on the big names she was chasing, despite the lure of free first-class air travel, hotels, interpreters and chauffeurs for as long as they stayed. Or lasted. Glenda Jackson and Rod Steiger were among those turning up – and losing. Winners in the mixed and men's doubles (no room for singles' egos) included such internationally renowned superstars as Robert Carradine and Cathy Lee Crosby.

These days a new kind of *festivalier* is noticeably increasing in number: the organizers, selectors and sundry other officials of the next events, fighting among themselves for the (few) films deemed worthy of future festival exposure and scurrying around selecting, collecting juryists, and the inevitable lofty name to head them. In Cannes, the jury presidents over the years have included Cocteau (three times), Pagnol, Fritz Lang, Sophia Loren, Visconti, Losey, René Clair, Tennessee Williams, Alan J Pakula, Rossellini and the controversial 1980 reign of Kirk Douglas. "Never again!", he swore after the row about *All That Jazz* tying with *Kagemusha* as Best Film and Peter Sellers (already dying on his feet) being passed over for his finest rôle in *Being There*.

The story grows that Kirk Douglas was never meant for the job in the first place. Ingmar Bergman had been invited and had to decline. He is supposed to have suggested a certain veteran German director, except the Cannes bosses misread the cable recommendation of. . .Sirk, Douglas.

With its preponderance of tributes to Hollywood's golden oldies, Deauville is known as Lana Turner – while Cannes is Pia Zadora. Not entirely true. I met them both in Deauville, which introduces as many newcomers as Cannes. Cannes is, or more thankfully was, Edy Williams. Every May, Edy locks up her fading pink house in the Hollywood hills, packs her case, travels light to the Midi and dutifully exposes herself. Cannes is thirty-nine next year. Edy is noticeably older. They've been together now, a steady item, for far too long. Biggest Cannes shock in the last two years is that Edy actually had films in the market.

The rest of the circuit's simplistic rule of thumb insists that Venice is plain wet and Berlin simply boring. Berlin is so meticulously organized, nothing ever goes

Edy Williams: dutifully exposes herself every year at Cannes.

wrong. Venice is so meticulously organized, everything goes wrong. (It's called, I believe, Italian Style.) Venice is also known as, allegedly, the most crooked festival. No surprises in its Golden Lion winners, as there often can be among Berlin's Golden Bears and Cannes' Golden Palms. That's not to say Venice trophies can be bought. They don't have to be. Juries seem to be handpicked to match the organizers' choice of winners. Not so in Cannes. Dirk Bogarde's 1984 jury was told that America had to win. It didn't. Milos Forman was said to have had similar instructions this year. Maybe he misheard them as South America, which collected three important awards, while Yugoslavia won its first Palme d'Or.

Cannes' awards are often as political as anything else – everything else! – in France. The festival legend is packed with factoids about arranged/bought/rewritten prizes.

France is a generous enough host, not having won Best Film since Lelouch's *Man and a Woman* tied for it in 1966. There is no escaping the fact, though, that when Visconti's *Death in Venice* lost out, ironically to Dirk Bogarde's other mentor, Joe Losey and *The Go-Between*, in 1971, the Italian cinemperor used language not quite in keeping with his artistic status. He packed and started to leave town, vowing never to set foot, etc (probably thinking he was *in* Venice) and thereby ended up with a special award for twenty-five years' movie-making. And in 1983 when William Styron's jury could not decide on who should win the Best Director award (an award not always given and never to the maker of the Best Film) they simply created a Creation Award. And then split it in two.

Three other French fests

Luchino Visconti: a 1971 Cannes 'special' prize and language not quite in keeping with his aristo status.

are organized by the same outfit, a publicity company, of course. It's optimistically called Promo 2000, although like most French institutions it's barely entered the twentieth century, much less the twenty-first. Admittedly, Avoriaz (on the ski-slopes), Cognac (in the cellars) and Deauville (on the coast) are friendly, warm, little affairs but you cannot escape the feeling they've been staged as parties for Promo 2000's friends. As thirty-five per cent of the combine was lately sold to the most influential advertising agency in Paris, which is already in cahoots with a leading film company and the *Liberation* newspaper in an FM radio station and a private TV channel to come – one wonders if there'll be room for anyone but their friends next year.

The new Rimini event is probably the most enjoyable festival of them all – along with the Chamrousse comedy

Bernardo Bertolucci: first met Jack Nicholson at Pesaro in 1965 ... or was it Cannes?

week. Both are fresh, trying hard to please, not yet out of control and/or ego. They also last one week only. Perfect! Two weeks in another town is for books . . . Rimini is a Common Market affair, with room for the Swiss and the Scandinavians. The countries' best films, according to local critics, plus their home box-office hits, are invited and there is an annual *hommage* to a screenwriter – Jean-Claude Carrière this year, getting better service than he does at Cannes, where he has compered those appalling opening nights. And the sole prize goes to the winner of a contest among film-school students – which is looking after tomorrow's *cineastes*. Hence the event is backed by more top directors than Cannes had on stage for its 35th birthday . . . and Fellini designed the festival logo.

Rimini is, then, rather like what Pesaro used to be. This Italian week still furthers New Cinema – but from India, only. It used to cover the world and is the festival most sixties' directors talk about with a certain nostalgic glow. It is where they started long friendships, and to exchange ideas, scripts, cameramen. It's where Coppola and Dusan Makavejev, for example, first met and saw the other side of the global film-making coin. Bertolucci remembers it well, too. "I first met Jack Nicholson there in ... ah, 1965. We met because we were following the same girl. And since she didn't want me or Jack, we became firm friends." Pause. "Or, was that at Cannes ...?"

I know the feeling.

LITTLE BRITISHERS

By James Park

"If I were English, I would have died of shame." That was how American actress Theresa Russell felt after the Cannes press conference for *Insignificance* at which critic Alexander Walker criticized Nicolas Roeg, the film's director, for bringing to the world's most prestigious film festival a picture featuring an American cast and set in a New York hotel. Surely he recognized a duty to put British life and manners on the screen? Roeg's answer to the argument could have been deduced from the fact that his previous films have been located in Jamaica, Morocco, Vienna, Australia, Venice and North America as well as Notting Hill Gate.

This black mark against Roeg's sense of national responsibility did not protect the British consul from attack a few days later when he made a slightly derogatory remark about the aforementioned film. David Gladstone was at a dinner attended largely by functionaries of the British industry. His sentiments were overheard by veteran producer Betty Box who took the luckless diplomat roundly to task for being so remiss in his duties in British Film Year.

The notion that British films should tell exclusively British stories – which would be laughed out of court if applied to theatre, painting or literature – still has strong support in movie-making circles. It is often combined with the contradictory compulsion to put a 'made-in-Britain' stamp on successful American films, such as *Superman* or *Indiana Jones and the Temple of Doom,* that were made in British studios by British technicians.

This concern with national culture and achievement partly explains why a Union Jack flutters as the logo for British Film Year. The event's main purpose is to secure a turnaround in the fortunes of Britain's cinema theatres. Thus the slogan – 'Cinema – The Best Place to See a Film'. But the flag suggests other meanings. Will going to see *Ghostbusters* help the national production industry? Should people go and see *The Company of Wolves* instead of *Ghostbusters* because the former is British? Is *Return to Oz,* made at Elstree, more or less British than Alan Parker's *Birdy,* which was made in Philadelphia?

The perplexing symbolism had a pragmatic justification. The British government, whose support was essential to the setting up of the Film Year, has generally been unsympathetic to the claims of film culture *per se.* Those who have campaigned for increased subsidy for production have over the years developed the argument that film is an excellent tool with which to encourage the export of British goods. If Coca-Cola could build its international market on the back of American films, couldn't successful British pictures do

'Insignificance': an American cast in a New York hotel.

'Birdy': made in Philadelphia.

the same for Sinclair computers and British Leyland cars? The argument had never worked before but it was successfully pitched by the organizers of British Film Year.

Some people, however, were touched by the appeal to patriotism. In its year of preparation, British Film Year replaced the weather as a favourite topic of conversation among film biz types. Up and down Wardour Street and in the dining hall of Pinewood Studios and elsewhere, people were asking each other about reports of squalls at the BFY's headquarters or the prospect of success for a series of events designed to put film-going back at the heart of the nation's life. As the launch bell was struck, everyone with a film to make was going to make it as a contribution to British Film Year. Cinemas were even opened by independent entrepreneurs in the same cause.

This strange fervour suggests the psychology of Third World revolutionaries rather than inhabitants of a metropolis at the centre of international film-making activity. The presence of American producers, directors and writers on British soil seemingly fosters

a sense that we have been overrun. For the struggling British film-maker, the sight of George Lucas or Jim Henson treating Elstree Studios as their own little playground is as galling as

'The Killing Fields': the American experience in South East Asia.

the sound of revelry from the High Commissioner's mansion on some imperial outpost in the Caribbean.

Ironically, the obsession with the Britishness of British films dates back to the

days when Britannia ruled the waves. That was a time when movies were seen as propaganda vehicles to convey the British way of life to those at the furthest reaches of Empire. As the flag was taken down, Ealing Studios under Michael Balcon clung to the idea of 'projecting' Britain. The concern now is an inverted obsession with films that will give the British back their sense of national identity.

It was the documentary film movement of the pre-war years that developed the idea that films should tell audiences about the communities in which they live. The concept retains its hold even though the responsibility has been shuffled off to television. There is a related argument, which has not been explicitly put in relation to British Film Year. It suggests that, where there is a vibrant national cinema which connects to the spirit of the times, there will be an increased interest in film-going generally to the benefit both of local producers and of film importers.

However, the current forms of cinematic nationalism were sharpened in the late seventies when the idea of a good British film, as defined by Lew Grade, consisted of a yarn about Americans getting tied up with emerald thieves in Mexico or trying to recover rare minerals from the wreck of a ship sunk in the North Atlantic. Grade was, in some ways, too easy an object of attack. His films, which had no cultural merit and failed commercially, eventually sank the company that made them. This collapse seemed to validate an argument couched in terms of the need for a national film culture, whereas the main problem with Grade's films was their lack of spirit, intelligence and wit. It would be a rather blind nationalism that criticized Goldcrest for making *The Mission,* a seriously-conceived film about Spanish Jesuits in seventeenth-century Paraguay, because it had no British characters, and applauded a piece of hokum like Thorn EMI's *Wild Geese II* or Rank's low-level comedy *The Chain,* simply because they were British.

The bind for film-makers everywhere is the need to have some form of success in the American market in order to recoup the costs of all but the most modestly-budgeted picture. A blockbuster picture like *Rambo: First Blood II* cleans up because it can speak directly to American chauvinism and frustration at what happened to their country in South East Asia. Roland Joffé's *The Killing Fields* also succeeded by taking a more oblique and personal approach to the same subject. It is now generally felt that for film-makers working outside the Hollywood system to second-guess the American psyche rather than work from their own convictions is a doomed course. The way in has to be through national films that rise above the parochial and the sort of international quasi-art movies which win Oscars and have a devoted following.

Social historians will, in fact, have plenty of cinematic evidence from which to build a picture of British concerns current in the first half of the eighties. The story of the Raj has been told from various angles in such pictures as *A Passage to India* and *The Assam Garden.* While *Dance with a Stranger* took a

Two Australians: Richard Franklin, director of 'Link'...

contemporary perspective on the repressive forces at work in Britain of the fifties, *Wetherby* tackled the nature of the bourgeois spirit head on. *Defence of the Realm*

opened up questions about the British media previously touched upon in *The Ploughman's Lunch.* Even the national obsession with snooker, a form of bar

...and Fred Schepisi, director of 'Plenty'.

billiards, has been charted in two projects – *Number One* and *Billy the Kid and the Green Baize Vampire.*

British directors do not, of course, have a monopoly on British stories. Last year, Australian director Fred Schepisi made an adaptation of David Hare's stage play *Plenty* for an American producer. It's the tale of an English woman, played by Meryl Streep, who attempts to recover the idealism of her youth. Another antipodean recently filmed a picture, *Link,* about a Yorkshire-based anthropologist who keeps apes. Richard Franklin explained that he set the film in Britain as the country whose antique civilization represents the opposite extreme to the jungle locations customary for films about man's primate predecessors.

Equally, British film-makers' palettes are not limited to local colour. There is no reason why they should be. Most directors and writers have intellectual and emotional experiences outside these islands which enable them to treat foreign subjects in an authentic way. Roland Joffé's *The Killing*

Fields focuses on the American experience in South East Asia, while Neil Jordan's *The Company of Wolves* is located in an imaginary world of forest, small villages and fairy-tales recreated at Shepperton Studios. Nicolas Roeg is going to a desert island for his next picture, *Castaway,* while Peter Greenaway's *A Zed And Two Noughts* travels to Rotterdam Zoo and is imbued with ideas and images from continental art and culture.

These works are clearly differentiated from the bulk of mainstream Hollywood, just as they are distanced from the quaint and literary aspects of much in Britain's cinematic history. One of the problems with British Film Year's attempts to celebrate the past history of UK film-making is that many of today's film-makers are attempting to construct new patterns of film-making that have more reference to the advances made in Europe and America over the past twenty years. That exercise is more relevant to a film culture that has stood still for twenty years than posturing behind nationalistic barricades.

It is difficult to quarrel with the methods chosen by British Film Year to revive cinema-going in the UK. Theatre managers in cities around the country have joined up with their competitors to organize programmes of events designed to draw people towards their screens and whet their palates for cinema. Early reports from Brighton, Lincoln, Nottingham and other places suggest that the action committees have managed to magic a spirit of invigorating carnival out of their desperate situations. Make-up and costume displays, lectures and competitions have been organized in association with a travelling roadshow. Cinema managers have been reintroduced to their audiences. Their houses again have a chance to thrive at the centre of their communities.

But British Film Year has also conjured up a nostalgia for the economics of the forties and the dream that the national cinema market could revive to the point where it might be possible for a large

batch of British films to recover their costs nationally. The aspiration may be a worthy one but it plays to film-makers' paranoia about the effects of 'international packaging' and the false dichotomy between the international film as something watered-down and uninteresting against the indigenous, which is seen as representing intellectual and aesthetic challenge. Too often, the celebration of the parochial and the reluctance to jump the hurdle to make films that will have an international audience is just an expression of deficient vision and cinematic courage.

British Film Year defines its other aim as that of "shouting about British films in a very un-British way". The emphasis is on promoting a recent group of pictures under the banner of 'The Revival Years'. By screening these movies in a package, BFY hopes to foster a sort of brand loyalty for British films so that audiences world-wide will have a preliminary 'want-to-see' for anything from the UK.

The commercial value of this exercise is in doubt. Most reasonably-proficient British films with any chance of scoring in offshore markets

Peter Greenaway: back from Rotterdam Zoo.

can secure some foreign distribution through the efforts of major UK sales companies or the network operated by the American majors. Films do not really benefit from brand labelling. British movies tend to do consistently better in Australia than elsewhere thanks to historic links between the two countries. In the US recently, UK movies have clearly benefited from a general increase in things British from pop music to fashion and theatre. But any film culture worthy of the name offers a diversity of output. The success of one

film rarely knocks on to another from the same production centre.

The key to more exposure in foreign markets for British films lies not in a reinforcement of the barriers of national separatism and self-promotion but in an opening up to new influences and forms of co-operation. It is partly because so many British film-makers have been trained in the artisan-like schools of television and commercials production that they are often timid in dealings with the outside world. The British dislike co-productions that would involve forging relationships with other industries and cultures, and the British voice has been largely absent from European discussions on ways to strengthen national film industries through collaboration. Many hide behind the quest for indigenous films or the ambition to compete with American producers to cover up their inability to engage with European and other routes towards a popular but cinematic film culture.

Ways of furthering the initiatives made by British Film Year are already under discussion. It is likely that a bureau will be set up to build on any short term success in bringing people back to the cinema. The industry would have taken a giant step forward if, on the international front, it abandoned nationalism and its inappropriate logo to seek ways to establish a free flow of ideas and resources between those working to make films in every part of the world.

Nicolas Roeg: on his way to a desert island.

THE AWARDS

THE ACADEMY OF PICTURE ARTS AND SCIENCES 'OSCARS'

BEST PICTURE
Amadeus

BEST DIRECTOR
Milos Forman
Amadeus

BEST ACTOR
F Murray Abraham
Amadeus

BEST ACTRESS
Sally Field
Places in the Heart

*BEST SUPPORTING
ACTOR*
Haing S Ngor
The Killing Fields

*BEST SUPPORTING
ACTRESS*
Peggy Ashcroft
A Passage to India

*BEST ORIGINAL
SCREENPLAY*
Robert Benton
Places in the Heart

*BEST SCREENPLAY
BASED ON MATERIAL
FROM ANOTHER MEDIUM*
Peter Shaffer
Amadeus

BEST CINEMATOGRAPHY
Chris Menges
The Killing Fields

*BEST FOREIGN
LANGUAGE FILM*
Dangerous Moves
(Switzerland)

*BEST ORIGINAL
SCORE*
Maurice Jarre
A Passage to India

*BEST ORIGINAL SONG
SCORE*
Purple Rain
Prince

*BEST ORIGINAL
SONG*
'I Just Called To Say I Love
You'
Stevie Wonder

*BEST COSTUME
DESIGN*
Theodor Pistek
Amadeus

BEST EDITING
Jim Clark
The Killing Fields

BEST MAKE-UP
Paul Leblanc, Dick Smith
Amadeus

*BEST ART
DIRECTION*
Patrizia Von Brandestein,
Karel Cerny
Amadeus

BEST SOUND
Marg Berger
Tom Scott
Todd Boekelheide
Chris Newman
Amadeus

*BEST VISUAL
EFFECTS*
Dennis Muren
Michael McAlister
Lorne Peterson
George Gibbs
*Indiana Jones and the Temple
of Doom*

THE BRITISH ACADEMY OF FILM AND TELEVISION ARTS FILM AWARDS

BEST FILM
The Killing Fields

BEST DIRECTOR
Wim Wenders
Paris, Texas

BEST ACTOR
Haing S Ngor
The Killing Fields

BEST ACTRESS
Maggie Smith
A Private Function

*BEST SUPPORTING
ACTOR*
Denholm Elliott
A Private Function

*BEST SUPPORTING
ACTRESS*
Liz Smith
A Private Function

*BEST ORIGINAL
SCREENPLAY*
Woody Allen
Broadway Danny Rose

*MOST OUTSTANDING
NEWCOMER*
Haing S Ngor

*BEST ADAPTED
SCREENPLAY*
Bruce Robinson
The Killing Fields

BEST CINEMATOGRAPHY
Chris Menges
The Killing Fields

BEST SCORE
Ennio Morricone
Once Upon a Time in America

*BEST PRODUCTION
DESIGN*
Roy Walker
The Killing Fields

*BEST COSTUME
DESIGN*
Gabriella Pascucci
Once Upon a Time in America

BEST EDITING
Jim Clark
The Killing Fields

BEST ORIGINAL SONG
Ray Parker Jr
Ghostbusters

*BEST FOREIGN
LANGUAGE FILM*
Carmen (Spain)
Emiliano Piedra
Carlos Saura

BEST SOUND
Ian Fuller
Clive Winter
Bill Rowe
The Killing Fields

*BEST SPECIAL
EFFECTS*
Dennis Muren
George Gibbs
Mike McAlister
Lorne Peterson
*Indiana Jones and the Temple
of Doom*

BEST MAKE-UP
Paul Engelen
Peter Frampton
Rick Baker
Joan Hills
Greystoke

THE AWARDS

STANDARD BRITISH FILM AWARDS

BEST FILM
Nineteen Eighty-Four
Michael Radford

BEST ACTOR
John Hurt
Champions, Nineteen Eighty-Four, The Hit

BEST ACTRESS
Helen Mirren
Cal

THE PETER SELLERS AWARD
Denholm Elliott
Trading Places

BEST SCREENPLAY
Bernard MacLaverty
Cal

MOST PROMISING NEWCOMER
Tim Roth
The Hit

BEST TECHNICAL ACHIEVEMENT
John Alcott
Greystoke

FRENCH CESAR AWARDS

BEST FILM
Les Ripoux

BEST DIRECTOR
Claude Zidi
Les Ripoux

BEST ACTOR
Alain Delon
Notre Histoire

BEST ACTRESS
Sabine Azema
Sunday in the Country

BEST ADAPTATION FROM A LITERARY WORK
Bertrand Tavernier, Colo Tavernier
Sunday in the Country

BEST CINEMATOGRAPHY
Bruno De Keyser
Sunday in the Country

BEST FOREIGN FILM
Amadeus

BEST EDITING
Les Ripoux

DAVID DI DONATELLO AWARDS

BEST FILM
Carmen
Francesco Rosi

BEST DIRECTOR
Francesco Rosi
Carmen

BEST ACTOR
Francesco Nuti
Casablanca, Casablanca

BEST ACTRESS
Lina Sastri
Secrets, Secrets

BEST SUPPORTING ACTOR
Ricky Tognazzi
Aurora

BEST SUPPORTING ACTRESS
Marina Confalone
Thus Spake Bellavista

BEST PRODUCER
Giuliani De Negri
Kaos
Fulvio Lucisano
Uno Scandalo per Bene

BEST DEBUTING DIRECTOR
Luciano De Crescenzo
Thus Spake Bellavista

BEST CINEMATOGRAPHY
Pasqualino De Santis
Carmen

BEST SET DESIGN
Enrico Job
Carmen

BEST MUSIC
Carlo Savina
The Pizza Connection

BEST FILM – FOREIGN
Amadeus

BEST DIRECTOR – FOREIGN
Milos Forman
Amadeus

BEST PRODUCER – FOREIGN
David Puttnam
The Killing Fields

BEST ACTOR – FOREIGN
Tom Hulce
Amadeus

BEST ACTRESS – FOREIGN
Meryl Streep
Falling in Love

BEST SCREENPLAY – FOREIGN
Woody Allen
Broadway Danny Rose

RENE CLAIR AWARD
Wim Wenders

LUCHINO VISCONTI AWARD
Istvan Szabo

VENICE FILM FESTIVAL

GOLDEN LION BEST DIRECTOR
Krzysztof Zanussi
The Year of the Quiet Sun

INTERNATIONAL CRITICS' PRIZE
Heimat
(West Germany)

SPECIAL JURY PRIZE
Otar Iosseliani
The Favourites of the Moon

SILVER LION – BEST FIRST FEATURE
Sonatine
(Canada)

SILVER LION – TECHNICAL AWARD
Pupi Avati
The Three of Us
(Italy)

BEST ACTOR
Naseeruddin Shah
Paar (The Crossing)
(India)

BEST ACTRESS
Pascale Ogier
Les Nuits de la Pleine Lune
(France)

PASINETTI AWARD
The Year of the Quiet Sun

PASINETTI – BEST ACTOR
Fernando Fernan Gomez
Los Zancos

PASINETTI – BEST ACTRESS
Claudia Cardinale
Claretta

VENEZIA DE SICA AWARD
Francesca Comencini
Pianoforte

THE DIRECTORS GUILD OF AMERICA AWARD

Milos Forman
Amadeus (US)

ACADEMY OF CANADIAN CINEMA GENIE AWARDS

BEST PICTURE
The Bay Boy

BEST DIRECTOR
Micheline Lanctot
Sonatine

BEST ACTOR
Gabriel Arcand
Le Crime d'Ovide Plouffe

BEST ACTRESS
Louise Marleau
La Femme de l'Hôtel

BEST SUPPORTING ACTOR
Alan Scarfe
The Bay Boy

BEST SUPPORTING ACTRESS
Linda Sorensen
Draw!

BEST SCREENPLAY
Daniel Petrie
The Bay Boy

BEST ART DIRECTION
Wolf Kroeger
The Bay Boy

BEST SOUND EDITING
Charles Bower
Peter Burgess
The Bay Boy

BEST CINEMATOGRAPHY
Pierre Mignot
Mario

BEST ORIGINAL SONG
Yves Laferriere
Marjolene Morine
Paul Baillargeon
La Femme de l'Hôtel

BEST MUSIC SCORE
François Dompierre
Mario

BEST FILM EDITING
André Corriebeau
La Guerre des Turques

SPECIAL ACHIEVEMENT AWARD
Ivan Reitman

SAN SEBASTIAN FILM FESTIVAL

INTERNATIONAL CRITICS' PRIZE
Rumble Fish (US)
Francis Ford Coppola

RUNNER-UP
Tasio (Spain)
Montzo Armendariz

CANNES FILM FESTIVAL

PALME D'OR
Father's Gone on a Business Trip
(Yugoslavia)

GRAND PRIX DU JURY
Birdy

BEST ACTOR
William Hurt
Kiss of the Spider Woman

BEST ACTRESS
Cher
Mask
Norma Aleandro
The Official Version

BEST DIRECTOR
Andre Techine
Rendez-Vous

JURY PRIZE
Colonel Redl
Istvan Szabo

BEST ARTISTIC CONTRIBUTION
Paul Schrader
Mishima

TECHNICAL AWARD
Insignificance
Nicolas Roeg

INTERNATIONAL CRITICS AWARD
The Purple Rose of Cairo
Woody Allen
Father's Gone on a Business Trip
Emir Kusturica

CAMERA D'OR
Oriane (Venezuela)
Fina Torres

PRIX DE LA JEUNESSE
Dance with a Stranger

BEST FRENCH FILM
The Harem of Archimedes

VARIETY CLUB OF GREAT BRITAIN AWARDS

BEST ACTOR
Anthony Hopkins
The Bounty

BEST ACTRESS
Helen Mirren
Cal

AUSTRALIAN FILM AWARDS

BEST FILM
Annie's Coming Out

BEST DIRECTOR
Paul Cox
My First Wife

BEST ACTOR
John Hargreaves
My First Wife

BEST ACTRESS
Angela Punch McGregor
Annie's Coming Out

BEST SUPPORTING ACTOR
Steve Bisley
Silver City

BEST SUPPORTING ACTRESS
Anna Jemison
Silver City

BEST CINEMATOGRAPHY
Dean Semler
Razorback

BEST ORIGINAL SCREENPLAY
Paul Cox
Bob Ellis
My First Wife

BEST ADAPTED SCREENPLAY
John Patterson
Chris Borthwick
Annie's Coming Out

CRITICS' CIRCLE AWARDS

BEST ENGLISH LANGUAGE FILM
Paris, Texas

BEST FOREIGN LANGUAGE FILM
Sunday in the Country
(France)

BEST DIRECTOR
Neil Jordan
The Company of Wolves

BEST SCREENPLAY
Philip Kaufman
The Right Stuff

BEST ACTOR/ACTRESS
Harry Dean Stanton
Paris, Texas
Albert Finney
Under the Volcano

MARI KUTTNA AWARD FOR ANIMATION
Iain McCall
Christmas for Sale

TAORMINA FILM FESTIVAL

GOLDEN CHARYBDIS
The Funeral (Japan)
Juzo Itomi

SILVER CHARYBDIS
Volley for a Black Buffalo
(France/Hunary)
Laszlo Szabo

BRONZE CHARYBDIS
The Death Jumper
Benno Trautman (Germany)

NATIONAL FILM JOURNALISTS UNION AWARD
A Private Function

GOLD POLYPHEMUS – BEST PERFORMANCE
Maggie Smith
A Private Function

SILVER POLYPHEMUS – BEST PERFORMANCE
Gerard Thoolen, Renee Soutendijk, Bruno Gantz
The Ice Cream Parlour

BRONZE POLYPHEMUS – BEST PERFORMANCE
Liz Smith
A Private Function

AGIS – BANCA NAZIONALE DEL LAVORO
Only for Love
Alessandro De Robilant

SPECIAL MENTION
John Gielgud
Leave All Fair

SPECIAL MENTION
The Ice Cream Parlour
Dimitri Frenkel Frank

MAX OPHUL'S PRIZE
Benno Trautman
The Death Jumper

BERLIN FILM FESTIVAL

GOLDEN BEAR
Wetherby (UK)
David Hare
The Woman and the Stranger
(East Germany)
Rainer Simon

SILVER BEAR SPECIAL JURY PRIZE
Flowers of Reverie
(Hungary)

SILVER BEAR BEST DIRECTOR
Robert Benton
Places in the Heart (US)

SILVER BEAR BEST ACTOR
Fernando Fernan Gomez
Stico (Spain)

SILVER BEAR BEST ACTRESS
Jo Kennedy
Wrong World (Australia)

SILVER BEAR – OUTSTANDING ACHIEVEMENT
Tolomusch Okejew for Art Direction
The Descendant of the Snow Leopard (Russia)
Tage Danielsson
Ronja, Robber's Daughter
(Sweden/Norway)

GOLDEN GLOBE AWARDS – US

BEST MOTION PICTURE – DRAMA
Amadeus

BEST DIRECTOR
Milos Forman
Amadeus

BEST ACTOR – DRAMA
F Murray Abraham
Amadeus

BEST ACTRESS – DRAMA
Sally Field
Places in the Heart

BEST SCREENPLAY
Peter Shaffer
Amadeus

BEST MOTION PICTURE – MUSICAL OR COMEDY
Romancing the Stone

BEST ACTOR – MUSICAL OR COMEDY
Dudley Moore
Micki & Maude

BEST ACTRESS – MUSICAL OR COMEDY
Kathleen Turner
Romancing the Stone

BEST SUPPORTING ACTOR
Haing S Ngor
The Killing Fields

BEST SUPPORTING ACTRESS
Peggy Ashcroft
A Passage to India

BEST FOREIGN FILM
A Passage to India

BOOKS

Reviewed by *Al Clark*, *John Walker* and *Nicholas Pole*

THE AGE OF THE DREAM PALACE
Jeffrey Richards
(Routledge & Kegan Paul)
Informative, well-researched account of cinema and society in Britain from 1930-1939 when Gracie Fields and George Formby were the country's biggest stars. It's written in that academic style where even the most obvious statements are backed up by footnoted quotations from other authorities, and where a sentence beginning "it goes without saying" is followed by three pages of saying what goes without saying.

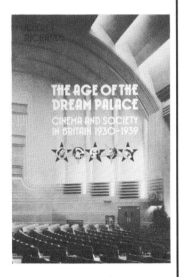

ALFRED HITCHCOCK PRESENTS
John McCarty and Brian Kelleher
(St Martin's Press)
A guide to the director's television series – *Alfred Hitchcock Presents* and *The Alfred Hitchcock Hour* – giving the background to the series, main credits, plot synopses and some photographs. As Paul Henreid, one of his regular directors, points out in his autobiography, the early programmes, based on classic short stories, were better than the later ones which relied on original scripts.

ALICE DOESN'T
Teresa De Lauretis
(MacMillan)
For those who believe that film theory – the business of watching ourselves watching films – has a future as a serious and popular discipline, semiology's obsessive concern with the re-interpretation of Freudian gospel must be one of the disasters of the decade. This book, doubly disappointing because of the importance of its subject ("Feminism, Semiotics, Cinema"), offers

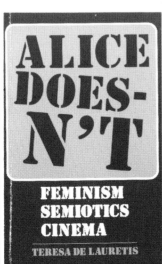

the general reader no relief. Inviting flashes of insight can occasionally be glimpsed – but seldom grasped – through barbed-wire thickets of jargon ("cinema is at once a material apparatus and a signifying practice in which the subject is implicated, constructed, but not exhausted"). This ritual torture of the English language is no way to advertise potentially valuable ideas, nor does it improve semiology's image of cultish introversion.

AMERICAN FILM AND SOCIETY SINCE 1945
Leonard Quart and Albert Auster
(MacMillan)
Though it took two Assistant Professors to write this slim volume, its intentions are academically unambitious. They put forward no new ideas about how film and society affect each other and are happy to consider

"Hollywood classics" and "American film" as synonymous. Taking the subject decade by decade, a brief assessment of the

political and economic climate is followed by a discussion of some of the most popular films of the time. Not a formula for surprises. Can successful films change public moods, or merely make a lot of money because they happen to reflect them? This is a question the authors never begin to ask, though they quote an ominously relevant comment by Coppola: "We made it *(Apocalypse Now)* the way America made war in Vietnam. There were too many of us, too much money and equipment, and little by little we went insane".

ASTAIRE, THE MAN, THE DANCER
Bob Thomas
(St Martin's Press/Weidenfeld & Nicolson)

"Can't act. Slightly bald. Also dances" was the studio reaction to Astaire's first screen test. From vaudeville to Broadway, where Gershwin was the rehearsal pianist, to films, Astaire tapped his way to the top. Written with the star's co-operation, Thomas tells how he did it. No surprises, but it's a good read and it includes details of his shows and films as well as an index.

BARBARA STANWYCK
Al Dioro
(Coward-McCann/W H Allen)
Clumsily written account of
the life of one of the most
enduring and professional of

movie actresses. She had bad
times early and late:
orphaned at two and reduced
to playing Elvis Presley's
mother in *Roustabout* at 61.
In between, came the
triumphs – *Stella Dallas*, *The
Mad Miss Manton*, *Union
Pacific* and many others –
which are inadequately dealt
with by an author who
confesses frequently that
much about Miss Stanwyck is
unknown (to him, at least).
There is a filmography, but no
index.

**BERNARDO
BERTOLUCCI**
Robert Phillip Kolker
(BFI)
Thorough critical study of a
(mostly) great director. Sound
in analysis if rather starchy
in expression.

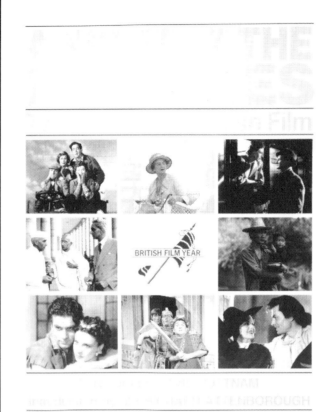

**THE BRITISH FILM
COLLECTION 1896-1984**
Patricia Warren
(Elm Tree Books)
**A NIGHT AT THE
PICTURES**
(Columbus Books/BFY)

**THE BIG BOOK OF
BRITISH FILMS**
Robin Cross
(Sidgwick & Jackson)
BRITISH SOUND FILMS
David Quinlan
(Batsford)

BRITISH CINEMA NOW
**Ed. Martyn Auty & Nick
Roddick**
(BFI)

THE ONCE AND FUTURE FILM
John Walker
(Methuen)

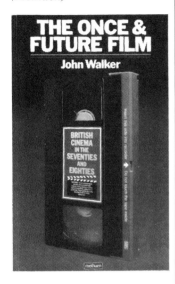

LEARNING TO DREAM
James Park
(Faber & Faber)
No less than seven books about British cinema preceded or coincided with British Film Year – four pictorial/historical, three more austerely analytical and rooted in the present. Richard Attenborough supplied the foreword to Patricia Warren's reverential picture history, separated into decades (the thirties are "booming", the sixties "swinging"), with a brief introduction in each case; otherwise, it's largely stills with captions. Attenborough also did the

introduction to BFY's official book *A Night at the Pictures* (subtitled 'Ten Decades of British Film') built around

two lengthy articles by Gilbert Adair and Nick Roddick and supplemented by a chronology and various lists. Robin Cross confines himself to the years 1939-1970 in his pithy, perceptive survey of British film history, while David Quinlan provides a complete directory of films between 1928 and 1959 with, rather unnecessarily, a star and film of each decade forming part of the introduction. The three books which deal with current British cinema all provide contrasting perspectives, despite the overlap in subject. *British Cinema Now* is a collection of essays dealing with different aspects of film; John Walker covers the last fifteen years by subdividing individual film-makers into groups, while James Park focuses more on illustrating themes and subjects. All are eminently readable.

CAHIERS DU CINEMA – THE 1950s
Ed. Jim Hillier
(Routledge & Kegan Paul/ BFI)
The first of four intended volumes from the influential French film journal, about equal parts provocative and pretentious. This one deals mainly with the French New Wave, Italian Neo-Realism and Hollywood, which really means *Cahiers* pets Ray (mostly), Hawks, Preminger, Hitchcock, Fuller, Mann and Boetticher. Enjoyable reading, if a little heavy going at times, and conveying at least a real excitement about cinema.

CHAPLIN: HIS LIFE AND ART
David Robinson
(Collins)
Definitive account of the great man, based on his papers, and grippingly detailing his career from Lambeth childhood and English music hall to swish Swiss retirement. Essential reading, particularly on the early, improvised days in Hollywood. It includes a chronology, filmography, who's who and detailed index.

CHOICES
Liv Ullmann
(Weidenfeld & Nicolson)
An odd mixture of windy philosophising and sharp-eyed observation on the idiocies of show business, the behaviour of men and the little incidents of life, like the time she sings for Richard Rogers and before her eyes he ages twenty years.

THE COTTON CLUB
Jim Haskins
(Robson Books)
The story of the Harlem
nightclub which purportedly
inspired Robert Evans' forty-
five-million-dollar folly:
owned by mobsters,
patronised by whites,
entertainment provided by
blacks. A lively account,
although a little heavy on the
name-dropping.

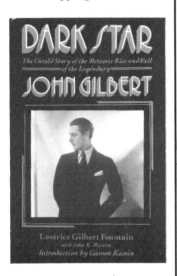

**DARK STAR: JOHN
GILBERT**
**Leatrice Gilbert Fountain
with John R Maxim**
(St Martin's Press)
Another legend bites the dust.
John Gilbert, lover of Garbo
and most charismatic of the
early stars, was not destroyed
because the coming of sound
revealed that he spoke in a
high-pitched squeak. It was
through the malice of the
vindictive and grossly
sentimental Louis B Mayer,
who didn't like the way
Gilbert talked about his
mother. Gilbert's daughter
restores his reputation in a
fascinating book that
includes an index and
filmography.

DIETRICH
Alexander Walker
(Thames & Hudson)
Lavish pictorial biography in
the style of Walker's previous
volumes on Garbo and
Crawford. Nothing
particularly new in it, but
intelligently written with
some remarkable
photographs.

ALEXANDER WALKER

**DINO – THE DEAN
MARTIN STORY**
Michael Freedland
(W H Allen)
The indefatigable and
anodyne Freedland reveals
Martin's claustrophobia and
decides that the big question
is whether he is going to
remarry the second of his
three wives. Interesting, eh?

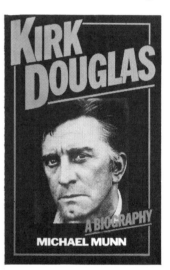

Michael Freedland

cared much for movies –
complete with index and
filmography.

KIRK DOUGLAS
Michael Munn
(Robson Books)
From Issur Danielovitch to
Kirk Douglas, from the son of
penniless immigrants to
successful star, must be a
more interesting trip than it
seems in this bland retelling.

DOUBLE LIFE

Composer in the Golden Years of Hollywood

DOUBLE LIFE
Miklós Rózsa
(The Baton Press)
Eastern fantasies (*The Thief
of Baghdad, The Golden
Voyage of Sinbad*),
psychological dramas (*Double
Indemnity, The Lost
Weekend*) and historical epics
(from *Quo Vadis* on) wouldn't
be the same without the
vibrant scores of Rózsa, a
violinist at the age of five,
who is also a composer of
concert works. His two lives
have encompassed everyone
from Hitler to Hollywood
dictators and he remembers
them all in a chatty, honest
autobiography – he never

There is, at least, an index
and a filmography as well as
an uninteresting selection of
stills.

**D W GRIFFITH AND THE
BIRTH OF FILM**
Richard Schickel
(Pavilion/Michael Joseph)
Not to be missed. One of the
most readable of critics on the
greatest of directors during
the formative years of
Hollywood. Schickel's
judgement can be
occasionally wrong –
Britain's greatest living

dramatist Rodney Ackland is dismissed as "a screen-struck playwright of no distinction" – but he provides, at great length, an engrossing account of a complex, self-destructive and neglected genius.

ELIZABETH TAYLOR
Christopher Nickens
(Hutchinson)
Subtitled 'A Biography in Photographs', this is also a "James Spada Associates Book", which means that it combines the blandest fan magazine prose with interesting pictures. Worth a glance, though not at the words.

EMPTY SEATS
Michael White
(Hamish Hamilton)
A producer whose occasional forays into film have resulted in *The Rocky Horror Picture Show*, *Moonlighting* and *The Ploughman's Lunch*, White delivers a mainly anecdotal account of his apprenticeship in the theatre, his emergence

as a force in London theatre recalling the staging of *Oh! Calcutta!* and the night an actor in *The Dirtiest Show in Town* substituted real for simulated sex on stage.

EVERYBODY'S MAN
Jhan Robbins
(Robson Books)
A biography of Jimmy Stewart, described by its

author as an "oral history profile" which, on the evidence of this book, can best be described as transcribing some extremely dull conversations in even duller prose. Robbins appears to have absolutely no interest in movies at all, least of all those made by his hero. Apart from their appearance in a detailed filmography, there's otherwise no mention of such films as *The Glenn Miller Story*, *The Far Country*, *The Man from Laramie* and *Two Rode Together*.

FANTASTIC CINEMA
Peter Nicholls
(Ebury Press)
An excellent, illustrated survey of the genre, covering science fiction and horror. There's a detailed filmography and rating of 700 films, 300 of which are discussed in greater detail. The main emphasis is on what has happened since 1968, defined as "the breakthrough year" – the time of Resnais' *Je t'aime, Je t'aime*, *Barbarella*, *Charly*, *Planet of the Apes*, and, of course *2001: A Space Odyssey*.

FASSBINDER, FILM MAKER
Ronald Hayman
(Weidenfeld & Nicolson)
Excellent account of the life (and death) of the celebrated film maniac, whose devotion to various forms of self-abuse was so excessive that by the time of his death at thirty-seven he already looked like a man in his fifties. A bisexual bully with "extraordinarily beautiful eyes" and a brilliant talent for getting his own way, he would rush into films without waiting to raise the money, either using his own or working on credit, so long as the idea still excited him. Not so much the-man-behind-the-image, as an examination of how inextricably the man, the films, and the image were all part of one great, prolific disaster area; as Hayman puts it, Fassbinder ended up by sacrificing himself to his own legend.

FILM FORUM
Ellen Oumano
(St Martin's Press)
Interviews with thirty-five directors, including Robert Altman, Claude Chabrol, Jean-Luc Godard, Michael Powell, Martin Scorsese and Joan Micklin Silver. The author has edited out her questions and divided the interviews into short takes on a number of topics: cinematography; sound; the actor; structure and rhythm; film and reality; writing, shooting and editing; the viewer; film and society; and the movie business. The result is a confusing read that raises more questions than it answers: why do only twelve of the thirty-five have anything to say on acting, for instance?

THE FRONT LINE
David Ehrenstein
(Arden Press)
The second in a series of annual reports and essential reading for those interested in the cinema's cutting edge. Ehrenstein encompasses the work of Jack Smith, Curt McDowell, Werner Schrotter, Luc Moullet, Lizzie Burden, Sally Potter and others, reserving a special place among the avant garde for the sublime trickery of Orson Welles.

THE FONDAS
Gerald Cole and Wes Farrell
(W H Allen)
Plenty of illustrations and an efficient retelling of the story of Henry and his two

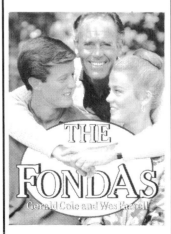

rebellious children Peter and Jane and how they all found fame and, finally, an understanding of each other. It would have been improved by a filmography and an index.

FILM REVIEW 1984-5
F Maurice Speed
(Columbus Books)
SCREEN WORLD 1984
John Willis
(Crown Publishers/Frederick Muller)
INTERNATIONAL FILM GUIDE
Peter Cowie
(Tantivy)
Another round for the defiant survivors among film annuals, in Speed's case his fortieth round-up of the British year. Despite the new larger format and a few structural changes (the stills are now integrated into the year's releases and there's a films-made-for-TV section), it's the familiar amalgam of opinion and reference, prefaced by Speed's customary 'over-view' (bad language and poor enunciation get a bit of a bashing this year). Marketing considerations have obviously dictated the

addition of the phrase 'including video releases' on the cover – which it doesn't at all unless you count the cinema films that had their video release within the same year. Willis's remains the definitive source book for American films, although the customary absence of any critical perspective limits its usage. It continues to bewilder that he should give such prominence to turkeys like *Trenchcoat* and *Man, Woman and Child* and so little to, say, *Under Fire* and *Rumble Fish*. Cowie's world survey remains alone in its sphere, but it would benefit from livelier contributions from its correspondents. Curious to see in its survey of the 1983 UK year Don Boyd's *Gossip* (abandoned in early 1983) and Derek Jarman's *Caravaggio* (not yet made) listed as 'recent and forthcoming' films.

FRENCH CINEMA
Roy Armes
(Secker & Warburg)
A comprehensive decade-by-decade history, seen largely through the careers of its best-known directors. Armes describes how rapidly the cinema was industrialized – by 1912 Pathé controlled one third of the world's film business and took seventy per cent of its profits from the US – and how the bulk of its early output "conformed to the inadequate social norms of a self-satisfied commercial bourgeoisie." He ends with a look at early eighties' big-budget production, dominated by inane plots and the lumbering egos of its superstars: Montand, Delon and Belmondo. Somewhere in between, told in refreshingly dispassionate prose, is the story of how France's best directors, from Gance to Godard, managed amid the mediocrity to produce their occasional masterpieces.

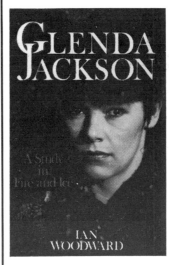

GLENDA JACKSON
Ian Woodward
(Weidenfeld & Nicolson)
Subtitled 'A Study in Fire and Ice', it chronicles with care and affection the career of possibly the best of contemporary screen and stage actresses, and certainly the least star-struck and most abrasive. It includes copious illustrations and details of her film, stage and television work and many awards.

GOLDIE
Peter Haining
(W H Allen)
Lots of pictures of Miss Hawn disguising her intelligence behind the familiar pose of a pop-eyed, giggling blonde decorate a solid account of her life, loves and work. There's a filmography but no index.

GLAMOROUS MUSICALS
Ronald Bergen
(Octopus Books)
Six essays on various aspects of the musical, into which the films themselves are somewhat uneasily squeezed – Nelson Eddy and Jeanette MacDonald are dealt with in a chapter on The European Touch, for instance. But the pictures are pretty.

THE GREAT BOOK OF MOVIE VILLAINS
Jan Stacey and **Ryder Syvertsen**
(Columbus Books)
A guide to the screen's meanies, tough guys and

bullies which treats them as real people, listing them by their names rather than by the actors who played them and providing advice on what you should do if you meet them. Joan Crawford (as played by Faye Dunaway) is the only star who makes it under her own name.

HOLLYWOOD BABYLON II
Kenneth Anger
(Dutton)
More squalid, ghoulish, misanthropic revelations about dead celebrities from the man whose childhood hobby was visiting cemeteries. Considering it's been twenty-five years since the last volume was originally published in France, some of the revelations are a little familiar, particularly in a long chapter on Hollywood suicides, but there are some extraordinary pictures (including Broderick Crawford and Robert Cummings in drag), and a florid and fascinating account of how George Cukor came to be fired from *Gone with the Wind*.

GUINNESS FILM FACTS AND FEATS
Patrick Robertson
(Guinness Superlatives)
Firsts, biggests, longests, mosts, youngests, earliests – all that kind of stuff, plus filmographies of Dracula, Cinderella, Tarzan, Hamlet, Napoleon, Sherlock Holmes, Buffalo Bill, US presidents, soccer, films that run over four hours, actors who have played themselves, non-actors who have played themselves and non-actors who have played somebody else. It also sets the record straight on the most hackneyed line in American cinema from 1938-74 ("let's get outta here" in eighty-four per cent of them, but only from a sample of 150 films); on how many takes Stanley Kubrick demanded of Shelley Duvall in one scene from *The*

Shining (127); on exactly how many names were on the end titles of *Superman* (457); and on the fact that all the Nazi concentration camp guards in Fuller's *The Big Red One* were played by Jews. It's also sobering to learn that the British actor still alive with most screen credits is Christopher Lee, acknowledged by everyone who has met him to be the world's most boring man. This last detail, of course, is not in the book.

HOLLYWOOD COLOUR PORTRAITS
John Kobal
(Aurum)
GREAT MOVIE ACTRESSES
Philip Strick
(Orbis)
CINÉ STARS
(Columbus Books)

The big three of the year's picture books. Kobal's is an

undisguised love-letter to the period of Hollywood history that was most dominated by lush colour images of the stars at work and play, prefaced by an informative history of the development of Technicolor and supplemented by brief biographical assessments. The heart of it, though, is in its remarkable pictures – the majority highly composed portraits, although it is the frontispiece still (Bing Crosby in an extraordinary set for *The Emperor Waltz*) which lingers in the memory ahead of Marlene Dietrich and Pal, the "Greer Garson in furs"

who played Lassie. Strick's book, with all mono stills and portraits, is at its best when his biographical note on each actress extends beyond simple data to consider what their special quality happens to be; at its worst, when it assumes familiar portraits are enough. Apart from a

brief introduction by James Cameron-Wilson, *Ciné Stars* doesn't bother with any words at all apart from filmographies of the actresses represented. A mixed bunch they are too, presented like a peculiarly elitist de-luxe casting directory with inclusion seemingly determined by whether or not they've been photographed by a prominent European-based photographer – Jamie Lee Curtis hasn't been but Charlene Tilton has. Good browsing material, though.

HOLLYWOOD DYNASTIES
Stephen Farber & Mark Green
(Delilah)
Absorbing chronicle of Hollywood's ruling families and their legacies, rooted in the premise that it is impossible to understand the film industry without unravelling the dynastic ties upon which it rests. A long, fascinating read of soap opera dimensions.

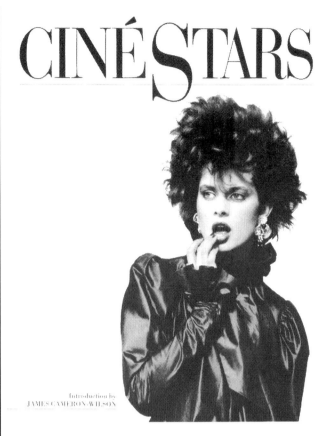

HOLLYWOOD FACTION: REALITY AND MYTH IN THE MOVIES
Bruce Crowther
(Columbus Books)
A volume dedicated to the proposition that most people get their knowledge of the past from the cinema. From this dubious premise, which overlooks the fact that most people do not go to the cinema, the author examines films based on real life and decides that Hollywood has trivialised the noble and turned into folk heroes the ignoble. So what else is new?

THE ILLUSTRATED GUIDE TO FILM DIRECTORS
David Quinlan
(Batsford)
THE UNIVERSAL STORY
Clive Hirschhorn
(Octopus Books)
Both of these precede the year under review but are first-class companion volumes to books we have recommended in the past. Quinlan's *Illustrated Director of Film*

Stars was one of the highlights of its year and his follow-up supplements it perfectly, with comparably perceptive summaries of directorial careers and complete filmographies. Indeed, some are a little too complete (John Carpenter's aborted *El Diablo* is listed and Quinlan credits *The Terry Fox Story,* a Canadian television movie directed by Ralph L Thomas, to British stalwart Ralph Thomas). Hirschhorn's epic studio history of Universal is, like his similarly styled *The Warner Bros Story* for the same publisher, a wonderfully illustrated chronological account of all the films made and released by the studio between 1913 and 1982. Plenty of opinion, too.

THE JACK WRANGLER STORY
Jack Wrangler and Carl Johnes
(St Martin's Press)
Light-hearted look behind the sleaze of porno films from a Hollywood child who went from soap operas to gay movies and heterosexual hardcore, modelled for a

plastic dildo and became the lover of Margaret Whiting, star of *Girls Four Girls,* which wasn't a sex film but a show in which she sang with her contemporaries Rosemary Clooney, Helen O'Connell and Rose Marie. Wrangler first made love to a woman at the age of thirty-one, while filming *Two China Sisters,* but whatever he lost, he's kept his sense of humour.

JACQUES TATI, FRAME BY FRAME
James Harding
(Secker & Warburg)
Exhaustive account of Tati's career from his beginnings as a mime-entertainer in amateur revues to his grumpy, bankrupt and disillusioned old age. Detailed but often pedantic descriptions of his working methods emphasize the intense seriousness of his approach. To prepare *Mon Oncle* he devoted himself to the full-time observation of Paris street life for two years.

JAMES DEAN: AMERICAN ICON
David Dalton & Ron Cayen
(St Martin's Press/Sidgwick & Jackson)
Yet another glossy attempt to wring significance from Dean's short, disturbed life, complete with an incoherent introduction from Martin Sheen ("James Dean was the strongest influence of any actor that ever stepped in front of the camera. Ever!") Photographs trace his development from intense bespectacled adolescent to moody actor. Much of the book, though, is given over to reprints of the tabloid and magazine gush that followed, and obviously continues to follow, his death.

JOAN COLLINS
Robert Levine
(Dell/Weidenfeld & Nicolson)
PAST IMPERFECT
Joan Collins
(W H Allen)
The only biographies worth
writing are those of people
who aren't going to write far
better (and more revealing)
ones of themselves. Joan
Collins already has and
although Levine's brisk
account is all right as far as it
goes, it isn't a patch on
Collins' own, from which
much of the information
appears to have been adapted.
Past Imperfect is one of the
funniest, trashiest and most
candid of showbiz biogs,
although the original 1978
edition was the truly
unexpurgated version that
this one claims to be – just
check out what Maxwell Reed
was *really* trying to do when
Joan came round from the
Mickey Finn for the second
time!

**JOLIE: THE STORY OF
AL JOLSON**
Michael Freedland
(W H Allen)
A new edition of a 1972
biography of the great
entertainer who ushered in
talking pictures in 1927 with
The Jazz Singer and, a
generation later, forgotten
and ill, still sung lustily with
one lung in *The Jolson Story*.
The story is well and
anecdotally told. There's an
index, but no filmography and
only a few stills.

**JUDI DENCH: A GREAT
DEAL OF LAUGHTER**
Gerald Jacobs
(Weidenfeld & Nicolson)
No doubt movie producers
and goers will discover the
great talents of classical
actress Judi Dench as late as
they did those of Peggy

Ashcroft. It's twenty years
since she won a prize in her
first full-length film rôle, in
Four in the Morning, and her
lack of screen opportunities
is, says Peter Hall, an
indictment of the film
industry. It has been theatre's
gain, as this charming
authorized biography, full of
funny anecdotes, makes clear.
It is, thankfully, informative
on her work as well as her life.

JULIE CHRISTIE
Michael Feeney Callan
(W H Allen)
Interesting, well-researched,
nicely illustrated biography
of the most stubbornly private
of British stars.

**KATHARINE HEPBURN
– THE THIRTIES AND
AFTER**
Andrew Britton
(Tyneside Cinema)
"The significance of the great
female stars of the Hollywood
cinema for feminist cultural
studies lies in the
contradictions they generate
within narrative structures
which are committed overall
to the reaffirmation of
bourgeois-patriarchal
norms," is how this book
begins. There's a lot more that
will be of greater interest to
students of deconstruction
than to *aficionados* of cinema
and creativity.

KID FROM THE BRONX
Michael Munn
(W H Allen)
Entertaining account of Tony
Curtis's life and career, from a
depression childhood in New
York to the personal
depression which sent him to
the Betty Ford Clinic last
year before his triumphant
return to form in
Insignificance. The tabloid
writing style gets wearying
though, and the cliché-count
is uncomfortably high.

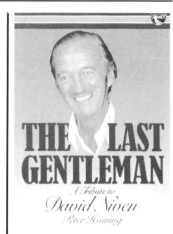

LADIES MAN
Paul Henreid with Julius Fast
(St Martin's Press)
Two forties classics, *Now Voyager,* in which he lit two cigarettes with a single match, one for Bette Davis, and *Casablanca* are still the films Henreid is best remembered for. It almost comes as a shock to realize that he's still around, if now retired after becoming a director following his blacklisting by HUAC. His memories are happy and

blunt, from complaints about Ricardo Montalban's diarrhoea to Hedy Lamarr's and Katharine Hepburn's acting. There's a filmography and an index.

THE LAST GENTLEMAN
Peter Haining
(W H Allen)
A tribute to David Niven, mainly from friends and acquaintances. A few are fascinating and even moving, most are dull and banal – the sort of material that would have been junked if it weren't

THE KILLING FIELDS
(Sydney Schanberg & Dith Pran)
(Weidenfeld & Nicolson)
A glossy souvenir of the film, more substantial than most such productions, providing background information on Cambodia and long interviews with the two protagonists, Schanberg and Pran, and with the film's makers. With illustrations of the reality and the movie's recreation of events, it's engrossing stuff even if you've not yet seen the film.

VIVIEN LEIGH
John Russell Taylor
(Elm Tree Books)
A slim volume of splendid photographs through which a few words wend their leisurely way, providing a cursory and occasionally overblown account of her life and work (only fourteen films in twenty-one years) which has been better dealt with elsewhere.

KNOCK WOOD
Candice Bergen
(Hamish Hamilton)
Hollywood from the inside: a story of coming to terms with fame from birth, with acting and with Charlie McCarthy, the obstreperous wooden figure who dominated her home and her famous ventriloquist father Edgar Bergen. And, after the traumas, there's a happy ending: she marries Louis Malle, who is very far from being a dummy.

over famous signatures. But all attest to the affection and regard in which he was held by those who knew him. There is a complete filmography from his appearance as an extra in *All the Winners* (1932) to his final appearance – his voice was dubbed – in the sad *The Trail of the Pink Panther* fifty years later.

JACK LEMMON
Michael Freedland
(W H Allen)
"The most outstanding film actor of our age", according to the author, who correctly describes this account as "a tribute". There's nothing sour about the Lemmon in these pages and his fans as well as lovers of sugar-coated prose, will love it. There's an inadequate index but no filmography.

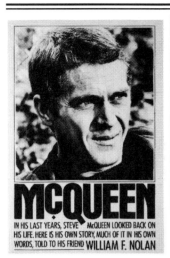

McQUEEN
William F Nolan
(Congdon & Weed)
Based, according to the blurb, on long talks that the star had with Nolan, a journalist who shared his interest in fast cars and bikes. McQueen, taciturn at the best of times, was not among the world's great conversationalists – even though he was intensely competitive about everything else. He set an increasingly high value on his time, demanding a million dollars a week if he were to act in *Apocalypse Now* and requiring a payment of $50,000 just to read a script, which maybe explains why he made so few films in the seventies. It's the work, not the life, that remains interesting. The book has an index and filmography.

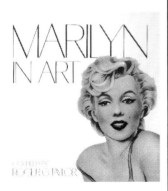

MARILYN IN ART
Roger G Taylor
(Elm Tree Books)
A picture book of an icon of our times, as portrayed by artists and illustrators and interspersed with quotes from colleagues and critics. All we need now is a book explaining

why she should have inspired so much tacky art and bad prose, even from Arthur "She's all woman, the most womanly woman in the world" Miller.

THE MATT DILLON SCRAPBOOK
Cheryl L Mead
(St Martin's Press)
It's all here, fans! More than sixty photos of delectable Matt. There's Matt in T-shirt, Matt without T-shirt and

Matt displaying his gamut of expressions: Matt smiling, Matt frowning and Matt sulking. And everything you wanted to know about him: he's cute, sexy and fun to kiss. And, it says here, a genuine superstar. Which only goes to show how far show-business propaganda has devalued the meaning of words.

MERYL STREEP
Diana Maychick
(Robson Books)
THE MERYL STREEP STORY
Nick Smurthwaite
(Columbus Books)
The first is a breathless, superficial and premature biography of a voraciously dedicated actress. Gems of

insight – "the private Meryl is often beset by periods of self-doubt" – are occasionally interspersed with interesting points: after weeks spent perfecting her Polish accent for *Sophie's Choice,* Streep was dismayed to find her own baby could no longer recognize her voice and would burst into tears whenever she tried to comfort him. The second is an uncritical career-so-far story with lots of glossy pictures; the only perceptive comments are the quotes from Pauline Kael.

MR LAUREL AND MR HARDY
John McCabe
(Robson Books)
A paperback edition of the best biography of the screen's finest clowns, first published in 1976.

An affectionate biography

THE MOVIE STARS STORY
Ed. Robyn Karney
(Octopus Books)
Part picture book, part star directory, part attempt at a Hollywood history, with career biographies of five hundred stars (varying length) written by five contributors (varying depth). Split into decades with an introduction in each case, some of the arbitrariness in the sub-dividing is rationalized in the preface,

although some remains bewildering: James Coburn, who rose to fame in the sixties, is included in the seventies' section, while Donald Sutherland, barely seen in the sixties, is viewed as part of that decade. A pity about the absence of filmographies, and inexcusable that among the paucity of eighties' entries Harrison Ford should be excluded on the grounds that he isn't a star.

THE MOVIEGOERS' QUIZ BOOK
F Maurice Speed
(Columbus Books)
Cheaper than *Trivial Pursuit* and appealing to the same audience, here are 1001 questions and answers on fifty-six topics, though those singled out for special treatment – Forman, Cronenberg, Hitchcock, Losey and Spielberg among directors and Burton, Gypsy Rose Lee, Astaire, Stallone, Streisand, Welch, Henry Fonda, MacLaine, McQueen, Olivier and Mason among

actors – seem an eccentric choice. If you don't know who said "After all, tomorrow is another day," then this compilation will enlighten you.

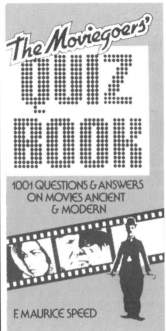

NATALIE
Lana Wood
(Columbus Books)
Subtitled 'A Memoir by Her Sister' this could just as easily be called *Lana*. As "a warm but devastatingly frank account", it promises a good deal more than it delivers, being mostly a familiar catalogue of details of a life which was conducted very much in the public eye.

NIVEN
(Hamish Hamilton)
Reissue in the same volume of *The Moon's a Balloon* (1971) and *Bring On the Empty Horses* (1975), David Niven's very funny, relentlessly anecdotal autobiographies, whose self-deprecating good humour has worn well.

NO BELLS ON SUNDAY
Ed. Alexander Walker
(Pavilion)
Rachel Roberts' diaries, written in the eighteen months before her suicide in 1980 and edited by Alexander Walker, who punctuates them with his own comments and those of the people who knew her. A harrowing read, to say the least.

PARIS, TEXAS
Ed. Chris Sievernich
(Road Movies/Greno)
INSIGNIFICANCE
Neil Norman & John Barraclough
(Sidgwick & Jackson)
Two commendable books-of-the-film. *Paris, Texas,* as lavish a record of a movie as has ever been published, features Sam Shepard's screenplay in three languages for what, proportionately, amounts to no more than a

prologue. From then on, it's four hundred pages or so of magnificent colour stills and identified location shots covering almost every moment of the film. *Insignificance* includes Terry Johnson's screenplay, a foreword by Nicolas Roeg and a format as engagingly kaleidoscopic as the film itself, whose spirit it nicely complements.

ROBERT MITCHUM
David Downing
(W H Allen)
Brisk, one-chapter summary
of the first twenty-five years
of Mitchum's life followed by a
useful if unrevealing career
biography. There is clearly a
great book about Mitchum to
be written, but one suspects
it'll be he who writes it.

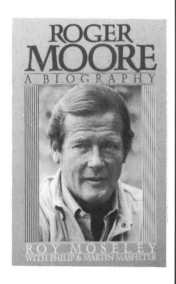

ROGER MOORE
**Roy Moseley with Philip
and Martin Masheter**
(New English Library)
The photos – of a bouffant-
haired Moore as Ivanhoe and
lifting an eyebrow as King
Henry II – are the best part of
what otherwise reads like an
uncritical, extended fan
magazine feature.

SCIENCE FICTION
Phil Hardy
(Aurum)
The second volume of
Aurum's film encyclopedia
series is every bit as
comprehensive as last year's
exemplary *The Western*, with
a chronological account of all
films in science fiction, horror
and fantasy genres,
extending beyond the
customary English language
tyranny to include movies
from other countries such as
Japan, Mexico, Spain and
Italy. A genuinely impressive
volume and the definitive
book on the subject for the
time being.

SEEING IS BELIEVING
Peter Biskind
(Pantheon Books/Pluto Press)
Subtitled 'How Hollywood
Taught Us to Stop Worrying
and Love the Fifties', this
came out before the coverage
period of the book but is
briefly noted and
recommended as a funny,
telling look at the hidden and
not-so-hidden messages in
American movies of the cold-
war years.

A SHORT HISTORY OF
THE MOVIES
Gerald Mast
*(Bobbs-Merrill/Oxford
University Press)*
The third edition of a reliable
guide – though at 450 double-
column pages, short it isn't.
Despite the preface
mentioning developments
into the eighties, the content
has hardly been updated since
the mid-seventies. Spielberg,
for instance, is discussed in
terms of *Jaws* and Lucas as
the maker of *THX 1138*.

STAR PROFILES
Ed. Marc Wanamaker
(Octopus Books)
Associated in some way with
The Hollywood Reporter,
although it is difficult to work
out precisely how, this has
seven contributors providing
two-page biographical
summaries of ninety-one
stars. The writing is
functional, the captions
erratic but there are some
good photographs,
particularly one
extraordinary small picture
of Marlon Brando buried up to
his shoulders in sand with a
bird standing on his head.

SUSPECTS
David Thomson
(Secker & Warburg)
Biographical sketches of
characters from Hollywood
movies, mostly *films noirs* or
their descendants. Some are
well known (Jake Gittes,
Vivian Sternwood, Norman
Bates), others quite obscure
(Henry Peterson from *Beat
the Devil*, Al from *The
Killers*). Thomson invents
lives for them (only some of
which is already known to us
from the screen) and makes
connections between them –

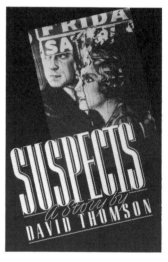

Julian Kay from *American
Gigolo* turns out to be the
illegitimate son of Joe Gillis
and Norma Desmond of
Sunset Boulevard. Well
written and quite enjoyable,
although the publicity takes
hyperbole into new realms by
comparing it with Borges,
Calvino and Marquez.

TRAVELS IN GREENELAND
Quentin Falk
(Quartet)
Thorough plod across often desolate terrain, but with occasional breathtaking landmarks. Some amusing stories and the details behind the making of *The Third Man* (Noel Coward almost played Harry Lime) do not entirely explain why anyone should devote a whole book to cataloguing the mediocre travesties which have been the usual result of attempts to turn Greenery into film. The man himself, we learn, "believes that adapting the novel must inherently result in a flawed production", and it is depressing to see how Greene, who was one of the finest film critics of the thirties, did so little to protect his own work from the slap-happy spare-part surgery of Hollywood adaptation. Mankiewicz's sanitised version of *The Quiet American* for example – which Greene called "a complete treachery" – came about because Greene had disposed of the film rights so that his daughter could buy a ranch.

TV MOVIES 1985-6
Leonard Maltin
(Plume)
Probably the best of the regularly updated film reference books, featuring listings of pretty much every theatrical and made-for-TV film imaginable, all capsule reviewed, rated and described. Nothing is too obscure for this book, not even *The Love Ins* (Arthur Dreyfuss, 1967), in which Richard Todd plays a character based on Timothy Leary.

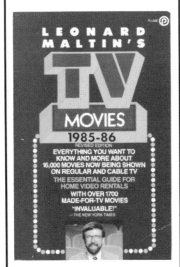

WAR MOVIES
Jay Hyams
(Gallery Books)
A mainly chronological plod through the genre, from *The Birth of a Nation* to *World War III*, taking in *Casablanca* on the way. Hyams concentrates on explications rather than analysis and stays starry-eyed: "War makes wonderful entertainment," he writes. It includes a good selection of stills.

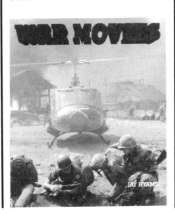

THE WARNER BROTHERS
Michael Freedland
(St Martin's Press/Harrap)
From a family of twelve children, there were four who went into the film industry although in the end only the youngest, Jack, really mattered. A familiar immigrant rags-to-riches story, blandly told, but incorporating much material from those who knew and suffered and triumphed at the studio that brought to an end cinema's silent days.

WORST MOVIE POSTERS OF ALL TIME
Gregory J Edwards & Robin Cross
(Sphere)
THE BIBLE ACCORDING TO HOLLYWOOD
THE HOLLYWOOD HISTORY OF WORLD WAR II
Robin Cross
(Ward Lock)
Add to this his *Big Book of*

British Films (see separate review), and Robin Cross becomes probably the most prolific film book author since the heyday of ghosted quickie biographies. Not that there's much writing in these, although what there is in the poster book is extremely funny, somehow conveying the right degree of awe in the face of awfulness, as a succession of quite terrible film posters with hysterical copylines are reproduced in gaudy splendour. The other two are collections of unidentified (but easy to identify) stills from biblical and war films: well researched, amusingly captioned but ultimately useless.

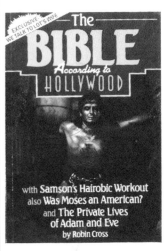

OBITUARIES

1 JULY 1984 – 30 JUNE 1985
Compiled by David McGillivray

DAWN ADDAMS

Addams' adventures as a starlet in the fifties have a storybook quality. Two years after her London stage debut in 1949 she was given a Hollywood contract by MGM but, after a few cheesecake parts, she was dropped. In

1954 she went to Italy and amidst much ballyhoo married Prince Vittorio Massimo. In 1957 Chaplin chose her as his leading lady in *A King in New York*, which was to be her only important film. Despite retaining a glamorous and likeable personality in middle age, she worked rarely and made her last film, *Vault of Horror*, in 1972. By 1982 she was in the TV soap opera *Triangle*. Died in London, 7 May, aged 55.

LUTHER ADLER

A member of a notable theatrical family, Adler was first on stage aged five and went on to play the title rôle in Clifford Odets' *Golden Boy* (New York 1937, London 1938). In films (from 1937) he was a powerful character actor in *Wake of the Red Witch* (1948), *M* (1951), *The Last Angry Man* (1959) and *The Brotherhood* (1968). He also played Hitler twice (in *The Magic Face* and *The Desert Fox*, both 1951). His last rôle was in *Absence of Malice*

(1981). Died in Kutztown, Pennsylvania, 8 December, aged 81.

EDWARD ANDREWS

In Broadway for four years prior to World War II, Andrews established himself in live TV during the fifties, then moved to films in 1955. Tall, heavily built and bespectacled, he looked like everybody else's hale and hearty next-door neighbour. Beginning in a variety of character rôles, he became almost exclusively associated with comedy from the early sixties and worked regularly for Disney and with Doris Day (both in films and TV's *Doris Day Show*). Inactive for the past ten years, he made a comeback in *Gremlins* (1984). Died in Santa Monica, California, 8 March, aged 70.

RICHARD BASEHART

Reporter turned actor Basehart's performance as the Scottish solider in the Broadway hit *The Hasty Heart* (1945) brought him to Hollywood. For five years he was a promising star of *film noir* and was outstanding as the would-be suicide in *Fourteen Hours* (1951).

Driven to Europe by the McCarthy purges, he was taken up by Fellini (*La Strada*, *Il Bidone*) and Huston (*Moby Dick*), then returned to the US to find his star had waned. For the rest of his career he was mainly on TV, but at the time of his death was largely forgotten as an actor – obituaries identified him as narrator for the 1984 Summer Olympics. Died in Los Angeles, 17 September, aged 70.

TOM BLAKELEY

Blakeley bridged two eras of British movie-making. From 1934 he was at his father John E Blakeley's Mancunian Films Corporation, producer-distributors of North country comedies. At their studios in Rusholme (Britain's only provincial feature film studio) Blakeley Jr produced second features starring such Lancashire favourites as Frank Randle and Norman Evans. The studios were sold to the BBC in the fifties and later demolished. From 1961-72 he ran the enterprising Planet Films, which made sub-Hammer horrors such as *Island of Terror* (1965) and *Night of the Big Heat* (1967), admired by some. Died in Manchester, 16 July, aged 67.

JOHN BOULTING

In 1937 identical twin brothers John and Roy Boulting formed Charter Films, a unique partnership in which the brothers alternated the duties of producer and director (and usually contributed to the scripts of their films). Their first big success came in 1942 with *Thunder Rock* and there followed two decades of Boulting Brothers productions which provided the backbone of the British film industry during the early years of its decline. After World War II the brothers

made brisk and adventurous dramas with topical themes. During the second phase of their career their name became a byword for sharp-witted satire; the foremost of a series of films poking fun at national institutions and starring the cream of Britain's character actors was *I'm All Right, Jack* (1959). From 1965 the brothers made conventional films in a number of genres. Their resignation as directors of the ailing British Lion in 1972 signalled the end of their partnership and of an era. John died in London, 17 June, aged 71.

SCOTT BRADY
(Gerald Tierney)

After World War II naval service Brady followed his elder brother Lawrence Tierney into thick-ear action pictures. Throughout the fifties he was the star of Westerns and crime melodramas, occasionally venturing into classier entertainment such as *The Model and the Marriage Broker* (1951) and *Gentlemen Marry Brunettes* (1955). When he returned to films after three years as TV's *Shotgun Slade* he was downgraded and spent most of the sixties and seventies as a fat villain in bizarre exploitation pictures. Latterly he had better rôles in *The China Syndrome* (1978) and his last film *Gremlins* (1984). Died in Woodland Hills, California, 16 April, aged 60.

WILFRID BRAMBELL

Brambell came from his native Ireland to Britain in the forties and played small film rôles as workmen and tramps from 1948 until he was cast as Albert Steptoe, the "dirty old man" of the long-running (1962-76) TV series *Steptoe and Son*. This led to his best known movie part as Paul McCartney's grandfather in *A Hard Day's Night* (1964). Brambell continued playing Steptoe, in two films and on radio, until the death of his co-star, Harry H Corbett, in 1982. In his last film, the 1983 short *Death and Transfiguration*, Brambell was almost unbearable to watch as a dying hospital patient. Died in London, 18 January, aged 72.

RICHARD BURTON

(Richard Jenkins)

In life and death Burton united his critics. Here is a man, they agreed, who could have followed in the footsteps of Gielgud and Olivier but, in opting for wild living and world fame, emerged a second-rate film star. His initial success stemmed from his stage performance in *The Lady's Not for Burning*, playing in London and New York in 1950. A Fox contract brought him good, well-received rôles in *My Cousin Rachel* (1952) and *The Robe* (1953). He then returned to England to play Hamlet, Othello and Coriolanus in a magnificent season with the Old Vic Company. His last prominent film rôle, prior to superstardom, was in *Look Back in Anger* (1959). Following *Cleopatra* (1962) and his scandalous affair with his co-star Elizabeth Taylor, whom he subsequently married and divorced twice, Burton became the world's highest paid film actor. During the sixties the Burtons, who made ten films together, were the screen's most celebrated love team even though their successes (*Who's Afraid of Virgina Woolf?*, *The Taming of the Shrew*) were rare and their follies (*Doctor Faustus*, *Boom!*) colossal. From 1970 Burton's career went into rapid decline and he is generally agreed to have redeemed himself only in his last film, *Nineteen Eighty-Four*. Died in Geneva, Switzerland, 5 August, aged 58.

EDWARD BUZZELL

A vaudeville and musical comedy star on Broadway from the early twenties, Buzzell began in Hollywood

as the star of *Little Johnny Jones* (1929) and other Vitaphone shorts. He was soon directing himself in shorts for Columbia and directed his first feature, *The Big Timer*, in 1932. From 1938–1949 he was a second division director at MGM, remembered today for his work with the Marx Brothers (*At the Circus*, *Go West*) and Esther Williams (*Easy to Wed*, *Neptune's Daughter*). In the fifties he moved to live television and directed Britain's first sex comedy, *Mary Had a Little*, in 1961. Ill health then forced his retirement. Died in Los Angeles, 11 January, aged 89.

JEANNE CAGNEY

Jeanne Cagney maintained that she was determined to make it without the help of her elder brother James. Briefly on stage, she won a Paramount contract and made her debut (as Jean Cagney) in *All Women Have Secrets* (1939). But although she worked regularly on Broadway and on TV in the fifties, her film career never took off and many of her appearances were small rôles in James' pictures, eg *Man of a Thousand Faces* (1957). She was last seen in *Town Tamer* (1965), a second feature Western. Died in Newport Beach, California, 7 December, aged 65.

TRUMAN CAPOTE

(Truman Persons)

Acclaimed, with the publication of his first novel *Other Voices, Other Rooms* in

1948, as a major new talent, Capote was spoiled by the success of two books, *Breakfast at Tiffany's* and *In Cold Blood*, both filmed. From the late sixties his finely-detailed, rhetorical writing virtually dried up while he courted notoriety as a gossipmonger on TV chat shows. Capote's screenplays included *Beat the Devil* (1954), *The Innocents* (1961) and *Trilogy* (1967). His last brushes with movies were in the seventies, when he was fired as the writer of *The Great Gatsby* and later played a flamboyant cameo in *Murder by Death*. Died in Bel Air, Los Angeles, 25 August, aged 59.

RICHARD DEACON

An instantly recognizable character actor (tall, bald and bespectacled), Deacon was a TV stalwart best known as Mel Cooley in *The Dick Van Dyke Show* (1961-6) but also a regular in another thirteen series. Most of his film rôles were in the fifties and sixties, when he played dozens of pompous managers and principals; his best parts were in *The Solid Gold Cadillac* (1956), *A Nice Little Bank That Should Be Robbed* (1956) (UK: *How to Rob a Bank;* 1958), and *The Gnome-Mobile* (1967). He returned to the big screen for the last time in *The Happy Hooker Goes Hollywood* (1980). Died in Beverly Hills, Los Angeles, 8 August, aged 62.

EDUARDO DE FILIPPO

(Eduardo Pasarelli)

De Filippo was chiefly the author of more than fifty boisterous Neapolitan comedies and as such was the most popular Italian playwright since Pirandello. But he was also an all-round master of the arts, acting in films from 1933 and directing from 1940. Outside Italy his best-known screenplay was for *Yesterday, Today and Tomorrow*, which won an Oscar for the Best Foreign Film of 1964. He also co-wrote *Marriage Italian Style* (1964). After *Shout Loud, Louder ... I Don't Understand* (1966) he became a lecturer at the University of Rome. Died in Rome, 31 October, aged 84.

JUNE DUPREZ

The daughter of American music-hall comic Fred Duprez, this strikingly beautiful actress began her career in Britain, going straight from drama school to a bit part in *The Amateur Gentleman* (1935). Spotted by Alexander Korda, who signed her for *The Four Feathers* (1939) and *The Thief of Baghdad* (1940), she then went with him to Hollywood and stayed there for *None But the Lonely Heart* (1944) and *And Then There Were None* (UK: *Ten Little Niggers*; 1945). She switched to the stage in 1947 and retired completely shortly afterwards. There was an unwise comeback in *The Kinsey Report* (1961). Died in London, 30 October, aged 66.

VALENTINE DYALL

Dyall had classical aspirations, making his stage debut at the Old Vic in 1930 and later appearing as the Duke of Burgundy in Olivier's film of *Henry V* in 1944. Fate, however, decreed a career in horror and crazy comedy. He was the sepulchrally voiced 'Man in Black' in *Appointment with Fear* on radio from 1941-53 and in a film version in 1950. He was also a regular on radio's *The Goon Show* and continued stooging on stage and screen for its star Spike Milligan until the late seventies. For many years he had supplied voice-overs for horror film trailers. Died 24 June, aged 77.

PEGGY ANN GARNER

A child actress too mature in manner to be described as a moppet, Garner enjoyed five years of popularity in prestige Fox pictures of the forties, winning an Honorary Oscar in 1945. She was the young Jane in *Jane Eyre* (1944) and was also in *A Tree Grows in Brooklyn* (1945) and *Daisy Kenyon* (1947) before fading out in the early fifties via *Bomba the Jungle Boy*. She married Albert Salmi and became an estate agent and a saleswoman for General Motors. Two comebacks in 1966 (*The Cat*) and 1978 (*A Wedding*) were unsuccessful.

Died in Woodland Hills, California, 16 October, aged 52.

JANET GAYNOR

(Laura Gainer)

In her silent and early sound pictures Gaynor was a child-woman in the Mary Pickford mould, idolized the world over especially for the ten romantic comedies (1927-34) she made with Charles Farrell. For the first of these, *Seventh Heaven*, she became the first actress to be awarded an Oscar. Her career faltered when she grew dissatisfied with ingenue rôles, but she eventually won the mature parts she deserved in *The*

Farmer Takes a Wife (1935) and the 1937 version of *A Star is Born*. She retired after marrying costume designer Adrian in 1939, but returned to work in 1953 and appeared sporadically until 1982. Died in Palm Springs, California, 14 September, as an indirect result of injuries she received in a car accident. She was 77.

CONNIE GILCHRIST

(Rose Constance Gilchrist)

On stage from her teens, Gilchrist was in her mid-thirties when an MGM talent scout spotted her in a play in Los Angeles. She made her screen debut in 1940 in *Hullabaloo* and for the next ten years played matronly housewives, nurses and domestics in nearly fifty MGM pictures. Well and truly typecast by the time her contract expired in 1949, she went on to play hard-working women throughout the fifities and early sixties, and was Purity in the film and TV versions of *Long John Silver* in 1955. She retired after *Some Kind of a Nut* in 1969. Died in Los Angeles, 3 March, aged 83.

JOHN GILLING

An assistant director from 1933, Gilling had his first screenplay filmed in 1947 and turned director the following year. After several second features he moved in the fifties to wide-screen adventures in Warwick Films. Then, on the strength of *The Flesh and the Friends* (1959), he was invited to join Hammer, where he made swashbucklers of no great interest and period horror in the style of Terence Fisher. Some critics think highly of *Plague of the Zombies* and *The Reptile* (both 1965). In 1970 he emigrated to Spain, where he directed his last film, *La Cruz del Diablo* (1974), and then became a painter. Died in Madrid, 22 November, aged 74.

RICHARD GREENE

A success on the London stage, Greene was sent to Hollywood to play one of the British title rôles in *Four Men and a Prayer* (1938), which so pleased Fox that they gave him a contract and more parts as dashing young chaps. He worked in Britain during the War years, but in 1947 returned to Hollywood, where he churned out minor costume dramas. His resurgence in TV's *The Adventures of Robin Hood* (1955-9) left him hopelessly typecast and he retired to Ireland to breed horses. A comeback in the late sixties led to occasional mature leads. After appearing in the TV series *Squadron* (1982) he underwent surgery for a brain tumour and never fully recovered. Died in Norfolk, 1 June, aged 66.

MARGARET HAMILTON

Hamilton made her Broadway debut in *Another Language* in 1932, repeated her rôle in the 1933 film and stayed in Hollywood to play sharp-tongued spinsters and busybodies. Her most famous rôle was the Wicked Witch of the West in *The Wizard of Oz* in 1939 (she also provided a voice for the worthless cartoon sequel *Journey Back to Oz* in 1971). A popular character actor until 1951, she spent most of her remaining years on TV. For

five years she promoted Maxwell House coffee, and reputedly made her last appearance in the video for the Damned's record 'Grimly Fiendish'. Died in Salisbury, Connecticut, 16 May, aged 83.

HENRY HATHAWAY

(Henri de Fiennes)

An 'old reliable' in the John Ford mould, Hathaway directed suspense dramas and tales of great outdooors for forty years. A former child actor who switched to production, he worked for Paramount as an assistant director and from 1932 a director. His first major films, both starring Gary Cooper, were *Now and Forever* (1934) and *Lives of a Bengal Lancer* (1935). Because of his experience in location shooting he was assigned to *The Trail of the Lonesome Pine* (1936), the first film made away from the studio in three-colour Technicolor. From 1940-60 he was at Fox, where his hard-edged thrillers included *The House on 92nd Street* (1945), *The Dark Corner* (1946), *Kiss of Death* (1947), *Call Northside 777* (1948), *Fourteen Hours* (1951) and *Niagara* (1952). In the sixties he became associated with high class Westerns such as *How the West Was Won* (1962) and *True Grit* (1969) and for his last film, *Hangup* (1973), he returned to the thriller format. Died in Los Angeles, 11 February, aged 86.

RICHARD HAYDN

Haydn's break came in 1938 when he went to Broadway with the Noël Coward revue *Set to Music*. He made his film debut in *Charley's Aunt* (UK: *Charley's American Aunt*) in 1940 and was a favourite supporting player for the next twenty-five years, often over-acting variations on the meek and adenoidal character ('Mr Carp') he invented for the stage. He also directed three films in the late forties. After *The Sound of Music* (1965) he was not seen again until *Young Frankenstein* (1974), his last film. Died in Los Angeles, 25 April, aged 80.

LOUIS HAYWARD

(Seafield Grant)

Although South African born, Hayward on screen was either

terribly British or mysteriously Latin. His career began in Britain, but soon after his film debut in 1932 he was off via Broadway to Hollywood. The first actor to play 'The Saint' on screen (in 1938), he also starred in the talkie remake of *The Man in the Iron Mask* (1939) and spent the rest of his career alternating between lounge suits and doublet and hose. After fading out in the mid-fifties, he made an unhappy comeback in the late sixties and finally retired after *Terror in the Wax Museum* (1973). Died in Palm Springs, California, 21 February, aged 75.

HAROLD HECHT

In 1947 Hecht (originally a dancer and choreographer) was working as a literary agent when he saw Burt Lancaster in a play and formed a company with the star to produce him in *The Crimson Pirate* (1952) and other hokum. Hecht and Lancaster (joined later by James Hill) were a successful producing partnership until the mid-sixties, by which time the Lancaster vehicles had become dramas with top-drawer credits, eg *Sweet Smell of Success* (1957), *Separate Tables* (1958) and *Birdman of Alcatraz* (1961). On his own Hecht produced *Cat Ballou* (1965) and *The Way West* (1967) and he was planning sequels to *Cat Ballou* and *The Crimson Pirate* when he died in Beverly Hills, Los Angeles, 26 May, aged 77.

IAN HENDRY

After attracting attention on TV (especially in the first series of *The Avengers* in 1961) Hendry was acclaimed as one of the most promising British newcomers of 1962 for his performance as the unscrupulous hire purchase salsesman in *Live Now Pay Later*. Throughout the sixties he was a much respected star, usually cast as a hard case but in a wide variety of good films. By 1970, however, hard living had got the better of him and he slipped into run-of-the-mill supporting rôles. His career ended tragically in bankruptcy and TV soap operas. Died in London, 24 December, aged 53.

OBITUARIES

DAVID HUFFMAN

Soon after making his off-Broadway debut in 1972 Huffman was in demand for TV movies. His first big screen rôle, as Sylvester Stallone's friend in *F.I.S.T.* (1978), evinced promising leading man material, but after three more films in 1979, his career faltered. In 1980 he was in a horror film *Blood Beach*, and he then drifted back to TV movies, the last being *Children in the Crossfire* (1984). On 27 February he was stabbed to death in San Diego, California, where he was appearing in *Of Mice and Men* at the Old Globe theatre. He was 40. His murderer has not been found.

H BRUCE HUMBERSTONE

Because so few people graduate from assistant director to director, Humberstone, who achieved the feat in 1932, was nicknamed 'Lucky'. For most of his career, ie 1935-50, he was at Fox making popular light entertainment movies of all kinds though often without much imagination. The best included an all-star musical *Sun Valley Serenade* (1941), a famous thriller *I Wake Up Screaming* (UK: *Hot Spot*; 1941), one of Danny Kaye's best comedies *Wonder Man* (1945) and two Gordon Scott *Tarzans* in the late fifties. He retired after *Madison Avenue* (1961). Died in Woodland Hills, California, 11 October, aged 81.

LEATRICE JOY
(Leatrice Joy Zeidler)

Largely forgotten for half a century, Leatrice Joy was one of the biggest stars of the silent screen, at her height in the early twenties when she popularised bobbed hair, married John 'The Great Lover' Gilbert, and made several pictures for Cecil B De Mille, notably *The Ten Commandments* (1923). She retired in 1931 but made comebacks in the late thirties and again in the late forties. Her last film was *Love Nest* (1951) after which she was not seen again until her appearance at the 'Night of 100 Stars' benefit in New York, in February 1985. Died in Riverdale, New York, 13 May, aged 91.

JENNIFER KENDAL
(Jennifer Bragg)

In 1953 Jennifer Kendal accompanied her parents to India, where the family (joined later by Jennifer's sister Felicity) toured the country performing 'fit-up' Shakespeare. In 1965 James Ivory made *Shakespeare-Wallah*, a fictionalised account of the family's adventures. Kendal then married Shashi Kapoor, a member of the company, and virtually retired when he became the Hindi cinema's top male star. She made only five more films spread over the next seventeen years, but in one of her last, *36 Chowringhee Lane* (1981), she gave an unforgettably moving performance as a spinster schoolteacher. Died in London, 8 September, aged 50.

ANTHONY NELSON KEYS

Having done most jobs on the studio floor, Keys (one of four film technician sons of comedian Nelson Keys) joined Hammer as an associate producer in 1956, became the general manager of Bray Studios in 1959 and a producer in 1962. His films reflected Hammer's eagerness to find another winning formula after their successes with Dracula and Frankenstein in the fifties. Keys left the company after *Frankenstein Must Be Destroyed* (1969), produced one independent horror film, *Nothing But the Night* (1972), and then took things easier as the secretary of the Stage Golfing Society. Died in Ham, Richmond, Surrey, 19 March, aged 74.

ROLAND KIBBEE

Kibbee began in the thirties as a radio gagwriter for Fred Allen, Fanny Brice and Groucho Marx. In Hollywood after World War II he proved a workmanlike, adaptable screenwriter, gradually moving away from comedy to take in musicals, adventures and Westerns. He was often associated with Burt Lancaster, for whom he wrote *The Crimson Pirate* (1952), *Vera Cruz* (1953), *The Devil's Disciple* (1959) and *Valdez Is Coming* (1970). In 1974 he and Lancaster produced, directed and wrote *The Midnight Man*, not a success. Kibbee continued to work in television. Died in Encino, California, 5 August, aged 70.

NORMAN KRASNA

This prolific writer, a former journalist, wrote his first play in 1931 and was snapped up by Hollywood shortly afterwards. For thirty years he alternated between stage and screen, sometimes adapting his work from one medium to another, and occasionally directing it as well. His thrillers included *Four Hours to Kill* (1935) and *Fury* (1936), but he became known for sophisticated comedies of confusion typified by *The Devil and Miss Jones* (1941), *Dear Ruth* (1947) and *Indiscreet* (1958). Later movies, the last being *I'd Rather Be Rich* (1964), were glossy trifles. His last play, *Lady Harry* (London, 1978), was written after his retirement to Switzerland. Died in Los Angeles, 1 November, aged 74.

ALBERT MALTZ

The writer of left-wing plays and films from the early thirties, Maltz came to the fore during World War II, when he wrote *Destination Tokyo* (1943) and *Pride of the Marines* (UK: *Forever in Love*; 1944) as well as two Oscar-winning documentaries, *Moscow Strikes Back* (1942) and *The House I Live In* (1945). He was one of 'The Hollywood Ten', film-makers who, in 1947, refused to tell the House Committee on UnAmerican Activities whether they were Communists, and were accordingly jailed. From 1952-62 Maltz lived in Mexico, writing under pseudonyms. His first screenplay for twenty-two years was *Two Mules for Sister Sara* (1970). *Scalawag* (1973) was his last. Died in Los Angeles, 26 April, aged 76.

JAMES MASON

With no previous acting experience, Mason bluffed his way into the theatre in 1931 and made his West End debut only two years later. His early films (from 1935) were 'quota quickies', but he gradually emerged as a red-blooded romantic hero with a tormented streak, topping British popularity polls after *The Man in Grey* (1943). On the strength of a string of international successes in the mid-forties – *The Seventh Veil, The Wicked Lady, Odd Man Out* – he emigrated to the US and made his debut there in 1949. His two most memorable Hollywood rôles were Captain Nemo in *20,000 Leagues Under the Sea* and Norman Maine in *A Star is Born* (both in 1954). Returning to Europe in 1960 he played distinguished character rôles in everything from Chekhov to Sidney Sheldon. His last great performances were in *Lolita* (1962) and *The Pumpkin Eater* (1964), but he was nominated for an Oscar as late as 1982 (for *The Verdict*). His last film was *The Assisi Underground* (1984). Died in Lausanne, Switzerland, 27 July, aged 75.

MARY MILES MINTER
(Juliet Reilly)

Little Juliet Shelby was a much-loved child star of stage and screen before World War I. In 1915 her name was changed again to Mary Miles Minter to allow her to progress to adult rôles. Adolph Zukor signed her to Paramount, and by the turn of the twenties only Mary Pickford was more popular. Between 1919-20 William Desmond Taylor directed Minter in four films. On 2 February 1922, he was shot dead. Although Minter was implicated, she was not suspected, but the controversy finished her career. She retired, aged twenty, the veteran of more than fifty films. (The Taylor murder mystery has never been solved.) Died in Santa Monica, 4 August, aged 82.

IVOR MONTAGU

The Hon Ivor Montagu, third son of Lord Swaythling, was a lifelong film fan who tried his hand at most aspects of the art, initially forming the first film society (1925) and making home movies with H G Wells (1928). Later a film

Left: James Mason

175

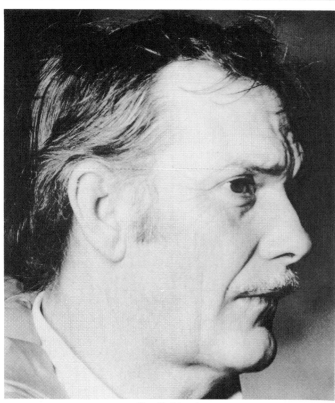

Sam Peckinpah

critic, he introduced Eisenstein's work to Britain and collaborated with the director on a number of unrealized projects. In the mid-thirties he co-directed *Wings Over Everest* and produced for Hitchcock, then produced propaganda films during both the Spanish Civil War and World War II. Co-scripting *Scott of the Antarctic* (1948) was his last active involvement with movies, but he continued writing about them until the end of his life. Died in Watford, Herts, 5 November, aged 80.

CLARENCE NASH

When animal impressionist Nash auditioned for the Disney Studio in 1934 he was hired to provide the voice for their new creation, Donald Duck, a job which, along with voicing other Disney characters (Dopey in *Snow White*, a bullfrog in *Bambi*), lasted him the rest of his life. He was semi-retired from 1971, but continued to make personal appearances, especially during Donald Duck's 50th birthday celebrations in 1984. The last film on which he worked was *Mickey's Christmas Carol* (1983). Died in Burbank, California, 20 February, aged 80.

EDMOND O'BRIEN

Impeccable stage credentials (in the thirties he was in Gielgud's *Hamlet* and worked with Orson Welles' Mercury Theatre) led O'Brien inevitably to Hollywood, where he was the juvenile lead in his first film, *The Hunchback of Notre Dame* (1939). Subsequently he appeared mainly as the hero or villain of tough thrillers, although he was Casca in *Julius Caesar* (1953) and won his Oscar for a comic rôle in *The Barefoot Contessa* (1954). Overweight, he moved into character rôles in the sixties and was extremely busy until his career stopped suddenly in 1974 after *99 and 44/100% Dead* (UK: *Call Harry Crown*). Died in Inglewood, California, 9 May, aged 69.

J(AMES) PAT(RICK) O'MALLEY

Not to be confused with American silent star Pat O'Malley, who died in 1966, this was a British actor who emigrated to the US before World War II and, from 1940, played all sorts of working-class character parts in films but only one lead (in *Blueprint for Robbery* in 1960). From the fifties he also provided British and Irish voices for Disney and Hanna-Barbera cartoons, and in 1973 starred opposite Shirley Booth in the TV series *A Touch of Grace* (the American version of *For the Love of Ada*). His last film was *Cheaper to Keep Her* (1980). Died in San Juan Capistrano, California, 27 February, aged 80.

SAM PECKINPAH

Peckinpah is already down in history as the man who, largely because of the slow-motion blood spurts in *The Wild Bunch*, made graphic violence acceptable in mainstream cinema; his commitment to depicting the harsh realities of the old West, however, was instrumental in the decline of the Western. He began his tempestuous career in 1953 as a 'gopher' for Don Siegel, and broke into directing via *The Rifleman*, the TV series he created in 1958. Although second features, his first two films, *The Deadly Companions* (1961) and *Ride the High Country* (UK: *Guns in the Afternoon;* 1962) were singled out by critics for their individual approach. Stormy relationships with producers limited his output in the mid-sixties, but he returned to favour when *The Wild Bunch* (1969) and *Straw Dogs* (1971) stirred up front page censorship debates. Peckinpah's only subsequent hit was *The Getaway* (1972), an action adventure with Steve McQueen. His remaining work, proficient but gloomy, was out of keeping with public taste and sharply divided the critics. By the turn of the eighties he was directing commercials and second units. He made two pop videos for Julian Lennon a month before his death in Inglewood, California, 28 December, aged 59.

WALTER PIDGEON

Pidgeon's fifty-year career breaks down precisely into youth, maturity and old age. He began as a supporting actor in silent films and was later a popular baritone in First National operettas. From 1937-56 he was under contract to MGM, although it was while he was on loan-out to Fox in *How Green Was My Valley* (1941) that he proved his star potential. In his mid-forties he was launched as a genteel leading man, paired with Greer Garson in eight films (1941-50), notably *Mrs Miniver*. From 1961 he was in dignified character rôles. After *Sextette* (1977), illness forced him to retire. Died in Santa Monica, California, 25 September, aged 87.

J(OHN) B(OYNTON) PRIESTLEY

A best selling novelist and playwright for over sixty years, Priestley was unanimously venerated as 'the grand old man of English literature'. In the thirties and forties his work, social comment often with a supernatural flavour, was regularly filmed: *The Good Companions* (1932 and 1956), *Dangerous Corner* (1934), *Laburnum Grove* (1936), *When We Are Married* (1942), *They Came to a City* (1943) and *An Inspector Calls* (1954). His own screenplays included *The Foreman Went to France* (1942) and *Last Holiday* (1950). The cinema lost interest in him after the mid-fifties, when he was considered middlebrow and old-fashioned. Died in Stratford-upon-Avon, Warwicks, 14 August, aged 89.

SIR MICHAEL REDGRAVE

A fine classical actor, celebrated for his Uncle Vanya, Redgrave lacked versatility, which kept him from the front rank of Britain's actor knights. A former teacher, untrained as an actor, he was most successful in films (from 1936) as dominant or introspective men of intellect, notably the tormented ventriloquist in *Dead of Night* (1945) and the teacher in *The Browning Version* (1950). Although he was rarely in comedy he made a perfect Algernon in *The Importance of Being Earnest* (1952). From the early sixties he played only supporting rôles and cameos (he was ill from 1965 with Parkinson's disease). His last film was *Nicholas and Alexandra* (1971) and he was last seen on stage, in a silent rôle, in *Close of Play* at the National in 1979. Died in

Denham, Bucks, 21 March, aged 77. His three children by Rachel Kempson (Vanessa, Corin and Lynn) are all actors.

DAME FLORA ROBSON

From an early age Dame Flora, never a beauty, favoured tense or strong-willed character parts. In the theatre (from 1921) these were often classical, eg Lady Macbeth, whom she played twice, but in the cinema (from 1931) she interspersed her queens and *grandes dames* with nuns and civil servants. From 1939-43 she was in Hollywood, blacking up for *Saratoga Trunk* (1941). In her

later years she was Britain's only titled actress lending her skills to the likes of *The Beast in the Cellar*. She was last seen as a witch in *Clash of the Titans* (1981). Died in Brighton, Sussex, 7 July, aged 82.

LEONARD ROSSITER

On stage from 1954 and in films from 1962 Rossiter was for most of his career a little-known small part player. His comic brilliance was first recognized in the 1969 play *The Resistable Rise of Arturo Ui*, but it was two TV series – *Rising Damp* (1974-8) and *The Fall and Rise of Reginald Perrin* (1976-80) – which made his rapid delivery and sarcastic throwaways famous. His only leading film rôles were in *Rising Damp* (1979), *Britannia Hospital* (1982) and *Water* (1984). He collapsed and died during a performance of *Loot* in London's West End, 5 October, aged 57.

ARTHUR SCHWARTZ

Schwartz gave up the law when the songs he contributed to Broadway revues became hits. He worked with a number of lyricists, but his most celebrated partnership was with Howard Dietz, who died in 1983; this collaboration produced the stage (1931) and film (1953) version of *The Band Wagon*. In Hollywood from 1930 Schwartz composed for comedies and musicals. He also produced two films, *Cover Girl* (1944) and the Cole Porter biopic *Night and Day* (1946). His gentle, sophisticated music became unfashionable in the fifties and, after a flop Broadway show *Jennie* (1963), he became inactive. Died in Pennsylvania, 3 September, aged 83.

ALEXANDER SCOURBY

Scourby made his stage debut in 1932, but from the late thirties to his death his radio and narration work made his rich bass voice more familiar than his face (he was known as 'The voice of the world'). During the fifties, however, he was often in films as a character actor. His most important rôle was the villain

of *The Big Heat* (1953), after which he played a number of professional types and historical statesmen. He made a comeback in *The Executioner* (1970) and his last film work was the narration of *Jesus* (1979). Died in Boston, Massachusetts (where he had announced a radio concert), 23 February, aged 71.

KENT SMITH
(Frank Kent Smith)

In the late twenties Smith was a member of an amateur company in Falmouth, Massachusetts, which also included James Stewart and Henry Fonda. Smith moved to Broadway in 1932 and films in 1936. During the forties he was normally a second lead, but co-starred in *Cat People* (1942), *The Curse of the Cat People* (1944) and *Nora Prentiss* (1947). By the mid-fifties he was in character parts. He was a regular in TV's *Peyton Place* in the sixties, and from 1970

practically all his films were TV movies. Died in Woodland Hills, California, 23 April, aged 78.

ROBERT L(EE) SURTEES

Formerly cameraman Gregg Toland's assistant at Universal, Surtees became a director of photography in 1942 and spent the next twenty years at MGM, where he became renowned for the beautiful colour of his epics and musicals. He won Oscars for *King Solomon's Mines* (1950), *The Bad and the Beautiful* (1952) and *Ben Hur* (1959). As a freelance he photographed many great films of the sixties and seventies including *The Graduate* (1967), *Sweet Charity* (1968), *The Last Picture Show* (1971) and *The Sting* (1973). His last film was *Same Time Next Year* (1978). Died in Carmel, California, 5 January, aged 78. His son, Bruce Surtees, is also a cameraman.

Leonard Rossiter

ERNEST TIDYMAN

Success came late in life and fleetingly to Tidyman, a crime reporter who turned novelist at the age of forty-two. The success of his books about black private eye John Shaft brought him to Hollywood, where he won an Oscar for his first screenplay, *The French Connection,* (1971). He also adapted two of his Shaft novels for the screen, beginning the 'blaxploitation' cycle of the early seventies. By 1978, however, he was scripting 'tough cop' TV movies and *A Force of One,* a martial arts programmer for Chuck Norris. In 1982 he was fired as the director of *The Last Plane Out,* a low-budget war film, and received only a screenplay credit; it was his last. Died in London, 15 July, aged 56.

MICHAEL TRUBSHAWE

Fans of David Niven will be well acquainted with Trubshawe, whom he first met in the thirties when they were serving with HM Forces in Malta, and who subsequently became a lifelong friend, cropping up throughout Niven's autobiography *The Moon's a Balloon.* Niven tried to drop Trubshawe's name into all his Hollywood films, eg *Wuthering Heights* (1939), which features Trubshawe the dog, and this publicity led to the real Trubshawe's film debut in 1950. Roguishly upper-crust, with a magnificent handlebar moustache, he played hilarious cameos in dozens of British comedies of the fifties and sixties, retiring after *The Magic Christian* (1970). Died 21 March, age unreported.

FRANÇOIS TRUFFAUT

One of the most important figures in post-war European cinema, Truffaut will be remembered for his warm, drily humorous and deceptively simple films about human relationships. A former film critic who, with Chabrol, Godard, Rohmer and Rivette, proposed the 'auteur' theory, he began making films in 1954 and soon became the most successful exponent of the so-called *Nouvelle vague.* His first feature, *Le Quatre Cent Coups* in 1959, featured Jean-Pierre Leaud as Truffaut's alter ego Antoine Doinel, a character who featured in four more films, ending with *L'Amour en Fuite* (1979). His third feature, *Jules et Jim* (1961), is thought to be his masterpiece. Following *Fahrenheit 451* (1966), Truffaut's first and only film in English, which was not liked, his work became variable, but he retained enormous popularity and is to this day the world's most famous French director. His other major films are *L'Enfant Sauvage* (1969), *La Nuit Américaine/Day for Night* (1973) and *Le Dernier Métro* (1980). He also appeared occasionally as a rather introverted actor, notably in *Close Encounters of the Third Kind* (1977). Died in Paris, 21 October, aged 52.

HARRY WAXMAN

A film technician from boyhood, Waxman became a camera assistant in 1929 and, while working for the RAF Film Production Unit during World War II, photographed his first feature, *Journey Together,* in 1944. In the forties and fifties he was one of Britain's most prolific and proficient black-and-white cameramen, responsible for *Brighton Rock* (1946) and *Father Brown* (1954). In the sixties he moved into colour productions with an international flavour: *The Swiss Family Robinson* (1960) and *The Roman Spring of Mrs Stone* (1961) were the best. The seventies brought a mixed bag of sex and horror, and his most recent credits were second unit assignments, the last being on *Flash Gordon* (1980). Died 24 December, aged 73.

OSKAR WERNER

(Josef Schliessmayer)
Born in Austria, where he began acting, Werner became a matinée idol in Germany after World War II, and was brought to Hollywood by Fox, who starred him in *Decision Before Dawn* (1951). Returning to Europe, he developed into Austria's greatest classical actor. In 1961 Truffaut persuaded him back to the cinema for *Jules et Jim.* This led to a few more rôles as an educated Continental charmer, but by 1968 his film career was virtually over, and he spent the last ten years of his life living as a recluse in Liechtenstein. Died in Marburg, West Germany, 23 October, aged 61.

WALTER WOOLF KING

Walter Woolf was a Broadway musical star of the twenties. Walter Woolf King (the same man) was a supporting player often seen in movies from 1930 to the mid-forties as dignitaries, stuffed shirts and bad men. He was an operatic stooge for the Marx Brothers in *A Night at the Opera* (1935) and Laurel and Hardy in *Swiss Miss* (1938). His occasional films in the fifties included *Call Me Madam* (1953) and *The Helen Morgan Story* (UK: *Both Ends of the Candle;* 1957). He retired after *Hong Kong Confidential* (1958) but had a cameo in *Rosie* (1967). Died in Beverly Hills, Los Angeles, 24 October, aged 88.

François Truffaut

REFERENCE

US PRODUCTION COMPANIES

ABC Motion Pictures
1330 Avenue of the Americas,
New York, NY 10019.
Tel: (212) 581 7777

and

2040 Avenue of the Stars
Century City, CA 90067,
Tel: (213) 553 2000.

Irwin Allen Productions
Columbia Plaza,
Burbank, CA 91505.
Tel: (818) 954 6000

The Almi Group
1585 Broadway,
New York, NY 10036.
Tel: (212) 975 8300

Arkoff International Pictures
9200 Sunset Blvd,
Penthouse 3,
Los Angeles, CA 90069.
Tel: (213) 278 7600

Bakshi Productions
5555 Melrose Avenue,
Los Angeles, CA 90038.
Tel: (213) 468 5000

Batjac Productions
9570 Wilshire Blvd,
Suite 400,
Beverly Hills, CA 90212.
Tel: (213) 278 9870

Warren Beatty Productions
5555 Melrose Avenue,
Los Angeles, CA 90038.
Tel: (213) 468 5000

David Begelman Productions
10202 West Washington Blvd,
Culver City, CA 90238.
Tel: (213) 468 5000

Brooksfilms
PO Box 900,
Beverly Hills, CA 90213,
Tel: (213) 203 1375.

Brut Productions
1345 Sixth Avenue,
New York, NY 10019.
Tel: (212) 581 3114

Buena Vista International
350 South Buena Vista Street,
Burbank, CA 91521.
Tel: (213) 840 5414

The Cannon Group
6464 Sunset Blvd,
Suite 1150,
CA 90028.
Tel: (213) 469 8124

John Cassavetes Productions
4000 Warner Blvd,
Burbank, CA 91522.
Tel: (213) 954 1871

CBS Theatrical Films
4024 Radford Avenue,
Studio City, CA 91604.
Tel: (213) 760 6134

Chartoff-Winkler Productions
10125 West Washington Blvd,
Culver City, CA 90230.
Tel: (213) 204 0474

Cine Media International
1 Transglobal Square,
PO Box 7005,
Long Beach, CA 90807.
Tel: (213) 426 3622

Dick Clark Productions
3003 West Olive Avenue,
Burbank, CA 91505.
Tel: (213) 841 3003

Columbia Pictures
Columbia Plaza,
Burbank, CA 91505.
Tel: (818) 954 6000
and
711 Fifth Avenue.
New York, NY 10022.
Tel: (212) 751 4400

Dino De Laurentiis Corporation
1 Gulf & Western Plaza,
New York, NY 10023.
Tel: (212) 399 0101

Walt Disney Productions
500 South Buena Vista Street,
Burbank, CA 91521.
Tel: (818) 840 1000

Blake Edwards Productions
1888 Century Park East,
Suite 1616,
Los Angeles, CA 90067.
Tel: (213) 553 6741

Embassy Communications
1901 Avenue of the Stars,
Suite 666,
Los Angeles, CA 90067.
Tel: (213) 553 3600

First Artists Production Company
2029 Century Park East,
Suite 3335,
Los Angeles, CA 90067.
Tel: (213) 557 0838

Samuel Goldwyn Productions
10203 Santa Monica Blvd,
Los Angeles, CA 90067.
Tel: (213) 552 2255

Group 1 Films
9200 Sunset Blvd,
Los Angeles, CA 90069.
Tel: (213) 550 8767

Hanna-Barbera Productions
3400 Cahuenga Blvd West,
Los Angeles, CA 90068.
Tel: (213) 851 5000

Larry Harmon Pictures Corporation
650 North Bronson Avenue,
Los Angeles, CA 90004.
Tel: (213) 463 2331

Home Box Office
2049 Century Park East,
Los Angeles, CA 90067.
Tel: (213) 557 9400
and
1271 Avenue of the Americas,
New York, NY 10020.
Tel: (212) 484 1100

Horizon Pictures
745 Fifth Avenue,
New York, NY 10151.
Tel: (212) 421 6810

Sandy Howard Productions
9336 Washington Blvd,
Culver City, CA 90230.
Tel: (213) 836 5537

ITC Productions
12711 Ventura Blvd,
Studio City, CA 91604.
Tel: (213) 760 2110
and
115 East 57th Street,
New York, NY 10022.
Tel: (212) 371 6660

Jalem Productions
141 El Camino,
Suite 210,
Beverly Hills, CA 90212.
Tel: (213) 278 7750

Norman Jewison Productions
9336 W Washington Blvd,
Culver City, CA 90230.
Tel: (213) 836 5537

Chuck Jones Enterprises
789 West 20th Street,
Costa Mesa, CA 92627.
Tel: (714) 548 7791

Elliott Kastner Productions
Universal Studio Bldg 463,
Universal City, CA 91608.
Tel: (213) 2071

Howard Koch Productions
5555 Melrose Avenue,
Los Angeles, CA 90038.
Tel: (213) 468 5000

Stanley Kramer Productions
Studio Center,
4024 Radford Avenue,
Studio City, CA 91604.
Tel: (213) 760 5000

Kurtz and Friends
2312 W Olive Avenue,
Burbank, CA 91506.
Tel: (818) 841 8188

The Ladd Company
4000 Warner Blvd,
Burbank, CA 91522.
Tel: (818) 954 4400

Edy and Ely Landau
2029 Century Park East,
Los Angeles, CA 90067.
Tel: (213) 553 5010

Walter Lantz Productions
6311 Romaine Street,
Hollywood, CA 90038.
Tel: (213) 469 2907

Jerry Leider Productions
12711 Ventura Blvd,
Studio City, CA 91604
Tel: (818) 760 2110

Joseph E Levine Presents
767 Third Avenue,
New York, NY 10017.
Tel: (212) 826 0370

Lion's Gate Films
1861 South Bundy Drive,
Los Angeles, CA 90025.
Tel: (213) 820 7751

Lorimar Productions
3970 Overland Avenue,
Culver City, CA 90230.
Tel: (213) 202 2000

Lucasfilm
PO Box 2009,
San Rafael, CA 94912.
Tel: (415) 457 5282

The Malpaso Company
4000 Warner Blvd,
Burbank, CA 91522.
Tel: (818) 954 6000

Manson International
9145 Sunset Blvd,
Los Angeles, CA 90069.
Tel: (213) 273 8640

Marble Arch Productions
12711 Ventura Blvd,
Studio City, CA 91604.
Tel: (213) 760 2110

MCA
100 Universal City Plaza,
University City, CA 91608.
Tel: (818) 985 4321
and

445 Park Avenue,
New York, NY 10022.
Tel: (212) 759 7500

Bill Melendez Productions
439 North Larchmont Blvd,
Los Angeles, CA 90004.
Tel: (213) 463 4104

MGM-UA
10202 West Washington Blvd,
Culver City, CA 90230.
Tel: (213) 558 5000
and
1350 Avenue of the Americas,
New York, NY 10019.
Tel: (212) 708 0300

Mirisch Corporation of California
100 Universal City Plaza,
Universal City, CA 91608.
Tel: (818) 508 1271

MTM Enterprises
4024 Radford Avenue,
Studio City, CA 91604.
Tel: (818) 760 4000

National Telefilm Associates
12636 Beatrice Street,
Los Angeles, CA 90066.
Tel: (213) 306 4040

NBC Film Productions
9336 West Washington Blvd,
Culver City, CA 90230.
Tel: (213) 836 5537

New World Pictures
1888 Century Park East,
Los Angeles, CA 90067.
Tel: (213) 551 1444

Orion Picture Corporation
(incorporating Filmways)
1875 Century Park East,
Los Angeles, CA 90067.
Tel: (213) 557 8700
and
540 Madison Avenue
New York, NY 10022.
Tel: (212) 758 5100

The Pakula Company
10889 Wilshire Blvd,
Suite 606,
Los Angeles, CA 90024.
Tel: (213) 936 2280

Paramount Pictures Corporation
1 Gulf & Western Plaza,
New York, NY 10023.
Tel: (212) 333 7000

and
5555 Melrose Avenue,
Los Angeles, CA 90038.
Tel: (213) 468 5000

Persky-Bright Organization
555 Madison Avenue,
New York, NY 10022.
Tel: (212) 421 4141

Polygram Pictures
8255 Sunset Blvd,
Los Angeles, CA 90046.
Tel: (213) 650 8300

Quinn Martin Films
1041 North Formosa Avenue,
Los Angeles, CA 90046.
Tel: (213) 850 2653

Rastar Films
Columbia Plaza West,
Burbank, CA 91505.
Tel: (818) 954 6000

The Walter Reade Organization
241 East 34th Street,
New York, NY 10016.
Tel: (212) 683 6300

RKO Pictures
129 North Vermont Avenue,
Los Angeles, CA 90004.
Tel: (213) 383 5525
and
1440 Broadway,
New York, NY 10018.
Tel: (212) 764 7000

Rollins/Joffé Productions
5555 Melrose Avenue,
Los Angeles, CA 90038.
Tel: (213) 468 5000

Rosemont Productions
1990 Westwood Blvd,
Suite 200,
Los Angeles, CA 90025.
Tel: (213) 474 4700

RSO
5555 Melrose Avenue,
Los Angeles, CA 90038.
Tel: (213) 468 5000

Mark Rydell
100 Universal City Plaza,
Universal City, CA 91608.
Tel: (818) 508 1078

The Richard Shepherd Co
10202 West Washington Blvd,
Culver City, CA 90230.
Tel: (213) 836 3000

Showtime Entertainment
10900 Wilshire Blvd,
4th Floor,
Los Angeles, CA 90024.
Tel: (213) 208 2340

Simon/Reeves/Landsburg Productions
260 South Beverly Drive,
Beverly Hills, CA 90212.
Tel: (213) 273 5450

Aaron Spelling Productions
132 South Rodeo Drive
Beverly Hills, CA 90212.
Tel: (213) 585 2000

Spiegel-Bergman Productions
2029 Century Park East,
Suite 1850,
Los Angeles, CA 90067.
Tel: (213) 552 0577

Steven Spielberg Productions
4000 Warner Blvd,
Burbank, CA 91522
Tel: (213) 954 3961

David Susskind Productions
10202 West Washington Blvd,
Culver City, CA 90230.
Tel: (213) 836 3000

Taft International Pictures
10960 Wilshire Blvd,
10th Floor,
Los Angeles, CA 90024.
Tel: (213) 208 2000

Thorn EMI Films
9489 Dayton Way,
Beverly Hills, CA 90210.
Tel: (213) 278 4770

Time Life Films
4024 Radford Avenue,
Studio City, CA 91604.
Tel: (213) 760 6300

Touchstone Films
500 South Buena Vista Street,
Burbank, CA 91521.
Tel: (218) 840 1000

Tri-Star
711 Fifth Avenue,
New York, NY 10022.
Tel: (212) 265 6130
and
1875 Century Park East,
Los Angeles, CA 90067.
Tel: (213) 201 2300

Twentieth Century-Fox Film Corporation
Box 900,
Beverly Hills, CA 90213.
Tel: (213) 277 2211
and
40 West 57th Street,
New York, NY 10019.
Tel: (212) 977 5500

United Artists Productions
3910 Overland Avenue,
Culver City, CA 90230.
Tel: (213) 202 0202

Universal Pictures
Universal City Studios,
Universal City, CA 91608.
Tel: (213) 985 4321
and
445 Park Avenue,
New York, NY 10022.
Tel: (212) 759 7500

Viacom Enterprises
10900 Wilshire Blvd,
Los Angeles, CA 90024.
Tel: (213) 208 2700

Warner Bros
75 Rockefeller Plaza,
New York, NY 10019.
Tel: (212) 484 8000
and
4000 Warner Blvd,
Burbank, CA 91522.
Tel: (213) 954 6000

Witzend Productions
1600 N Highland Avenue,
Los Angeles, CA 90028.
Tel: (213) 462 6185

World Wide Pictures
2520 W Olive Avenue
Burbank, CA 91505.
Tel: (818) 843 1300

Wrather Corporation
270 North Canon Drive,
Beverly Hills, CA 90210.
Tel: (213) 278 8521

Zanuck-Brown Company
202 North Canon Drive,
Beverly Hills, CA 90210.
Tel: (213) 274 0261

Zoetrope Studios
1040 North Las Palmas,
Hollywood, CA 90038.
Tel: (213) 469 9011

UK PRODUCTION COMPANIES

Acorn Pictures
49 Old Bond Street,
London W1.
Tel: (01) 493 1420

Allegro Films
27b Elsworthy Road,
London NW3 3BT.
Tel: (01) 586 1443

Allied Stars
Pinewood Studios,
Ivor Heath,
Bucks SL0 0NH.
Tel: (0753) 651700

Anderson Burr Pictures
Bray Studios,
Water Oakley,
Windsor, Berks.
Tel: (0628) 22111

Ariel Productions
162-170 Wardour Street,
London W1.
Tel: (01) 437 7700

Arts International
32 Eccleston Square,
London SW1 1PB.
Tel: (01) 834 6811

Astramead Ltd
43 Whitfield Street,
London W1.
Tel: (01) 636 8622

AZ Productions
Lorrimer House,
47 Dean Street,
London W1.
Tel: (01) 734 4568/437 7349

Boyd's Co
9 Great Newport Street,
London WC2.
Tel: (01) 836 5601

Brent Walker
9 Chesterfield Street,
London W1X 7HF.
Tel: (01) 491 4430

Britannic Films
Pinewood Studios,
Iver Heath, Bucks.
Tel: (0753) 651700

British Film Institute Production Board
29 Rathbone Street,
London W1P 1AG.
Tel: (01) 636 5587

Burrill Productions
51 Lansdowne Road,
London W11 2LG.
Tel: (01) 727 1442

The Callender Company
39 Long Acre,
London WC2 9JT.
Tel: (01) 240 8644

Cannon International
167-169 Wardour Street,
London W1.
Tel: (01) 437 9844

Charisma Films
90 Wardour Street,
London W1V 3LA.
Tel: (01) 434 1351

Children's Film and Television Foundation
Thorn EMI Elstree Studios,
Boreham Wood, Herts.
Tel: (01) 953 1600

Columbia (British) Productions
19-23 Wells Street,
London W1.
Tel: (01) 580 2090

Consolidated Productions
56 Ennismore Gardens
London SW7.
Tel: (01) 589 2262

Cosgrove Hall
Albany House,
2 Albany Road,
Chorlton-cum-Hardy,
Manchester M21 IBL.
Tel: (061) 881 2305

Courier Films
Shepperton Studios,
Studio Road,
Shepperton TW17 OQD.
Tel: (09328) 62611

Walt Disney Productions
31 Soho Square,
London W1V 6AP.
Tel: (01) 734 8111

Dumbarton Films
Dumbarton House,
68 Oxford Street,
London W1N 9LA.
Tel: (01) 631 4926

Embassy Pictures
3 Audley Street,
London W1Y 5LR.
Tel: (01) 409 1925

Ian Emes Animation/Timeless Films
132 Royal College Street,
London NW1.
Tel: (01) 267 7625

Enigma Productions
15 Queensgate Place Mews,
London SW7 5BG.
Tel: (01) 581 0238

Eon Productions
2 South Audley Street,
London W1Y 5DQ.
Tel: (01) 493 7953

Euston Films
365 Euston Road,
London NW1 3AR.
Tel: (01) 387 0911

Falcon International Productions
Twickenham Film Studios,
St Margaret's,
Twickenham, Middx.
Tel: (01) 892 4477

Film and General Productions
10 Pembridge Place,
London W2 4XB.
Tel: (01) 221 1141

Film Contracts
2 Lower James Street,
London W1R 3PN.
Tel: (01) 437 7015

Films of Record
73 Saint James's Street,
London SW1.
Tel: (01) 491 2585

S Benjamin Fisz Productions
51 South Audley Street,
London W1.
Tel: (01) 493 7428

Flamingo Productions
47 Londsdale Square,
London N1 1EW.
Tel: (01) 607 9958

Mark Forstater Film Productions
42a Devonshire Close,
Portland Place,
London W1N 1LL.
Tel: (01) 631 0011

Bob Godfrey Films
55 Neal Street,
London WC2.
Tel: (01) 240 1889

Goldcrest Films and Television
180 Wardour Street,
London W1V 3AA.
Tel: (01) 437 8696

Golden Communications
(Golden Harvest)
47 Greek Street,
London W1V 5LQ.
Tel: (01) 439 1431

GPA Films
22 Romilly Street,
London W1.
Tel: (01) 734 6994

Grand Slamm Animation
100 St Martin's Lane,
London WC2N 4AZ.
Tel: (01) 240 2273

Greenpoint Films
145c St George's Road,
London SE1 6HY.
Tel: (01) 928 0670

Colin Gregg Film Productions
Floor 2,
1-6 Falconberg Court,
London W1.
Tel: (01) 439 0257

Grenadier Films
The Coach House,
High Road,
Chigwell,
Essex IG7 5BJ.
Tel: (01) 500 0936

Val Guest Productions
9 Clifford Street,
London, W1.
Tel: (01) 286 5766

Halas and Batchelor Animation
3-7 Kean Street,
London WC2.
Tel: (01) 240 3888

Hammer Film Productions
Thorn EMI Elstree Studios,
Borehamwood,
Herts WD6 1JG.
Tel: (01) 953 1600

HandMade Films
26 Cadogan Square,
London SW1X OJP.
Tel: (01) 584 8345

Hanstoll Films
4 New Burlington Place,
London W1.
Tel: (01) 734 3864

Hartswood Films
12 Stratford Place,
London W1N 9AF.
Tel: (01) 408 2355

Hemdale
21 Albion Street,
London W2 2AS.
Tel: (01) 724 1010

Henson International Television
2 Old Brewery Mews,
Hampstead High Street,
London NW3 1PZ.
Tel: (01) 435 7121

Horizon Pictures
31 Dover Street,
London W1.
Tel: (01) 493 9292

Hudson Films
11 Queens Gate Place Mews,
London SW7.
Tel: (01) 581 3133

Island Pictures
22 Saint Peter's Square,
London W6 9NW.
Tel: (01) 741 1511

ITC Entertainments
ACC House,
17 Great Cumberland Place,
London W1.
Tel: (01) 262 8040

Kestrel Films
5 Bramerton Street,
London SW3.
Tel: (01) 351 1706

Kestrel II
23 Hamilton Gardens,
London NW8.
Tel: (01) 286 8602

Ladbroke Films
4 Kensington Park Gardens,
London W11 3HB.
Tel: (01) 727 3541

Legion Films
16 Bloomfield Terrace,
London SW1.
Tel: (01) 730 9581

Limehouse Productions
Limehouse Studios,
Canary Wharf,
West India Docks,
London E14 9SJ.
Tel: (01) 636 8622/987 2090

Euan Lloyd Productions
Pinewood Studios,
Iver Heath, Bucks SLO ONH.
Tel: (0753) 651700

London Film Productions
44a Floral Street,
London WC2E 9DA.
Tel: (01) 379 3366

Lorimar Services
16 Berkeley Street,
London W1X 5AE.
Tel: (01) 493 1564

Lucasfilm (UK)
Thorn EMI Elstree Studios,
Borehamwood, Herts WD6 1JG.
Tel: (01) 953 1600

MCA Television
170 Piccadilly,
London W1.
Tel: (01) 408 0188

Bill Melendez Productions
32-34 Great Marlborough Street,
London W1.
Tel: (01) 439 4411

Memorial Films
Lee International Studios,
128 Wembley Park Drive,
Wembley, Middx HA9 8JE.
Tel: (01) 902 1262

Merchant Ivory Productions
54 Marshall Street,
London W1.
Tel: (01) 437 6249

Mersham Productions
41 Montpelier Walk,
London SW7 1JH.
Tel: (01) 589 8829

Metropolis Pictures
8-10 Neal's Yard,
London WC2.
Tel: (01) 836 1056

MGM-UA
UIP House,
Beadon Road,
London W6.
Tel: (01) 741 9041

Moving Picture Company
25 Noel Street,
London W1.
Tel: (01) 734 9151

MPL Communications
1 Soho Square,
London W1.
Tel: (01) 439 6621

Norfolk International Pictures
107 Long Acre,
London WC2E 9NT.
Tel: (01) 240 0863

Orion Pictures Company
31 Soho Square,
London W1V 4AP.
Tel: (01) 437 7766

Palace Productions
16-17 Wardour Mews,
London W1V 3DG.
Tel: (01) 734 7060

Paramount Pictures (UK)
162 Wardour Street,
London W1V 4AB.
Tel: (01) 437 7700

The Alan Parker Film Company
Pinewood Studios,
Iver Heath, Bucks SL0 ONH.
Tel: (0753) 655052

Peerford
Twickenham Film Studios,
St Margaret's,
Twickenham TW1 2AW
Tel: (01) 892 4477

Pennies From Heaven
83 Eastbourne Mews,
London W2.
Tel: (01) 723 7326

Picture Partnership Productions
73 Newman Street,
London W1.
Tel: (01) 637 8056

Portman Productions
Tennyson House,
159 Great Portland Street,
London W1N 6NR.
Tel: (01) 637 2692

Poseidon Films
113 Wardour Street,
London W1V 3TD.
Tel: (01) 734 4441

Primetime Television
Seymour Mews House,
Seymour Mews,
Wigmore Street,
London W1H 9DE.
Tel: (01) 486 1362

Python (Monty) Pictures
25 Newman Street,
London W1P 3HA.
Tel: (01) 935 0307

Quintet Films
Station House,
Harrow Road,
Wembley,
Middx HA9 6EH.
Tel: (01) 903 5111

The Rank Organization
Pinewood Studios,
Iver Heath,
Bucks SL0 ONH.
Tel: (0753) 651700

Recorded Picture Co
8-12 Broadwick Street,
London W1.
Tel: (01) 434 1192

Rediffusion Films
Carlton House,
Lower Regent Street,
London SW1Y 4LS.
Tel: (01) 930 0221

Geoff Reeve Associates
11 St James's Chambers,
2 Ryder Street,
London SW1Y 6QB.
Tel: (01) 930 0123

RKO Productions
33 Dover Street,
London W1X 3RA.
Tel: (01) 629 4799

RM Productions
1 Rockley Road,
London W14.
Tel: (01) 734 3474

Satellite Television
Craven House,
25 Marshall Street,
London W1.
Tel: (01) 439 0491

Sandfire Productions
Pinewood Studios,
Iver Heath,
Bucks SL0 ONH.
Tel: (0753) 651700

Rosemont Productions
Pinewood Studios,
Iver Heath,
Bucks SL0 ONH.
Tel: (0753) 651700

Roymark
112 Wardour Street,
London W1V 3LD.
Tel: (01) 437 9121

Salon Productions
13-14 Archer Street,
London W1V 7HG.
Tel: (01) 734 9472

Scimitar Films
6-8 Sackville Street,
London W1V 1DD.
Tel: (01) 734 8385

Silver Chalice Productions
10 Dover Street,
London W1.
Tel: (01) 629 0500

Skreba Productions
145c St George's Road,
London SE1 6HY.
Tel: (01) 928 7700

Robert Stigwood Group,
118 Wardour Street,
London, W1V 3LA.
Tel: (01) 437 2512

Sunn Classic Productions
37 Great Marlborough Street,
London W1.
Tel: (01) 437 9556

Sword and Sorcery Productions
20 Stradella Road,
London SE24 9HA.
Tel: (01) 274 3215

Third Eye Productions
82 Wardour Street,
London W1V 3LF.
Tel: (01) 437 7687

Thorn EMI Films
30 Golden Square,
London W1.
Tel: (01) 437 9234

Trident Films
Thorn EMI Elstree Studios,
Borehamwood,
Herts WD6 1JG.
Tel: (01) 953 1600

Twentieth Century-Fox Film Company
31 Soho Square,
London W1V 6AP.
Tel: (01) 437 7766

Umbrella Films
111a Wardour Street,
London W1.
Tel: (01) 437 5357

United British Artists
73 St James's Street,
London W1.
Tel: (01) 629 5276/491 4893

Video Arts
Dumbarton House,
68 Oxford Street,
London W1N 9LA.
Tel: (01) 580 0652

Virtue Consolidated
56 Ennismore Gardens,
London SW7 1AJ.
Tel: (01) 589 2262

Virgin Vision
328 Kensal Road,
London W10 5XJ.
Tel: (01) 968 8888

Warner Bros Productions
135 Wardour Street,
London W1.
Tel: (01) 437 5600

Michael White
13 Duke Street,
London SWY 6DB.
Tel: (01) 839 3971

Who Films
112 Wardour Street,
London W1V 3LD
Tel: (01) 439 8411

David Wickes Television
Twickenham Studios,
St Margaret's,
Twickenham TW1 2AW.
Tel: (01) 892 4477

Richard Williams Animation
13 Soho Square,
London W1V 5FB.
Tel: (01) 437 4455

Winkast Programming
Pinewood Studios,
Iver Heath, Bucks SL0 ONH.
Tel: (0753) 651700

Witzend Productions
4 Queensborough Studios,
London W2 3SQ.
Tel: (01) 221 1383

World Film Services
10 Mount Row,
London W1Y 5DA.
Tel: (01) 493 3045

Zenith Productions
8 Great Titchfield Street,
London W1P 7AA.
Tel: (01) 637 7941

UK FILM DISTRIBUTORS

Alpha Films
Unit 1, McKay Trading Estate,
Kensal Road, London W10 5BX.
Tel: (01) 960 8211

Ambassador Film Distributors
25 Parkways Avenue,
Oulton, Leeds LS26 8TV.
Tel: (0532) 820911

Anglo-American Distributors
68 Wardour Street,
London W1.
Tel: (01) 437 1563

Apollo Film Distributors
303 Wimbourne Road,
Bournemouth BH9 2AA.
Tel: (0202) 533577

Artificial Eye Film Co
211 Camden High Street,
London NW1 7BT.
Tel: (01) 267 6036

Avatar Communications
Imperial Studios,
Imperial Road,
London SW6.
Tel: (01) 756 6304

Barber International Films
38 Dover Street,
London W1X 3RB.
Tel: (01) 499 9416

Blue Dolphin Films
15-17 Old Compton Street,
London W1V 6JR.
Tel: (01) 439 9511

Bordeaux Films International
92 Wardour Street,
London W1.
Tel: (01) 434 3459

Brent Walker Film Distributors
9 Chesterfield Street,
London W1.
Tel: (01) 491 4430

British Film Institute Film and Video Library
81 Dean Street,
London W1V 6AA.
Tel: (01) 734 6451

Butcher's Film Distributors
6-7 Great Chapel Street,
London W1.
Tel: (01) 437 7282

Cannon Distributors
167-169 Wardour Street,
London W1.
Tel: (01) 437 9844

Cinegate
Gate Cinema,
87 Notting Hill Gate,
London W11.
Tel: (01) 727 2651

Columbia-EMI-Warner
135 Wardour Street,
London W1V 4AP.
Tel: (01) 734 8400

Connoisseur Films
167 Oxford Street,
London W1R 2DX.
Tel: (01) 734 6555

Contemporary Film
55 Greek Street,
London W1V 6DB.
Tel: (01) 434 2623

Crawford Films
15-17 Old Compton Street,
London W1V 6JR.
Tel: (01) 734 5298

Curzon Film Distributors
38 Curzon Street,
London W1Y 1EY.
Tel: (01) 626 8961

Walt Disney
See UK Production Companies.

Eagle Films
15-17 Old Compton Street,
London W1V 6JR.
Tel: (01) 437 9541

Enterprise Pictures
113 Wardour Street,
London W1.
Tel: (01) 734 3372

Entertainment Film Distributors
60-66 Wardour Street,
London W1.
Tel: (01) 734 4678

Essential Cinema
122 Wardour Street,
London W1.
Tel: (01) 437 8127

Facelift Film Distributors
Suite 4,
60-62 Old Compton Street,
London W1.
Tel: (01) 439 2047

Gala
See Cannon.

Golden Communications
47 Greek Street,
London W1.
Tel: (01) 439 1431

Golden Era Film Distributors
Cinema House,
225 Oxford Street,
London W1R 1AE.
Tel: (01) 734 8595

Grand National Film Distributors
26 Oak Grove,
Ruislip, Middx HAA 8UF.
Tel: (01) 866 9757

GTO Films
36 Soho Square,
London NW1 5DQ.
Tel: (01) 439 0921

HandMade Films (Distributors)
26 Cadogan Square,
London SW1X OJP.
Tel: (01) 584 8345

Hemdale Leisure
21 Albion Street,
London W2.
Tel: (01) 724 1010

ICA Projects
12 Carlton House Terrace,
London SW1Y 5AH.
Tel: (01) 943 0493

ITC Film Distributors
5-7 Carnaby Street,
London W1V 1PG.
Tel: (01) 439 6611

London Films
44a Floral Street,
Covent Garden,
London WC2E 9DA.
Tel: (01) 379 3366

Mainline Pictures
37 Museum Street,
London WC1A 1LP.
Tel: (01) 242 5523

MGM
See UIP.

Miracle International Films
92-94 Wardour Street,
London W1V 4JH.
Tel: (01) 437 0507

New Realm Film Distributors
Townsend House,
22 Dean Street,
London W1V 5AL.
Tel: (01) 437 9143

Osprey Film Distributors
120 Pall Mall,
London SW1Y 5EA.
Tel: (01) 839 3292

The Other Cinema
79 Wardour Street,
London W1V 3TH.
Tel: (01) 734 8508

Palace Pictures
16-17 Wardour Mews,
London W1V 3DG.
Tel: (01) 734 7060

Paramount
See UIP.

Premiere Releasing
93 Wardour Street,
London W1.
Tel: (01) 437 6516

Rank Film Distributors
127 Wardour Street,
London W1V 4AD.
Tel: (01) 437 9020

Sunn Classic
37-39 Great Marlborough Street,
London W1V 1DA.
Tel: (01) 437 9556

Supreme Film Distributors
Suite 6,
60-62 Old Compton Street,
London W1.
Tel: (01) 437 4415

Target International
5-7 Carnaby Street,
London W1V 1PG.
Tel: (01) 439 6611

TCB Releasing
Stone House, Rudge,
Frome, Somerset.
Tel: (0373) 830769

Thorn EMI Classics
30 Golden Square,
London W1A 4QX.
Tel: (01) 437 4415

Tigon Film Distributors
5-7 Carnaby Street,
London W1V 1PG.
Tel: (01) 439 6611

Twentieth Century-Fox
See UK Production Companies.

UIP (United International Pictures)
Mortimer House,
37-41 Mortimer Street,
London W1A 2LJ.
Tel: (01) 636 1655

UK Film Distributors
31-33 Soho Square,
London W1V 6AP.
Tel: (01) 734 8111

United Artists
See UIP.

Universal
See UIP.

Virgin Vision
328 Kensal Road,
London W10 5XJ.
Tel: (01) 968 8888

Watchgrove
6 New Road,
Ham, Richmond,
Surrey TW10 7HY.
Tel: (01) 948 5839

FILM STUDIOS

AUSTRIA
Schönbrunn Film
Neubaugasse 1,
1070 Vienna.
Tel: (0222) 932265

WDS Film
Göllnergasse 8-10,
1030 Vienna.
Tel: (0222) 735436

Wien Film
Engelshofengasse 2,
1238 Vienna.
Tel: (0222) 882541

CANADA
David Bier
1085 St Alexander Street,
Montreal, Quebec H2Z 1P4.
Tel: (514) 861 3469

Magder Studios
793 Pharmacy Avenue,
Toronto, Ontario M1L 3K3.
Tel: (416) 752 8850

Studio Centre
2264 Lakeshore Blvd W,
Toronto, Ontario M8V 1A9.
Tel: (415) 255 6857

Studio 523
523 Richmond Street E,
Toronto, Ontario M5A 1R4.
Tel: (416) 862 0523

Toronto International Film Studios
11030 Highway 27, Box 430,
Kleinburg, Ontario LOJ 1CO.
Tel: (416) 851 2201

Yorkville Studio
47 Scollard Street,
Toronto, Ontario M5R 1GI.
Tel: (416) 961 5283

FEDERAL REPUBLIC OF GERMANY

Arnold & Richter Cine Technik
Turkenstrasse 89,
8000 Munich 40.
Tel: (089) 38 09 240

Bavaria Atelier Gesellschaft
Bavariafilmplatz 7,
8022 Geiselgasteig.
Tel: (089) 649 91

Berliner Union Film
Oberlandstrasse 26-35,
1000 Berlin 42.
Tel: (030) 75 94 1

Internationale Film Union
Haus Calmuth,
Postfach 1250,
58 Remagen/Rhein.
Tel: (02642) 220 41

Studio 57
Grunerstrasse 119,
4 Dusseldorf.
Tel: (0211) 62 63 11

Studio Hamburg
Tonndorfer Haupstrasse 90,
2000 Hamburg 70.
Tel: (040) 66 88 2246

Taunus Film
Unter den Eichen,
PO Box 690,
6200 Wiesbaden 1.
Tel: (06021) 521025

TBS Studio Berlin
Mühlenstrasse 52,
1000 Berlin 46.
Tel: (030) 775 5026

FRANCE
Eclair
Rue du Mont 10,
93800 Epinay.
Tel: (01) 821 63 03

Images de France
Rue Vernet 29,
Paris 8.
Tel: (01) 720 53 17

Paris Studio Cinema
Quai du Point du Jour 50,
Billancourt.
Tel: (01) 609 93 24

Studios de Boulogne
Avenue Jean Baptiste
Clement 137,
92100 Boulogne.
Tel: (01) 605 65 69

Studios Francoeur
Rue Francoeur 6,
Paris 18.
Tel: (01) 257 12 10

Victorine Studios
Avenue Edouard Grinda 16,
06200 Nice.
Tel: (93) 72 54 54

IRELAND
**National Film Studios of
Ireland**
Ardmore,
Bray, Co Wicklow,
Tel: Bray 862971

ITALY
Cinecitta
Via Tuscolana 1055,
00174 Rome.
Tel: (06) 74 641

Dear International
Via Nomentana 833,
00137 Rome.
Tel: (06) 826 801

De Paolis – In.Ci.R.
Via Tiburtina 521,
00159 Rome.
Tel: (06) 43 85 341

Filmauro
Via della Vasca Navale 58,
00173 Rome.
Tel: (06) 55 84 875

ICET De Paolis
Via Lumiere 4,
20093 Cologno Monzese,
Milan.
Tel: (02) 25 43 184

RAP – Elios
Via Tiburtina Km 13, 600,
00131 Rome.
Tel: (06) 61 90 195

Vides Cinematografica
Via Concesio Km 1 800,
00188 Prima Porta,
Rome.
Tel: (06) 69 10 181

MEXICO
Estudios America
Calzada de Tlalpan 2818,
Mexico 21, D.F.
Tel: (05) 549 3106

Estudios Churubusco
Atletas 2, Country Club,
Mexico 21, D.F.
Tel: (05) 549 3060

NETHERLANDS
Cinetone Studios
Duivendrechtsekade 83-85,
1096 AJ Amsterdam.
Tel: (020) 93 09 60

Cinevideo Studios
Ambachtsmark 3,
1355 EA Almere-Haven.
Tel: (03240) 12324

Metamedia
's-Gravelandseweg 80,
1217 EW Hilversum.
Tel: (035) 13851

SPAIN
Cinearte SA
Plaza Conde Barajas 5,
Madrid 12.
Tel: (01) 266 5407

**Estudios Cinematograficos
Roma**
Carretera de Irun Km 11, 7000,
Madrid 34.
Tel: (01) 734 2050

Estudios Isasi
Esplugas de Llobregat,
Barcelona.
Tel: (03) 271 1404

Estudios Macian
Av. Hospital Militar 252,
Barcelona 6.
Tel: (03) 248 1818

Vallehermoso
Vallehermoso 59,
Madrid 15.
Tel: (01) 446 1450

SWEDEN
AB Europa – Film
Box 20065,
S-161 20 Bromma.
Tel: (08) 98 77 00

Accord Film
Fiskhamnsgatan 10,
S414 55 Götenborg.
Tel: (031) 12 12 11

Svenska Filminstitutet
Filmhuset, Box 27 126,
S-102 52 Stockholm.
Tel: (08) 63 05 10

UK
Bray Studios
Down Place, Windsor Road,
Water Oakley,
Windsor, Berks.
Tel: (0628) 22111

Bushey Film Studios
Melbourne Road,
Bushey, Herts.
Tel: (01) 950 1621

**Edinburgh Film and TV
Studios**
Nine Mile Burn, Penicuik,
Midlothian EH26 9LT.
Tel: (0968) 72131

Isleworth Studios
Studio Parade,
484 London Road,
Isleworth, Middx TW7 4DE.
Tel: (01) 568 3511

**Lee International Film
Studios**
Wembley Park Drive,
Wembley, Middx.
Tel: (01) 902 1262

Limehouse Studios
Canary Wharf,
West India Docks,
London E14 9SJ.
Tel: (01) 987 2090

Pinewood Studios
Iver Heath,
Iver, Bucks SLO ONH.
Tel: (0753) 651700

The Production Village
100 Cricklewood Lane,
London NW2.
Tel: (01) 450 8969

St John's Wood Studio
87a St John's Wood Terrace,
London NW8 6PY.
Tel: (01) 722 9255

Shepperton Studio Centre
Studios Road,
Shepperton,
Middx TW17 0QD.
Tel: (09328) 62611

Thorn EMI Elstree Studios
Borehamwood,
Herts WD6 1JG.
Tel: (01) 953 1600

Twickenham Film Studios
St Margaret's,
Twickenham, Middx.
Tel: (01) 892 4477

US
ABC Television Center
4151 Prospect Avenue,
Los Angeles, CA 90027.
Tel: (213) 557 7777

CBS/Fox Studios
4024 Radford Avenue,
Studio City, CA 91604.
Tel: (818) 760 5000

Columbia Pictures
Columbia Plaza,
Burbank, CA 91505.
Tel: (818) 954 6000

**Consolidated Film
Industries**
959 Seward Street,
Los Angeles, CA 90038.
Tel: (213) 462 3161

**Walt Disney
Productions**
500 South Buena Vista Street,
Burbank, CA 91503.
Tel: (818) 840 1000

**Jerry Fairbanks
Productions**
826 North Cole,
Los Angeles, CA 90038.
Tel: (213) 462 1101

Falcon Studios
5526 Hollywood Blvd,
Los Angeles, CA 90028.
Tel: (213) 462 9356

Samuel Goldwyn Studios
1041 North Formosa Avenue,
Los Angeles, CA 90046.
Tel: (213) 650 2500

Hollywood Center Studios
1040 North Las Palmas Avenue,
Hollywood, CA 90038.
Tel: (213) 469 9011

International Studios
486 Cahuenga Blvd,
Los Angeles, CA 90038.
Tel: (213) 466 3534

**Major Independent Film
Studios**
1207 North Western Avenue,
Los Angeles, CA 90029.
Tel: (213) 461 2721

MGM-UA Studios
10202 West Washington Blvd,
Culver City, CA 90230.
Tel: (213) 558 5000

NBC Television
3000 West Alameda Avenue,
Burbank, CA 91503
Tel: (818) 845 7000

Paramount Studios
5555 Melrose Avenue,
Los Angeles, CA 90038.
Tel: (213) 468 5000

Producers Studio
650 North Bronson Avenue,
Los Angeles, CA 90004.
Tel: (213) 466 3111

Production Group
1330 North Vine Street,
Hollywood, CA 90028.
Tel: (213) 469 8111

Television Center Studios
846 North Cahuenga Blvd,
Los Angeles, CA 90038.
Tel: (213) 466 1351

Twentieth Century-Fox Film Corporation
10201 West Pico Blvd,
Los Angeles, CA 90035.
Tel: (213) 277 2211

Universal City Studios
Universal City Plaza,
Universal City,
CA 91608.
Tel: (818) 985 4321

UPA Pictures
4440 Lakeside Drive,
Burbank, CA 90621.
Tel: (213) 556 3800

Warner Bros
4000 Warner Blvd,
Burbank, CA 91522.
Tel: (818) 954 6000

MAGAZINES

Afterimage
1 Birnham Road,
London N4.
Ed: Simon Field, Guy L'Eclair
Irregular

American Cinematographer
ASC Holding Coporation,
1782 N Orange Drive,
Hollywood, CA 90028.
Ed: Richard Patterson
Monthly

American Film
American Film Institute,
John F Kennedy Center for the
Performing Arts,
Washington DC 20566,
Ed: Peter Biskin
Ten issues pa

L'Avant-Scene (Cinema)
Rue Lord Byron 1,
75008 Paris.
Ed: Claude Beyie
Monthly

Bianco e Nero
Via Tuscolana 1524,
00173 Rome.
Editorial Board
Quarterly

Cahiers du Cinema
Passage de la Boule-Blanche 9,
75012 Paris.
Ed: Serge Toubiana
Monthly

Chaplin
Filmhuset, Box 27 126,
S-102 52 Stockholm.
Ed: Lars Ahlander
Bi-monthly

Cineaste
200 Park Avenue South,
New York, NY 10003.
Ed: Gary Crowdus, Dan Geogaka,
Lenny Rubenstein
Quarterly

Cine Cubano
Calle 23 no 1155,
Habana, Cuba.
Ed: Julio Garcia Espinoso
Irregular

Cinefantastique
PO Box 270, Oak Park, IL 60303.
Ed: Frederick S Clarke
Five issues pa

Cinema 85
Rue Cadet 7, 75009 Paris.
Ed: Joel Magny
Monthly

Cinema
Kino Verlage,
Milchstrasse 1,
2000 Hamburg 13.
Ed: Jörg Altendorf, Willi Bär
Monthly

Cinema Canada
834 Bloomfield Avenue,
Montreal, Quebec.
Ed: Connie Tadros, Jean-Pierre
Tadros
Monthly

Cinema Journal
Department of English,
Box 4348,
University of Illinois at Chicago,
Chicago, IL 60680.
Ed: Virginia Wright Wexman
Bi-annual

Cinema Nuovo
Edizione Dedalo,
Casella Postale 362,
70100 Bari, Italy.
Ed: Guido Aristarco
Bi-monthly

Cinema Papers
644 Victoria Street,
North Melbourne 3051, Australia.
Ed: Nick Roddick
Quarterly

Cinema Sessanta
Piaza dei Caprettari 70,
00186 Rome.
Ed: Mino Argentieri
Bi-monthly

Continental Film and Video Review
PO Box 1, Barking,
Essex IG11 8AZ.
Ed: Ann Totterdell
Monthly

Dirigido Por
Rbla de Catalunya, 108 3° 1°,
Barcelona.
Ed: Edmundo Orts Climent
Monthly

Film
British Federation of Film
Societies,
Film Society Unit,
British Film Institute,
81 Dean Street,
London W1V 6AA.
Ed: Peter Cargin
Monthly

Film Comment
140 West 65th Street,
New York, NY 10023.
Ed: Richard Corliss
Bi-monthly

Film Criticism
Allegheny College,
Meadville, PA 16335.
Ed: L Lloyd Michaels
Three issues pa

Film Dope
45 Lupton Street,
London NW5 2HS.
Ed: David Badder,
Bob Baker
Irregular

Film Directions
8 Malone Road,
Belfast BT9 5BN.
Ed: Michael Open
Irregular

Film Echange
Avenue Marceau 50,
75008 Paris.
Ed: Rene Thevenet
Quarterly

Filmkritik
Filmkritiker-Kooperative,
Kreittmayrstrasse 3,
8000 Munich 2.
Editorial Board
Monthly

Film Quarterly
University of California,
Berkeley, CA 94720.
Ed: Ernest Callenback
Quarterly

Film Reader
Film Division,
Northwestern University,
1905 Sheridan Road,
Evanston, IL 60201.
Editorial Board
Irregular

Film Review
EMI Cinemas Ltd,
Old Court House,
Old Court Place,
London W8 4PL.
Ed: Peter Haigh
Monthly

Films (On Screen and Video)
22024 Buckingham Palace
Road,
London SW1.
Ed: Edwina Wynyard
Monthly

Films and Filming
Brevet Publishing Ltd,
43b Gloucester Road,
Croydon CR0 2DH.
Ed: John Russell Taylor
Monthly

Films in Review
PO Box 589,
Lennox Hill Station,
New York, NY 10021.
Ed: Robin Little
Ten issues pa

Framework
English and American Studies,
University of East Anglia,
Norwich NR4 7TJ.
Ed: Paul Willeman
Irregular

Interview
860 Broadway,
New York, NY 10003.
Ed: Robert Hayes
Monthly

Jump Cut
PO Box 865,
Berkeley, CA 94701.
Ed: John Hess,
Chuck Kleinhans,
Julia Lesage
Quarterly

Literature/Film Quarterly
Salisbury State College,
Salisbury,
MD 21801.
Ed: Thomas L Erskine,
James M Welsh
Quarterly

Media, Culture and Society
28 Banner Street,
London EC1Y 8QE.
Editorial Board
Quarterly

Monthly Film Bulletin
81 Dean Street,
London W1V 6AA.
Ed: Richard Combs
Monthly

Movie
25 Lloyd Baker Street,
London WC1 9AT.
Editorial Board
Irregular

Movie Maker
1 Golden Square,
London W1R 3AB.
Ed: Chris Sheldon
Monthly

October
MIT Press Journal,
28 Carlton Street,
Massachusetts 02142.
Ed: Rosalind Kraus,
Annette Michelson
Quarterly

Photoplay/Movies and Video
1 Golden Square,
London
W1R 3AB.
Ed: Lisa Dewson
Monthly

Positif
Nouvelles Editions Opta,
Quai Conti 1,
75006 Paris.
Editorial Board
Monthly

Primetime
c/o Illuminations,
16 Newman Passage,
London W1.
Editorial Board
Irregular

Quarterly Review of Film Studies
Redgrave Publishing Co,
380 Adams Street,
Bedford Hills,
New York 10507.
Ed: Ronald Gottesman, Beverley Houston
Quarterly

La Revue du Cinema
Rue Recamier 3,
75341 Paris 07.
Ed: Jacques Zimmer
Monthly

Screen
29 Old Compton Street,
London W1V 5PL.
Ed: Mandy Merck
Five issues pa

Screen Digest
37 Gower Street,
London WC1E 6HH.
Ed: David Fisher
Monthly

Screen International
King Publications,
6-7 Great Chapel Street,
London W1.
Ed: Terry Ilott
Weekly

Sight and Sound
British Film Institute,
81 Dean Street,London W1V 6AA
Ed: Penelope Houston
Quarterly

Stills
6 Denmark Street,
London WC2H 8LP.
Ed: Nicolas Kent
Six issues pa

Variety
154 West 46th Street,
New York,
NY 10036.
Ed: Syd Silverman
Weekly

Undercut
London Filmmakers
Co-op,
42 Gloucester Avenue,
London NW1.
Editorial Board
Irregular

Wide Angle
Ohio University Press,
Box 388,
Athens, OH 45701.
Ed: Peter Lehman
Irregular

US FILM SCHOOLS

ALABAMA
University of Alabama
Department of Broadcast and
Film Communication,
PO Box D,
University, AL 35486.
Tel: (205) 348 6350

ARIZONA
University of Arizona
Department of Radio-Television,
221 Modern Languages Building,
Tuscon, AZ 85721.
Tel: (602) 626 4731

ARKANSAS
University of Arkansas, Fayetteville
The Film Program,
417 Communication Center,
Fayetteville, AR 72701.
Tel: (501) 575 2953

CALIFORNIA
American Film Institute Center for Advanced Film Studies
501 Doheny Road,
Beverly Hills, CA 90210.
Tel: (213) 278 8777

Art Center College of Design,
Film Department,
1700 Lida Street,
Pasadena, CA 91103.
Tel: (213) 577 1700

Brooks Institute
Cinema/TV Department,
School of Photographic Art and
Science,
2190 Alston Road,
Santa Barbara, CA 93108.
Tel: (805) 969 2291

California College of Arts and Crafts
Film/Video Department,
5212 Broadway,
Oakland, CA 94618.
Tel: (415) 653 8118

California Institute of the Arts
School of Film and Video,
24700 McBean Parkway,
Valencia, CA 91355.
Tel: (805) 255 1050

California State University, Fresno
Department of Radio-TV-Cinema,
Cedar and Shaw Avenues,
Fresno, CA 93740.
Tel: (209) 487 2627

California State University, Humboldt
Theater Arts/Film Department,
Arcata, CA 95521.
Tel: (707) 826 3566

California State University, Northridge
Radio-TV-Film Department,
18111 Nordhoff Street,
Northridge, CA 91330.
Tel: (213) 885 3192

Columbia College, Hollywood
Department of Cinema,
925 North La Brea Avenue,
Hollywood, CA 90038.
Tel: (213) 851 0550

Loyola Marymount University
7101 West 80th Street,
Los Angeles, CA 90045.
Tel: (213) 642 3033

New College of California
777 Valencia Street,
San Francisco, CA 94110.
Tel: (415) 626 1694

San Diego State University
Telecommunications and Film
Department,
College Avenue,
San Diego, CA 92182.
Tel: (714) 286 6575

San Francisco Art Institute
Filmmaking Department,
800 Chestnut Street,
San Francisco, CA 94133.
Tel: (415) 771 7020

San Francisco State University
Film and Creative Arts
Interdisciplinary Department,
1600 Holloway Avenue,
San Francisco, CA 94132.
Tel: (415) 469 1629

Stanford University
Communication Department,
Cypress Hall,
Stanford, CA 94305.
Tel: (415) 497 4621

University of California, Los Angeles
Theater Arts Department,
405 Hilgard Avenue,
Los Angeles, CA 90024.
Tel: (213) 825 7891

University of California, Santa Barbara
Film Studies Program,
Santa Barbara, CA 93106.
Tel: (805) 961 2347

University of California, Santa Cruz
Theater Arts Board,
Santa Cruz, CA 95064.
Tel: (408) 429 2974

University of Southern California
Division of Cinema/Television,
School of Performing Arts,
University Park,
Los Angeles, CA 90007.
Tel: (213) 743 2235

CONNECTICUT
University of Bridgeport
Cinema Department,
84 Iranistan Avenue,
Bridgeport, CT 06602.
Tel: (203) 576 4430

Western Connecticut State College
Photography, Film and TV
Department,
181 White Street,
Danbury, CT 06001.
Tel: (203) 797 4047

DISTRICT OF COLUMBIA
American University
School of Communication,
Washington, DC 20016.
Tel: (202) 686 2055

University of the District of Columbia, Mount Vernon Square Campus
Communicative Arts
Department,
916 G Street NW,
Building T-10,
Washington, DC 20001.
Tel: (202) 727 2717

FLORIDA
Florida State University
Department of
Communication,
Diffenbaugh Building,
Room 356,
Tallahassee, FL 32306.
Tel: (904) 644 5034

University of Florida
Film Studies Program,
408 GPA Building,
Gainesville, FL 32601.
Tel: (904) 392 0777

University of Miami
Communications Department,
PO Box 248127,
Coral Gables, FL 33124.
Tel: (305) 284 2265

GEORGIA
University of Georgia
Radio-TV-Film Department,
School of Journalism,
Athens, GA 30602.
Tel: (404) 542 3785

ILLINOIS

Columbia College
Film Department,
600 South Michigan Avenue,
Chicago, IL 60605.
Tel: (312) 663 1600

Northwestern University
Radio, Television and Film
Department,
School of Speech,
Evanston, IL 60201.
Tel: (312) 492 7315

**School of the Art Institute of
Chicago**
Filmmaking Department,
Columbus Drive and Jackson
Blvd,
Chicago, IL 60603.
Tel: (312) 443 3700

**Southern Illinois University at
Carbondale**
Department of Cinema and
Photography,
Carbondale, IL 62901.
Tel: (618) 453 2365.

**University of Illinois, Urbana-
Champaign**
Cinematography Program,
Department of Art and Design,
129 Fine Arts Building,
Champaign, IL 61820.
Tel: (217) 333 0855

INDIANA

**Indiana University, Purdue
University at Fort Wayne**
Communications
Department,
2101 Coliseum Blvd E,
Fort Wayne, IN 46805.
Tel: (219) 482 5348

KANSAS

University of Kansas
Radio-Television-Film
Department,
217 Flint Hall,
Lawrence, KS 66045.
Tel: (913) 864 3991

KENTUCKY

**Northern Kentucky
University**
Department
of Communications,
Highland Heights, KY 41076.
Tel: (606) 292 5435

LOUISIANA

University of New Orleans
Drama and Communications
Department,
Lakefront,
New Orleans, LA 70122.
Tel: (504) 283 0317

MARYLAND

John Hopkins University
The Humanities Center,
Baltimore, MD 21218.
Tel: (301) 338 7616

**University of Maryland at
College Park**
Radio-Television-Film Division,
College Park, MD 20742.
Tel: (301) 454 2541

**University of Maryland,
Baltimore County**
Visual Arts Department,
5401 Wilkens Avenue,
Catonsville, MD 21228.
Tel: (301) 455 2150

MASSACHUSETTS

Boston University
Department of Broadcasting and
Film,
School of Public
Communication,
640 Commonwealth Avenue,
Boston, MA 02215.
Tel: (617) 353 3483

Emerson College
Department of Mass
Communication,
148 Beacon Street,
Boston, MA 02116.
Tel: (617) 578 8500

Hampshire College
Film and Photography
Department,
Route 116,
Amherst, MA 01002.
Tel: (413) 549 4600

MICHIGAN

**Central Michigan
University**
Broadcast and Cinematic Arts
Department,
340 Moore Hall,
Mount Pleasant, MI 48858.
Tel: (517) 774 3852

University of Michigan
Program in Film and Video
Studies,
131 Old A & D Building,
Ann Arbor, MI 48109.
Tel: (313) 764 0147

MINNESOTA

**Minneapolis College of Art
and Design**
Design Division,
133 East 25th Street,
Minneapolis, MN 55404.
Tel: (612) 870 3161

MISSOURI

**University of Missouri –
Columbia**
Area of Radio-
Television-Film,
Speech and Dramatic Art
Department,
200 Swallow Hall,
Columbia, MO 65201.
Tel: (314) 882 3046

MONTANA

Montana State University
Department of Film and
Television Production,
Bozeman, MT 59717.
Tel: (406) 994 2484

NEVADA

**University of Nevada, Las
Vegas**
Department of Film Studies,
4505 Maryland Parkway,
Las Vegas, NV 89154.
Tel: (702) 739 3325

NEW JERSEY

Jersey City State College,
Media Arts Department,
2039 Kennedy Blvd,
Jersey City, NJ 07305.
Tel: (201) 547 3207

NEW YORK

Adelphi University
Department of Communications,
South Avenue,
Garden City, NY 11530.
Tel: (516) 294 8700

Bard College
Film Department,
Annandale-on-Hudson,
NY 12504.
Tel: (914) 758 6822

**City University of New York,
Brooklyn College**
Film Department,
Bedford Avenue and Avenue H,
Brooklyn, NY 11210.

**City University of New York,
City College**
Leonard Davis Center for the
Performing Arts,
138th Street and Convent
Avenue,
New York, NY 10033.
Tel: (212) 690 8173

**City University of New York,
Hunter College**
Department of Theater
and Film,
695 Park Avenue,
New York, NY 10021.
Tel: (212) 570 5747

Columbia University
School of the Arts,
513 Dodge Hall,
116 Street and Broadway,
New York, NY 10027.
Tel: (212) 280 2875

Cornell University
Theater Arts Department,
College of Arts and Sciences,
Lincoln Hall, Ithaca, NY 14853.
Tel: (607) 256 3533

Ithaca College
Department of Cinema Studies
and Photography,
School of Communications,
Danby Road, Ithaca, NY 14850.
Tel: (607) 274 3242

New York University
Undergraduate Institute of Film
and Television,
65 South Building,
Washington Square,
New York, NY 10003
Tel: (212) 598 3702

Pratt Institute
Film Department,
215 Ryerson Street,
Brooklyn, NY 11205.
Tel: (212) 636 3766

Sarah Lawrence College
Film Department,
Bronxville, NY 10708.
Tel: (914) 337 0700

School of Visual Arts
Film Department,
209 East 23rd Street,
New York, NY 10010.
Tel: (212) 679 7350

**State University of New York
at Binghamton**
Cinema Department,
Vestal Parkway,
Binghamton, NY 13901.
Tel: (607) 798 4998

**State Univesity of New York at
Buffalo**
Center for Media Study,
310 Hochstetter,
Buffalo, NY 17222.
Tel: (716) 831 2426

**State University of New York
College at Purchase**
Film Program,
Lincoln Avenue,
Purchase, NY 10577.
Tel: (914) 253 5000

Syracuse University
College of Visual and Performing
Arts,
Syracuse, NY 13210.
Tel: (315) 423 2214

University of Rochester
Film Studies Program,
Rush Rhees Library,
River Station, NY 14627.
Tel: (716) 275 2121

Vassar College
Drama Department,
Poughkeepsie, NY 12601.
Tel: (914) 452 7000

NORTH CAROLINA

**University of North Carolina
at Chapel Hill**
Department of Radio, Television
and Motion Pictures,
College of Arts and Sciences,
Swain Hill O44A,
Chapel Hill, NC 27514.
Tel: (919) 933 2313

Wake Forest University
Speech, Communication and
Theater Arts Department,
PO Box 7347,
Winston-Salem, NC 27109.
Tel: (919) 761 5406

OHIO

**Bowling Green State
University, Bowling Green**
Radio-Television-Film Area,
School of Speech
Communication,
413 South Hall,
Bowling Green, OH 43403.
Tel: (419) 372 2138

Cleveland Institute of Art
Photography Department,
11141 East Blvd,
Cleveland, OH 44106.
Tel: (216) 421 4322

Denison University
Department of Theater and
Cinema,
Granville, OH 43023.
Tel: (614) 587 0801

Ohio State University
Department of Photography and Cinema,
Columbus, OH 43210.
Tel: (614) 422 1766

Ohio University, Athens
Film Department,
Lindley Hall 378,
Athens, OH 45701
Tel: (614) 594 5138

University of Cincinnati
Film and Media Program,
Mail Location 184,
Cincinnati, OH 45221.
Tel: (513) 475 2551

Wright State University
Department of Theater Arts,
Dayton, OH 45435.
Tel: (513) 873 3072

OKLAHOMA
Oklahoma State University
Radio-Television-Film Department,
Stillwater, OK 74078.
Tel: (405) 624 6354

University of Oklahoma
Video-Film Program,
520 Parrington Oval,
Norman, OK 73019.
Tel: (405) 325 2691

OREGON
University of Oregon
Film Studies Area,
Department of Speech,
Villard Hall,
Eugene, OR 97403.
Tel: (503) 686 4228

PENNSYLVANIA
Pennsylvania State University
Department of Theater and Film,
University Park, PA 16802.
Tel: (814) 865 7586

Philadelphia College of Art
Photo-Film Department
Broad and Spruce Streets,
Philadelphia, PA 19102.
Tel: (215) 893 3140

Temple University
Department of Radio-Television-Film,
Philadelphia, PA 19122.
Tel: (215) 787 8423

RHODE ISLAND
Rhode Island College
Film Studies Program,
600 Mount Pleasant Avenue,
Providence, RI 02908.
Tel: (401) 274 4900

SOUTH CAROLINA
Bob Jones University
Unusual Films,
Division of Cinema,
1700 Wade Hampton Blvd,
Greenville, SC 29614.
Tel: (803) 242 5100

TEXAS
Baylor University
Division of Radio-Television,
Waco, TX 76706.
Tel: (817) 755 1511

North Texas State University
Radio-Film-Television Division,
Denton, TX 76203.
Tel: (817) 788 2537

Southern Methodist University
Broadcast-Film Arts Department,
Binkley and Bishop Street,
Dallas, TX 75275.
Tel: (214) 692 3090

Stephen F Austin State University
Communication Department,
PO Box 13048, SFA Station,
Nacogdoches, TX 75962.
Tel: (713) 569 4001

UTAH
Brigham Young University
Theater and Cinematic Arts Department,
D-581 HFAC,
Provo, UT 84602.
Tel: (801) 378 4574

University of Utah
Film Studies Program,
205 Pioneer Memorial Theater,
Salt Lake City, UT 84112.
Tel: (801) 581 6356

WISCONSIN
University of Wisconsin, Milwaukee
BA/BFA in Film,
Curtin Hall,
PO Box 413,
Milwaukee, WI 53201.
Tel: (414) 963 5970

University of Wisconsin, Oshkosh
Radio-Television-Film Division,
Speech Department,
Arts and Communication Center,
Oshkosh, WI 54901
Tel: (414) 424 3131

UK FILM SCHOOLS

City of Birmingham Polytechnic
Department of Visual Communication,
Birmingham B42 2SU.
Tel: (021) 359 6721

Bolton Metropolitan College
Department of Art and Design,
Hilden Street,
Bolton BL2 1JB.
Tel: (0204) 31411

Bournemouth and Poole College of Art and Design
Department of Photography,
Film and Television,
Off Wallindown Road,
Poole,
Dorset BH12 5HH.
Tel: (0202) 533011

University of Bristol
Department of Drama,
29 Park Row,
Bristol BS1 5LT.
Tel: (0272) 24161

Croydon College
School of Art and Design,
Barclay Road,
Croydon CR9 1DX.
Tel: (01) 688 9271

Derby Londsdale College of Higher Education
School of Art and Design,
Kedleston Road,
Derby DE3 1GB.
Tel: (0332) 47181

Dewsbury and Batley Technical and Art College
School of Art and Design,
Cambridge Street,
Batley,
West Yorkshire WF17 5JB.
Tel: (0924) 474401

Goldsmiths' College
University of London,
Lewisham Way,
London SE14 6NW.
Tel: (01) 692 7171

Gwent College of Higher Education
Faculty of Art and Design,
Clarence Place,
Newport,
Gwent NPT OUW.
Tel: (0633) 59984

Harrow College of Higher Education
Faculty of Art and Photography,
Northwick Park,
Harrow, Middx HA1 3TP.
Tel: (01) 864 6422

University of Hull
Department of Drama,
Cottingham Road,
Hull HU6 7RX.
Tel: (0482) 46311

Humberside College of Higher Education
School of Visual Communication,
Design and Fine Art,
Queens Gardens,
Hull HU1 3DH.
Tel: (0482) 224121

Kingsway-Princeton College
Photography Department,
Hugh Myddleton Annexe,
Sans Walk,
London EC1.
Tel: (01) 837 8185

Lanchester Polytechnic
Faculty of Art and Design,
Gosford Street,
Coventry CV1 5RZ.
Tel: (0203) 24166

Leeds Polytechnic
School of Creative Arts and Design,
Calverly Street,
Leeds LS1 3HE.
Tel: (0532) 462439

Liverpool Polytechnic
Faculty of Art and Design,
Department of Graphic Design,
2a Myrtle Street,
Liverpool L7 7DN.
Tel: (051) 709 9711

London College of Printing
Department of Photography,
Film and Television,
Elephant and Castle,
London SE1 6SB.
Tel: (01) 734 8484

London International Film School
24 Shelton Street,
London WC2H 9HP.
Tel: (01) 240 0168

Maidstone College of Art
Oakwood Park,
Oakwood Road,
Maidstone,
Kent ME16 8AG.
Tel: (0622) 57286

Manchester Polytechnic
Faculty of Art and Design,
Capital Building,
School Lane,
Didsbury,
Manchester M20 OHT.
Tel: (061) 434 3331

Medway College of Design
Fort Pitt,
Rochester,
Kent ME1 1DZ.
Tel: (0634) 44815

Middlesex Polytechnic
Humanities Department,
White Hart Lane,
London N17.
Tel: (01) 801 3434

National Film School
Beaconsfield Film Studios,
Station Road,
Beaconsfield,
Bucks HP9 1LE.
Tel: (04946) 71234

Newcastle-upon-Tyne Polytechnic
Faculty of Art and Design,
Squires Building,
Sandyford Road,
Newcastle-upon-Tyne
NE1 8ST.
Tel: (0632) 326002

North East London Polytechnic
School of Art and Design,
Greengate Street,
London E13.
Tel: (01) 590 7722

Polytechnic of Central London
School of Communication,
18-22 Riding House Street,
London W1P 7DP.
Tel: (01) 486 5811

Portsmouth Polytechnic
Department of Fine Art,
Lion Terrace,
Portsmouth PO1 3HF.
Tel: (0705) 827681

Ravensbourne College of Art and Design
Department of Television,
Wharton Road,
Bromley,
Kent BR1 3LE.
Tel: (01) 468 7071

Royal College of Art
School of Film and Television,
Kensington Gore,
London SW7 2EU.
Tel: (01) 584 5020

Saint Martin's School of Art
Film and Video Unit,
27-29 Long Acre,
London WC2E 9LA.
Tel: (01) 437 0611

Sheffield City Polytechnic
Faculty of Art and Design,
Brincliffe,
Psalter Lane,
Sheffield S11 8UZ.
Tel: (0742) 56101

Trent Polytechnic
Department of Fine Art,
Dryden Street,
Nottingham.
Tel: (0602) 58248

West Surrey College of Art and Design
Department of Audio-Visual Studies,
Falkner Road,
The Hart, Farnham,
Surrey CU9 7DS.
Tel: (0252) 722441

Wimbledon School of Art
Merton Hall Road,
London SW19 3QA.
Tel: (01) 540 0231

FILM ARCHIVES/LIBRARIES

AUSTRALIA
Australian Film Institute
47 Little Latrobe Street,
Melbourne.
Tel: (03) 662 1944

National Film and Sound Archive of Australia
GPO Box 2002,
McCoy Circuit,
Canberra 2601 ACT.
Tel: (062) 621 111

AUSTRIA
Osterreichisches Filmarchiv
Rauhensteingasse 5,
A-1010 Vienna,
Tel: (0222) 529936

Osterreichisches Filmmuseum
Augustinerstrasse 1,
1010 Vienna 1.
Tel: (0222) 523426/526206

BELGIUM
Cinematheque Royale de Belgique
Ravenstein 23,
1000 Brussels.
Tel: (513) 41 55

CANADA
Cinematheque Quebecoise
Boul de Maisonneuve Est 335,
Montreal H2X IKI.
Tel: (514) 845 8118

National Film, Television and Sound Archives
395 Wellington Street,
Ottawa,
Ontario K1A ON3.
Tel: (613) 995 1311

Ontario Film Institute
770 Don Mills Road,
Don Mills,
Ontario M3C IT3.
Tel: (416) 4100

CZECHOSLAVAKIA
Czechoslovak Film Institute
(Ceskoslovensky filmovy ustav)
Narodni trida 40,
110 00 Prague 1.
Tel: (02) 260087

DENMARK
Det Danske Filmmuseum,
St Søndervoldstraede,
1419 København K.
Tel: (01) 576500

FRANCE
Centre National de la Cinematographie – Service des Archive du Film
Rue Alexandre Turpault 7,
78390 Bois d'Arcy.
Tel: (03) 4602050/4602879

Cinematheque de Toulouse
Rue Roquelaine 3,
3100 Toulouse.
Tel: (061) 489075

Cinematheque Française
Rue du Colisée 9,
75008 Paris.
Tel: (01) 553 21 86

GERMAN DEMOCRATIC REPUBLIC
Staatliches Filmarchiv der D.D.R.
Hausvogteiplatz 3-4,
1080 Berlin.
Tel: (02) 2124324

GERMAN FEDERAL REPUBLIC
Bundesarchiv-Filmarchiv
Am Wöllershof 12,
D 5400 Koblenz.
Tel: (0261) 3991

Deutsches Filmmuseum/ Deutsches Institut für Filmkunde
Schaumainkai 41,
D 6000 Frankfurt 70.
Tel: (069) 212 3369

Stiftung Deutsche Kinemathek
1000 Berlin 19,
Pommernalle 1.
Tel: (030) 3036234

GREECE
Tainiothiki tis Ellados
1 Kanari Street,
Athens 138.

HUNGARY
Hungarian Institute of Film Science and Archives
Nepstadion ut 97,
1143 Budapest.
Tel: (01) 429599

INDIA
National Film Archive of India
Ministry of Information and Broadcasting,
Law College Road,
Poona 411 004.
Tel: (0212) 58516

IRELAND
Liam O'Leary Film Archives
Garden Flat,
74 Ranelagh Road,
Dublin 6.

National Film Institute of Ireland
65 Harcourt Street,
Dublin 2.
Tel: (0001) 753638

ISRAEL
Archion Israeli Leseratim
PO Box 4455,
Hebron Road,
Jerusalem 91403.

ITALY
Centro Studi Cinetelevisi
Casella Postale 165,
47100 Forli.

Cineteca Italiana
Via Palestro 16,
20121 Milan.
Tel: (02) 799224

Cineteca Nazionale
Via Tuscolana N 1524,
00173 Rome.
Tel: (06) 749 0046

Museo Nazionale del Cinema
Piazza San Giovanni 2,
10122 Torino.
Tel: (011) 510370

JAPAN
The Kawakita Memorial Film Institute/Japan Film Library Council
Ginza-Hata Building,
4-5, 4-chome,
Ginza, Chuo-ku,
Tokyo.
Tel: (03) 561 6719

MEXICO
Cineteca Nacional
Orizaba No.139,
Col. Roma C.P.,
06700 Mexico.

NETHERLANDS
Stichting Nederlands Filmmuseum
Vondelpark 3,
1071 AA Amsterdam.
Tel: (020) 831646.

NEW ZEALAND
New Zealand Film Archive
150 Wakefield Street,
PO Box 9544,
Wellington.
Tel: (04) 850 162

NORWAY
Norsk Filminstitutt
Militärhospitalet,
Grev Wedels Plass,
Postboks 482,
Sentrum, 0105 Oslo 1.
Tel: (02) 428 740

POLAND
Filmoteka Polska
ul. Pulawska 61,
00-975 Warsaw.
Tel: (022) 455074/455404

PORTUGAL
Cinemateca Portuguesa
Rue Barata Salgueiro 39,
1200 Lisbon.
Tel: (01) 41244

SPAIN
Filmoteca Nacional de España
Carretera de la Dehesa de la Villa s/n,
Madrid 35.
Tel: (01) 2434795

SWEDEN
Cinemateket
Filmhuset, Box 27126,
S-102 52 Stockholm 27.
Tel: (08) 4686511

SWITZERLAND
Cinemathèque Suisse
Casino de Montbenon,
Case Ville 2512,
Esplanade de Montbenon,
1002 Lausanne.
Tel: (021) 237406

UK
Barnes Museum of Cinematography
Fore Street,
St Ives, Cornwall.

British Film Institute: Library Services
127 Charing Cross Road,
London
WC2H OEA.
Tel: (01) 437 4355

British Film Institute: National Film Archive
81 Dean Street,
London W1V 6AA.
Tel: (01) 437 4355

Imperial War Museum
Lambeth Road,
London SE1 6HZ.
Tel: (01) 735 8922

The John Grierson Archive
University of Stirling,
Stirling FK9 4LA, Scotland.
Tel: (0786) 3171

National Museum of Photography, Film and Television
Princes View,
Bradford, Yorks,
Tel: (0274) 727448/723377

Scottish Film Archive
74 Victoria Crescent Road,
Glasgow G12 9JN.
Tel: (041) 334 9314

USA
Academy of Motion Picture Arts and Sciences
Margaret Herrick Library,
8949 Wilshire Blvd,
Beverly Hills, CA 90211.
Tel: (213) 278 8990

American Film Institute: John F Kennedy Center for the Performing Arts
Washington DC 20566.
Tel: (202) 828 4000

American Film Institute: Louis B Mayer Library
PO Box 27999,
2021 North Western Avenue,
Los Angeles, CA 90027.
Tel: (213) 278 8777

George Eastman House
Department of Film,
900 East Avenue,
Rochester, NY 14607.
Tel: (716) 271 3361

Library of Congress
Motion Picture, Broadcasting and Recorded Sound Division,
Washington DC 20540.
Tel: (202) 287 5840

Museum of Modern Art
Department of Film,
11 West 53rd Street,
New York, NY 10019.
Tel: (212) 956 4121 (Study Center)/959 4209 (Stills)

Pacific Film Archive
University Art Museum,
2621 Durant Avenue,
Berkeley,
CA 94720.
Tel: (415) 642 1413

USSR
Gosfilmofond
Byelye Stolby,
Moskovskaja oblast.
Tel: (095) 136 0516

FESTIVALS

ANNECY
Annecy International Festival of Animation
BP 399,
74013 Annecy Cedex,
France.
Tel: (50) 51 78 14
Held: June

ADELAIDE
Adelaide International Film Festival
GPO Box 354, Adelaide,
South Australia 5001.
Tel: (08) 278 6330
Held: June

ANN ARBOR
Ann Arbor Film Festival
PO Box 7283,
Ann Arbor, MI 48107.
Tel: (313) 663 6494
Held: March

AVORIAZ
Avoriaz International Fantasy Film Festival
Promo 2000,
Avenue MacMahon 33,
Paris 75017.
Tel: (01) 755 71 40
Held: January

BERLIN
International Film Festival
Budapester Strasse 50,
D-1000 Berlin 30.
Tel: (030) 263 41
Held: February

Berlin International Radio and Television Competition
Prix Futura Berlin,
Sender Freies Berlin,
Masurenallee 8-14,
D 1000 Berlin 19.
Tel: (030) 308 2302
Held: April

BRIGHTON
British Film and Video Festival
c/o British Industrial and Scientific Film Association,
102 Great Russell Street,
London WC1E 3LN.
Tel: (01) 580 0962
Held: June

BRUSSELS
Brussels International Film Festival
Avenue de l'Astronomie 32,
1030 Brussels.
Tel: (02) 218 12 67
Held: January

CAIRO
Cairo International Film Festival
9 Oraby Street,
PO Box 2060, Cairo.
Tel: (02) 741112
Held: November

CAMBRIDGE
Cambridge Film Festival Arts Cinema
Market Passage,
Cambridge CB2 3PF.
Tel: (0223) 352001
Held: July

Cambridge Animation Festival
PO Box 17 6 St Edward's Passage,
Cambridge.
Tel: (01) 341 5015
Held: September

CANNES
Cannes International Film Festival
Rue du Faubourg St Honoré 71,
75008 Paris.
Tel: (01) 266 92 20
Held: May

MIP-TV
Avenue Victor Hugo 179
75116 Paris.
Tel: (01) 505 14 03
Held: April

CARTHAGE
Carthage International Film Festival
Journées Cinematographiques de Carthage,
BP 1029, 1045 Tunis RP,
Tunisia.
Tel: (01) 242 189
Held: October

CHICAGO
Chicago International Film Festival
415 North Dearborn Street,
Chicago, IL 60610.
Tel: (312) 644 3400
Held: November

CORK
Cork International Film Festival
38 MacCurtain Street,
Cork, Eire.
Tel: (0002) 502221
Held: October

EDINBURGH
Edinburgh International Film Festival
Film House,
88 Lothian Road,
Edinburgh EH3 9BZ.
Tel: (031) 228 6382
Held: August

FLORENCE
Festival dei Popoli
Via Fiume 14,
50123 Florence.
Tel: (055) 294 353
Held: December

HONG KONG
Hong Kong International Film Festival
Room 807,
New World Office Building,
Tsim Sha Tsui,
Kowloon,
Hong Kong.
Tel: (03) 678873
Held: March/April

KARLOVY VARY
Karlovy Vary International Film Festival
c/o Ceskovensky Filmexport,
Jindrisska 34,
11206 Prague 1.
Tel: (02) 22 37 51
Held: July

LOCARNO
Locarno Film Festival
Via Balli 2,
PO Box 186,
CH-6600 Locarno,
Switzerland.
Tel: (093) 31 82 66
Held: August

LONDON
London International Film Festival
National Film Theatre,
South Bank,
London SE1 8XT.
Tel: (01) 928 3842
Held: November

London Market
c/o Chris Snowden
Dennis Davidson Associates,
57 Beak Street,
London W1R 3LF.
Tel: (01) 439 6391
Held: October

LOS ANGELES

Los Angeles International Film Exposition (Filmex)
Berwin Entertainment Complex,
6525 Sunset Blvd,
Hollywood, CA 90028.
Tel: (213) 469 9400
Held: March

MELBOURNE

Melbourne Film Festival
21 Victoria Street,
Fitzroy, Melbourne,
Australia 3065.
Tel: (03) 417 3111
Held: June/July

MILAN

MIFED – International Film, TV Film & Documentary Market
Largo Domodossola 1,
20145 Milan.
Tel: (02) 4997 267
Held: April/October

MONTREAL

World Film Festival
1455 Blvd de Maisonneuve Est,
Montreal, Quebec H3G IM8.
Tel: (514) 879 4057
Held: August

MONTREUX

Montreux TV Festival
Direction du Concours de la Rose
d'Or de Montreux, PO Box 97,
1820 Montreux, Switzerland.
Tel: (021) 63 12 12
Held: May

MOSCOW

Moscow International Film Festival
Sovinterfest, 10 Kokhlovsky per,
Moscow 109028.
Tel: (095) 297 76 45
Held: July

MUNICH

International Munich Film Festival
Turkenstrasse 93,
8000 Munich 40.
Tel: (089) 393011
Held: June

NEWCASTLE-UPON-TYNE

Tyneside Film Fesitval
Tyneside Cinema,
10-12 Pilgrim Street,
Newcastle-upon-Tyne.
Tel: (0632) 321507
Held: October

NEW DELHI

International Film Fesitval
National Film Development
Corporation,
13-16 Regent Chambers,
208 Nariman Point,
Bombay 400021.
Tel: (022) 224924/222926
Held: January

NEW YORK

International Film and TV Festival of New York
251 West 57th Street,
New York,
NY 10019.
Tel: (212) 246 5133
Held: November

New York Film Festival
The Film Society of the
Lincoln Center,
140 West 65th Street,
New York,
NY 10023.
Tel: (212) 765 5100
Held: September/October

OBERHAUSEN

Oberhausen International Festival of Short Films
Westdeutsche Kurzfilm Tage,
Grillostrasse 34,
4200 Oberhausen 1,
Federal Republic of Germany.
Tel: (0208) 825 2652
Held: March

OXFORD

Oxford International Film Festival
123 South Bank House,
Blackfriars Road,
London SE1.
Tel: (01) 587 1060
Held:

ROME

Prix Italia
c/o RAI,
Viale Mazzini 14,
00195 Rome.
Tel: (06) 3878 4118
Held: September/October

ROTTERDAM

Rotterdam Film International
Westersingel 20,
30104 GP Rotterdam.
Tel: (010) 363111
Held: February

SAN SEBASTIAN

San Sebastian International Film Festival
Apartado Correos,
397 Reina Regente s/n,
San Sebastian,
Spain.
Tel: (43) 424 106
Held: September

SAN FRANCISCO

San Francisco International Film Festival
3501 California Street,
Suite 201,
San Francisco,
CA 94118.
Tel: (415) 211 9055
Held: April

SYDNEY

Sydney Film Festival
Box 25, PO Glebe,
NSW 2037.
Tel: (02) 660 3844
Held: June

TAORMINA

Taormina International Film Festival
c/o Ente Provinciale Turismo,
Via Calabria,
Isol 346,
98100 Messina,
Italy.
Tel: (090) 360 84 30
Held: July

THESSALONIKI

Thessaloniki International Film Festival
Thessaloniki 36,
Greece.
Tel: (031) 220 440
Held: September/October

TORONTO

Canadian International Animation Festival
Box 5009, Station F,
Toronto, Ontario M4Y 2T1.
Tel: (416) 364 5924
Held: August

Festival of Festivals
Suite 206,
69 Yorkville Avenue,
Toronto, Ontario M5R 1B8.
Tel: (416) 967 7371
Held: September

VARNA

World Animated Film Festival
Organizing Committee,
135a Rakousky Street,
1000 Sofia, Bulgaria.
Tel: 595061
Held: October

VENICE

La Biennale di Venezia
Ca' Giustinian,
San Marco,
30100 Venice.
Tel: (041) 700 311
Held: August/September

VIENNA

Viennale
Künstlerhaus, Karlsplatz 5,
1010 Vienna.
Tel: (0222) 56 98 23
Held: April

ZAGREB

World Festival of Animated Films
c/o Zagreb Film,
Nova Ves 18,
41000 Zagreb,
Yugoslavia.
Tel: (041) 276 636
Held: June

GOVERNMENT ORGANIZATIONS

ALGERIA

Office National pur le Commerce et l'Industrie Cinématographique
(National Office for Commerce and the Film Industry)
Immeuble les Asphodeles,
Ben-Aknoun,
Algiers.
Tel: 782255

ARGENTINA

National Institute of Cinematography
Lima 319,
1073 Buenos Aires.
Tel: (01) 378429

AUSTRALIA

Australian Film Commission
8 West Street,
North Sydney,
New South Wales 2060.
Tel: (02) 922 6855

AUSTRIA

Bundesministerium für Handel, Gewerbe und Industrie (Ministry for Trade and Industry)
Sektion 1,
Abt. Filmwirtschaft,
Stubenring 1,
1010 Vienna.
Tel: (0222) 7500

Bundesministerium für Unterricht und Kunst
(Ministry for Art and Education),
Sektion IV,
Film und Lichtbildwesen,
Freyung 1,
1010 Vienna.
Tel: (0222) 66200

BELGIUM

Ministry of Education and Culture
(Cinema Department)
Quai du Commerce 7,
1000 Brussels.
Tel: (02) 217 4190

BRAZIL

Consuelho Nacional do Cinema (National Cinema Council),
Rua Visconde de Inhauma 58,
Rio de Janeiro.
Tel: (021) 233 8329

CANADA

Canadian Film Development Corporation
Suite 2220,
Tour de la Bourse,
C.P. 71, Montreal,
Quebec H4Z 1A8.
Tel: (514) 283 6363

and

Suite 602,
111 Avenue Road,
Toronto,
Ontario M5R 3J8.
Tel: (416) 966 6436

CHINA
China Film Corporation
25 Xin Wai Street,
Beijing.
Tel: 667831

CUBA
**Cuban Institute of Arts and
the Film Industry**
Calle 23, no 1155,
entre 10 y 12,
Vedado, Habana.
Tel: (07) 305041

CZECHOSLOVAKIA
**Central Management of the
Czechoslovak Film**
Jindrisska 34,
112 06 Prague 1.
Tel: (02) 223751

DENMARK
**Danish Government Film
Office**
Vestergade 27,
1456 Copenhagen K.
Tel: (01) 132686

FRANCE
**Centre National de la
Cinématographie,**
Rue de Lubeck 12,
75784 Paris.
Tel: (01) 505 1440

DEMOCRATIC
REPUBLIC OF
GERMANY
DEFA
c/o DEFA Aussenhandel,
Milastrasse 2,
Berlin 1058.
Tel: (02) 440 0801

FEDERAL REPUBLIC
OF GERMANY
**Bundesministerium für
Wirtschaft** (Federal Ministry for
Economic Affairs)
Villemombler Strasse 76,
Bonn-Duisdorf.
Tel: (0228) 6151

**Filmförderungsanstalt des
Offentlichenrechts**
(Office for the Administration of
Film Aid)
Budapester Strasse 1,
PO Box 301/87, 1000 Berlin 31.
Tel: (030) 261 6006

HUNGARY
**Central Board of Hungarian
Cinematography**
Szalai U. 10,
1054 Budapest.
Tel: (01) 126417

Mafilm
Lumumba U. 174,
1145 Budapest.
Tel: (01) 6311473

INDIA
**National Film Development
Corporation**
1st Floor,13-16 Regent Chambers,
208 Nariman Point,
Bombay 400021.
Tel: (022) 231861

IRELAND
**Department of Industry,
Commerce and Tourism**
Kildare Street,
Dublin 2.
Tel: (0001) 789411

Irish Film Board
65 Pembroke Lane,
Dublin 2.
Tel: (0001) 607544

ITALY
**Ministry of Tourism and
Entertainment**
Via della Ferratella 51,
Rome.
Tel: (06) 7732

JAPAN
Agency for Cultural Affairs
3-2-2 Kasumigaseki,
Chiyoda-ku, Tokyo 100.
Tel: (03) 581 4211

MEXICO
**Direccion General de Radio
Television y Cinematography**
Guanajuato 125,
Col. Roma.
Tel: 584 5077

NETHERLANDS
**Ministry of Cultural Affairs
Recreation and Social
Welfare,**
Steenvoordelaan 370,
PB 5406,
Rijswijk ZH.
Tel: (070) 949233

**Netherlands Information
Service**
Communication Techniques
Department,
Anna Paulownastraat 76,
2518 BJ The Hague.
Tel: (070) 614181

NEW ZEALAND
**New Zealand Film
Commission**
PO Box 11-546,
Wellington.
Tel: (04) 859754

POLAND
Ministry of Culture and Art
Central Board of
Cinematography,
Warsaw.
Tel: (022) 267489

SPAIN
**Direccion General del Libro y
de la Cinematografia**
Ministerio de Cultura,
Paseo de la Castellana 109,
Madrid 16.
Tel: (01) 455 2600

SWEDEN
Svenska Filminstitutet
Filmhuset, Borgvagen,
Box 27126,
S-102 52 Stockholm 27.
Tel: (08) 651100

SWITZERLAND
**Federal Office of Cultural
Affairs**
Film Section,
Postfach 3000, Bern 6.
Tel: (031) 619271

UK
**Arts Council of
Great Britain**
105 Piccadilly,
London W1V OAU.
Tel: (01) 629 9495

**Arts Council of Northern
Ireland**
181a Stanmillis Road,
Belfast BT9 5DU.
Tel: (0232) 44222

**Department of Education and
Science**
Office of Arts and Libraries,
Elizabeth House,
York Road,
London SE1 7PH.
Tel: (01) 928 9222

**Department of Trade – Films
Branch**
16-20 Great Smith Street,
London SW1P 3DB.
Tel: (01) 215 7877

**National Film Finance
Corporation**
22 Southampton Place,
London WC1 2BP.
Tel: (01) 831 7561

Scottish Film Council
Dowanhill,
74 Victoria Crescent Road,
Glasgow G12 9JN.
Tel: (041) 334 9314

Welsh Arts Council
9 Museum Place,
Cardiff CF1 3NX.
Tel: (0222) 394711

USA
**International
Communications Agency**
1776 Pennsylvania Avenue NW,
Washington DC 20546.
Tel: (202) 376 7806

US Department of Commerce
Economics,
Bureau of Industrial
Consumer Goods and Services
Division,
Washington DC 20230.
Tel: (202) 377 0337

USSR
**State Committee of
Cinematography
of the USSR
Council of Ministers**
7 Maly Gnesdnikovsky Pereulok,
Moscow.
Tel: (095) 229 9912